Founding
CORPORATE
POWER
IN EARLY NATIONAL
PHILADELPHIA

Founding
CORPORATE
POWER
IN EARLY NATIONAL
PHILADELPHIA

ANDREW M. SCHOCKET

NORTHERN
ILLINOIS
UNIVERSITY
PRESS

© 2007 by Northern Illinois University Press

Published by the Northern Illinois University Press, DeKalb, Illinois   60115

Manufactured in the United States using acid-free paper

All Rights Reserved

Design by Julia Fauci

Library of Congress Cataloging-in-Publication Data

Schocket, Andrew M.

Founding corporate power in early national Philadelphia /

Andrew M. Schocket.

p.   cm.

Includes bibliographical references and index.

ISBN-13: 978-0-87580-369-2 (clothbound : alk. paper)

ISBN-10: 0-87580-369-5 (clothbound : alk. paper)

1. Corporations—Pennsylvania—Philadelphia—History.

2. Philadelphia (Pa.)—Commerce—History. I. Title.

HD2798.5.P4S36 2007

338.7'4097481109033—dc22

2006016686

TO DEBORAH

CONTENTS

LIST OF ILLUSTRATIONS

PICTURES

CHARTS & TABLES

•   ACKNOWLEDGMENTS   •

$\mathcal{U}$nfortunately, the amount of space and time that can be dedicated to acknowledgments compared to the rest of the book is in inverse proportion to the pleasure of their composition and the depth of the many intellectual, professional, and personal debts I have incurred. This project began about ten years ago as a couple of exploratory graduate seminar papers at the College of William and Mary, became my dissertation, and has gone through numerous significantly different drafts before its final version, and at each stage I have been the beneficiary of wonderful people and institutions.

As an exemplary dissertation director, Ronald Hoffman advised, cajoled, critiqued, and edited far beyond the call of duty. He has continued to be a mentor, offering sage advice concerning both the content of the book and the process of getting it into print. Carol Sheriff acted as almost a second director, cheerfully and patiently offering guidance, encouragement, and commiseration. Like many students at William and Mary, I am also indebted to Jim Whittenburg for his patience and encouragement, as well as to Tom Sheppard (from whom I learned much about teaching and professional dedication) and John Selby, who are both greatly missed. The graduate community at William and Mary is among the most cohesive anywhere, and I do not exaggerate when I say that I may not have been able to finish my graduate studies, much less this project, without the support of Lynn Nelson, Suzanne Cooper-Guasco, Anthony De Stefanis, Robert Galgano, Kelly Gray, Mike Guasco, Emily Mieras, and Sheila Phipps. As with Larry Peskin, Jacob Jones, and Inga Rost-Jones, who continue to be respected colleagues and dear friends, their contributions to my sanity (such as it is) have been at least as important as those to my scholarly development, and they have continued to offer companionship and timely advice.

In addition to those friends, many people have enriched this project by offering their comments and advice on parts or all of this project in various forms, including dissertation chapters, conference papers, article drafts, and manuscript drafts. They include Sean Adams, Sven Beckert, Michael Carroll, Clyde Haulman, Graham Hodges, Roger Horowitz, Tom Humphrey, Brooke Hunter, John Larson (who read both the dissertation and two manuscript drafts), Bob Lockhart, Cathy Matson (who has supported and commented on the project through several of its stages), David Nye, Jonathan Prude, Dan Richter, Donna Rilling, Billy Smith (who also graciously provided Philadelphia tax data and publishing guidance), Barbara Toth, Mike Zuckerman, and the anonymous reviewer for Northern Illinois University Press, as well as the participants in colloquia at the McNeil Center for Early American Studies, the Newberry Seminar on Technology, Politics, and Culture, and the Policy History Program at Bowling Green State University; attendees at the Michael P. Malone Memorial Conference on Class & Class Struggles in North America and the Atlantic World, 1500–1800; and attendees at annual meetings of the Society for the History of Technology, the Society for the History of the Early American Republic, the Business History Conference, the Pennsylvania Historical Association, and the Omohundro Institute for Early American History and Culture.

Over the course of this project I have received considerable support from numerous institutions. These include the College of William and Mary, the Sons of Cincinnati, the Society for the History of Technology, the Center for the History of Business, Technology, and Society at the Hagley Museum and Library; the Huntington Library, the Program in Early American Economy & Society at the Library Company of Philadelphia, the Bowling Green State University Faculty Research Council, the Bowling Green State University College of Arts & Sciences, and the Graduate Program in Policy History at Bowling Green State University.

History books are only as good as the research on which they are based, and that research is only possible because of the hard work and amiable assistance of librarians, archivists, and their support staff. The staffs of the Library Company of Philadelphia (especially Jim Green, Phil Lapsansky, and Wendy Woloson), the Historical Society of Pennsylvania, the Hagley Library, the Philadelphia Free Library, the Philadelphia City Archives (especially Jefferson Moak), the Pennsylvania State Archives, the Huntington Library, and the library systems of the College of William and Mary, the University of Pennsylvania, Purdue University, Ball State University, and Bowling Green State University contributed greatly to my ability to locate often difficult-to-find documents and publications.

Colleagues and friends at Bowling Green State University have offered guidance, support, advice, and camaraderie, especially Rob Buffington, Paul Cesarini, Ed Danziger, Liette Gidlow, Walter Grunden, Scott Martin, Don Nieman, Ted Rippey, Peter Way, and Leigh Ann Wheeler. While the Department of History no doubt would continue without us, the entire university might crumble without the competence, cheer, and hard work of Tina Amos and DeeDee Wentland.

Friends and relatives have provided places to stay, cheerful encouragement, and not a small bit of gentle teasing. Alan Schocket will be the first to know when my twelve-hour prime-time documentary on the Philadelphia waterworks hits PBS; Bob Colnes, Laura Lomanto, Becca and Sam were far more compelling than the musty manuscripts I looked through when I visited them; I hope to return to the East Coast to see dear cousins Jacob and Ruth Casper again soon; and Lorraine Griffith made a stay in Pasadena seem like a visit to a long-lost favorite aunt.

I submitted this book to Northern Illinois University Press largely on the basis of the reputation of Melody Herr, its history acquisitions editor. Her competence, professionalism, and responsiveness more than warrant the praise that other authors and fellow editors offered, unsolicited, on her behalf. Indeed, the entire staff at NIUP has displayed these qualities in abundance. Tom Willcockson of Mapcraft Cartography composed the wonderful map of Philadelphia-area internal navigations.

This project could not have been completed (nor would it have been worth completing) without the support and love of family. As only a loving mother can, Sandy Schocket gave constant needling, support, and encouragement; in addition, her perseverance in writing and publishing her own book has been an inspiration. Lyn and Rob Houk cheerfully tolerated my constant tapping away at the computer during numerous stays with them. To answer your question, asked many sweet times over an extended period, darling Sophie, yes, Daddy's book is now published! Thank you for your love and encouragement; you are an endless joy.

Finally, this book is for Deborah Houk Schocket. We met in Philadelphia soon after I began research on this project, and for most of the time since, she has lived with this work as much as I have. More than all the other people combined that I have mentioned, she has provided advice, editing, encouragement, and humor that have enriched this book and made it possible. But even after having composed all the words that follow, I am unable to express the measure of my debt to Deborah, in her tenderness and love, who made this volume, and my life, worthwhile.

Founding
CORPORATE
POWER
IN EARLY NATIONAL
PHILADELPHIA

heights. Nonetheless, the attending local and even statewide elected officials were only ornamental, there to bask in the navigation's reflected glory.

Rather, the thirteen board members of the navigation company with whom Heister shared the first boat had the greatest reason to be satisfied. The Schuylkill Navigation Company was a type of organization that made its North American debut during the American Revolution: a business corporation, chartered by the Pennsylvania state government both to improve transportation and to make a profit for its investors, and this new kind of institution was central to the transformation of Philadelphia and its hinterland. The names of the first two boats proved particularly telling: the first, the *Thomas Oakes,* was named after a company engineer who had died the previous year, while the second, the *Stephen Girard,* was named after the spectacularly wealthy and wily Philadelphia financier who had parlayed his investment in the company into a mortgage on the entire waterway. Because the Schuylkill Navigation Company was a business corporation and because of the way that corporations operated, its board members—not the public, or even, for that matter, most of its stockholders—decided upon the routing and the technology to be used. Within certain limits, the board members would decide what prices to charge on tolls for various commodities. The board members would decide what kind of boats would be allowed in the navigation. The board members would decide to whom they would sell the river's valuable waterpower, and for how much. The board members would decide who would be employed on the navigation and who would get valuable construction and maintenance contracts. Though not individually named in local newspaper accounts, these well-connected corporate insiders held great influence over the shape of development in the Schuylkill River Valley. These men almost all hailed from Philadelphia, where they made decisions about the navigation not in public but in the company's offices.[2]

The opening of the Schuylkill Navigation signaled more than a triumph of finance, technology, and administration; it was an episode in the unfolding of a new landscape of opportunity and power in the early republic. The era after the American Revolution marked a transformation from a republic to a democracy, from a deeply hierarchical society to one of social egalitarianism, from limited economic horizons to seemingly boundless possibility. As the right to vote became extended to include most white men, American politics and society burst into riotous bloom: at least in spirit and in tone, the early republic became an age for the common, albeit white, man in which the average farmer was exalted and even the most well born of politicians claimed humble roots and pedestrian tastes. Gone were the days when members of the local gentry could depend upon election based on their status as a "father of the people"; the age of everyman, "friend-of-the-people" politicians had arrived, with its party campaigns taking the place of informal personal appeals. Economic opportunities seemingly abounded, too. So many Americans took advantage of cheap land, inexpensive transportation, and easy credit that already-established cities found their adolescent growth spurts while new farms, towns, and cities sprouted in what to many people appeared to be the sunny spring-time of the new nation. If only for white men, the American dream of eco-nomic competency and political freedom seemed within grasp.[3]

But a close examination of the institutions most central to that economic growth—the business and municipal corporations that administered the fi-nancial and physical infrastructure fertilizing such expansion—reveals a tableau at odds with the sunny vision of broad equality and easy success during the decades following the American Revolution. This cloudier picture shows some avenues of economic and political opportunity broadening at the same time that economic power and some forms of political leverage be-came more concentrated in fewer hands. Despite the increasingly open and raucous display of democratic politics, certain kinds of economic questions, ones especially crucial to the shape of economic growth and how its oppor-tunities and rewards would be distributed, came to be decided more and more outside the public arena, closed off from the reach of an increasingly confident and demanding electorate. Historians have puzzled over what they generally have described as these seemingly contradictory phenom-ena—democracy and opportunity on the one hand, consolidated power on the other. Some scholars have emphasized the former, some the latter, and others have recognized both without reconciling them.[4]

This book offers an explanation of this apparent contradiction. As such, this work is about power, specifically, the origins of corporate power in America. It argues that, rather than being paradoxical processes, the early re-public's diffusion of political and economic opportunity and its consolida-tion of capital and influence were complementary developments. The men who founded and dominated early corporations used them to forge a new, more secure, and in some ways more far-reaching economic elite than the colonial one that it superseded. As much as any other force or phenomenon, corporations served to bind together the fledgling republic's centrifugal and centripetal forces, and it was in Philadelphia as much as anywhere during the republic's first fifty years where these institutions took full form and their officers came to possess such power.

In the decades following the American Revolution, citizens of the new na-tion did more than create a new set of national identities, separate and dif-ferent from Britain's. They also worked out the foundations of a new society, one vastly different from its colonial predecessor. Part of this transformation had been occurring for some time before the Revolution: an increased desire for consumer goods and access to markets, a breakdown of traditional pat-terns of deference, a shift from a book-credit economy to a cash economy, and a transition from influence based mostly on face-to-face, personal con-nections to one in which power became mediated through institutions. The increasingly egalitarian tone of early national politics left northern urban economic elites in an unfamiliar position in that they no longer had their hands on the controls of state government. Accordingly, a small group of men imported a British institution, the corporation, and used it to build a base of power from which to formulate and enact economic policies more to their likings than to those of state legislatures. The initial formation of corporations reflected an implicit compromise over economic power and ideology between the state government and local urban economic elites.[5]

Corporations soon grew deep roots in the United States, but the seeds had come from Britain, having grown over centuries from musty medieval holdovers to large-scale, modern endeavors. In eighteenth-century Anglo-American legal theory, the corporation served to harness the energy and resources of private citizens for the interests of the state. As its name suggests, a corporation was a body politic. Monarchs granted charters to groups of subjects to allow them to use their own resources to pursue goals that dovetailed with the Crown's interests. A corporate charter represented the granting of a tiny bit of sovereignty on the part of a monarch or a republic's elected officials: a government-within-a-government endowed with certain privileges that otherwise were reserved to the state, such as the exercise of eminent domain or permission to print banknotes that passed for money. In addition, a corporate charter endowed the authority to act as a legal "person" in that a corporation could sue and be sued in court, could buy and sell property, and could hire and fire employees and contractors to carry out its mission.[6]

The greater community received the benefits of the corporation, such as improved transportation or greater availability of credit, without having to spend public money on it. Generally, membership in corporations was defined through some kind of contribution to the institution: either by paying in upon its establishment (buying shares in the case of business corporations) or by making regular payments (paying taxes in the case of municipal corporations). The members of the corporation then composed their own by-laws and set up an administration by corporate officers—usually an elected board of directors or board of managers, who in turn hired employees—whose decisions were to be legally binding upon all the shareholders. For their part, the owners of the corporation secured the privilege to profit from this arrangement as long as they kept to the bounds of the charter. Furthermore, many charters were good for only a limited term (often twenty, fifty, or one hundred years), after which the sovereignty and privileges they conferred would revert to the ultimate sovereignty, the state.

Although the corporate form had a long English heritage, it still represented a strange, new, and even frightening departure for Americans in an economic landscape dominated by individuals and partnerships. Most Americans farmed, and even the largest agricultural operations—southern plantations with hundreds of slaves—were owned by individual families. In cities, tradesmen's shops or businesses were generally small operations, owned by a master and sometimes with numerous journeymen and apprentices, but still run by a single proprietor. Some merchants operated on their own, while others got together in two- or three-man partnerships to share risk and to extend their activities but still were small operations. In all of these cases, businessmen operated on their own, with no direct help from the government, and with the risk that, if their businesses went under, their creditors could go after not only business assets but also personal property, potentially landing failed men in debtors' prison.

In contrast, through their very size, corporate institutions effectively limited the liability of investors while also receiving state authority for privileges that other economic actors—even individuals or firms—did not have. For many citizens of the new United States, corporations conjured up the greatest excesses of the British Empire they had so violently rejected. Americans were familiar with what the British press referred to as the "three moneyed companies"—the Bank of England, the East India Company, and the South Seas Company—and how "stock jobbers" seemed to derive profits from them seemingly out of thin air, surely a sign of the corruption of the economy. They had thrown East Indies Company tea into the Boston harbor to protest how Parliament, encouraged by that corporation's shareholders, enacted policy enforcing the corporation's monopoly on tea at the colonists' expense, surely a sign of the corruption of governance. And they had seen how Parliament had raised taxes on colonists to help pay off government debts held by the Bank of England, surely a sign of corruption of the British constitution itself.

Lending organizations, internal improvements, or urban infrastructure did not inherently threaten the balance between democracy and centralized—and thus potentially dangerous—economic power. Indeed, Americans clamored for more paper money, wider access to credit, more efficient transportation, and better drinking water, and were not averse to setting up institutions to supply them, including private banks, state-run loan banks, private lending associations, and commissions run by publicly appointed officials, the most famous being New York State's Canal Board, which supervised the Erie Canal. But many observers also understood both the advantages and the perils of tying control over capital or crucial technologies and services to the corporate form. They saw that corporations could allow a small group of individuals to control vast resources with the power of the state behind them but with little oversight, and thus the corporate form could be a recipe for constructive entrepreneurship, for self-interested exploitation of the public trust, or for downright rascality less likely than with public institutions and on a scale far greater than with private institutions. Corporations bore the potential to be more effective but also more dangerous than other forms of administration.

Despite these widespread anxieties and misgivings concerning corporations, a few men in several American cities saw the Revolution as an opportunity to establish corporations, now that they had banished the British imperial authorities who had forbade them from doing so. First in Philadelphia, but soon in Boston, New York, Baltimore, Richmond, and eventually throughout the country, corporations seemed to sprout everywhere. For their founders, such institutions represented a chance to diversify investments, improve credit and public transportation, govern localities, and decrease business risks. Although individual states generally chartered corporations no faster than did the British parliament, which continued to issue them throughout the eighteenth century, in sum American legislatures issued an increasing stream of charters. Eventually, corporations and the services that they provided allowed the consolidation of control over credit and precious resources crucial to growing cities and their increasingly interconnected hinterlands, not only greatly accelerating this process of intensive economic growth but also laying the foundations for the ability of a small metropolitan elite to be able to project power over space on an unprecedented scale. Corporate leaders in state after state initiated the process of creative destruction that ravaged the economic foundations of old, local structures of influence and replaced them with the building blocks of the corporate power. Such uses of the corporation would eventually come to predominate throughout the nation. How and why corporate power was born in the early national United States is the subject of this book.[7]

While the story that follows—the construction of corporate power—is clearly one with great implications for the nation and its development, it is a case study of that process in one place and time. The site of a good historical case study must offer at least one of two things: either it must have served as a precedent for future, broader developments or it must be somewhat typical of similar developments in other places and times. Early national Philadelphia provides the ideal time and place to consider the origins of corporate power because the Quaker City not only hosted the nation's first business corporations and first major municipal waterworks but also functioned as the erstwhile capital of the United States and of Pennsylvania, the state with the most radical and fractured politics in the early republic. Pennsylvanians were among the first Americans to sift through the consequences and contradictions of democratic capitalism, and the Quaker City served as a bellwether for the twin phenomena of democratization and corporate power that would later spread throughout the North and Old Northwest in the early republic and eventually to the entire nation. And while Philadelphia's corporate founders blazed trails in some areas—banking and urban water supply—they progressed along the same paths as men in other cities in other corporate endeavors—internal improvement. Through analyses of the publications and internal records of the Corporation of Philadelphia (the city's municipal government), Philadelphia's corporate banks, local corporate internal improvements, the personal journals and correspondence of the people who came in contact with these institutions, state and local legislation, and the newspapers of the day, the following pages relate why early national Philadelphians chose the corporate form, how they shaped and used it, and to what immediate and lasting consequences.[8]

The men who founded and ran Philadelphia's early corporations wielded power in various ways during the early republic. Power involved the ability of some people to affect or constrain others' options in ways favorable to the first group. The most glaring—though least used—power was manifested through corporate officers' right under certain circumstances to use the state's monopoly on authorized physical force to apply their will, as bank managers did to have counterfeiters arrested and city and internal improvement company officers did to have punished those who physically harmed corporate facilities. More often, their power stemmed from their control of large amounts of capital, mostly raised from stockholders or bondholders with little interest in how the money was administered, and corporate insiders' leverage over resources essential to others' economic success, each of which came with endless economic, political, and even social possibilities for offering carrots and brandishing sticks. Through careful calibration of these two factors, corporate men put themselves in a position to encourage political support, which the municipal council members did through their ability to hand out rich contracts; to compel others to do their bidding, such as when canal companies rounded up petition signatures for desired legislation; or to limit others' options for action, for example, when newspaper publishers became reluctant to criticize bank managers publicly lest they lose their lines of credit.[9]

Furthermore, Philadelphia's increasingly coherent, if contentious, corporate elite worked to set aside a corporate sphere of activity at once sheltered from the public but also projecting its power in a way that set policies that otherwise might have been the purview of state government. By the 1830s, Philadelphia corporate power touched not only the population of the city proper but also that of its contiguous suburbs and an increasingly populous and productive hinterland stretching from northern Delaware to central Pennsylvania. Thus, not only did corporate men transform the methods of projecting power, but they also greatly extended the geographic scale on which economic power could be extended.

Still, the corporations of the early republic might seem like small, harmless creatures compared to the corporate behemoths that strode the American landscape from the second half of the nineteenth century onward. Early corporations did not exhibit all of the hallmarks of the large corporations that both contemporary observers and later scholars attributed to later institutions: they did not employ cadres of middle managers to control or supply far-flung operations, they were not of national scope, they were not vertically or horizontally integrated industrial giants, they did not effect broad monopolies on basic commodities, and the amount of money they had at their disposal would look like molehills next to later corporate capital mountains.[10] Furthermore, corporate activities did not even fully dominate early national Philadelphia, home to perhaps the nation's most entrepreneurial independent businessmen, among them printers, builders, engine makers, and other small-scale manufacturers operating on their own or in limited partnerships, who all contributed greatly to the city's transformation from the sparkling "Athens of America" in the eighteenth century to the gritty industrial metropolis it would become in the nineteenth century. These thousands of enterprising people primarily used partnerships as the most prevalent model of enterprise throughout the period.[11] Corporations and their employees faced opposition on many fronts: in the statehouse, in court, in coalfields and along the routes of navigations. Even Philadelphia's early corporate elite was only a subset of the city's economic and social upper crust, though the two became increasingly synonymous as decades passed.[12]

But just as twentieth-century corporations dwarfed their nineteenth-century predecessors in terms of global reach and access to capital, Philadelphia's early-republic corporate captains commanded capital and operated on a scale that was unheard of before the American Revolution. Generally elite merchants and lawyers, the men who served on corporate boards availed themselves of powers conferred by the state government to corporate institutions in combination with the large pools of capital they were able to raise through taxes or the sale of shares. The ability of a board of directors or a few members of a city council to control hundreds of thousands of dollars of other people's money, to invoke the state's authority for eminent domain, or to control technologies used by tens or hundreds of thousands of people marked a huge shift from previous bases of power, which depended mostly upon imperial connections and family fortunes. In doing so, they contributed to a fundamental shift in the nature of economic power in the early republic.

Philadelphia's corporate pioneers established institutional frameworks, both formal and informal, and set long-term precedents as to how the region's (and nation's) economy would be ordered. These models ranged from the adoption of internal rules and customs that governed behavior within corporations, to ways of raising and distributing capital, to the methods corporate men used to effect favorable legislation at the state, and eventually national, level. Furthermore, a new corporate elite emerged that differed from Philadelphia's previous mercantile elite, one that would come to be reflected among corporate elites in other cities; this new corporate community had a less prominent political profile but more economic power than its mercantile predecessor, and was far more stable because of the new kinds of investments that corporations offered. Traditionally, historians have emphasized the quantitative distinction of scale between early and later corporations, but a central premise of this work is that the qualitative issues of corporate power—its forms, its uses, and its results—were worked out in the early republic, only to be repeated and elaborated upon by later practitioners.

Three central processes contributed to the rise of corporate power. First, the men who established and ran corporations considered them to be more than utilitarian institutional structures for administration, the collection of capital, the provision of specific services, and—for business corporations— a source of profit: corporate founders also used them as an instrument to shape economic policy, mostly outside the realm of popular politics they found so threatening. Second, corporations served as a prism that broadly diffused some economic benefits (transportation, money supply, water, employment) while consolidating others (profits and power). Corporate leaders used a variety of tools to accomplish these ends, from the shaping of internal by-laws to the negotiation of legislative charters, from financial sleight of hand to economic blackmail, and from the placing of neighborhood fire hydrants to the rerouting of mighty rivers. Third, corporate men did not gain such power on their own; rather, they could do so only because corporations served to fill broad economic needs that private individuals or partnerships were unable to fulfill and that the state was unwilling to fulfill. This book integrates the adoption and use of corporations into the central debates concerning democratization and the market revolution during the early republic.

In addition to investigating these processes, by considering the nation's first corporations as media for the distribution of power, this work challenges two staples of our nation's historical narrative, the one that appears in American history textbooks, documentaries, and historical fiction. When considering what historians call the "Revolutionary settlement," scholars have generally emphasized the establishment of governmental structures and customs (the state and federal governments, American jurisprudence, political parties, and so forth) in Americans' jockeying for power following the break with Britain. What this book demonstrates is that we should consider the founding and entrenchment of corporations as part of that process of creating new institutions reflecting new political and economic realities. In addition, this work moves forward historians' traditional narrative of the rise of corporations from the late nineteenth century to the nation's first decades. Rather than following the familiar trope of the origins of corporate power being tied to large-scale industrial capitalism on a national scale, this study demonstrates that early national corporate men exploited the corporate form far before the development of railroad networks and vertically integrated manufacturing corporations. American corporate power was born in Revolutionary-era America as exemplified in Philadelphia and reached its adolescence there in the space of two generations.[13]

The scholarly conversation concerning early American corporations has developed along several lines, all of them pursuing important avenues of inquiry but none of them taking the issue of early corporate power head-on. One ongoing debate has concerned the degree to which state and local governments have encouraged and regulated corporate enterprise, that is, business corporations; there, the primary fault lines have been over the extent to which early state legislatures encouraged and regulated corporations, and the motivations and timing of state and local investments in business corporations.[14] Meanwhile, other historians have considered municipal corporations, investigating the ways that city governments have regulated their citizens and worked out the tensions between public needs and private desires.[15] Scholars have increasingly and convincingly demonstrated the extent to which state and local governments acted both to promote and to regulate a very wide swath of economic behavior, from the size of loaves of bread to the establishment of highly capitalized corporations. But while they have spent much energy on the state side of the equation—that is, how governments defined and influenced the early national economy—historians have not adequately addressed the ways that corporate officers sought to shape economic activity and economic expansion.

Defining the role of and methods by which business corporations participated in economic expansion has also elicited much valuable work, though scholars have shown less interest in considering the role of corporations in how that growth was distributed. Both economists and historians have delved into corporate banking operations, including the effectiveness of bank lending practices and money supply policies. They have also studied the sources of investment in internal improvements and those projects' role in fostering different kinds of economic growth. Despite their zeal and effectiveness in measuring the mechanisms and quantity of economic growth, scholars have not focused much attention on the quality and distribution of corporate-led expansion, that is, the ways that corporate officers designed their institutions, methods, and technologies in ways that benefited some people or communities more than others. Such consequences were neither incidental nor accidental; rather, they were the result of conscious policies on the part of corporate men to shape an economy that would grow in ways that benefited themselves, their families, their class, and their city. That is, they exercised economic and social power. When historians have looked at the issue of corporate power in politics and society, they have nearly exclusively looked beyond the early republic to consider the corporate leviathans of the Gilded Age and beyond, paying little such attention to their precedents.[16]

The one place that scholars of the early national period have lavished attention on the issue of corporate power has been the corporate-owned and corporate-run factories of Lowell, Massachusetts. Nonetheless, the so-called Boston Associates (a label invented by a twentieth-century historian) who established the first of those factories did not do so until 1814, nearly two generations after the founding of the first American corporation in Philadelphia in 1781. And just as they were not the first corporate trailblazers, the Boston men did not inspire many to follow in their path. Though their corporate officers did show great ingenuity in their development of corporate, water-power textile manufacturing, the Lowell mills provoked so much contemporary and later scholarly inquiry exactly because they represented such an anomaly on the American landscape for decades after their first waterwheels began turning—even in Massachusetts, as their unincorporated Fall River Valley competitors could attest. In order to keep those wheels in motion, the "Boston Associates" did develop some of the same technologies as the officers of some Philadelphia-area improvements and used similar devices (literal as well as figurative) in their dealings with local landowners, fishermen, and boaters. By the 1810s, nearly every state had incorporated banks, municipalities, and internal improvements, but none had chartered many manufacturing establishments. Not until well after the Civil War would corporate manufacturing begin to become a national phenomenon, while the vines of corporate power planted by Philadelphia's first corporate men had already been creeping slowly but steadily across the country for a century.[17]

Though covering some of the same territory as previous scholars, I aim in this work to conceptualize that intellectual ground in a different way. Rather than considering the state's actions toward corporations, it asks how corporate men influenced the state through the activities of corporate insiders and allies, such as lobbying, applying financial leverage, and mobilizing voters dependent upon corporate officers' good graces. Rather than delineating the mechanisms and measuring the degree of economic growth, it investigates the means by which corporate men sought to shape economic growth, the distribution of its fruits, and its political consequences. Rather than denoting the level of economic regulation and activism by municipal corporations, it analyzes the ways that city officials found to insulate themselves from public scrutiny while extending their geographic and administrative reach. And rather than dissecting the sinews of corporate power after patterns of corporate behavior and the institutional structure of American corporations had already been established, it demonstrates that the founding and development of corporations and corporate power were bound inextricably with the founding and development of American democracy.

In so doing, this book places the corporation front and center as one of the principal engines not only of the increased economic activity of what historians of the early national period have called the "market revolution" but also of the social and political upheavals that accompanied increasingly intensive market activity. In the decades following the American Revolution, a small community of Philadelphia men used corporations to amass unprecedented pools of capital, and corporate officers did not shrink from using that money to foster economic growth in ways that clearly benefited themselves and their friends. Investments in banks, internal improvement companies, insurance companies, and municipal bonds became a basis for stable family fortunes, thus contributing to the coalescence of a Philadelphia capitalist elite distinct from its mercantile predecessor. By selectively doling out credit and by dictating routes and the technological details of the city waterworks and regional internal improvements, corporate insiders had great leverage over who would be winners and who would be losers as the region's economy grew.

Meanwhile, thousands of city and hinterland craftsmen, farmers, and entrepreneurs took advantage of the expansion of credit, the availability of plentiful water and waterpower, increasingly inexpensive transportation, and cheaper sources of energy that corporations provided. Between these energetic people and those who found steady employment within the burgeoning corporate structure, corporate activity contributed significantly to the establishment of an urban and suburban middle class. In turn, employment for working people expanded, and the quality of urban life improved because of greater public water distribution and cheaper heating fuel, but class lines hardened because of differing access to credit and investment opportunities and the class segregation partly fostered by clever routing of public water mains. In sum, the establishment and use of corporations helped transform the United States from a mercantile and agrarian society composed of orders to a capitalist world divided by class.[18]

Like any work of history, this book is a study of people in the past, what they thought and believed, and why they behaved in the ways they did. Thus, it is populated by modest toll takers and by cynical politicians, by aspiring farmers and by urban vandals, by merchant princes and by desperate debtors. But history is also the study of deeper trends transcending individual actions, processes resulting from complex interactions between and among many cooperating and competing people and factions, sometimes with outcomes that none of them intended and often that few of them foresaw or desired. In light of that view of history, this book describes a process of economic, social, legal, and political change that transformed the landscape of power. The United States of the 1830s was very different from the United States of the 1780s, largely because of the improvised dance of thousands of women and men who ended up in formations and configurations that they never could have conceived of when their parents had first begun moving to the rhythms of the new nation. This book, then, attempts not only to illuminate the dancers and the idiosyncrasies of their steps but also to choreograph the larger patterns of the dance itself.

The following pages offer an analysis of the first decades of Philadelphia's corporate leaders, the institutions they ran, and the processes that they helped to set in motion. Chapter 1 demonstrates that the foundation of the first corporations was far from inevitable and reflected a choice among options; in addition to the form's utility, a small subset of Philadelphia's economic elite saw corporations as a vehicle to help them reclaim some of the power they had lost in the Revolution, as well as providing for a mediated settlement of the bifurcation of economic and political power that had occurred in Pennsylvania's revolution. That said, the establishment of corporations provoked considerable debate and opposition. Chapter 2 analyzes the terms of that debate and the methods that corporate boosters used to defeat or co-opt rivals and opponents. Chapter 3 considers corporate men's use of the least concrete but most controversial type of early American corporation, corporate banks, focusing on the Bank of Pennsylvania, while Chapter 4 follows the development of a much more tangible project, the Philadelphia municipal corporation's waterworks system. Corporate leaders operated banks for profit, and bank officers tried to keep a healthy distance between their institutions and state authorities, while city corporate men ostensibly worked for the public good and used their state-delegated authority to the fullest. Internal improvement companies were somewhere in between, in that they administered and built complex technological systems and their insiders sought profits, but they also did not shy away from manipulating their charter-granted rights when it suited them. Chapter 5 investigates this phenomenon through a consideration of the Schuylkill Navigation Company.

Shifting away from the examination of specific institutions, Chapter 6 moves on to the corporate community at large, explaining how, by the 1810s, the officers of the organizations began to coordinate corporate activities and develop a distinct intracorporate culture, and illuminating the coalescence of a new corporate elite—distinct from its colonial predecessor—as a subset of elite Philadelphia society. Finally, the Conclusion examines the results of corporate consolidation in Philadelphia and eastern Pennsylvania, showing the ways these worked as precedents for later corporate development and considering the greater ramifications of these developments for American democratic capitalism in the nineteenth century and beyond. Philadelphia corporate officers and insiders did more than establish the first American corporations: they eventually established the first beachhead of American corporate power.

1

ESTABLISHING
CORPORATIONS

$\mathcal{W}$hen Virginians in Williamsburg tore the royal crest from the walls of the colonial Governor's Palace and Bostonians cheered the first reports of the Declaration of Independence, American revolutionaries did more than simply change allegiances: they set about a process that resulted in a complex rearrangement of who would be in positions of power and in what ways that leverage would be wielded. People and groups jockeyed for political and economic power in an ever-shifting kaleidoscope of alliances based on party allegiances, philosophical proclivities, economic aspirations, geographic interests, personal ambitions, ethnic backgrounds, religious affiliations, and class considerations. At the same time that Americans struggled to reshape their polity, they began to confront other, more down-to-earth economic problems that seemed to require collective rather than individual action.

The citizens of the new nation had encountered some of these old problems before, such as how to provide credit and an adequate money supply for people in an economy and population whose growth, as Benjamin Franklin had pointed out, appeared to spiral upward with no end in sight. Other challenges were new ones that came about as a result of that expansion and, if solved, would contribute further to it, including a healthy water supply for fast-growing cities and better transportation between town and country. Furthermore, Americans had to figure out how to pay for and administer the solutions to these problems. Projects could be undertaken by private individuals or partnerships, by the state government, or by groups of individuals with some level of state sanction and oversight; Americans considered all possibilities. These conditions and questions resulted in a half century of conflicts, experiments, and half starts as well as the beginnings of more permanent formal and informal institutions and organizational structures that became the foundations for capitalist democracy. And in each case, city by city and state by state, the various groups worked out new political and economic arrangements that were neither inevitable nor predictable but that functioned to distribute power in ways that reflected new realities.[1]

No one confronted these issues more directly and with greater deliberation and long-term result than the people of Philadelphia. Philadelphia's peers— New York, Boston, and eventually Baltimore—simply did not face the same economic or political challenges. In contrast to New York and its Hudson River, and to Baltimore and its nearby Susquehanna River, Philadelphia did not have a broad, navigable river to offer easy access to its rich hinterlands. New York, Boston, and Baltimore would not face yellow fever epidemics serious or often enough for their citizens to undertake a large-scale water-supply system in the opening decades of the republic. Just as crucially, in both New York and Boston a substantial section of the mercantile elite had been active enough in the Revolutionary effort to have significant influence over the crafting of their state constitutions and state governance to continue to wield considerable influence over state economic policy. Indeed, from the point of view of the Shays regulators who put a great scare into the Boston mercantile elite with their protests in 1786, rich Boston men like Massachusetts governor James Bowdoin had too much say over economic policy. In both New York and Boston, enough of local elites had ridden the surge of Revolutionary disturbances to emerge in positions of considerable power in the 1780s and 1790s. Thus, while both those cities hosted chartered corporations, the precarious political position of Philadelphia's elites in combination with the state's early radicalism resulted in a peculiar disconnect between moneyed men and political power.

Philadelphia was different. It faced geographic challenges that its rival cities did not. Further, proportionately more of its economic elites found themselves on the outs politically because of Revolutionary chaos. Members of one particular subsection of Philadelphia's elite that survived the Revolution resented their being thrust out of control of state economic policy and found the corporation to be the perfect vehicle to put economic matters in their own hands while solving some of the city's most pressing economic problems. Men like William Bingham and Thomas Willing used their personal and reading knowledge of British corporations to design their own corporations, while outsiders with more technical expertise, such as B. Henry Latrobe, contributed to and benefited from corporations but learned the line between employer and employee.

*A*s Philadelphia recovered from its occupation by the British army, the city quickly reclaimed its place as the largest and most culturally sophisticated city on North America's Atlantic seaboard. By the mid-1780s, about

40,000 people lived in Philadelphia or its suburbs, temporarily still ahead of close rival New York City. "Penn was not mistaken when he conceived its plan in such a way as to make it one day the capital of America," French general François Jean, the marquis de Chastellux gushed about Philadelphia's grid of streets and squares. The city's wide streets and grand buildings drew compliments from many travelers, as did its lively cultural and social scene. "Philadelphia may be considered the metropolis of the United States," observed de Chastellux's countryman, J. P. Brissot de Warville, in 1788, long enough after the Revolution for the repainting of facades, the replacement of windows, and the mending of streets to have taken place. "It certainly is the finest town, and the best built; it is the most wealthy, though not the most luxurious. You find here more men of information, more political and literary knowledge, and more learned societies." He was referring to well-grounded institutions, including the American Philosophical Society, founded there in 1743, the Pennsylvania Hospital, opened in 1752, the College of Philadelphia, chartered in 1755, and the Library Company of Philadelphia—America's first lending library—organized in 1731. Philadelphia's cultural wealth reflected its commercial wealth, manifested in the grand, three-story brick mansions built for the city's richest men. Commerce was the lifeblood of all waterfront cities in the Atlantic world in the eighteenth century, and the Quaker City was no exception.[2]

Some visitors expressed less complimentary views of Philadelphia. Englishman Isaac Weld allowed that from a "distance it looks extremely well" but carped that closer up "the city makes a poor appearance, as nothing is visible from the water but confused heaps of wooden storehouses, crowded upon each other." Although in 1682 William Penn had planned the city to span a one-mile-wide, two-mile-long stretch of land between the Delaware and Schuylkill rivers, a century later it remained mostly hunched along the western bank of the Delaware. The Delaware not only was deeper and less likely to freeze than the Schuylkill (though both often froze during the frigid eighteenth-century winters); it was also navigable for many miles above the growing commercial capital, well into New York State. But by the 1780s, city habitations reached less than a mile inland, a densely settled six or seven blocks beyond the convergence of thickets of masts and jumbles of warehouses at the water's edge. Inside the large blocks Penn had laid out sat warrens of narrow streets and alleyways smelling of the human and industrial refuse typical of the early modern city: busy taverns and messy stables sat cheek-by-jowl with crowded residences. Brewers and tanners plied their trade on the city's outskirts, but their activities no doubt smelled more immediate to downwind neighbors. Nonetheless, residents boasted about Philadelphia's city plan, its copious markets, and its broad, tree-lined, well-lit paved avenues, with their brick sidewalks and gutters.[3]

Comparing American social conditions to his native France, visitor de Chastellux claimed that in Philadelphia, "every citizen is about equally well-off." Certainly the eyes of a European aristocrat saw nothing in the comfortable

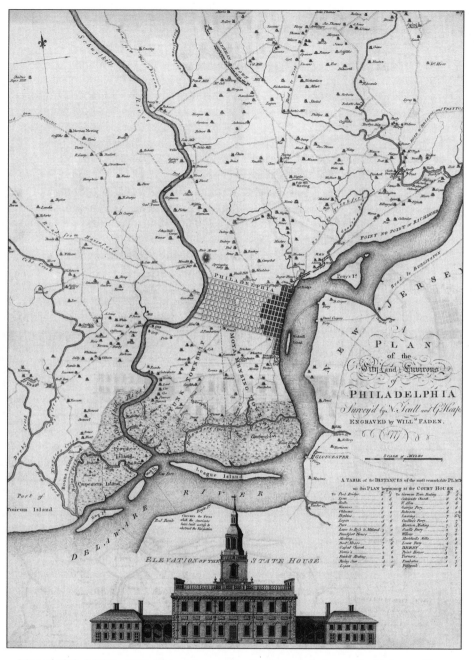

Map of Philadelphia, 1777. The grid spanning the distance between the Delaware River on the east and the Schuylkill River on the west represents Penn's plan; the shaded blocks are those actually built upon by the 1770s. Note the many country seats of wealthy Philadelphia families, labeled by family name, mostly north of the city. From Nicholas Scull, *A Plan of the City and Environs of Philadelphia, survey'd by N. Scull and G. Heap* (London: W. Faden, 1777). Map Collections, Library of Congress.

townhouses of the Quaker City's most well-to-do that he had not seen in mere middling gentry houses back home, and, though he probably caught a glimpse of a few of Philadelphia's enslaved people, de Chastellux did not see the widespread abject poverty that so struck visitors to Paris or London. Nonetheless, over the course of the eighteenth century, the gap between Philadelphia's rich and poor had widened. In 1693, those below the 60th percentile in taxable wealth held 17.4 percent of the wealth, while those in the top 10 percent held 46 percent; in 1774, the bottom 60 percent of the population held 5.1 percent of the wealth, while the top 10 percent held 72.3 percent. The city's wealthier merchants and lawyers could expect to leave sizable estates to their families upon their deaths, and a map produced in 1777 showed the countryside dotted with their country homes, to which they retreated from Philadelphia's summer humidity.[4]

The wealthy made their money primarily through trade. Provisioner merchants purchased flour, beef, and wood not only from the Delaware River Valley but also as far afield as upstate New York and much of the Chesapeake Bay region, bought locally from suppliers—another mercantile specialty—and sold globally. Dry goods merchants did the opposite, importing mostly finished goods to be sold to distributors (yet another layer of commercial complexity) in the Delaware Valley and beyond. Of course, not all merchants were wealthy. They ranged from fabulous to struggling, with nine of Philadelphia's 341 merchants in 1772 below the eighteenth-century equivalent of the poverty line. Conversely, not all the rich were merchants. Some highly successful artisan-entrepreneurs also joined the economic elite, as did well-to-do professionals—lawyers and brokers—who socialized with doctors and pastors whose other attainments put them in society's upper crust.[5]

Clerks, notaries, and a smattering of city, colony, and imperial officials garnered steady pay, joining a broad middling sort of successful artisans who contributed to the city's commerce in trades like shipbuilding and sailmaking as well as to the local community through brewing, printing, smithing, baking, building, and a host of other trades: groups representing forty-four different specialties marched in the 1788 parade celebrating the adoption of the new federal constitution. In these walks of life, too, some made good and others struggled, leading the uncertain life of journeymen and often lucky to stay one step ahead of poverty, which was the constant lot of many laborers. Worst of all, in the early 1770s about 1,400 Philadelphians lived a life of enslavement, although the number fell to about 400 by the end of the Revolution. Philadelphia society did not reach the heights of European society and may have had a broader middling sort, but it also reached greater depths by allowing the subjugation of slavery.[6]

Pennsylvania politics could be as complicated as its population was diverse. During the opening decades of the eighteenth century, elite Quakers, most of them merchants, had dominated both the city government and Pennsylvania's colonial government, of which Philadelphia was capital. But the 1750s and 1760s brought new growth, new groups, new pressures, and new crises that pushed the elites' iron grasp on politics to the limits before it melted away in the crucible of revolution. Despite the Penn family's return to Anglicanism, eastern Quakers had managed to keep a grip on political power, partly through their continued strength in numbers, partly through sectarian solidarity, and partly because the colonies' three eastern counties held a disproportionately high number of seats in the colonial legislature. Two political factions vied for the allegiances of Pennsylvania's fractious electorate—an "assembly" party composed mostly of Quakers and Anglicans that opposed the Penn family (still the proprietors of the colony) and supported making Pennsylvania a royal colony; the other, a "proprietary" faction largely Presbyterian-led and closer to the Penn family.

In the mid-1760s, much of this competition came to a head with bitterly fought colonial elections over fundamental issues of defense (many westerners resented the Quakers' pacifistic Indian policy), colonial governance (the assembly faction pushed for the Crown to take over the colony from the Penns), and imperial taxes (the proprietary party opposed the Stamp Act more vociferously than the assembly party) prompting hot debate and record turnouts. But by the mid-1770s, that antipathy had largely subsided: even during the imperial crisis of 1775, only a third of Philadelphia voters showed up to cast ballots in colony elections. Despite competition within elites and among various groups, control both of Pennsylvania's colonial legislature and of Philadelphia's city government stayed in few hands with little turnover, lending a veneer of political stability to a complex, heterogeneous, and rapidly changing society. Indeed, in 1775 two-thirds of the city council membership were among the richest 5 percent of Philadelphia's population. Governmental power and economic power were for the most part intertwined in the sense that the wealthy dominated political office, with many of the most affluent Philadelphians gaining office and reinforcing their wealth through political connections.[7]

That condition came to an abrupt end between 1774 and 1776. In most colonies, the main political factions assumed one of two postures: either they took opposite sides over resistance to and independence from imperial authority, or they even competed to see which one would lead that movement. But because of Pennsylvania's peculiar relationship with the proprietor Penns, the assembly faction had positioned itself over the previous decade to get closer to rather than further from the imperial administration, while the proprietary faction, despite its suspicion of imperial policy, supported the status quo. This is not to say that affluent Philadelphians all opposed revolution; actually, their allegiances during the Revolution nearly exactly reflected those of the city's general population, insofar as religion and ethnicity tended to be larger determinants of political proclivities than did pocketbook size. Nonetheless, because of their relationship to the Penns or attachments to Britain, wealthy Philadelphians generally approached the Revolution more cautiously than their less prosperous neighbors.[8]

Accordingly, while the leaders of both factions continued to concentrate on local issues in the colonial assembly and to move extremely carefully when it came to resistance to royal authority, artisans and lesser merchants came to lead the extralegal committees of correspondence that spearheaded the Revolutionary movement. In 1774, over half of the members of the Philadelphia Committee of Observation—the extralegal group overseeing the city's Revolutionary activities—owned assessed wealth over £100; two years later, nearly two-thirds of the members of the now larger committee were assessed at under £44. The shift in the occupations of successful politicians showed an even more drastic change: of the first committee, about three-quarters of the members were merchants or professionals, but in 1776, the practitioners of such prestigious pursuits had dropped to little more than a third of the total. Once independence was secured, these new leaders designed and got elected to the new state legislature that replaced its colonial predecessor. Before the Revolution, the colonial legislature was composed of thirty-eight members, twenty-four of whom came from Bucks, Chester, and Philadelphia counties. But the constitution of 1776 resulted in a transformed polity. Under this most radical of state founding documents, all taxpaying freemen who declared their allegiance to the new government had the franchise, and they annually elected members of a unicameral legislature that, in deep contrast to its predecessor, overrepresented sparsely settled western counties. In this new political environment, all the old bets were off, especially those on the wealthy and well connected to have more than a fraction of the political prominence they had held just a few years before.[9]

Because of this dramatic shift in political power, Pennsylvania faced a situation uncharacteristic among the new states—and Philadelphia, unusual among cities—that is, a significant bifurcation between those seated in political office and those holding economic power. Enough of Boston and New York's colonial elites had joined the Revolution early on and taken the lead in forming their respective state governments, thus positioning themselves strongly for participation in post-Revolutionary governance. Boston had grudgingly hosted British troops from 1768 through 1775, and its merchant and legal community nearly unanimously supported the Revolutionary cause, got involved in early efforts to coordinate resistance to British authority, and participated in the formation of the state government. Such was their political persistence that in the 1780s among the states they passed the most draconian financial measures designed to shore up the state's finances and thus the value of the financial instruments mostly in the hands of the merchant community. In addition, James Bowdoin, a fairly conservative Boston merchant, served as the state's governor from 1785 to 1787. In New York, the colonial assembly had been dominated from 1768 to 1775 by men who became loyalists, and when the British army took New York City, they scattered the new state's most radical mechanics, thus leaving much of the political field open to elite lawyers, merchants, and landowners. New York's farmers and mechanics would control the state legislature for a few years in the 1780s, though working under a constitution much more conducive to elites than Pennsylvania's. Meanwhile, during the late 1770s, many of Philadelphia and Pennsylvania's most economically potent men, that is, the ones with the most access to capital and the widest colonial and Atlantic world connections, found themselves thrust out of office. In some ways, this development represented the wildest dreams come true for many central and western farmers and Philadelphia mechanics and laborers.[10]

Perhaps they had not been careful enough in their wishes. Wealthy Philadelphia men like Robert Morris would spearhead the movement to replace Pennsylvania's radical charter with one more to their liking, eventually succeeding in 1790. But during the 1770s and 1780s, the reins of government were out of the hands of the old elites, and the carriage of state could be driven in directions that better served middling or even lower Philadelphians and inland farmers. Nonetheless, that carriage would not get far without being hitched to anything, and therein lay the rub: with the old economic elite out of the picture, the state did not have access to money to meet its needs. Conservative Philadelphia attorney James Allen encapsulated the feelings of many elite Philadelphians about the new state of affairs, lamenting that Pennsylvania "may be divided into 2 classes of men, viz. those that plunder and those that are plundered. . . . The most insignificant now lord it with impunity & without discretion over the most respectable characters." In short, wealthy Philadelphia felt endangered by the new order and soon enough began seeking a way to reconsolidate political and economic power.[11]

At the same time that a faction of wealthy Philadelphians began their maneuvering over the distribution of power, its members struggled with pressing economic issues. In working through these challenges, they would remake not only the landscape of their city but also the topography of political and economic power in the new republic. Runaway inflation was one of the most pressing of these issues, undermining both stable government and people's ability to make a living. For a variety of reasons—most notably the novelty of state and national government, their difficulty in collecting taxes in wartime, and the subsequent lack of public confidence in the value of government-issued money—the nation in general and Pennsylvania in particular suffered from highly unstable currency, a situation exacerbated by "convulsions of credit" and "maneuvers of speculation" that made paper money nearly worthless. And, just as with transportation difficulties, the City of Brotherly Love experienced more than its share of the crisis. Philadelphia had become, in one man's miasmic metaphor, "the great sink wherein all the speculation of America terminates and mingles." While money's ever-changing value vexed Philadelphians, so did their inability to borrow money at reasonable rates of interest. Almost no one was willing to lend at less than usurious rates in such an uncertain atmosphere, and even in the less troubled times before the Revolution, few men had great reserves of money to put out. Furthermore, because any monetary policy inherently favored some residents over others, any solution to the problems of credit and currency would be crucial to determining winners and losers in the fledgling economy.[12]

The problem of money sometimes seemed esoteric and abstract, but nearly all city residents faced a much more mundane and physical challenge: finding potable water. Eighteenth-century cities struggled with inadequate supplies of fresh water, Philadelphia more than most. The city had no central water source; rather, most residents got their water from private wells or from public pumps situated along city streets. But they also disposed of their waste in privies and buried their dead in graves dug into the same high water table, leading to water that sometimes held a ghastly taste. Even when the water was good enough to drink, it often ran out when residents tried to clean the streets or, far more perilously in a city built mostly of wood, when they scrambled to put out fires. Soapboilers, brewers, tanners, blacksmiths, innkeepers, and other tradesmen struggled to get enough water to complete their work all year round. Simply digging more or deeper wells was not the answer. If money was a vital resource, water was even more so, and Philadelphians would clash over how to get it, who would have access to it, and who could control it.[13]

Philadelphia merchants and the residents of the city's sprawling and primarily farming country also desired and required much more reliable and extensive methods of travel and transport. Even in well-settled areas, travelers encountered "rough roads" that were often "difficult and rather wild." Nearly everyone complained of the mud, wheel ruts, stumps, and rocks that hindered speedy travel, reducing overland movement to a constant struggle in which even urgent progress, as one frustrated traveler put it, came only "as soon as the badness of the roads would permit." Nor did inland water transportation, besides a few rivers, offer anything better. On the rim of the Atlantic world in the eighteenth century, waterways provided the fastest and cheapest mode of transportation: it cost less to send Pennsylvania flour over a thousand miles to the West Indies than fifty miles overland. But one voyager found that in the United States most rivers were "neither navigable nor fordable," thus hindering more than helping farmers to sell their produce and merchants to distribute their wares. Here, too, Philadelphia's obstacles symbolized those of the nation. Of the city's two rivers, one natural waterway—the Delaware—offered access to the Atlantic Ocean and some travel upstream, but a traveler remarked that the other, the Schuylkill, "is ornamental rather than useful to this city and its commerce . . . on account of its shallow and rocky bed." Philadelphians wrangled with the questions of who would pay for, build, and maintain the new roads, or better yet, canals, necessary for the country to prosper and grow. Further complicating the issue, many Americans realized that control over transportation represented a crucial source of leverage over local economies and politics.[14]

Quaker City residents had at their disposal several general categories of options for who would finance and oversee the solutions to their money, water, and transportation woes. Philadelphians could seize the initiative as private citizens, either individually or in small groups, for each different problem. The Pennsylvania state government could step in to finance and run the necessary projects. Or the state could authorize groups of citizens to tackle these problems while providing some level of oversight. Americans in general and many Philadelphians in particular had extensive familiarity and varying degrees of comfort with each of these kinds of organization and would experiment with them and employ them in different forms throughout the early national period. Each of them had their respective practical merits and demerits that certainly weighed on the minds of those who had to choose among them. But a particular group of elite Philadelphians who took the greatest initiative in these areas considered more than practicality: the attendant issues of the distribution of political and economic power also entered their calculations. Accordingly, the organizational solution that they championed reflected not only financial, administrative, and legal nuts and bolts but also the greater American political engine of which they were a part.

Perhaps the most immediate possibility to many Philadelphians was for private citizens either as individuals or in small groups to take on these challenges. In the decades before the American Revolution, Quaker City residents had been among the colonies' most enterprising and public-minded people. Massachusetts embraced its imperious Mathers and the Chesapeake cradled its cavalier Carters, but only Philadelphia's Benjamin Franklin helped to found the British continental colonies' first fire company, its first lending library, and its first public hospital. Such organizations inspired individuals to join together to take on problems bigger than any one person could tackle but that colonial city governments would not undertake, and these institutions would persist in many forms in the early republic. Fire companies were simply voluntary associations. Other civic organizations structured as joint-stock companies raised their original capital by selling shares that could then be passed on to family members or sold to others. They did not pay dividends, but shareholders might have special privileges, depending upon the organization.[15]

Philadelphians also adopted the joint-company structure to raise larger amounts of money in pursuit of profit: land speculators collaborated to purchase vast tracts in the hopes of developing them and selling them to eager settlers. Of course, that did not mean that individuals did nothing on their own; many property owners initially addressed the water supply problem by having wells dug on their property, though later the city government took over the task of putting in public pumps. Merchants and tradesmen had long experience both running their own individual businesses and banding together in partnerships to pool resources, share talent, and distribute economic risk. They lent each other money, insured each other's shipping ventures, and, especially in Philadelphia, engaged in manufacturing on what became an impressive scale. Private initiative had accomplished a great deal in colonial Philadelphia and would continue to do so in early national Philadelphia.[16]

Nonetheless, individuals on their own and in concert could not cure the larger ills that plagued the city. Though useful for getting people together to fight fires or for overseeing small businesses, their efforts tended to suffer from a lack of resources, could be unstable, and did not have the legal standing necessary for these particular kinds of projects. Philadelphians' impressive private efforts at public safety and to take up the slack from ineffective governance from 1776 to 1789 did not mask the necessity of greater resources. Lending sums to a few neighbors and associates paled next to the challenge of providing credit and money supply for the nation's largest city and one of its largest states. Not until the 1810s would an individual Philadelphian have the resources to try private banking on a considerable scale, when rich merchant Stephen Girard would establish his own bank backed by perhaps America's largest fortune. Men with a lesser reputation or lesser fortunes were hard-pressed to gain the widespread trust necessary for their notes to be widely accepted. In addition to a lack of resources, private bankers—men running unincorporated banks—lacked the imprimatur of the state. Their banknotes were not legal tender, that is, they could not be used to pay taxes, and while anyone had the option to accept them as money (and many creditors did), no one was legally obligated to—not exactly a good basis for running a cash-based economy.[17]

If a lack of resources and state backing proved difficult for money and credit, it presented an insuperable obstacle for transportation projects or for urban water supply. Water systems and internal improvements were enormously costly, more so than anything any American individual or even any small group could afford. River water belonged to the public, and while landowners on riverbanks had a limited right to divert some water for millraces, no private citizen could legally divert water on a scale to supply a city or provide for boat traffic, much less to charge tolls for boats to travel on any such project. And even if a group of landholders along a river got together to make a canal along their properties, any property holder whose lands would be affected could kill the project. While many private companies and partnerships lasted generations, the form could also be unstable and unwieldy. Partnerships worked best when only a few people were involved, when there were clear lines of succession, and when not a great deal of administration was required; but undertakings like banks or internal improvements required a larger bureaucratic apparatus in terms of clerks and managers than most partnerships could handle. Furthermore, all members of the partnership were personally liable for any debts the partnership might incur, meaning a potential loss of property and debtors' prison for group failure. Partnerships, then, implied a great degree of trust. No doubt most merchants could relate at least one tale of some acquaintance's ruination through the bad luck or malfeasance of erstwhile partners. And using business partnerships to solve Philadelphia's problem would require more than just trust among partners. A covenant between its proprietors and the public was also needed. Who could guarantee that a private partnership designed for profit would not put its own avarice ahead of the common weal?

Given that private efforts would not suffice, another option was for the

Pennsylvania state government to administer projects that would address Philadelphians' economic needs. The treasury was the largest pool of capital in the state, and the state legislature could authorize the rights-of-way and eminent domain necessary for water supply or transportation projects. In addition, colonial Pennsylvania had been more successful than most of its neighbors in solving credit and money-supply woes. The Quaker colony had employed two strategies that many other colonies had adopted to ensure a stable and plentiful currency. One consisted of issuing "fiat money," paper currency so called because it was established simply because of the declaration of the government. That said, it was backed by the colony's power to tax in order to gain revenue to buy back its notes, and Pennsylvania always redeemed them fully within a few years, even through the financial crisis of the Seven Years War. As one Pennsylvanian later reminisced, "it is in the memory of every gentleman, that, before the beginning of the Revolution, every State issued paper money; it answered the exigencies of Government in a considerable degree." Runaway inflation during and after the Revolutionary War rendered nearly all fiat money in circulation almost valueless, but even in the late 1770s and early 1780s, while the continental lost nearly all of its practical value, Pennsylvania currency generally held its ground better than most other state-issued notes. The lesson of the Revolution was that for fiat money to be successful, the issuing agency needed to convince jittery investors that it could generate revenue sufficient to cover whatever liabilities the government might incur through the use of paper money.[18]

The other colonial governmental solution to inadequate levels of cash, and one especially popular with farmers, was the loan office, often referred to as a land bank, which printed currency to be loaned for long-term mortgages on land. These loans tended to be in small amounts, as low as £25, and the revenue generated from the interest resulted in significant income for the colonial treasury. Loan offices also made credit available across the colony and to people of middling means. After the Revolution, land banks still held their appeal and fulfilled their mission to offer credit and supplement the money supply. In 1785, the Pennsylvania legislature authorized an establishment of a land bank whose notes circulated until the last of the bills trickled back into the state treasury sometime around the turn of the nineteenth century. Some Pennsylvanians would long remember the success of land banks and think of them as a viable policy option. As late as 1820, members of the Pennsylvania Senate would propose the establishment of a land bank as a solution to a perceived lack of credit and circulating medium in the wake of the Panic of 1819. Land banks and fiat money provided revenue for the state, thus aiding state finance while also providing needed public credit and currency. That said, from the point of view of Philadelphia merchants engaged in transatlantic commerce, land banks offered little: merchants wanted investments and short-term loans based upon expectations of profit rather than state-run ventures that provided them with no profit opportunity, and long-term loans based upon land they did not have.[19]

Furthermore, state governments could not solve every problem. Though loan banks and fiat currency could serve well in everyday business affairs and their administration could fill government coffers, Pennsylvania's colonial government had enjoyed no success in internal improvement. Accordingly, Pennsylvanians could harbor at least some confidence in the new state government's ability to address the problem of money, but little such faith in other areas, and most of the early national period legislators balked at having the state administer such projects. After all, in a state with an electorate so hostile to taxes that its citizens forcibly resisted them several times before the turn of the nineteenth century, rare was the legislator with the courage—or perhaps foolhardiness—to go back to his constituents to explain why he voted public funds (their taxes) for a canal through someone else's district, thereby giving their competitors cheaper transportation to market.

During its infancy, the state was simply not ready or willing to undertake large projects. Only in the 1820s, when Keystone Staters envied the brilliant success of neighboring New York's state-financed Erie Canal, did the state legislature back a state-run project, and then only because Pennsylvania's new Main Line system, an overly costly engineering feat combining canals with inclined planes, would connect much of the state. And though it first succeeded, it soon became bogged down with extra spurs insisted upon by those through whose counties it did not originally go. Meanwhile, central and western hostility to Philadelphia ensured that the state would not finance city projects; Philadelphians would be left to their own devices. In addition, a great many Pennsylvanians from all areas remained suspicious of establishing a state bureaucracy. No doubt many remembered that one of their primary grievances against the Crown had been their perception that the imperial bureaucracy gave ministers the opportunity to reward their friends with jobs and contracts and so establish tyranny. Furthermore, Pennsylvanians could reasonably be wary that the state would spend money inefficiently and possibly be intrusive besides. As one naysayer denigrated a proposal for a state-run project in 1808, "the work would be unreasonably procrastinated, and finally cost twice as much as if committed to individuals who had an interest in its speedy completion." Thus, while individuals and partnerships were unable to rise to the task of meeting Philadelphia's big challenges, voters hesitated to have the state take them up, either.[20]

Another possibility remained: corporations. In theory, this solution allowed for the state government to authorize large groups of people to assume problems that neither the state nor partnerships could. Americans, and especially Philadelphians, had long experience with municipal corporations, that is, city governments chartered by the colony. The city of Philadelphia first obtained a charter in 1701, a begrudging admission by proprietor William Penn that while he still held political authority in his American province, his power was limited. His fears were confirmed, as his opponents soon controlled Philadelphia government. Membership in the corporation consisted of being an adult male, having established two years' residence, and owning a certain amount of property; upon meeting these strictures, members elected corporate officers (councilmen and alders) who in turn governed the city. The colony granted the corporation's officers the right to make laws and ordinances and to regulate markets, though it stopped short of allowing them to tax inhabitants. Still, the corporation proved up to some considerable tasks, including channeling and eventually covering over Dock Creek, a stream that wended its way through the city to the Delaware, when the small waterway became too polluted for residents to bear. And other British colonial municipal corporations had completed even larger projects, such as Boston's Long Wharf. The formation of Pennsylvania's new state government in 1776 swept away the Philadelphia corporation, as many radical legislators from the city and the country finally exercised long-held grudges against the closely ruled body; they substituted a jury-rigged system barely functional during peacetime and certainly not up to the task of governing the city during the war. Nonetheless, a municipal corporation seemed the most appropriate long-term answer to administering the state's capital city, which suffered from governmental inattention even as state legislators stayed there while the government was in session.[21]

Despite their long medieval heritage, corporations—especially business corporations—were among the largest, most active, and most important economic institutions in eighteenth-century Britain. Under British rule, Americans had been forbidden from chartering business corporations but certainly had knowledge of them. Philadelphians read and heard about a range of British contemporary corporate business activities that the Crown had chartered to channel private interests to public ends. From its inception in 1694, the Bank of England had supplied a steady line of credit to the Crown, allowing Britain to finance the military machine that undergirded its empire while delivering steady profits to investors; Scotland's three corporate banks had pioneered the use of banknotes as a way to bolster a developing economy's money supply and the opening of branch offices to geographically extend the availability of credit. Indeed, Scottish philosophers such as Adam Smith credited Scottish banks as being central to that country's spectacular economic growth. Meanwhile, by the early eighteenth century the British began building inland navigations from mining regions to the coast or to regional population centers. The construction of corporate canals greatly accelerated in the 1760s, as more inland manufacturing and mercantile centers strove to be better connected to what was quickly becoming a national market. Pennsylvanians followed these developments with great interest, to the point where one broadside wit could mention "the hydrophobia of a Brindly"—James Brindley was England's most celebrated canal engineer and one of its most enthusiastic promoters—with the expectation that his audience would understand the reference. Despite widespread wariness of corporations in Britain immediately after a stock-trading bubble broke in 1720, the British increasingly used business corporations throughout the eighteenth century, and Parliament's chartering of new corporations—especially internal improvement companies—accelerated sharply from the 1760s forward. Though Americans had not constructed business corporations of their own, they had ample British blueprints from which to borrow.[22]

In between state government or fully private solutions to Philadelphia's pressing needs, corporations combined some of the advantages and liabilities of both of those extremes while introducing new factors present in neither. Through the chartering process, corporations could obtain the legal authority necessary for the success of financial institutions, internal improvements, or urban infrastructure, while the state government could place reasonable limits on corporate behavior and institute oversight mechanisms that private efforts largely avoided. Unlike with state governmental programs, the people most interested in solving the particular need would be the ones to put up the initial capital, whether that would be private investors in the case of business corporations or local taxpayers in the case of municipal corporations. They would also provide the energy, leadership, and expertise required by such endeavors without their getting paralyzed in the gridlock of legislative affairs, and, because of their commitment in time and money, would presumably run the project more efficiently and with a lower cost than could the state government. Unlike partnerships, corporate investors would not be liable for company debts, thus freeing corporate investors to risk ventures that partners, with their unlimited liability, might not (though shareholders were perhaps legally liable for corporate debts, the practical difficulties of collecting from hundreds of shareholders gave them de facto limited liability). Corporations could also be structured to administer complex operations, as Britain's large corporations had demonstrated. At the same time, the state government could demand a portion of business corporation stock or a percentage of their dividends so that both the shareholders and the treasury would gain revenue from successful ventures. In these ways, corporations offered the best of both worlds.[23]

But corporations also posed new difficulties as a result of their hybrid nature. A group of private citizens could accomplish much good if given access to state authority for such legal privileges as eminent domain, right-of-way, the privilege of printing notes that served as legal tender; they could also abuse it to their own benefit. While individuals and partnerships had to be efficient to survive against endless competition, states tended to grant corporations monopolies, leading to the same kinds of bloat, inefficiencies, and potential for gouging that accompanied state enterprises. Limiting liability encouraged risk, but it could also leave a corporation's creditors holding the bag because of corporate officers' incompetence or malfeasance. And the practice of granting some people charters while others struggled without the advantage of incorporation seemed antithetical to Pennsylvania's new egalitarian bent. In sum, corporations offered a practical, if imperfect, option.

Philadelphians understood that governance and the economy were inextricably tied together in innumerable ways, but to a certain small coterie of the Quaker City's more wealthy merchants and lawyers, corporations offered a way to cut that Gordian knot. To them, the American Revolution appeared to replace a misruling king with an unruly mob. By the 1780s, many members of the economic elite perceived themselves as the Philadelphians whose existence was most precarious. Such a view was, of course, outrageously self-centered, in that they had the greatest pool of resources to ride out even the Revolution with at least some of their fortunes remaining; unlike the city's legions of day laborers who resorted to begging, destitute women forced into casual prostitution, and ever-growing numbers admitted to the poorhouse, these men never feared for their next meal or had to shift for a warm, dry place to sleep. But such advantages apparently offered little reassurance.[24]

Accordingly, a small group of Philadelphia men addressed their political insecurities by focusing upon a critique of policies that they characterized as antithetical to the dictates of sound fiscal management and of eighteenth-century domestic and transatlantic commerce. A subsection of the city's economic elite, these Philadelphians tended to be among the wealthiest provisioner merchants whose primary profits came from exporting, men such as Thomas Fitzsimons, Robert Morris, Thomas Willing, and William Bingham. Their primary business interests would remain in international commerce, pursued through the partnerships with which they were so familiar, but they looked for new institutional opportunities through which to effect policy in ways that complemented their principal business pursuits. This core was joined by a smattering of other merchants, lawyers, and others depending upon the nature of subsequent corporate ventures. Wealthy men of every stripe speculated in land and so provided a broad base of support for the first internal improvement projects—men such as solicitor James Wilson, instrument maker David Rittenhouse, and College of Pennsylvania professor William Smith, who all joined the rush. The majority of this group had been Anglicans and supporters of the colonial Assembly faction, and the core came from several interconnected family circles that included the Allens, the Willings, the Binghams, and a few other well-established clans.[25]

Two instances proved particularly telling of the bifurcation between popular rule and members of what would become the nascent corporate elite, the first one involving wealthy Philadelphia merchant Robert Morris; the second one, eminent Philadelphia lawyer James Wilson. By the late 1770s, in response to the state's struggles to keep money at a steady valuation, local governing committees began to institute draconian price controls and various measures against engrossing (buying up at wholesale and selling later at monopoly prices) and forestalling (buying goods at prices lower than available to the public). Many lower-sort radicals favored these policies in order to ensure the affordability of basic necessities, but such rules were anathema to many artisans and nearly all merchants, especially those engaged in international trade. In March 1779, Morris arranged to purchase grain for local sale from a ship already anchored in port; he then sat on it for a month, during which local prices doubled because of shortages, before selling the grain at a fabulous profit—at least a borderline case of engrossing, though Morris later claimed that he was the victim of translation problems with the ship's French-speaking captain. Meanwhile, Morris had also been engaged in what could be construed as forestalling: he had bought grain in Wilmington, Delaware, and had avoided price controls there through equally shady tactics, including, apparently, smuggling barrels of flour under cover of darkness that later appeared in his Philadelphia warehouses (he later claimed he did so to keep the grain out of the hands of loyalist partisans). As a result of these twin offenses, a Philadelphia town meeting deputized a committee to charge Morris with engrossing and monopolizing goods at the expense of the public. Though Morris protested his innocence and avoided penalty, his reputation suffered considerable damage.[26]

Portly financier Robert Morris in 1785, looking something between dignified and put upon; the painting very well captured his general demeanor. Portrait by Robert Edge Pine, c. 1785. Courtesy of National Portrait Gallery, Smithsonian Institution.

On October 4 of that same year, a crowd of militiamen proceeded down the streets, keen on harassing opponents of price regulations. The marchers placed several merchants under extralegal arrest and then proceeded to James Wilson's house, where twenty self-described "gentlemen" had holed up in fear—or defiance, as they later bragged. A ten-minute firefight ensued, during which one man in the house—later dubbed "Fort Wilson"—was killed before the militia was chased off by some City Troop cavalry and members of a Continental cavalry brigade. To men like Morris and Wilson, the underlying problem appeared to be that economic instability had led to social instability. These men began to wonder how they could live, much less conduct business, under these uncertain conditions, in which the state government, to their eyes, appeared incapable of administering a stable economy or keeping social order.[27]

Morris, Wilson, and other sympathetic men perceived corporations to be a solution to Philadelphia's economic problems that would also allow them, rather than elected officials, to set economic policy in ways that they believed better served society and, not coincidentally, could also line their pockets. Their first such project resulted in the first business corporation in the United States. Writing in the spring of 1781, ambitious young Alexander Hamilton asserted to Morris, the Continental Congress's newly designated superintendent of finance, that "the people have lost all confidence in our public councils," and "our friends in Europe are in the same disposition." The nation looked increasingly unable to fund the war effort, much less confront its ever-burgeoning debt. For Hamilton, the only way to accomplish these aims was to remove "the reins of administration" from Congress and have them "intrusted to individuals of established reputation and con[spicuous] for probity, abilities, and fortune." In other words, to shift control over fiscal policy away from publicly elected representatives and to the elite merchants, lawyers, and gentlemen whom Hamilton trusted more than the people at large. Furthermore, Hamilton sought a device that would "inspire confidence in monied men in Europe as well as in America" to lend money to the flagging cause.[28]

Hamilton's method: establishing an incorporated national bank. His lengthy letter to Morris in late April 1781 included an extended discussion of the nation's financial distress, its potential resources, his rationale for a bank, and even a detailed plan for one. Hamilton's letter may have inspired Morris, or perhaps the rich merchant had already been thinking along parallel lines. He had certainly entertained similar notions before: fifteen years earlier, as an ambitious young man himself, Morris had suggested the formation of a corporate bank in Pennsylvania. And the year before Hamilton contacted the superintendent, Morris and others had allied to form and invest in an unincorporated Pennsylvania bank to raise money for the war effort. Less than three weeks after receiving Hamilton's letter, Morris submitted his own plan for a national bank to the Continental Congress and to Pennsylvania's General Assembly. He and his associates named the institution the Bank of North America, and when the Continental Congress that Hamilton so derided expressed legitimate concerns regarding its authority to charter corporations, Pennsylvania legislators quickly voted the proposal into law with few changes.[29]

While the Bank of North America was a new kind of institution for Philadelphians, the revival of the city corporation in 1789 represented a reincarnation of one that had fallen into temporary disuse, and came under different circumstances and with somewhat different champions than the incorporated bank. The Bank of North America had been formed in the crucible of the Revolution; by 1789, Pennsylvania moderates had tempered Revolutionary radicalism and were hammering out institutions more to their liking. In 1776, Pennsylvania's radical-dominated new unicameral state government had revoked the city's charter as a relic of the hierarchical, aristocratic colonial power structure; however, legislators did not offer a replacement, instead choosing to govern the capital city themselves. In terms of its ability to run itself, during the 1780s Philadelphia was worse off than it had been in 1700. While the men who pushed for business corporations mostly hailed from the old Assembly faction, the ones who pushed for a new municipal charter mainly had been part of the old proprietary elite, men like Samuel Powel, who wanted to regain at least a modicum of their old political standing. After thirteen years of alternating periods of rebuffs and inattention at the hands of a legislature dominated by westerners largely unsympathetic or even hostile to the nation's largest city—during which time eventually even the legislature admitted that "the administration of government within the city of Philadelphia is, in its present form, inadequate"—Philadelphia's representatives finally managed to push through a new corporate charter.[30]

Claiming to "to invest the inhabitants thereof with more speedy, vigorous, and effective powers of government," this document elaborated in much greater detail than the previous charter the new city corporation's powers, limits, and modes of operation, while opening up its membership to all eligible voters. As before, aldermen fulfilled the judicial function of justices of the peace and sat as judges in local courts, and a thirty-member common council wrote and passed ordinances, laws, and budgets. Reflecting the nation's new republican ethos and the state's 1776 constitution, though, these men were to be elected: aldermen for seven years and council members annually. The General Assembly gave this corporation a somewhat longer leash than the last one had enjoyed; the charter allowed that "as often as any doubts shall arise touching this act, the same shall . . . be construed and taken most favourably for the said Corporation." Checks on the new government included stipulations that the council have all ordinances and budgets printed in city newspapers, that any officer could be impeached, and that decisions by justices of the peace and by city courts could be appealed. In a 1796 move to bring the structure of city government in line with the state government under the 1790 constitution, the Pennsylvania legislature amended the charter to provide for an upper legislative body, the Select

Council, whose members served three-year terms. This revised framework remained untouched for over half a century.[31]

Though the Philadelphia corporation's legal structure thereafter remained stable, as with many American city governments that would undertake a wide variety of services, the functions it performed and how it performed them changed considerably with the massive undertaking of building a city-wide water supply system in the late 1790s. Philadelphians had successfully offered a British corporate solution for credit and transportation problems, but it took a native Briton to come up with a way to address the city's water problems. Massive yellow fever plagues in 1793, 1797, and 1798 claimed thousands of lives, emptied the city to a ghost town in late summer, and convinced city residents that unless they prevented further such calamities, "the reputation & salvation of the City [was] at stake." Doctors and laymen hotly debated the cause of the epidemics, but they generally agreed that the city's current inadequate combination of private wells and public pumps probably contributed to the spread of the dreaded disease. Despite Governor Thomas Mifflin's warning that "the general prosperity of our state will be immediately endangered" unless everyone worked "to avert, as far as human agency can avail, the recurrence of so awful a visitation," the state legislature seemed content to let the city deal with the problem.[32]

The Philadelphia city corporation began negotiating with a chartered canal corporation, the Delaware and Schuylkill Canal Company, to route the canal through the city not only for commerce but also with aqueducts for water supply, at the same time that city officials lobbied the state government for funds to help the deal go through, but the efforts failed. Meanwhile, in 1798, British engineer and architect B. Henry Latrobe proposed a city-run, steam-powered water supply system that would be funded through municipal bonds rather than directly through city taxes. Because of a lack of confidence that the canal corporation would be able to finish the job, suspicion of cost overruns, and concerns regarding who would actually have control over the canal's water, the city councils opted for Latrobe's system. The municipal corporation would build the first of its grand water systems, using bonds to pay for it.[33]

While the founding of the first bank may have been a reaction to what a group of Philadelphia businessmen considered an overreaching state government, and the reestablishment of the City Corporation of Philadelphia and its building its own water system may have been a result of state governmental neglect, the establishment of internal improvement companies can be seen as an energetic response to a lack of state legislative leadership. Philadelphians sought institutional structures to gather the capital and administrative resources necessary to build canals and river navigations connecting the city to its hinterland, and they demanded new artificial inland navigations that, in the words of canal booster Charles Paleske, would "secure the grand objects of conveying the products of the interior country to the metropolis, and returning with the imports or manufactures of the latter."

Significant progress in this arena did not occur until 1791, with the formation of the Society for Promoting the Improvement of Roads and Inland Navigation by Robert Morris, John Nicholson, William Smith, and a handful of other Philadelphia notables. Arguing that "neither the state alone, nor any number of companies without public regulation and assistance, can be adequate to the great work in all its parts," the group petitioned the Pennsylvania legislature with a plan for coordinating public supervision and finance with private investment to connect all parts of the state with roads, canals, and river improvements.[34]

The plan called for a legislature-appointed Board of Commissioners that would decide what roads and canals to run where and which ones were to be financed out of the public coffers, through a combination of public and private money, or entirely through private investment. In the last two cases, the board would subcontract to time-limited corporations—still answerable to the board—to construct the works, maintain them, and collect tolls. The investors would be guaranteed a return of 6 percent by the state, but should the company begin to make more than 6 percent a year, the state would buy out the investors. This thorough scheme allowed for public oversight of internal improvement while taking the politically charged decisions of routes and funding out of the notoriously contentious Pennsylvania legislature. It answered all the potential political, institutional, and financial difficulties of internal improvement. The scheme made enough of an impression to last: a modified but similar proposition appeared in a Philadelphia paper as late as 1812. But it was never close to being enacted, failing to reach the floor for a legislative vote. The state had dropped the ball.[35]

Accordingly, most of the same body of men who had decided to take policy into their own hands by establishing business corporations with control over credit and money supply proceeded to found the same kinds of institutions in the field of internal transportation. Having had their scheme for a state-administered system of internal improvements rebuffed by the legislature, members of the road and inland navigation society proceeded on their own, lobbying successfully to establish two internal improvement business corporations, the Delaware and Schuylkill Canal Navigation Company and the Schuylkill and Susquehanna Canal and Lock Navigation Company, both chartered by Pennsylvania in the spring 1792 session. Many Bank of North America founders contributed to the establishment of these Philadelphia-area projects; some sat on the boards of several of these institutions, a connection cemented by the bank's subsequent ownership of seven shares in the Delaware and Schuylkill Canal Company.[36]

The individuals who founded corporations, especially business corporations, also primarily designed them, and they did so with considerable British know-how. The four men most closely involved in the establishment of the Bank of North America—William Bingham, Robert Morris, Thomas Willing, and James Wilson—had an ample store of knowledge concerning British corporate banks. All were familiar with the commerce-oriented publications that claimed a wide readership among well-informed merchants in the Anglo-Atlantic world. Alexander Hamilton's correspondence leading up to his letter to Morris in which he proposed a national bank revealed a common set of readings for businessmen in the know about current British practices. He wrote to a colleague asking to borrow particular books and the works of certain authors: "Have you any tract written by *Price* in which he estimates the specie & current cash of Great Britain? Have you Hume's Essay's, *Lex Mercatoria* or Postlethwait?" That he referred to these texts in such an abbreviated way indicated the familiarity with which he regarded these works and the clear expectation that his correspondent, too, would know them without further elaboration. The publications Hamilton requested, Richard Price's *Observations on Civil Liberty* and his *Additional Observations on the Nature and Value of Civil Liberty,* David Hume's *Political Discourses,* Wyndham Beawes's *Lex Mercatoria Rediviva: or the Merchant's Directory,* and Malachy Postlethwayt's *The Universal Dictionary of Trade and Commerce,* were all part of a commonly read and referred-to corpus of works used by eighteenth-century American merchants that included detailed descriptions of British business corporations and corporate practice.[37]

The latter two publications, Beawes's *Lex Mercatoria* and Postlethwayt's *Universal Dictionary,* were oft-consulted references for merchants in the English-speaking Atlantic world, each issued in numerous editions in the 1760s and 1770s. The Library Company of Philadelphia (the city's lending library that Franklin helped found) owned copies of both, indicative of the value attributed to them by its members, mostly composed of the merchant class. William Bingham and Robert Waln, each involved in the Bank of North America's founding, later headed the committee designated to order books for the Library of Congress, and the two works would be included among the first ordered, further evidence of their general currency in the period. The *Lex Mercatoria* was virtually an encyclopedia of world trade. Billed by publishers as "a Complete Guide to All Men in Business," it included profiles of various nations and ports the world over, entries describing British economic institutions, including the Bank of England, and selections on business practices, including the buying and selling of corporate stocks. The *Universal Dictionary* offered detailed treatment of banks in general and the Bank of England in particular. Along with brief descriptions of private and government banks, it defined corporate banks as "consist[ing] of a company of monied men, who, being duly established and incorporated by the laws of their country, agree to deposit a considerable fund or joint stock, to be employed for the profit and advantage of the whole society . . . of which kind is the bank of England." The Bank of North America, as (unsuccessfully) proposed by Hamilton and as planned and operated by Morris, Bingham, Willing, Wilson, and its board of directors, operated exactly on these general principles.[38]

In name, form, and operation, founders of Philadelphia-based banks closely followed British precedent, beginning with remarkable similarities in their charters. British bank charters required a majority of electors to amend company by-laws, that the companies' governor, lieutenant governor, and directors be elected annually during a specified one-month time frame, and that the directors be English (or, in the case of Scotland's banks, Scottish) subjects, and stated that a majority of directors constituted a quorum for official business. The Bank of North America and the Bank of Pennsylvania's charters stipulated that by-laws be amended by a majority of electors, that the president and directors be elected annually on a specific date, that directors be citizens of the United States—or in the case of the Bank of Pennsylvania, Keystone State citizens—and that a majority of directors constituted a quorum. They raised capital in similar ways, too: both British and American banks placed a limit on the initial capital, set a maximum on individuals' initial investment, and collected their capital through subscription. They even operated under similar limitations, including charter-mandated capital ceilings, the condition that dividends be issued out of profits rather than paid-in capital, and prohibitions against engaging in other trades. And once Philadelphia was home to several banks, company officers met to coordinate money policy the same way Scottish banks did. Philadelphia bankers clearly emulated British bankers through their adoption of such similar methods and structures. As a governor of Pennsylvania pointed out in 1814, specifically referring to the Bank of England, "the principles of that institution are substantially those adopted in all the banking establishments of the United States." Indeed, he argued that "British institutions and practices [contained] the principles which have generally been adopted as the basis of every branch of financial policy in the United States."[39]

Connections between British and American internal navigation companies grew even more extensive than those of banking corporations. America's first wave of canal corporations was chartered during exactly the same period as Britain's 1790s canal-building frenzy, suggesting that the canal craze was a transatlantic phenomenon rather than strictly a British one. From 1791 to 1796, state governments chartered forty-two canal companies, peaking at eleven in 1792 and 1796, more than in any five-year period in the United States until the Erie Canal–inspired boom of the early 1820s. The British Parliament authorized fifty-two canal corporations during the same five-year stint, suggesting that the mother country was still blazing trails for its postcolonial offspring to follow.[40]

The Delaware and Schuylkill Canal Navigation Company and the Schuylkill and Susquehanna Canal and Lock Navigation Company showed considerable debts to British precedent. Just as in banking, American knowledge and modeling of British internal navigation corporations was widespread and detailed. In his efforts to promote the two companies, College of Pennsylvania president William Smith wrote America's most complete treatise on internal navigation during the 1790s. The pamphlet includes long passages expounding upon the benefits of internal navigation companies and the waterways they built and administered. Smith argued that "by *canals,* a people may be supplied . . . with grain, forage, fuel, materials for building, and also all other heavy and raw materials for manufactures, which otherwise would remain of little value at a distance from the place where they are wanted"—quoting directly (though without attribution) from Charles Villancey's *A Treatise on Inland Navigation*, a popular British book promoting several British canal corporations. Smith's work also includes passages that appeared in several British sources, and that he most likely lifted from *The History of Inland Navigations*, a book that doubled as treatise and corporate propaganda. The latter work and other British publications such as *A General History of Inland Navigation, Foreign and Domestic* and *The Advantages of Inland Navigation* became standard references for British and American internal-improvement boosters.[41]

American canal-corporation pioneers learned much from their British internal-navigation corporate predecessors. In 1766, English canal booster Richard Whitworth published a pamphlet that could be read as a manual for an internal navigation company's bid to secure financing and a charter. His suggestions typified organizers' efforts: advertise widely, explaining the proposed route and announcing a time and place for interested parties to meet; hold meetings at multiple locations to drum up financial and political support; encourage attendees to sign a solicitor-composed petition to Parliament to charter the company; ask for subscriptions to defray costs associated with the charter legislation process, the money for which would be returned upon successful application; generate subscriptions for backing the actual project; get local landholders and merchants to sign sympathetic petitions; finally, apply to Parliament. Whitworth even included sample language for the various resolutions and petitions.[42]

Philadelphia-area project boosters followed suit, from the first two projects in 1791 through the 1820s. They advertised meetings along the proposed route, took subscriptions and composed petitions, had a lawyer draw up a charter, and campaigned for local political support, in the form of sympathetic petitions, and financial support, in the form of subscription shares. The phrasing and structure of early Philadelphia-area internal-improvement company charters also echoed their British counterparts, including sections devoted to the adjudication of disputes between the companies and the owners of lands through which the canals would flow. Just like corporate bank charters, canal company charters on both sides of the Atlantic contained clauses providing for the annual election of directors to ensure the will of the stockholders, and—as a sop to wary legislators—graduated voting systems designed to limit the influence of large stockholders. American internal-improvement company officials followed their British counterparts closely.[43]

Such detailed knowledge of British practice and the willingness to follow it shows that early corporate men came from a small economic and political slice of the American population. Though clearly tied into the Atlantic world, Philadelphia's early corporate founders were tied even more to each other, both by class and by politics. Nearly to a man, early Bank of North America insiders shared a common outlook. Nothing could be more demonstrative of their views on society, how it should be run, and by whom than the prohibitive $400 asking price for Bank of North America shares. Indeed, bank supporters openly referred to themselves as "the most respectable characters among us" and almost universally supported a political and economic program that supported their belief that government would be best run by opulent men. On the national level, many had served in or for the Continental army and the Continental Congress, decried the weaknesses of the Articles of Confederation, and became ardent Federalists, certain that the 1787 Shays's "rebellion" (as they called it) in Massachusetts and Pennsylvania's Carlisle riots of the late 1780s heralded a descent into leveling chaos. In Pennsylvania politics, too, they opposed the current structure of government, in this case the state's radical constitution passed in 1776. Bank of North America men like Ebenezer Hazard, Thomas Fitzsimons, and Robert Morris politicked hard as members of the state's Anti-Constitutional faction to rid Pennsylvania of what they perceived to be a weak and overly democratic state governmental structure.[44]

These elite men were not elitists in the sense of believing that their lineages rendered them superior to others; after all, the group was willing to admit new members, and more than a few of their number were self-made. Rather, they believed that their wealth in combination with education and worldliness marked them as part of what many of the nation's well-heeled referred to as a "natural aristocracy," more capable of ruling than those men with lesser social and economic attainments. Taken this way, Quaker City corporate founders could positively interpret their own elitism as merely resisting what they perceived as Pennsylvania's potential decline into demagogic tyranny; they convinced themselves that the best way to counter such a decline would be to put financial institutions, in the words of one sympathetic Philadelphian, "in the hands of men of fortune probity and moderation." They perceived themselves as taking the risks and potentially reaping the rewards of economic leadership that they believed that other Pennsylvanians and their elected representatives could not provide.[45]

A look at three men deeply involved in the founding of Philadelphia corporations offers a deeper sense of the emerging corporate culture, its politics, its social makeup, and its sources of thought. Thomas Willing and William Bingham, two of the city's wealthiest merchants and investors, personified the founding generation of Philadelphia's corporate elite. Merchant and banker Thomas Willing was born in Philadelphia in 1731; his mother, Mary, was from the prominent Pennsylvania Shippen merchant family, and his father, Charles, was English. His parents sent him to England to study at age nine, and he eventually read law at Inner Temple (perhaps England's most prestigious place to learn law) before returning to take over his father's merchant firm when that man died in 1754. Those familial connections placed him among the stalwarts of Philadelphia's antiproprietary elite clique. In addition, for all of his professional life, he corresponded with his paternal uncle, also named Thomas, who was a London merchant. In the 1760s, Willing was instrumental in founding America's first unincorporated marine insurance company, but the firm had liability and solvency worries because of its partnership status—a condition that incorporation would have obviated. Before independence, he served as the chairman of the Second Continental Congress's Secret Committee, charged with acquiring arms and supplies for the Continental army; during the war he bitterly opposed the state's unicameral legislature, and by the late 1780s he was an ardent Federalist. In the 1780s Willing further strengthened his British ties by opening trading relations with the House of Baring. He also speculated in land and was a founding director of the Schuylkill and Susquehanna Canal Company and of the Delaware and Schuylkill Canal Company; he became the first president of the first Bank of the United States; and he eventually also held stock in the Phoenix Insurance Company, Schuylkill Navigation Company, the Chesapeake and Delaware Canal Company, the Pennsylvania Company for Insuring Lives and Granting Annuities, and the Farmers and Mechanics Bank. His career connected the old colonial elite with the new economic order.[46]

William Bingham also was born and bred in Philadelphia and a member of a prominent merchant family. At age twenty-three, Bingham was appointed secretary to the Continental Congress's Committee for Secret Correspondence (charged with drumming up international support for the Revolutionary cause) and later operated in Martinique as a secret agent for the Continental Congress, obtaining supplies while ostensibly representing Morris and Willing's mercantile partnership. In 1780, he courted and married Anne Willing, Thomas Willing's eldest daughter. Although committed to the Revolution, Bingham was no radical: he firmly believed that economic order as defined by men like Morris and Hamilton underlay social and economic stability. He was one of the leaders of Pennsylvania's 1780s Republican faction—that is, he was opposed to Pennsylvania's radical 1776 constitution that provided for a unicameral legislature and weak executive. He represented Pennsylvania in the Continental Congress for the 1786 and 1787 sessions and became a staunch Federalist, arguing that "the Confederation is . . . an evil of an alarming nature. It does not possess sufficient power." Two years later, Bingham signed the petition that led to Pennsylvania's 1790 constitutional convention.[47]

In business, Bingham engaged in typical activities for Philadelphia's provisioning merchants—overseas trade, investment in government securities, and land speculation—and he cultivated personal and professional associations with Britain. As early as the summer of 1776, Robert Morris and Benjamin Franklin thanked him for the Richard Price pamphlets that Bingham had sent from London to Philadelphia, and importuned him to send "a constant and ample supply of the English, Irish, & French Newspaper, Political publications, &c." Also while in London, Bingham struck up what would became a long-standing correspondence with Price and began building his considerable library. Few men in post-Revolutionary America could have known more British economics, business, and society than did Bingham, and he put

William Bingham commissioned Gilbert Stuart to paint a portrait of George Washington in 1796; apparently Bingham liked it so much he himself posed for Stuart in 1797. This painting portrays a man of action, standing in front of a busy desk by the halls of power, handing off important papers. Gilbert Stuart, 1797. Courtesy of ING Bank N.V., London Branch.

his knowledge and British experience to use in a number of ways. Ever the anglophile, he made sure that his Philadelphia residence was, in the words of one visitor, "a magnificent house and gardens in the best English Style." He established a mercantile relationship with the House of Baring in the 1790s, a connection confirmed through the marriages of his two daughters to sons of House founder Francis Baring; eventually, the Barings bought into Bingham's sprawling Penobscot land grant in Maine. And, in 1781, Bingham wrote the by-laws for the Bank of North America, the first business corporation in the United States.[48]

Unlike Willing and Bingham—the first two members of this composite portrait—the last of the trio never became a member of the corporate elite. But the knowledge and expertise he brought was essential to the corporate project, and his complex relationship with corporate men exhibited the class tensions inherent in early corporate management. Benjamin Henry Latrobe (he referred to himself by his middle name) seemed to have spent all his life readying to design and build the Philadelphia Waterworks. He was born outside Leeds, England, in 1764. Latrobe's father was the "provincial helper" of Great Britain—the chief Moravian of the realm—and his mother had grown up in Bethlehem, Pennsylvania, and married the elder Latrobe after immigrating to London in 1743. Young Latrobe packed off to study at Moravian schools in Saxony at age twelve and returned to London in 1784, eight years later. He spent a couple of years in the Stamp Office before leaving the government to join celebrated engineer John Smeaton as an apprentice. Smeaton was especially known for designing steam engines that a contemporary described as "distinguished by juster proportions and greater nicety of detail than had yet been realised." Just as significantly for Latrobe, Smeaton had built a steam engine for the New River Company, one of the concerns supplying London with drinking water. Thus, Latrobe received training in canal surveying and steam engines from England's most capable engineer. Latrobe continued his occupational development as a draftsman and then architect in the office of Samuel Pepys Cockerell, the famous London architect. Finally setting out on his own, the young professional prospered his first few years in practice, but his obvious skills were offset by poor business sense and his political leanings toward revolutionary France. By 1793, when Britain declared war on France, the bottom fell out of the economy, and Latrobe's practice with it.[49]

Latrobe's personal life turned bleak, too. In November 1793 came what he described as "the most melancholy event that could ever befell" him: at the end of his wife Lydia's third pregnancy, she died giving birth, as did their baby. Latrobe languished. Perhaps when he told tales to his children at night, he remembered stories his mother had told him about the land of her childhood. Through his mother's family, Latrobe held sizable tracts of land in western Pennsylvania. Leaving his children under his brother's care, in 1795 Latrobe shipped off to Virginia. He earned some money by designing houses but lost more through his efforts on the Virginia State Penitentiary.

B. Henry Latrobe, soon after he made his name in the United States. Unlike an earlier portrait that displayed a somewhat whimsical young man and a later one that would picture a man whose troubles had caught up with him, this image of Latrobe shows a serious professional. Charles Willson Peale, c. 1804. Courtesy of White House Historical Association (White House Collection) (445).

The ambitious man wrote to a Philadelphia friend in January 1798 that he "should be happier in the active pursuit of professional reputation." Friends in high places turned out to be his salvation. In early 1798, Latrobe traveled to Philadelphia, armed with letters of introduction from Thomas Jefferson. There, Latrobe met Samuel Fox, who asked for a design proposal for a new building to house the Bank of Pennsylvania. Latrobe's design was approved that fall. In December 1798, he wrote his proposal for the waterworks, officially titled "View of the Practicability and Means of Supplying the City of Philadelphia with Wholesome Water," including a complete survey of the available options, detailed measurements of his own technological solution, and even a subscription model of payment that was later adopted.[50]

Latrobe's professionalism marked him as separate from but essential to the emerging corporate elite. On the one hand, Latrobe personified the transfer of technological, organizational, and even financial knowledge from Britain that was so essential to American corporate projects. On the other hand, he was the product of an English tradition of architects and engineers as independent professionals. Further complicating matters, Latrobe believed that his polished education and sophisticated manners in combination with early republican egalitarianism made him the peer of corporate men, though they thought differently. Philadelphia corporation Common Council member Thomas Cope viewed Latrobe as an employee—and a conniving, incompetent, and perhaps corrupt one, at that. When the project was struggling in 1801, Cope growled that "not a hydrant or other device of his contrivance answers the purpose," evidence of Latrobe's "injudicious experiments . . . [and] blunders & waste." In Englishman Latrobe's code, engineers were paid a percentage of the job's total costs and reimbursed for expenses, but when the waterworks went over budget—largely because of the conditions beyond Latrobe's control—his request for more money was rebuffed. For Cope, employees were entitled to what they contracted for—no more, no less—and were to be seen and not heard, unlike Latrobe, who seemed to have advice for the corporation on nearly every water-related topic. At one point their relationship bordered on the comical when the easygoing, equitable, and cash-poor Moravian Latrobe approached the starched, self-righteous, and niggardly Quaker Cope for a personal loan. The controversy between Latrobe and Cope revealed a central tension within corporations between the elite notions of the men who ran them and the egalitarian strivings of the men who worked for them. Latrobe and his successors might be corporate men, and their expertise and labor necessary for corporate success, but they would never be members of the corporate elite like Thomas Willing and William Bingham. Over the following decades, corporate leaders worked to extend the reach of their corporations while drawing lines within them.[51]

Willing, Bingham, and Latrobe all consciously lived in an Anglo-American Atlantic world. The adoption of corporations as opposed to private or state solutions entailed consequences well beyond who would manage these projects and how: they also involved significant redistribution of wealth and further integrated the United States into the Atlantic economy beyond the adoption of similar institutions. Indeed, the Bank of North America nearly failed, surviving at one point only because of a sudden influx of specie from Cuba. And through the creation of legal entities whose ownership could be divided into shares, the incorporation of American banks allowed for foreigners to buy stock in United States business ventures. One Philadelphia broker informed a Caribbean correspondent anxious to buy bank stock that shareholding in the Bank of North America "is but small and Ch[ie]fly owned in Europe & our Monied men here," although other banks' stocks were somewhat more readily available. Nonetheless, it was an opportunity that wealthy British investors did not pass up: by 1803, they owned over $34 million in the stock of state banks and the Bank of the United States. The British would also invest heavily in American internal navigation projects once the Erie Canal's spectacular success seemed to bode so well for such endeavors. Meanwhile, American corporate officers borrowed more than money, also continuing to adopt new British financial methods, including the use of preferred stock (also known as preference shares) to raise money from reluctant investors. Such common efforts showed their ultimate fruition in the development of railroad technologies and corporations on both sides of the Atlantic in the 1820s and 1830s.[52]

The foundation of corporations thus contributed significantly to the coalescence of a stable economic elite in the early republic. Heavy European investment provided an economic underpinning of Philadelphia's upper crust. Bank founders, especially men such as Robert Morris, Thomas Willing, and William Bingham, explicitly stated that Bank of North America shares would sell at the high price of $400 so as to limit shareholding to monied men, thereby both admitting a sense of elite solidarity and limiting the opportunity of bank stock ownership to the rich. With banks stocks quickly rising to over $500, and with the average Philadelphian possessing only in the $600s in total property, the opportunities for most Quaker City residents to share in the benefits of stockholding were slim at best. Given the cost of stocks, the number of shares available, the median holding of shares, the size of the total population, and median wealth figures, probably no more than 10 percent of Philadelphia's population could realistically expect to be able to invest in bank stock. Because wealthy Philadelphians always took up all of a bank's initial issues of stock, subsequent European purchases of stock on the open market entailed a large transfer of money into the hands of the Quaker City's well-off. Continued transatlantic interest in bank stocks meant that the establishment of every new corporate Philadelphia bank would result in the flow of capital from wealthy Europeans to their Philadelphia counterparts. In turn, the banks' ability to draw investment provided confidence in the banks and gave them adequate assets to lend without fears of a run on the bank. Banks' fairly regular dividends could provide a source of steady income that elite Philadelphians had craved for so long, thus contributing to family financial stability; the practice of establishing stock-owning trusts for widows and children testified to such motivations. Furthermore, lending policy ensured that the banks' capital would be used to bolster the fortunes of well-to-do merchants and allow them to weather the inevitable ups and downs of transatlantic and continental commerce. Even Philadelphia's municipal corporation, through the use of interest-bearing bonds, would redistribute wealth from taxpayers and renters to investors willing and able to afford such investments.[53]

While benefiting a wide swath of the population, corporations clearly held the most potential for a small percentage of Philadelphia's residents. Nonetheless, by definition the creation of corporations occurred only through the approval of the state government and, at least implicitly, the voting public. Furthermore, the Corporation of Philadelphia would be an institution at least nominally responsive to the voting public. Regardless of the motives of corporative founders—and legislators' suspicion of them—they had something that the state neither had on hand nor had the political courage to get, namely, money. The Bank of North America garnered the quick approval of the Continental Congress precisely because the national government had run out of ways to come up with the funds to continue the war effort, but investors snapped up the expensive stock in a matter of days. Over the coming decades, while Pennsylvania legislators heeded the call of their constituents to keep taxes down at all costs, they could count on the revenue from bank stocks and from taxes on bank dividends to contribute a hefty portion of the state's annual budget. Rather than dickering over which counties deserved state monies for roads and canals, the state legislature could hand out internal improvement charters like candy (charters were free, after all) and dole out small bits of aid everywhere in large omnibus bills without funding an entire system—at least, until the Erie Canal made inaction seem too risky. And rather than having representatives from all over the state spend their time and their constituents' money on the intricacies of water supply for a metropolis that most of them resented, by incorporating the City of Philadelphia, legislators could leave the problem to the locals.[54]

At the same time, by putting clauses in charters such as twenty-year terms for banks, prohibitions against internal improvement companies from engaging in land speculation, and limits on municipal government reach, state legislators hoped to prevent the most easily foreseeable abuses most tempting to corporate officers. Corporations seemed to offer state representatives relatively painless solutions to otherwise thorny problems. Accordingly, the founding of corporations represented a tacit power-sharing arrangement that could further the goals both of the legislators and of Philadelphia's economic elite.

Of course, Pennsylvania was not the only state to charter corporations. All the states had done so before 1800. Pennsylvania had by that time chartered twenty-three business corporations, New York twenty-eight, New Hampshire thirty-two, and Massachusetts a whopping sixty. Marked another way, Pennsylvania actually lagged behind other states: it ranked only eleventh among them in terms of charters granted proportional to its population. But the contrast of Pennsylvania's early political radicalism with the leveraging of capital by moneyed Philadelphia men put the establishment of Philadelphia corporations into stark and illuminating relief, best presaging the political and economic conditions that would occur in state after state over the coming decades. The founding and operation of Philadelphia corporations both constituted one of the main ingredients of the rearrangement of power that resulted from the American Revolution and served as a harbinger of future developments in other states.[55]

As in other states, in Pennsylvania corporations were far from the only factors in this process: the federal constitution of 1787 affected intrastate political dynamics, the Pennsylvania constitution of 1790 put the state on less radical political footing, and Keystone State voters and politicians on the local and state level spent much energy making the political culture and working out the ideas that established democracy and capitalism alongside each other. The uneasy truce between capitalism and democracy happened not only through the support of rich men, but as an accommodation among the myriad of Pennsylvania interests and groups. Many of the middling sort, especially in Philadelphia, supported the new state constitution after having lived through what they perceived as the state's mismanagement of the previous decade. Even some dyed-in-the-wool radicals approved of parts of the new program; Thomas Paine shocked many of his supporters with his staunch defense of the Bank of North America.[56]

Nonetheless, as corporate men founded and fostered their institutions, corporations would function as a way for a small group of men suddenly marginalized from the political process at the state level to establish an alternate base of power. By parlaying limited success in municipal elections and their access to capital, these men used corporations to forge a new arrangement that offset their newfound impotence in electoral politics at the state level, while state legislators could argue, with some validity, that private capital was being used to support public ends. This implicit arrangement of power signified the end of the Revolutionary upheaval in Pennsylvania. Nonetheless, it constituted merely the establishment of corporations, not the full establishment of corporate power. That would take the work of two generations, and against much resistance.

2

INCORPORATING
THE OPPOSITION

♦

In 1785, the Pennsylvania General Assembly—the state's legislature—responded to thousands of petitioners by voting to revoke the charter of the Bank of North America, at that point the state's only business corporation. While bank opponents vehemently presented nearly a dozen different and partly contradictory reasons for their opposition, a majority of representatives apparently agreed with a pamphleteer who stated flatly that "the Bank is an institution incompatible with the interest and welfare of the state." The nascent movement to establish corporations seemed to have run into a political brick wall. Nonetheless, rather than the opposition to corporations being an immovable object, in time corporate boosters proved to be an irresistible political and economic force. Less than thirty years later, in what would have appeared to their predecessors an obscene legislative orgy, frenzied Pennsylvania representatives authorized a whopping forty-one banks distributed throughout the state, all established in one act, and with enough bipartisan support to override popular Governor Simon Snyder's spirited veto. In the meantime, they had also rechartered the Bank of North America, handed out charters to three other banks, and granted charters to dozens of canal, bridge, and turnpike companies. Pennsylvania's political climate had completely reversed, from one of widespread hostility to incorporated banks in particular and corporations in general to one in which corporations were either tolerated or encouraged in every part of the state. Why the dramatic change? What had happened during the intervening years that led to such a dramatically different corporate landscape?[1]

Corporations were first established in Pennsylvania from the early 1780s to the early 1790s, but the main struggle over the legitimacy of the corporate form occurred from the 1780s through the 1810s. In the first decades of the early republic, leaders of corporations faced strong resistance. As with any major change in economics and politics, critics offered an abundance of objections, from the philosophical to the practical, and used tactics ranging from petitioning and ballot stuffing to speechifying and editorializing. People like John Nicholson acted in various combinations of high principle, grubby interest, burning ambition, smoldering resentment, admirable companionship, and unseemly aggrandizement, and sometimes even switched sides in the debate. William Findley and other opponents to corporations, through their objections and political force, to some extent shaped the structure of corporations, while others decided that the only way to compete with established corporations was to found their own. For their part, corporate promoters like James Wilson used the public presses to parry ideological attacks while making their own thrusts; they also used the money at their disposal and the joint-stock structure of corporations to co-opt some of their fiercest critics. Ironically, the primary objection to corporations—that they fostered monopoly—resulted not in the banishment of the corporate structure but rather in a numerical and geographical proliferation of the corporate form that guaranteed their survival while, in the long run, reinforcing the economic and political power of the people who led them.[2]

*T*hose who debated the propriety and role of corporations in American life infused the conversation with much more than the particular institutions at issue. Early national disputes over the extension of slavery represented to many a fight over the fundamental nature of American democracy and how national political power would be distributed. Similarly, those involved in the battles over corporations perceived themselves as participating in a conversation concerning the fundamental structure of the economy, who would have power in it, and how that power would be distributed geographically and along class lines. Furthermore, as with the slavery debate, people brought great passion to controversies concerning corporations because they considered their actions to be precedents for the nation's development. For staunch opponents, corporations posed nothing less than the threat that, through the incorporating process, not only would the state grant some citizens (stockholders and corporate officers) economic privileges denied to other citizens within a given geographic community, but also that those new privileges might even go to people outside that community. In other words, not only might the rich and well-connected get perks and powers that others would not: control of local services and resources might reside in the metropolis rather than being distributed among local communities.[3]

To the strongest corporate proponents, corporations offered more than an institutional form for business and local government. They also represented an opportunity to provide for stewardship of the economy, for the mobilization of private capital for public ends, and for economic growth that would integrate local communities into national and even international commercial and financial networks. Those on the far sides of the debate, as in many such conversations, often talked past each other. But most people found themselves somewhere along that broad spectrum, desiring the benefits that corporations might bring while hoping to temper the institutions' most dangerous possibilities, and these compromisers were the ones to find the middle ground that allowed for corporate proliferation (and, ironically, for modes of corporate power that many of them abhorred). Just as the initial establishment of corporations represented a new arrangement of powers in institutional form, the survival and proliferation of corporations—especially business corporations—reflected arrangements that satisfied the prevailing ideologies of early national America.[4]

The debate over corporations occurred at the intersection of the three main bodies of American thought regarding how the society and economy should be structured and who should run it. None of these loose groupings of ideas was fully defined in detail, and many Americans picked and chose tenets of each depending upon time and context. Still, each of these ways of thinking inflected the debate over corporations in important ways. What early Americans identified as "republican" thought held a republic could only be as strong as the virtue of its citizens and counseled suspicion of government power, though willing to use public authority to pursue public ends. Citizens should put the common weal (as they defined it) above their own individual interests. Other Americans took what later nineteenth-century thinkers would call a more "liberal" economic worldview. Following a line of reasoning skeptical that anyone could be truly virtuous, liberal thought sought to channel self-interest in constructive ways, turning the economy into a free-for-all with the assumption that, en masse, individual interest would add up to the public interest, with government only serving to make sure that everyone followed the rules. Finally, a third, less formalized set of ideas forwarded the proposition of a moral economy in which members of local communities would ensure a balance between fair profits on the one hand and broad access to goods and resources on the other. The proponents of this system of thought were willing to support an active government to enforce community ideals.[5]

Corporations came to be seen, legislated on, and operated in light of each of these loose and sometimes contradictory ideologies. To some extent, the formation of corporations to pursue the public ends of transportation and money supply—and the main restraints put in their charters—jibed well with the republican concept of putting the public good above private interest and with devolving power away from the state government. Also consistent with traditional republican thought, corporate founders at first portrayed themselves as being above the economic fray and therefore better stewards of the economy than those whose economic standing forced them to follow their economic interests; it was a self-serving view, to be sure. Corporate leaders would change their stance to a more liberal one by the 1820s, increasingly expounding upon the legitimacy of their pursuing their own economic interests while resenting governmental efforts to impinge upon their decision-making. And not only did they make the argument for themselves, but corporate boosters also began to argue that corporations would help others pursue their own interests. Meanwhile, the moral economic desire for local control over economic affairs and broad access to resources led to the wide proliferation and geographic distribution of corporations. Thus, just as the establishment of corporations represented a compromise of economic and political interests and powers, it also marked a confluence of the main ideological tropes that Americans brought to bear upon their construction of political and economic institutions.[6]

Like the corporate structure, opposition to it originated in England and migrated across the Atlantic. In 1658, English legal scholar Edward Coke excoriated the very idea of corporations, complaining that "they cannot commit treason, nor be outlawed, nor excommunicate, for they have no souls." Over a century later, another English jurist echoed Coke's sentiments. "Corporations have neither bodies to be punished, nor souls to be condemned, they therefore do as they may," groused attorney-general Edward Thurlow. Many Americans were no less critical of corporations when the corporate form was planted in American soil. American opponents to the Bank of North America took up the English baton and ran in the same direction, quoting British critics of the Bank of England when they bemoaned "the establishment of a monopoly in any corporation, immense in its magnitude . . . and which may, by that establishment, be enabled to control the whole national powers of public and private credit." They also noted that in 1721 Britain's House of Commons rejected an application to incorporate the Bank of Ireland, admonishing the Crown "to deliver them from the *apprehension they lie under, of the POWER and INFLUENCE of a public Bank*." Those objections echoed through the decades of the early republic. As late as the 1830s, a group of Philadelphians met to condemn "corporate monopolies, in which individuals control not only their own property, but that of many others, tend to give the wealthy that undue influence, so dangerous, and so prejudicial" to a republic, further arguing that "it has been through the undue influence of overgrown wealth, that aristocracies have been established, and, the liberties of nations destroyed."[7]

Of all kinds of corporations, chartered banks drew the most unease and scrutiny. The specter of a cabal of wealthy men getting privileges from the state to gain huge profits without physically producing anything—regardless of the extent to which such visions had any basis in reality—certainly played a part. Compared to internal improvement companies or municipal corporations, which the state legislature eventually incorporated seemingly willy-nilly, banks encountered significant opposition. At least private, unincorporated bankers (though there were only a few, and they could not afford to operate broadly) were fully liable for any debts they accrued, no one was required to accept their notes, and the state did not give them a boost by accepting their notes for payment of taxes, whereas corporate banks could go under with little penalty to their investors. Incorporating banks then seemed to give a few men who had special access to the legislative process a chance to enrich themselves further with less risk than other economic actors. Nonetheless, farmers, miners, and other Pennsylvanians did use anticorporate rhetoric at times to oppose other kinds of corporations, such as municipal corporations, canal companies, and coal mining companies. Thus, despite differing intensities of opposition, nearly all corporate supporters had to find ways to explain the necessity of their institutions and to justify their establishment and continued operations.

Business corporations held an obvious attraction to the rich merchants and lawyers connected to them, but Philadelphia was made up of more than wealthy men, and the Commonwealth of Pennsylvania was made up of more than Philadelphia. The city's tradesmen and the state's farmers tended to be hostile to the establishment of corporations, especially banks; petitioners to the state complained pointedly that "moneyed men by means of the bank receive near three times the rate of common interest, and at the same time to receive their money at a very short warning, whenever they have occation for it," but that "it will ever be impossible for the husbandmen or mechanic to borrow on the former terms of legal interest and distant payments of the principal." For many Pennsylvanians, who elected the most radical of all the early state legislatures, the national founding represented an opportunity to establish a more virtuous society, one free of what they perceived as the financial, political, and moral corruption of the metropolitan elites. To them, corporations looked like the Cerberus incarnate.[8]

Like that mythical three-headed beast, corporations represented a trio of dangers to the legacy of the American Revolution. One head, the target of republican thought and moral economists, conjured up suspicions of speculators and stockjobbers that long predated independence but had become more acute with the adoption of the Stamp Act, the Townshend Acts, and the general willingness of Parliament to raise revenue from the colonists to pay for the huge bills left over from the Seven Years War. In the 1770s, Pennsylvania radicals had joined those of other colonies in railing against the British stockjobbers and speculators who made their money not through labor but through mysterious financial machinations and by buying the British government debt, goading the Crown to go to war to raise taxes to go further into debt so that the speculators would make more money on government bonds. That the financial interests of a few could pervert government policy seemed to strike at the heart of their republican notion of a government that reflected the will of all its citizens. Thus, the founding of American banking corporations that would gain their profits through buying government debt—as did the Bank of England—seemed a perverse result of their victorious Revolution. This use of this rhetorical trope would continue well into early-republic Philadelphia; in 1796, one newspaper scribbler skewered the "stock-jobbers and speculators" who enriched themselves on government securities whose interest came from taxes.[9]

What one group of rural petitioners to the state legislature called "the inequality introduced" by corporations represented the second of corporations' nasty heads. Objecting to the activities of canal companies, the signers contended that "a country cannot long preserve its liberty, where a great inequality of property takes place. Is it not therefore, the most dangerous policy in this infant republic, to combine the wealthy in order to make them powerful?" Banks' detractors went even further, charging that a bank officer "essentially has the power to decide who will succeed and who will not," and so had the capacity to be "destructive of that equality which ought to take place in a free country." Great disparities in wealth had not suddenly appeared after or as a result of the Revolution, of course. Since its founding, Pennsylvania had been home to royal proprietors, merchant princes, farmers, master tradesmen, journeymen, redemptioners, laborers, indentured servants, and slaves. Inequalities in the distribution of wealth had increased markedly during the eighteenth century, especially in the Quaker City. Moreover, a quick walk down a few blocks of Philadelphia in the 1780s or by its poorhouse would dispel any notion that barring corporations would magically bring the rich and the poor any closer to economic parity. Still, the prospect of business corporations violated any sense of a moral economy that put a premium on everyone getting a fair shake rather than some getting rich at the expense of others.[10]

The fact remained that business corporations had the potential to enrich directly only their investors, as opposed to the other proposed solutions to Pennsylvania's money supply and transportation problems that returned profits to the state for the benefit of the wider community. Nor could just anyone invest in the corporations most likely to be profitable. Just like the Bank of England's initial stock offering at £400 a share, the Bank of North America set its initial share price at $400. In a city where the annual cost of bare necessities—that is, food, shelter, clothing, and fuel—for a family of four ran $264, and where a tailor's annual wages averaged about $215, only a small slice of Philadelphians could afford that enriching opportunity. While the state of Pennsylvania eventually did acquire bank stock as part of the chartering process for the Bank of Pennsylvania and subsequent banks, and eventually garnered significant revenue from its shareholdings, it garnered only a small fraction of the profits to be gained with loan offices. Thus, rather than the whole community benefiting from all the proceeds of a credit-granting institution, those individuals with the money or connections to buy shares profited disproportionately from the adoption of corporations. Of course, investors countered by arguing that they also shouldered all of the risk by supplying capital when neither the state nor other individuals were willing to pay in.[11]

The third objection to business corporations focused on accusations that a company's "directors can obtain unfair advantages in trade for themselves and their friends." To some extent, this accusation implied monopoly, which early corporate leaders did their utmost to secure, thereby contradicting the liberal tenet of free competition. But this last charge also encompassed a whole range of resentments, some specific, others vague. Even corporate banks' most sheepish boosters did not deny that a banking company was far more likely to lend to merchants than it was to extend credit to farmers or mechanics, who would in turn be better served by a state-sponsored loan office. Merchants composed over two-thirds of the Bank of North America's most active customers in the mid-1780s—and the bank offered nominally short-term loans rather than the long-term credit that farmers or aspiring tradesmen required. In contrast, three-quarters of the borrowers from the Pennsylvania loan bank in 1775 were yeoman farmers; the rest were mostly tradesmen, with only a smattering of merchants and gentlemen.[12]

To some extent, bankers could argue that restricting most loans to the merchant community made sound policy for banks, because merchants tended to have an idea of others' financial condition and because they were likely to be able to pay back loans more quickly than tradesmen or farmers. In practice, though, despite being nominally ninety-day notes, many loans to merchants got rolled over indefinitely, essentially becoming long-term loans, anyway. Bank minutes are riddled with cases in which the discount committee turned loans over multiple times. Furthermore, whether banks considered only a prospective client's ability to pay back a loan, rather than factors such as political or social considerations, seems questionable at best. New banking syndicates always cited that kind of potential discrimination when applying for bank charters of their own. Finally, there were those potential borrowers whose unlikelihood of getting loans from banks probably was perfectly legitimate—from bankers' point of view, that is—because they did not have enough collateral or earning potential. Many people, then, opposed corporations and corporate banks in particular because of occupational concerns, political differences, and simple disgruntlement.[13]

All of these philosophical objections to corporations became entangled in the complex web of Keystone State politics. Pennsylvania had been the most pluralistic colony nearly from its founding; riven by geographic, religious, partisan, and class differences, it remained a highly contentious polity throughout the early republic. Charles Biddle, a state representative in the 1780s, observed that "those from the westward look upon the people in any of the commercial towns, as little better than swindlers; while those of the east consider the western members as a pack of savages." Pennsylvanians living east of the Appalachians viewed their western brethren as rough-hewn, unsophisticated country bumpkins who were always crying for a more active government but were unwilling to pay the taxes necessary for such interventions. In the rugged band of mountains running southwest from the state's northeast border to the Maryland line, many farmers sent their goods down the Susquehanna River to the Chesapeake and Baltimore; beyond the hills, farmers rafted their products down the Ohio to the Mississippi and New Orleans. Both groups extolled what they considered to be their more simple virtues compared to the corrupt city-folk of Philadelphia, whom they blamed for a strong central government seemingly insensitive to western realities and needs. Meanwhile, Scotch-Irish Presbyterians, English Quakers and Anglicans, and German pietists competed with many other sects and groups for political leverage and social authority, but none of these groups acted as a coherent bloc come election day.[14]

In addition to being geographically, ethnically, and religiously splintered, Pennsylvania politics also featured constant and often byzantine partisanship. In the late 1770s and the 1780s, the Constitutionalists (their strength mostly in the western counties and among the middling or lower sort) and Republicans (mostly though far from exclusively eastern and well-to-do) faced off over the state's radical 1776 founding document; generally, the antagonists reversed positions on the more conservative federal constitution of 1787. Once Pennsylvania adopted its own less radical constitution in 1790, its parties aligned themselves more closely with their national counterparts, the former Constitutionalists becoming Republicans and the former Republicans becoming Federalists, respectively. But these parties, too, fractured in terms of geography, ethnicity, and political philosophy. Finally, class distinctions cut across all these divisions. Just as Philadelphia was home to merchant princes and lame paupers, rural areas included wealthy gentry farmers and professionals as well as itinerant laborers; on issues regarding people's pocketbooks, people with different-sized wallets often voted in different ways. All in all, it was no wonder that Pennsylvania politics proved so fractious.

Furthermore, corporations' proponents and opponents did not form two coherent groups; rather, individuals might support some corporations while desiring to limit or banish others. Banks' most stalwart supporters generally emerged from among the ranks of those who expected to be able to own stock or get loans from the institution in question, while often opposing the charters of other men's banks; indeed, of all kinds of corporations, banks tended to be the ones for which private interest tended to be the best indicator of attitude toward the institution. Internal improvement corporations, on the other hand, usually enjoyed much broader support, even in rural areas that were often hostile to banking. Here, even when voters, legislators, or pamphlet writers did not expect to become stockholders or use a canal themselves, they expected higher property values and cheaper goods, often at little personal cost. Still, many Pennsylvanians remained wary of corporations.[15]

Through his initial opposition to the Bank of North America, conversion to the Bank of Pennsylvania, and changing political beliefs, John Nicholson symbolized the institutional and ideological expansion of the corporate community as well as anyone. Born in Wales in 1757, and migrating to America in the 1770s, Nicholson signed with the Continental army, serving as a sergeant in the First Pennsylvania Regiment. He quickly exhibited talents for keeping accounts, shifting with political winds, and latching onto more powerful men; in October 1778 he wangled a position as clerk in the Chamber of Accounts of the Continental Congress's Board of Treasury, and three years later became auditor of accounts for the Pennsylvania state government. In the early 1780s, Nicholson became one of the Pennsylvania constitution's staunchest defenders, painting its opponents as "a certain aristocratic party joined with those who were unfriendly to the late Revolution." He opposed the initial chartering and rechartering of the Bank of North America out of concerns about concentrated power, monopoly, and aristocracy—in other words, all the usual ideological suspects.[16]

Nonetheless, the finagling Nicholson partnered with Robert Morris to build one of the nation's largest land speculation empires, amassing millions of acres in Pennsylvania and beyond. Because of his interest in land development, he became active in the Society for the Improvement of Roads and Inland Navigation in the State of Pennsylvania and helped found the Delaware and Schuylkill Navigation Company and the Susquehanna and Schuylkill Canal Navigation Company. Like many other former Constitutionalists-become-Republicans, he found common ground with men like Morris when it came to canals and roads. The same could not be said for banks, though, where politics ran thicker than even his partnership with Morris. Accordingly, Nicholson was shut out of the credit that Morris and his cronies availed themselves of through the Bank of North America. The always-enterprising Nicholson wrote to fellow Republican George Meade, "For gods sake let us have our own a bank a going and we shall be able to get some [loans]." He joined the syndicate that put together, lobbied for, and established the Bank of Pennsylvania, which soon became a center of credit for well-to-do Republicans the way that the Bank of North America continued to function for well-to-do Federalists. Though Bank of North America partisans had fought tooth-and-nail against the expansion of the corporate franchise, that growth had the effect of ensuring the Bank of North America's political survival. Corporate men had taken one step back but two steps forward.[17]

The eternally stormy waters of Pennsylvania politics not only ensured that corporate advocates could rarely count on smooth sailing but also forced them to tack constantly to the shifting political winds. Bank boosters had the most difficult time. Philadelphia hosted all four of the banks chartered in Pennsylvania before 1814. When the Bank of North America regained its charter in 1787, voting in the General Assembly divided pretty closely on geographical lines, with the bank getting the majority of its support from Philadelphia and surrounding counties. Six years later, the Bank of Pennsylvania's charter bid provoked exactly the opposite reaction. This time, representatives from the mountains and west strongly supported a new bank, proving that anticorporate stances could be inspired by circumstances as much as by principle. Once chartered, the Bank of Pennsylvania rewarded its generally rural, generally Republican supporters by sprinkling five branches across the state over the following decade. In turn, western and mountain district representatives would oppose the charters of Philadelphia-based banking groups that would compete with the Bank of Pennsylvania but not make loans outside of the city. In addition to sectionalism, bank boosters had to contend with party politics, class antagonisms, and the peculiar circumstances of each bank's relationship to the legislature.[18]

But an increasing minority of Republican-Democrats (having once again changed their name, this time from Republicans) willingly allied with the Quids (a new political faction, many of them former Federalists) to incorporate each of these banking institutions. Unlike the concentration of banks, the wide distribution of internal improvement companies resulted in fewer and less heated statehouse battles. Road, canal, and navigation companies could always count on local support, but sponsors often had to team up with representatives from other districts who were also pushing pet projects. Passing internal improvement charters and especially getting aid to internal improvement companies gave legislators the perfect chance to hone their logrolling skills. Nor did the corporation of Philadelphia receive a free ride; its representatives struggled to get authorization for its waterworks and to raise bond issues but failed in their efforts to receive any funding for it, even when the city still served as the state capital. Corporate sponsors and opponents learned quickly that any debate involving a corporation could open a Pandora's box of sectional, party, and class animus.

What some early opponents of corporations possessed in great abundance was an incisive grasp of the consequences of corporations for American life. William Findley personified the conflicted early objections to the Bank of North America in particular and corporations in general. Born in northern Ireland in 1741, he learned the trade of weaving; motivated by political unrest, economic upheaval, or perhaps some combination of the two, the young Scotch-Irish Presbyterian immigrated to Pennsylvania in 1763. He was able to scrounge up enough cash for the journey, thus avoiding the more typical immigrant fate of having to indenture himself, as poor, single, male immigrants tended to do—that is, paying off his Atlantic passage by working several years as a servant in America. Findley also demonstrated dedication to principle, later writing that his "aversion to slavery" convinced him to reject promising offers to go to the slave-plantation Carolinas in favor of becoming, for a time, a schoolteacher in Pennsylvania, where slavery was less prevalent. Findley saved up and purchased farmland in Cumberland County, on the eastern edge of the mountains, married a local resident, and joined the local Presbyterian church. He established political credentials by supporting the Pennsylvania constitution of 1776, which increased legislative representation for counties beyond the Delaware Valley compared to the colonial charter; by fighting in the local militia during the Revolutionary War; and by serving in various posts in local government in the late 1770s. By 1783, he had moved beyond the Appalachians to Westmoreland County. His neighbors quickly elected him to the General Assembly; it was the beginning of a thirty-three-year period that he spent nearly continuously in elec-

tive office, either in the state legislature or the federal House of Representatives. As a farmer, as a westerner, as a Scotch-Irish Presbyterian, and as a man
with a common touch, Findley clearly captured much of the spirit of the
people who elected him year after year. At the same time, he lent a steady
and reasonable voice to Pennsylvania politics, claiming credit for "reconciling the parties" for and against amending the state's constitution in 1789.
He offered the philosophical objections to corporations that also had a basis
in both legitimate, practical concerns and real-world jealousies and resentments toward the urban, mercantile, elitist group at the center of the Bank
of North America and early internal improvement companies.[19]

Findley led the opposition to corporations in the 1780s. He countered the incorporation of the city of Philadelphia for much of the 1780s, arguing that
granting the city a charter would entrench men who had "designed incorporation to establish an aristocratic influence in the city." Findley voiced his opposition to the Bank of the North America, and indeed all corporations, when the
General Assembly debated whether to recharter the bank in 1786. In 1781, he
had been lukewarm on the subject of the bank, not completely against it but

William Findley, whose gray-
flecked hair and eyebrows
reflected the aging and partial
mellowing of a former radical
who had stuck to his principles
through many political battles.
William Findley by Rembrandt
Peale, from life, 1805. Courtesy
of Independence National
Historical Park.

later privately admitting to being "in favour of substituting a smaller bank in its place." In 1786, Findley railed against the idea that the legislature "may incorporate bodies for the sole purpose of gain, with the power of making bylaws, and of enjoying an emolument of privilege, profit, influence, or power"; he called the nation's first incorporated business "inconsistent with our laws—our habits—our manners." For Morris and his colleagues, corporations may have represented the culmination of their American Revolution through the establishment of institutions that the British limited or forbade, but for Findley corporations symbolized a retreat from the Revolution's egalitarian ideals.[20]

Like other corporate critics, Findley articulated several connected objections to restoring the bank's state imprimatur. Findley labeled the bank "in the common popular sense a monopoly," if not "in the strict legal sense of the word." He noted that stock-holding legislators had secured for the bank "peculiar privileges by obtaining partial laws in their own favour." Most importantly, though, Findley argued that corporations violated the "right to equal protection, power, privilege, and influence." If the state could "incorporate bodies for the sole purpose of gain, with the power of making byelaws, and of enjoying an emolument of privilege, profit, influence, or power," then the assembly might eventually "parcel out the commonwealth into little aristocracies." In short, even the possibility not just of incorporated banks but of any corporations put the government in the position "to bestow unequal portions of our common inheritance on favorites." Such policies, Findley suggested, undermined the code of equality upon which the nation was based. Monopoly, government corruption, the enriching of the few at the expense of the many: Findley rolled liberalism, republicanism, and a moral economic ethos all into one in his objections.[21]

Just as important as the principles that Findley articulated were the objections he left unsaid but which his constituents certainly brought up in taverns and on court days, that pertained to the particular nature of an incorporated bank and how this one operated. The bank offered only forty-five-day loans, too short for farmers who needed either accommodation loans long enough to last at least for a season or two or long-term loans to buy land or animals. Furthermore, while renewing such loans was a theoretical possibility, it remained impractical for people who lived a week's journey from Philadelphia. Meanwhile, the existence of the bank politically precluded the establishment of a loan bank with local offices that would serve westerners' needs. For Findley and the people he represented, the practical operations of the bank reinforced the underlying political and social challenge that corporations represented.

Corporate opponent Findley faced his opposite equal in corporate booster James Wilson. Both British, born one year apart, Presbyterian, raised in rural areas, well-educated, immigrants to Pennsylvania within two years of each other, beginning their American careers as educators, living for a time in Cumberland County, marrying daughters of prominent locals, strong believers in the voice of the people, active in the Revolution, and leaders in

Pennsylvania politics, they nonetheless showed the diverging paths of thought and interest that led to diametrically opposed views concerning early corporations. Wilson was born in Scotland in 1742 and attended the University of St. Andrews and St. Mary's College. Short of funds, he studied merchant bookkeeping for a while before immigrating to Philadelphia in 1765, where, after a stint teaching at the College of Pennsylvania, he studied law under John Dickinson. He moved to Reading in 1767 and on to Carlisle, in the Cumberland Valley, in 1770. Wilson quickly got caught up in the conflict between Whigs and Tories; he joined the county's Committee on Correspondence and penned an influential pamphlet arguing that because Americans did not vote for members of Parliament, that body had no authority over them. He sat in the Continental Congress, signed the Declaration of Independence, and continued his national service by serving in the Confederation Congress and the Constitutional Convention, where he used his sophisticated knowledge and understanding of political philosophy to influence debate. Wilson became a strong advocate of the proposed federal constitution and of replacing Pennsylvania's constitution of 1776. Meanwhile, he became involved in land speculation and with the founding of the Bank of North America; he served on the board and was the bank's lawyer. Indeed, he was most likely the primary source of American bankers' information concerning Scottish incorporated banks. Just as Findley was conscious that every step the new nation took could lead down a path that could not be retraced, the always-lawyerly Wilson, too, perceived that well-set precedents would "have a salutary, a decisive, and a permanent Influence upon [the nation's] future Fortune and Character." He sat as an associate justice of the Supreme Court before his land speculation debts caught up with him, and he died in debtors' prison in North Carolina in 1798.[22]

Like that of many corporate advocates, Wilson's strong defense of corporations highlighted their potential role in enhancing economic growth while eliding the questions of how that growth would be distributed or of what would be the extent of corporate power. In particular, bank backers tended to emphasize banks' role in offering credit and increasing the amount of circulating money, and this Philadelphia lawyer proved no different. In a 1785 pamphlet supporting the rechartering of the Bank of North America, Wilson stressed "the most material advantages resulting from a Bank." Wilson aimed twin barrels at his opposition. With the first, he elaborated upon the many merits of increasing the nation's money supply, which he contended "is of peculiar importance in young and flourishing countries, in which the demands for credit, and the rewards of industry, are greater than in any other." He further referred to personal experience, noting that the introduction of three corporate banks to Scotland had contributed significantly to that country's economic expansion in the eighteenth century. Wilson then moved on to banks' role in offering credit, especially to merchants. "TRADE," he wrote, "derives great support and assistance from a bank." In addition to these two arguments, he voiced several others, including corporate banks' ability to facilitate government borrowing during wartime and to provide a medium for citizens to pay their taxes. Just as notable as what Wilson mentioned was what he chose not to address: that other options, such as land banks, could perform many of the same functions while distributing credit more widely. Corporate advocates always made sure to emphasize the quantity of economic growth rather than its quality for all Philadelphians.[23]

Wilson sent opening salvos of a long ideological campaign by and on behalf of the men running both banking and internal improvement corporations, and just as Wilson emphasized national development when advocating for the Bank of North America, so did canal boosters when talking up their projects. One major strain in pro-corporate rhetoric touted the ability of such large institutions to unite a fractious union. The appeals of the Society for the Improvement of Roads and Inland Navigation and Philadelphia's first two canal companies forwarded the cause of corporations by emphasizing one great goal, according to Robert Morris, "to combine the interests of all the parts of the state, and to cement them in a perpetual commercial and political union, by the improvement of [Pennsylvania's] natural advantages." The Pennsylvania legislature agreed, asserting that "the opening of a communication by water . . . will greatly tend to strengthen the bands of union between citizens inhabiting distant parts" of the state. Inland navigation boosters consistently emphasized the theme of uniting disparate economic and geographical interests. In 1795, William Smith optimistically predicted that the two canals would bind Pennsylvania "together in one flourishing and civilized whole, sensible of a common interest, and rejoicing in the common prosperity." For Smith and others, good roads and canals made good neighbors.[24]

Proponents recycled this argument whenever they applied for charters, asked the legislature for funding, solicited investment, or addressed their stockholders. In his 1811 address to the legislature, Governor Simon Snyder claimed state-funded canals could "form an indissoluble bond of union . . . forever banish the idea of a severation of the States . . . create new and strong ties and dependencies . . . and excite new sympathies and affections among the children of the same American family." The very next year, the Union Canal Company's petition for state aid reminded the legislature that "the strength of the individual members of the union demands imperiously a proportionally powerful cement to bind them together." Clearly, they projected the canal to be that adhesive. As late as 1825, a Philadelphia city council subcommittee endorsed a plan to cut a canal across the city connecting the Schuylkill and the Delaware rivers by claiming that it would "make a unity of interest between the east and west [city wards] . . . and make the city united in all its great interests of trade and commerce." That canal was never built, but the sentiment that inland navigations could unite disparate interests remained. Canal boosters suggested that internal navigation had nearly magical, inherent qualities guaranteeing prosperity and union, with the alternative being an undeveloped, fragmented economy eventually leading to social and political chaos.[25]

To counter the claim that corporations would engender political and economic divisions, canal and river navigation supporters offered their institutions as the solution to one of the most vexing philosophical and political problems facing the new nation. The conundrum of conflicting interests had played a central role in political economy for centuries; the notion that a republic could survive only through at least some modicum of public virtue and the occasional placing of the common weal above private interest formed a cornerstone of American political economy. Both colonists and Britons had argued that the divergence of American interests from Britain's had precipitated the American Revolution. A number of the men involved in the Susquehanna and Schuylkill Canal and the Delaware and Schuylkill Canal had served in the Continental Congress or under Washington in the Continental army and thus had firsthand knowledge of the numerous ways that sectional, class, state, and occupational interests could threaten the young republic's very survival.[26]

Meanwhile, Philadelphians who put a high premium on social and economic stability, including corporate men like Ebenezer Hazard and George Clymer, had immediate proof that intrastate unity was as fragile as the national compact. Through much of the 1780s and 1790s, Pennsylvania farmers blocked roads and disrupted court days in their efforts to delay tax collections and farm foreclosures. In the early 1790s western Pennsylvanians protested, sometimes violently, the federal excise tax on whiskey, leading to the federal march to put down the Whiskey Rebellion in late 1794. Western Pennsylvanians, at least partly because they sent their goods west down the Ohio River to the Mississippi and on to New Orleans, had different economic interests than did Philadelphians. At the same time, settlers and two groups of speculators—one from Pennsylvania, the other representing Connecticut claimants to the same territory—continued wrangling over disputed land titles in northern Pennsylvania. To many Philadelphia Federalists, the message must have been clear: that Pennsylvanians in the mountains and beyond perceived their interests as being at odds with those of East Coast speculators and governments. Something was needed to secure the loyalty of westerners. The integration of western areas into the economic fabric of the Atlantic ports seemed to be the best solution.[27]

Corporation supporters shrewdly exploited clear indications that, both in other states and at the national level, Americans of nearly all political persuasions held lofty opinions of the potential influence of internal navigation upon the economy and the polity. In response to an 1807 congressional request for a comprehensive review of internal navigation, secretary of the treasury (and Pennsylvanian) Albert Gallatin, in his well-received and much-praised report on roads and canals, predicted that better inland transportation "will shorten distances, facilitate commercial and personal intercourse, and unite by a still more intimate community of interests, the most remote quarters of the United States." In Gallatin's opinion, "no other single operation . . . can more effectually tend to strengthen and perpetuate that union, which secures external independence, domestic peace, and internal liberty." An open letter from Robert Fulton, added as an appendix to Gallatin's report, put the cabinet member's sentiments in more practical terms. "What stronger bonds of union can be invented," the steamboat entrepreneur rhetorically asked, "than those which enable each individual to transport the produce of his industry [1,200] miles for 60 cents the hundred weight?" He answered that "here then is a certain method of securing the union of the states, and of rendering it as lasting as the continent we inhabit." Philadelphia-area canal boosters did not exaggerate much when lauding "the wish at this time so universally expressed, in favour of internal improvement."[28]

Just about every community, in fact, did want a canal or river navigation running through its backyard because the alternative—poor transportation—hurt a locality in a variety of ways. Most obviously, it meant being shut out of economic development. Pamphlet after pamphlet touting the benefits of inland navigation projects compared the costs of water transport to overland transport, a difference that could affect a farmer's bottom line significantly. That in turn influenced property values, sending land prices in canal-fed areas skyward and depressing those in landlocked localities. Compounding matters, some of the taxes local residents paid to the state might go to projects that helped other areas connect to Philadelphia. No locality wanted its state tax dollars to finance the undercutting of its own ability to sell its produce profitably by building a canal for farmers in other districts. Consequently, Pennsylvania legislators tended to distribute money to very small projects fairly equally across the state but was often stingy with major projects that would benefit only one area (that is, until the Pennsylvania Main Line Canal, a public project so huge that it promised something to nearly every county and eventually almost bankrupted the state in the process). Meanwhile, the projects most likely to be defeated were those that funneled Pennsylvania goods to seaports in other states, thereby demonstrating the flip side of the unification argument: Philadelphians did not want Pennsylvania farmers to unify their interests with those of out-of-state merchants.

By the 1820s the more pompous strains of "uniting the union" tended to be relayed in a shorthand in which Philadelphia-area boosters needed only to mention the connection between two specific geographic areas to imply the commingling of interests that would occur should a given project be completed. Popular familiarity with both the projects and the terms of the debate certainly played a role. Beginning with the Delaware and Schuylkill Canal Company and the Schuylkill and Susquehanna Canal Company in the 1790s and continuing with their successor, the Union Canal Company, in the 1810s, boosters had bombarded the public and the legislature with pamphlets and petitions. The Schuylkill Navigation Company, the Lehigh Coal and Navigation Company, the Delaware and Hudson Canal Company, the Delaware and Raritan Canal Company, and a host of others later took up the same refrain. As of 1822, Pennsylvania had chartered eighteen canal companies, some of which had applied to the General Assembly in more than one legislative session and nearly all of which were the subjects of multiple acts of the legislature over several sessions. Perhaps equally important, by the 1820s the men proposing, administering, and legislating such ventures thought Pennsylvania's polity to be far less fragile than had their fathers in the 1790s. They felt less self-conscious about appealing to the interests of different groups and regions, knowing that their audiences did not fear for the state's fragility. Nonetheless, the repetition of their message and its undertones left no doubts that the great majority of Pennsylvanians considered inland navigation projects to be a uniting influence.[29]

Despite such sustained efforts to convince corporate critics, not everyone bought into corporate boosters' rhetoric. Much to the chagrin of Robert Morris, local resistance played a part in the collapse of the Schuylkill and Susquehanna Company. In the fall of 1793, Morris wrote in disbelief to Pennsylvania governor Thomas Mifflin that "among those difficulties one has arisen, that was the least expected, that is an opposition to the work, by the very persons who will be most materially benefited by the completion of it, some of the landholders along the track of the canal." A number of farmers along the projected canal route had decided that the annoyance of a canal outweighed its potentially unifying and remunerative benefits. Some so strongly opposed the tearing up of their lands that Morris feared "that the land holders will arm themselves to oppose" the courts from exercising the corporation's legal right to eminent domain. While these men backed down, others did not. Later that winter, a quarrel between Dauphin County resident Martin Glass and a canal worker escalated into fisticuffs, "and a violent riot and attrocious assaults and battaries were committed," with the local men coming out on the winning end. Not to be outdone, the next day around a hundred canal workers, "all armed with Clubs," descended on the town and skirmished a bit before both sides calmed down. Such disturbances certainly made property owners more reluctant to sell their land, driving up canal costs to a point where some projects became untenable.[30]

In the face of such opposition that slowed down construction, internal navigation company promoters reworked another of the liberal ideological arguments they used to justify the privatization of waterways: that the private interest of investors and company officers would ensure that boards of managers built quickly and efficiently. In a deft flip, company promoters also reversed the logic. If the profit motive inherent in incorporated companies legitimized those corporations, then any profits turned by internal improvement companies, too, were proper gains as long as the pursuit of them did not conflict with the public interest. Petitioners to the Pennsylvania legislature did not "hesitate to avow . . . that views of individual profit had a share in the motives of inducement" to found and invest in internal improvement companies. Nonetheless, they only gained "individual profit connected with public advantage, —the pursuit of a lawful, a necessary, and a laudable end, by fair, lawful, and honourable means—persuaded . . . that their efforts were in accordance with the views of the Pennsylvania legislature." According to internal improvement company investors, the possibility of profits made internal navigation companies good, and the lofty goals of internal improvement companies made profits good—too bad, they privately lamented, that the companies rarely made good profits. And here was a great irony: because they wanted investors, internal improvement corporate boosters did not want to admit that they lost money and so were actually subsidizing cheaper transportation at considerable costs to themselves.[31]

The talk of profits, of course, reinforced the new liberal theme of legitimizing individual interest. The changing appeals of the Union Canal Company to potential investors, public and private, showed a subtle shift from playing on anxieties over the republic's fragility to extolling the virtues of economic development through the collected strivings of individuals. Despite an initial flurry of activity in the early 1790s, the Schuylkill and Susquehanna and the Delaware and Schuylkill Canal companies floundered because of financial and technical setbacks. In 1807, a syndicate of original investors and speculators new to the projects sought to combine the companies under a new charter from the state legislature. At first, Union Canal Company supporters recycled familiar arguments, claiming that "the facility of transportation by water . . . greatly tends to strengthen the bands of union between citizens inhabiting different parts of a country." They blamed past failures upon "the baleful effects of local interests," including "short sighted individuals" who demanded "unreasonable prices for slips of land, far exceeding the proportional value of the remainder of the farm." A letter to the Philadelphia *Aurora* exhibited the same logic, tracing canal troubles in general to "various efforts of speculation and the influence of private over public interests . . . and the infidelity and artifices of persons who sacrificed every principle of public duty to an unjustifiable selfishness." At first, then, the canal company and its friends charged that the property owners put their own interests ahead of the greater good by demanding exorbitant amounts for property through which the canal would travel. Union Canal Company backers claimed to represent the public against the unseemly pursuit of individual interest.[32]

Nonetheless, those same men were not above manipulating that line of reasoning in creative ways. The Union Canal Company's 1811 petitions to the legislature for state aid hinted at the justification of private interest while using the old familiar terms. When "the powerful motive of individual interest is combined and united with the more exalted sentiment which Patriotism and Public Spirit inspire to hasten its completion," company officials argued, their canal would provide great service to the commonwealth. In other words, canal backers were once again asking for state investment to supplement funds raised through the sale of stock to individuals in the building of the canal. The harnessing of "the powerful motive of individual interest" to promote the general good did not represent a new idea, at least to anyone who had read David Hume, Adam Smith, or the many newspaper editors and politicians influenced by their ideas. Also, the Union Canal

Company officers still characterized "Patriotism and Public Spirit" as being a "more exalted sentiment" than the desire for private gain. However, unlike in previous lobbying efforts, this time boosters were not warning of the divisive dangers of interest and the subsequent need to unite potentially disruptive private ends. Instead, they portrayed individual economic efforts as potentially valuable when properly directed. Naturally, they considered their own project a proper direction. Private interest, these petitioners implied, was not an inherently disjunctive force, separating individuals from society so as to pull it apart; rather it represented a neutral impulse, one that could be either positive or negative depending upon how it was channeled. The authors of the Union Canal Company petition argued that internal improvement would point private interest in a constructive direction.[33]

Corporate boosters also made more individualized appeals to personal interest. For many corporate opponents, money talked louder than words. Accordingly, corporate boosters found ways to co-opt opponents who objected to corporate cronies' ability to get access to credit. After all, this was a charge as much about being shut out from credit as it was anticorporate principle. The simplest way, of course, was to give a piece of the action to those who cried "monopoly." At first, sure that the establishment of other banks would destroy their brainchildren, corporate leaders resisted any possibility of competition. But in such a politically volatile climate, the insularity of those British-inspired business corporations—the Bank of North America and the two canal companies—was too cozy to last, though their officers did their best to fend off potential challengers. Just as Bank of North America directors would be accused of political favoritism, their monopoly of corporate banking in Pennsylvania depended upon the Anti-Constitutional party beating back rivals' attempts to form their own corporate banks. Although in theory anyone could buy Bank of North America stock, few shares changed hands in the 1780s; furthermore, whether accurately or not, many Philadelphia merchants and mechanics perceived the bank as a closed institution lending only to insiders and their families, associates, and political allies.

Doubtless, many of incorporated banks' potential opponents decided to join them when they could not beat them. More than the marginally-profitable-at-best early internal improvement companies, banks actually made money. The corporate Bank of England and nearly every American loan bank had generated steady revenue streams and impressive dividends for their investors, public and private. As hybrid imitations of the Bank of England and of Scottish corporate banks, Pennsylvania's incorporated banks had two potential sources of profit. The Bank of North America, the Bank of Pennsylvania, and other of Philadelphia's corporate banks lent large sums to the government at or below the going market rate, as did the Bank of England. That guaranteed the banks steady income. And like Scottish incorporated banks, American banks routinely lent money to merchants, brokers, and, increasingly, manufacturers and tradesmen at the full market rate. Because banks made these loans by issuing banknotes, rather than by handing out the specie on hand, banks could lend out several dollars for every dollar of gold sitting in their vaults. Thus, they could earn 12 or 18 percent interest on their capital. In practice, bank profits rarely reached that level, because Philadelphia bankers tended to stay cautious in order to instill confidence in their institutions and because banks had operating costs, including salaries, rent, and printing. Nonetheless, investors expected and received good returns on their bank stock.

Those rising expectations won over many men who had at first been skeptical of banking. Some early naysayers jumped on the bandwagon once the Bank of North America and especially the Bank of Pennsylvania proved that not only one but multiple banking institutions could survive and thrive in the same city. Banking corporations raised huge sums of capital—at least on paper—in seemingly the blink of an eye. The Bank of North America's 1781 charter called for raising $400,000 in capital, the Bank of Pennsylvania's 1793 charter authorized a $2,000,000 capital, and the Bank of Philadelphia's charter allowed a capital of $1,000,000. That nominal capital limit did not represent actual cash paid in. A few banks held back shares, preferring to make sure they could sell out their first offerings. Banks sometimes permitted stock purchasers to pay with United States bond issues, or even the stock of other banks. Also, some banks allowed favored customers to take out loans using their shares as collateral; these customers could then purchase their shares with the borrowed money (a circular practice of dubious legality and risky to banks). Eventually, of course, they were obligated to pay up, but, given that banks often rolled indefinitely the loans of stockholders, it might not be for a long time. But by 1808, the banks in Philadelphia controlled about $4.5 million dollars, or close to $88 for each city resident. And everyone who owned stock in one of those banks became invested in corporations in more than just a strictly financial sense: in buying into the institutions, they had also bought into the principle of incorporation.[34]

Control over that big a pile of money allowed bankers to use their leverage over credit to mute those who had not yet bought in. Furthermore, because the incorporation of banks necessitated political activity on the part of bank boosters, banking officials brought their leverage to bear to affect the political process in any way that they could. Merely the perception of the possible uses of such power led less-connected Philadelphians to gauge their actions accordingly. Even the bravest publishers remained cowed by the chance that their flow of credit would run dry. In 1809, a proposal for the state to sell off part of its stock in the Bank of Pennsylvania almost never saw the light of day. John Taylor submitted a piece advocating that position to William Duane, publisher of the newspaper *Aurora*, but, as Taylor confided to a friend, "Mr. Duane being once a director thereof, he Conceived it would be some what indelicate for him to publish an Article of that kind, which would tend to lowering the Stock of said Bank." Duane was no shrinking violet. In the 1790s, he had run afoul of the Sedition acts and later was held in contempt of the Senate for publishing scathing editorials against numerous Federalists. Nor was it loyalty to his former colleagues that stayed the publisher's hand. Rather, Duane "owes that Bank some money & they might be illiberal enough to Curtail his discounts which at this season of the year would be inconvenient to him." As evidence of general awareness of the power that bank directors held over current and potential borrowers, Taylor admitted that he fully sympathized with Duane's plight. Sometimes subtle, sometimes blunt, bankers' ability to sway the terms of debate or to muzzle their critics certainly played a role in their success.[35]

Eventually, corporate backers' combination of ideology, co-optation, and intimidation overwhelmed the remaining voices of opposition. No one shouted louder into that rising wind than Simon Snyder. Snyder's parents emigrated from what is now Germany to Lancaster, Pennsylvania, the center of German settlement in the colony, in 1758; Simon was born a year later. He apprenticed at tanning before setting up shop as a storekeeper; he then established a mill on a creek near the Susquehanna River in central Pennsylvania. Despite getting into a tiff with his new neighbors over water rights, they respected him enough to appoint him a county justice of the peace and voted to send him to Pennsylvania's 1789–90 constitutional convention. Beginning in 1797, Snyder spent a decade in the Pennsylvania Assembly, where his colleagues elected him speaker for four terms. He gained election to the post of governor on his second try, in 1808, and cruised to easy victories in 1811 and 1814. He then sat in the state Senate in the two years before his death. Snyder often opposed anything that smacked of eastern, urban, or otherwise established interests. As a legislator, he worked to limit both gubernatorial and judicial power; as a governor, he championed better support for public education, debtor relief measures, and state support for internal improvements. Snyder's politics perfectly symbolized the cultural and political values of backcountry Pennsylvania, as well as the region's ascendant electoral power.[36]

Snyder also bitterly and staunchly opposed the expansion of corporate banking in Pennsylvania, twice vetoing omnibus bills chartering dozens of banks. In his veto messages, Snyder cogently articulated the main objections to corporations in general and to banks in particular. In 1813, he sent back a bill calling for the incorporation of thirty-five new banks—this in a state that at the time hosted only four such institutions. He objected to the potential proliferation on numerous grounds, beginning with the philosophical and progressing to the practical. On grounds of principle, Snyder argued that "corporation are privileged orders" that undermine equality. That went double, he continued, for "moneyed institutions . . . the undue influence of which has often been the subject of well founded complaint." He questioned whether Pennsylvania needed any more paper currency, suggested that the notes of so many new banks would prove a boon to counterfeiters, and pointed out that wartime was no time "to try experiments," given that the state garnered the lion's share of its revenue from its current bank stock. Finally, ever the politician, Snyder noted that while some petitioners had

Simon Snyder's somewhat imperious gaze did not belie the strong and combative governor. Simon Snyder by Charles Willson Peale, from life, 1810. Courtesy of Independence National Historical Park.

asked for banks, none had proposed so extensive an expansion in banking; furthermore, the bill had barely passed. The next year, the stubborn governor stuck to his guns despite an overwhelming majority. In addition to his previous objections—he instructed the assembly to look at his previous veto message—he added one more. Despite the measure's popularity among legislators, it did not seem to inspire the voters. Snyder could not "divest [himself] of the fear that . . . it would tend only to enrich the wealthy and the speculator, while it would in various forms heap burdens on the poor and the industrious." Taken together, the messages offered a stinging indictment of the proposed banking system. But those objections carried less constitutional weight than the legislature's supermajority, and the state extended the offer of a charter to forty-one new institutions.[37]

In the long run, Snyder's efforts proved impotent at best and counterproductive at worst. Individual companies and the corporate community would continue to face opposition in Pennsylvania, but the 1814 explosion effectively marked the permanent establishment of corporations. With so many institutions established in so many parts of the state, every district had a powerful constituency with a significant stake in the continued existence of banks, the most threatening corporations of all. From then on, opponents to corporations found themselves slipping inexorably down the long, slippery slope to Pennsylvania's general incorporation law of 1847, which provided a routinized, bureaucratic process by which anyone could apply for a corporate charter, thus making incorporation available to any citizen regardless of partisan or legislative connections. Pennsylvania's bankers had fought tooth and nail to protect their cartel; little did they know that by losing the battle they won the war. Coupled with corporate insiders' more intentional tactics of persuasion, co-optation, and occasional intimidation, the 1814 measure that passed despite the opposition of established bankers nonetheless led to their triumph over their more numerous but less organized and undercapitalized anticorporate opponents.

The expansion of corporations resulted in the geographic broadening of the corporate community, with practical political implications but also answering the main ideological objections to corporations. The wide spatial distribution of corporations throughout the state guaranteed that nearly every legislative district would have an ox to be gored should the greater principle of incorporation be threatened. Pennsylvania chartered 307 business corporations between 1800 and 1825; of those, three-quarters were transportation companies, mostly turnpikes, crisscrossing the Keystone State in a network that connected nearly all the state's towns that could practically be reached through early nineteenth-century road technology. Any attempt to stop further construction certainly would have been futile, given

PENNSYLVANIA CORPORATE BUSINESS CHARTERS

	1781– 1785	1786– 1790	1791– 1795	1796– 1800	1801– 1805	1806– 1810	1811– 1815	1816*– 1820*	1821– 1825*	1826– 1830
Banks	1	0	1	0	1	1	41	2	2	6
Manufacturing	0	0	0	0	1	1	7	6	0	1
Insurance	0	1	2	0	4	4	2	1	3	2
Internal Improvement	0	0	8	6	20	38	72	74	27	93
TOTAL	1	1	11	6	26	44	122	83	32	102

Sources: Davis, "Charters," 432–35; Miller, "Note," 155–59; Hartz, *Economic Policy*, 38.
*Rechartering of pre-existing corporate banks

that another ninety-one transportation companies gained charters in the following five years, with that trend only accelerating until the Panic of 1837 temporarily dampened interest in further investment. And though the forty-one banks of the class of 1814 did not include every county and not all of them would actually open their doors, between the ones that did conduct business and the Bank of Pennsylvania's branches, nearly all the state's densely populated areas hosted at least one chartered bank or bank branch. The expansion in stock ownership further insulated corporations from political pressure. Ownership in Pennsylvania internal improvement companies tended to be local; the same was true of most banks incorporated in 1814. There would be continued localized resistance to particular charters, but the geographic distribution of business corporations meant that any attempt to return to a corporate-free state would have to transcend sectional rivalries, perhaps through partisan politics that could unite enough regions of the state to turn back the institutional clock.[38]

But politics is the art of the possible, so even had they not been divided in so many ways, Pennsylvania politicians were unlikely to be able to stop time. Rather, the establishment of so many new corporations blunted partisan opposition to corporations generally and to banks especially. The Bank of North America remained an Anti-Constitutionalist and then a Federalist institution for decades, but the founding of the Bank of Pennsylvania, the Philadelphia Bank, and especially the Farmers and Mechanics Bank (all of them based in Philadelphia) broke the Federalist monopoly on corporate credit; similarly, the banks of the class of 1814 mostly represented Democratic-Republicans rather than Federalists. By providing investment and credit opportunities to all the state's major political factions, state legislators effectively eliminated the charges of political favoritism that corporate opponents had used to club corporate boosters. Meanwhile, desire for internal improvement, whether through the corporate form or otherwise, generally transcended party politics. Though the Society for the Promotion of Roads and Internal Navigations had boasted a mostly Federalist membership, the movement for internal improvement would include men such as William Findley and Tench Coxe, a prominent Antifederalist economic thinker, as well. Because politicians of all stripes could now avail themselves of corporate credit and show their constituents that they were responsive to calls for better transportation, significant and lasting partisan opposition to corporations became increasingly unlikely. Indeed, in Pennsylvania after the 1814 bank bill, while many individual corporations encountered resistance to their policies and actions, opposition to the principle of incorporation became increasingly sporadic and localized, with little sustained, effective statewide support. Even during the bitter partisan debates of the late 1820s and early 1830s, though Whigs tended to be far more approving of legislation than did Democrats, generally enough of the latter crossed party lines to vote for corporations or at most to put restrictions on corporations, rather than to kill them altogether.[39]

One particular source of anticorporate rhetoric and politicking demonstrated the extent to which resistance to corporations could become only marginally successful: the opposition to coal-mining corporations. Once the market for anthracite coal took off in the mid-1820s, individuals, partnerships, and corporations all competed to buy up coal lands and to bring the black rock to market from the rich coalfields in eastern Pennsylvania down the Schuylkill or Lehigh navigations down to market. Here as in other economic arenas, men on all sides of corporate questions claimed the high ground of principle while taking positions that also coincided with their interests. In 1825, several Philadelphia syndicates that included corporate insiders Joshua Lippincott and Manuel Eyre allied with prominent Schuylkill County men in a failed effort to obtain coal-mining company charters; the upriver men then encouraged out-of-state companies to bring capital to the region, apparently with little local opposition. But within a few years, once local men realized the magnitude and accessibility of the coal deposits, they changed their minds and began to stir against corporations to protect their new investments.[40]

In both the Schuylkill and the Lehigh valleys the local mining entrepreneurs directed much of their fire at New York–chartered corporations that began buying up coal lands in the mid-1820s. As one anticorporate writer typically put it, "the incorporation of coal companies will result in the destruction of the individual coal dealers." And not only the miners would suffer; so would "the large population of individuals, coal masters, merchants, and mechanics, who now fill our towns and villages," because "the stockholders will reside in Philadelphia, NY, &C. and all the profits of the trade will go to those places." Thus, just as their pro-corporate opponents did, local mining entrepreneurs mixed ideologies, often with contradictory results. Essentially, the would-be mining moguls argued that locals should control local resources, thereby drawing from moral economy thought. But they also championed free trade, a central tenet of liberalism.[41]

Lehigh Valley mine operators often targeted the Lehigh Coal and Navigation Company, which not only owned the main transportation route to market but also had a charter granting it the privilege to own land and to mine coal. In one of the more amusing volleys, a pamphleteer claiming to be "a backwoods-marksman [and] humble . . . shinglemaker" imagined a conversation between Lehigh Coal and Navigation Company cronies. Among other things, the anonymous author accused insiders of using shady tactics to increase company landholdings beyond the limits of its charter; plotting to get their company president, Josiah White, appointed to be head of a state-sponsored canal along the Delaware so that the company would control it; and supporting new bank charters in the legislature in exchange for votes to authorize higher company tolls. And while this was one of the more creative voices in the debate, the general anticorporate tone certainly resonated strongly among mining locals. George Taylor, a former Pottsville newspaper editor, railed in 1833 against an institution operated by a "distant board of directors" that controlled both the trade and local communities.[42]

Because of such strong resentment and usually favorable rhetoric in Harrisburg, mine operators' complaints got some degree of legislative traction in the Pennsylvania statehouse. In 1833, they persuaded the legislature to limit out-of-state corporate mining activity but at the same time left the door open for those corporations to gain Pennsylvania charters. In so doing, legislators gave the distinct impression that they were more concerned with sovereignty over Pennsylvania affairs than with scaling back corporate activity. Groups seeking charters to establish coal-mining corporations faced legislators and governors who often questioned whether incorporation was necessary in an industry that featured many successful proprietorships, and who let few promoters through the legislative gauntlet to incorporation. As with banks after 1814, that reluctance can be credited both to the political strength of established corporations, especially the Lehigh Coal and Navigation Company, and to strong anticorporate feelings.[43]

The high tide of this anticorporate movement came in 1834, when a Pennsylvania Senate investigation into the complaints against the corporations in general and the Lehigh company in general recommended that the state buy out the Lehigh navigation—an offer that Josiah White in some ways welcomed (the navigation may not have been worth the trouble that its tolls brought in) but the state could not afford. In the end, nothing was done to challenge seriously either the Lehigh Coal and Navigation Company or the general principle of incorporation. And because the issue affected only a small part of the state, corporate promoters could look to legislators from other regions to push charters through. Still, at least in this one industry, the state applied the brakes to corporate advancement.[44]

Just as importantly and with even more profound long-term consequences as the blunting of partisan and geographic challenges to incorporation, the profusion of the corporate form at least partly provided answers to many of the philosophical objections to corporations. Corporate boosters achieved an ideological balance analogous to the institutional balance established through corporations' functioning as a counterpoint to the state legislature. The ability of local rather than state or metropolitan interests to control local banks and transportation improvements helped to allay the fears of those whose belief in a moral economy emphasized the ability of locals to have a say over their economy. The state's oversight over corporations, its gaining revenue from banks, and its distribution of aid to internal improvement companies answered the republican emphasis on government for the common good rather than for individual striving. In addition, the simultaneous breaking up of the banking monopoly and the opportunity for so many Pennsylvanians to avail themselves of the opportunities available through credit and especially transportation improvements fit in perfectly with the strengthening liberal ethos.

While brushing back their opponents' republican ideological concerns, the ideology of corporate boosters became increasingly liberal, though with a liberalism tempered in a number of ways, and the very structure of corporations would eventually lend themselves to liberalism in ways that even some of their founders might have found alarming. True, officers of struggling corporations would continue to invoke republican ideals when asking the state for funding or for legislative favors, and courts did to some extent continue to protect local and individual interests over corporate ones. And they would invoke the public good when threatened with expansion of the corporate form, citing the dangers of "ruinous competition," but that was more to protect their interests than those of the public at large. Corporate men would also work to resist state efforts at monitoring and oversight, and indeed nearly any legislative or chartered restriction on their activities. Furthermore, because of the nature of corporations' ownership structure, corporations that began by being mostly locally owned could be bought out by metropolitan investors; the expansion of the availability of incorporation also opened the possibility of city men incorporating internal improvements with almost no input from the localities the projects ran through. Corporate supporters continued to employ republican and even occasionally moral economy rhetoric when it suited them. Nonetheless, despite their dependence upon the state for their institutional existence and continued use of state authority for their operation, corporate men ultimately embraced economic liberalism. This pattern would be repeated on both state and national scales innumerable times increasingly during the nineteenth century.[45]

Because of the mitigation of the geographical, partisan, and ideological opposition to corporations and through the co-option of the elite of all major political factions, corporate leadership became less divided over politics and more united in terms of class solidarity. Certainly in economic terms, the corporate elite remained mostly limited to Philadelphia's more wealthy men. Perhaps membership in the Dancing Assembly provided the best barometer of social standing in late eighteenth-century Philadelphia. Founded in 1748, the Philadelphia Dancing Assembly comprised the city's social elite, offering several opportunities for the city's self-appointed upper crust to see and be seen, to dance, to show off, to flirt, and to mingle. In early 1792, the organization undertook a subscription to build a dance hall; its subscription list functioned as a social register. Over a third of Philadelphia's business corporate officers signed their names, including William Bingham and John Nicholson. The high proportion is particularly striking given that while only Philadelphians subscribed, a generous proportion of the corporate officers at this point were from out of town (including appointed members of the Bank of Pennsylvania and a few canal company managers), and the subscribers also included men active in corporations but not corporate officers, such as Samuel Powel and Andrew Bayard. Even more striking, over 68 percent of the subscribers owned stock in at least one Philadelphia-area corporation. The same would be true of Philadelphia's political leadership, as indicated by members of the Philadelphia municipal corporation, its representatives to the state legislature, and its congressional representatives. Although charter provisions often forbade bank officers from concurrently holding public office, there nonetheless was considered to be some overlap between the corporate community and Philadelphia's political leadership. So, while the corporate elite, the political elite, and the social elite were not coequal, there was considerable overlap among Philadelphia's high society, its rich, its elected representatives, and its corporate leadership. This trend would continue in the first two decades of the nineteenth century with the incorporation of new Philadelphia-area banks and internal improvement companies.[46]

While a small group of Philadelphians worked in concert with allies across the state to ensure the perpetuation of the corporate form, developments at the federal level reinforced their efforts. In 1815, four years after President James Madison and a Republican-led Congress allowed the charter of the first Bank of the United States to expire, Madison and another Republican-led Congress overwhelmingly chartered the Second Bank of the United States. And four years later, the Supreme Court ruled in *Dartmouth College v. Woodward* that the New Hampshire state legislature could not amend a corporate charter. Together, these events demonstrated that, under the right conditions, a legislative majority on a national scale could support corporations and that a legislative action in a state could not banish them.

As for the Keystone State, the combination of corporate proliferation and the co-option of corporate opponents put the principle of incorporation on solid ground. Nor was Pennsylvania alone: in state after state—and especially in New York and Massachusetts, the other leaders in corporate activity—the proliferation of the corporate form, by allowing men of the various political factions and different geographic regions to participate, blunted the strongest political challenge to incorporation. Certainly, corporate men would continue to face legislative resistance on a range of particular issues; nonetheless, in Pennsylvania as well as in other states they could be assured that their institutions would not face en masse or even for the most part individually the existential political threats that the Bank of North America had beaten back in the 1780s. Though corporations themselves competed to some extent for customers and legislative favors, corporate leaders' business and class interests would generally transcend their partisan and competitive differences. Merely founding institutions and ensuring their survival did not make those organizations powerful; that took place over decades and with much meticulous effort. But the struggles to establish corporations resulted in state-authorized, highly capitalized institutions that could beat back ideological and political assaults. Having withstood their most serious political and ideological challenges, corporate men soon set to extending their power, taking advantage of all the financial, economic, technological, legal, and cultural tools at their disposal.[47]

3

• INCORPORATING MONEY •

In January 1810, a group of Pittsburgh citizens petitioned the Pennsylvania state legislature on behalf of the Philadelphia-based Farmers and Mechanics Bank, requesting that legislators allow the bank to open a branch there. By now the home of a Bank of Pennsylvania branch, the Pittsburgh community had already seen that one bank office had "put in circulation amongst us an active and productive capital," but only "to a limited amount." The petitioners listed the many benefits that banking expansion could impart: not only would a new bank branch lead to increased property values, greater trade, and more reliable money supply, but also "every merchant, manufacturer and mechanic of our country would be able to extend his business; would make a greater profit to himself; give constant employment to a greater number of industrious laborers"; and "a better and more extensive market would be provided for the surplus produce of the agriculturalist." In short, a new bank branch could help the entire community prosper.[1]

But just as banks seemingly created wealth, they also had the power to destroy it. Ten years after the Pittsburgh petition, Pennsylvania suffered in the grip of a dreadful economic depression, and a special state Senate committee convened to investigate the reasons for the state's dismal economic condition. Until the spring of 1819, Pennsylvania's economy had been booming, but over the past year the bubble had burst, leaving "ruinous sacrifices of landed property . . . numerous bankruptcies and pecuniary embarrassments . . . a general scarcity of money . . . a general suspension of labor . . . a stagnation of business . . . [and] vexatious losses," all leading to "a mass of evils" that left a "dispirited" people. Capturing both their constituents' mood and the gist of prevailing economic theory, the legislators located the genesis of the depression "chiefly in the abuses of the banking system, which abuses consist first in the excessive number of banks, and secondly in their universal bad administration." The frustrated senators lay the problem at the feet of the institutions themselves, raging against not only their deleterious economic effects but also their corrosive social and political consequences, thundering that "the incorporation of the monied interest already sufficiently powerful of itself, was but the creation of odious aristocracies, hostile to the spirit of free government, and subversive of the rights and liberties of the people." While corporate bank issuing policies from 1816 to 1823 may actually have helped to mitigate the depression's worst effects, Pennsylvania's legislators articulated the popular consensus concerning the roots of the state's economic woes.[2]

Regardless of the ambiguity with which Pennsylvanians viewed banks, Philadelphia bankers set the pace for state corporate banking in the United States. They established both the first corporate bank (the Bank of North America) and the first bank to serve as a commercial bank and as a state bank and to open branches (the Bank of Pennsylvania). In addition, Pennsylvania began the national trend of greatly expanded access to corporate banking with its chartering of forty-one such institutions in 1814. In each of these ways, Philadelphia led New York and Boston in the establishment of corporate banking. Thus, while Philadelphia was one of many cities that hosted corporate banks in the early republic, at the very least it was first among equals. More than those of the other big eastern cities, the pattern of Philadelphia banking in terms of the loose coordination of many institutions became the norm among most states in the middle decades of the nineteenth century.

But Philadelphia bankers were preoccupied with concerns more immediate than simply leading their urban rivals. More than with other corporate institutions, state elected officials hoped to keep a close rein on bankers, so banking provided the most contentious battles between corporate men and legislators over who had ultimate control over corporate actions. From the 1780s through the 1820s, Philadelphia corporate bank insiders and promoters worked to establish their institutions, to ward off competitors, and to gain independence from state oversight. And as keen observer Mathew Carey would later complain, the bankers generally succeeded on all these points.

*P*recisely because of their desire to wrest economic policy from the hands of state officials, delegates to the federal constitutional convention had inserted a clause into the national document that specifically denied states the authority to "coin Money; emit Bills of Credit" or "make any Thing but gold and silver Coin a Tender in Payment of Debts." Certainly the delegates were concerned about the prevailing economic situation in which the various state currencies had differing values, but when the federal congress met it did not choose to issue a national currency. Whether under the Constitution the states retained the authority to delegate others to issue currency remained open to question, but, regardless, the states looked to agents to issue notes to circulate as a medium of exchange. Nearly all of the states incorporated banks run by private citizens rather than publicly elected officials—exactly the result desired by convention delegates like Robert Morris and James Wilson.[3]

On the face of things, banking corporations in the early republic appeared to be perfect partnerships between state governments and private investors. Through the granting of a charter that functioned as a conditional license for a group of wealthy investors to go into business, state governments could foster economic growth, monitor money supply and credit, have access to large loans at short notice and on reasonable terms, and skim some revenue from banks' profits. In exchange for providing those considerable services to the public, investors received ample benefits, including de facto limited liability, the official imprimatur of the state, monopolies or at least limits on competition, and the right to print notes acceptable as legal tender. And no evidence of the tying together of public and private seems more emblematic of that partnership than state government ownership of corporate stock. Many charters allotted most of a corporation's shares for private investors while reserving a significant slice of ownership to the state.[4]

The granting of a charter offered assurances to the state, to a bank's investors, and to the general public that unincorporated banks (also called "private banks") could not. The bankers received legal protection from counterfeiters and were provided with a legal structure that allowed for the easy buying and selling of shares and a legally recognized mechanism for renewing organizational leadership. Furthermore, their notes were accepted by the state government for the payment of taxes, thus ensuring that they would to some extent keep their value. For its part, the state often demanded a monetary bonus from the banks' investors in exchange for a charter and gained a significant portion of its tax revenues out of banks' profits. And the public was assured that, at least in theory, the state would provide some level of oversight. Some individuals and groups did take up private banking, but, at the behest of already incorporated banks, the Pennsylvania legislature several times passed laws forbidding private banking. Much to the annoyance of incorporated bankers, the state could not always enforce the law, as Stephen Girard demonstrated through his personal banking efforts from 1812 until his death in 1829. But, given that the officers of several unincorporated banks campaigned heavily to be included in the 1814 omnibus bank charter, many early national Pennsylvanians clearly perceived the advantages of incorporated banks over unincorporated ones.[5]

Corporate banks played two crucial roles in the economy, one at a small-scale, individual level and the other at a large-scale, regional, and even national level, and though they were not alone in providing such services, banks became essential to Philadelphians' economic and social ambitions.

The small-scale function of banks was to loan money to individuals. City residents continued to use older modes of credit, including book credit (allowing customers to buy goods now but pay for them later), personal loans, ground rents (a kind of land title generally peculiar to Philadelphia that allowed developers to build on speculation), and commercial paper (IOUs that could be bought and sold). Some men became big players on or near the scale of incorporated banks, including Stephen Girard, whose enormous personal fortune backed his personal private bank, and commercial paper broker Nathan Trotter, who conducted transactions amounting to millions of dollars over the course of his long career. Essentially, the sum of all these loans—plus other circulating mediums of exchange such as gold and silver coins—constituted the money supply.[6]

Because corporate banks were the biggest lenders with the most money, in aggregate their lending policies had great effect on the local, state, and even national money supply, and so bank policy affected large-scale economic trends, too. Both of these functions—credit and money supply—proved central to Philadelphia's economic well-being, so control over them provided great leverage both over individuals' fortunes and over that of the city. Though a great many ambitious, hardworking, and lucky Philadelphians became economically successful through individual credit and stayed that way because of the city's stable money supply in good times, a great many also failed when their credit ran out, especially during depressions either caused or exacerbated by banking policies.[7]

Pennsylvanians understood that of all corporations, banks could be the most wonderful and the most dangerous, because the establishment of corporate banks meant nothing less than the incorporation of money itself. From the institutions' very beginnings, bankers had notes printed, used big, heavy ledgers, and rented offices or built impressive buildings to house their operations. Reflecting these physical manifestations, banks represented the most wonderful, frightening, and bewildering form of incorporation, mysterious instruments for creating wealth. Although banks were not the only powerful corporations and notwithstanding that many, if not most, of the struggles concerning the growth of corporate power occurred in venues besides the statehouse and bank boardrooms, the battles among banks and between bankers and legislators concerning how banks would be structured, who would run them, and how became the most publicly, politically contested battleground in the greater fight over the role of corporations in early American life.[8]

The negotiation necessary to obtain charters amounted to a tollbooth on the turnpike of success for Pennsylvania corporations, especially banks. Corporate leaders considered the acquisition of a charter the most onerous and perilous task required for setting up a capital-intensive business, just as the election of a board, the raising of capital, and the hiring of employees were all necessary to the successful administration of their projects. The chartering process became one of negotiated authorization. On the one hand, corporate organizers gained control over their ventures and secured permission from civil authorities for company officials to proceed with the activities they had proposed, organized, and initiated. On the other, legislators did their best to provide for the interests of residents on proposed canal routes, for the integrity of the financial system, for the growth of the economy, and for corporations to contribute a fair share of their profits to the greater community.

More than that of any other Philadelphia corporation, the Bank of Pennsylvania's ambiguous and ever-changing relationship with Pennsylvania state government and with other corporate banks typified the evolution of state–corporate and intercorporate relations, especially those of banks, in the early republic. The Bank of Pennsylvania served as the prototype of early national state banks: its charter contained provisions obliging it to lend money to the state, requiring legislature-appointed members of the board of directors, and reserving a large block of stock for the state treasury. From its chartering in 1793, the Bank of Pennsylvania did make money for its private stockholders and for the state, in addition to lending the state significant sums. So far, so good. But a close examination of the Bank of Pennsylvania and its rival institutions clouds that optimistic view. Corporate officers in general and bankers in particular did not look upon their elected officials as ideal partners. Indeed, the travails of the Bank of Pennsylvania tell the story of a continual struggle for power among the leaders of various banks and state officials. Rather than working together with legislators through consultation to achieve common goals—the hallmarks of any successful partnership—corporate leaders often strove to use the auspices of the state while retaining tight control of companies free from state oversight. They did so along three parallel tracks.

First, in their negotiations with the state legislature to gain incorporation, renew charters, or acquire additional privileges, bankers struggled to drive hard bargains and to limit state investment. Instead of seeking partnership, then, bankers hoped to avoid it, thereby strengthening their own hand in running their institutions. Second, despite their wariness of politics, bankers endlessly sought leverage to use the legislature for their own purposes or to project images of their institutions as engaged in public service. They did so through their efforts to prevent the chartering of potential rival institutions while constructing buildings, issuing notes, and publishing pamphlets all testifying to banks' solidity and their role in economic growth. Finally, bankers tried at every turn to counter state oversight of their operations: they informally excluded state-appointed directors from decision making, lobbied for the elimination of state-appointed directors, resisted state investigations, and found ways to shield corporate officers from civil suits. Bank of Pennsylvania officers and supporters used all of these techniques against economic and political rivals and to exert control over their institution and over the state economy. In doing so, they grasped the reins of economic policy from elected representatives and put them into the hands of a small group of Philadelphia bankers.

From their inauspicious initial gambit to their later defeats, stalemates, and victories, Bank of Pennsylvania backers experienced the entire range of permutations in the complex chess match of bank-chartering politics. Their first effort demonstrated the capacity of incumbent institutions to divide and conquer an association of potential rivals. On January 19, 1784, a group of 153 eager investors signed a broadside signaling their plans for "establishing another Bank in the City of Philadelphia, by the name of the Bank of Pennsylvania." While praising the "utility" of its corporate predecessor, this syndicate subtly indicated its members' frustrations with the Bank of North America: the group wanted to found an institution "as nearly similar to it as shall be found proper, in order that the benefits arising therefrom may be extended to a greater length than one institution of that kind can be expected to reach." In other words, having been excluded from Robert Morris's banking club, they wanted a club of their own. This new group had several gripes with the already-established institution. From the very beginning, investment in the Bank of North America had been limited: its initial offering was only 1,000 shares, the great majority of which were reserved in the hands of a small crowd of Republicans (of the 1780s Pennsylvania vintage) and their associates or foreign colleagues. People outside the circle of Morris, Willing, Bingham, and friends—especially political opponents—thus had little opportunity to share in the Bank of North America's significant dividends.[9]

Even more than they privately grumbled about being excluded from the bank's profits, Constitutionalists strongly objected to what they called the "undue influence" of insiders over Bank of North America affairs—that is, the power that a few self-selected men held over banking policy. The bank's one-share, one-vote system of director elections "gave Morris & his Different Partners a decided majority over all the other stockholders," complained men like Constitutionalist merchant Thomas Wistar. During the first twenty years of its existence, thirty-one out of the thirty-four men who sat on the bank's board counted themselves as Pennsylvania Republicans (Federalists after 1787). Those directors showed no reluctance in rewarding their political friends to the detriment of their opponents. Constitutionalists sourly noted that they could not get loans from the bank. Wistar railed against "the great partiality in the discounting shewn to the hangers on, of Morris." The bank's policy of lending primarily to friends meant that outsiders found themselves excluded from the city's only institutional, state-sanctioned source of credit. If Constitutionalist merchants could not buy stock or get loans, they reasoned, they would push to get a bank of their own. For them, getting a new bank had little to do with public service and everything to do with access to and control over credit.[10]

But rather than letting potential borrowers have, in Morris's words, "two shops to go to," and thereby diluting insiders' own influence, Morris and company successfully pushed back. Bank of North America backers countered the upstarts with arguments partly based on legitimate fears that "two capital banks operating in one city . . . might, perhaps, act in opposition to each other and, of course, destroy each other," partly out of the concern that competition might eat into their dividends, and partly out of jealous protection for the bank's monopoly status. Hoping that widening the banks' stockholder base would dampen criticism and lessen the enthusiasm for a new institution, bank president Thomas Willing and his board reacted swiftly, proposing to enlarge the stock of the bank, selling off a thousand additional shares of stock (though at $500, rather than the $400 price of original shares only three years before). Not deterred, the rival group went ahead with an application for a charter; Bank of North America officers countered by increasing their offering to four thousand shares and lowering the price back to $400.[11]

Meanwhile, Morris and his allies mobilized partisans in the General Assembly to oppose the establishment of another bank. Combined with representatives opposed to an expansion of banking and with those against corporations in general, Bank of North America sympathizers managed to stymie the new group in the legislature. Willing also made assurances that the new stock sale would be open to new stockholders only. While that did not prevent insiders' friends, relatives, and associates from buying in, it was enough of a sop to legislators and to some of the more vocal Bank of Pennsylvania supporters to prevent the establishment of a new bank. For the new investors who simply wanted a shot at bank stock, the move to prod the Bank of North America into selling off more shares worked. For those who also wanted some say over banking policy so as to have a basis of economic and political power similar to the established bank, the incident offered a clear lesson. Establishing a bank involved much more than simply gathering capital: it also required garnering enough political leverage to sway the finicky state legislature.

That educational experience paid off nine years later, when a similar group managed to obtain a charter for a new Bank of Pennsylvania. The composition of this new association illuminates the murky mix of money and politics so central to corporate banks in the early republic. Much of the nucleus of the old association joined the new one: at least twenty-five of the individuals pledged to invest in the 1784 effort lined up to buy stock when the new incarnation came into being in 1793. If these men had ever held any aversions to banks, they had long since shed them. One new investor, though, clearly had changed his position: none other than William Findley, who had vigorously opposed rechartering the Bank of North America in 1785. Given that Findley objected most loudly to the old bank's opportunity to abuse its monopoly, Findley was perhaps willing to join a new institution that would counter the old one, or maybe he just grabbed a good chance when he saw one. A few shareholders crossed lines from the other direction: Ebenezer Hazard had been a member of the founding coterie of the Bank of North America. Nonetheless, most of the men active in establishing the new bank placed themselves solidly in the Democratic-Republican camp. Its first two presidents, John Barclay and Samuel M. Fox, both called themselves Democratic-Republican. The latter was also a correspondent and political ally of Thomas Jefferson. Other prominent Democratic-Republicans included Jonathan Dickinson Sergeant, John Swanwick, and Caspar Wistar. Politically, the new bank had a much different complexion than its predecessor.[12]

Still, when the founders of the Bank of Pennsylvania looked in the mirror they saw men who lived, dressed, and worked very much like their Bank of North America rivals. Despite one Bank of Pennsylvania director's claim that the Federalists "have always been the most wealthy, and generally the most respectable of our inhabitants," these Democratic-Republicans did not seem far behind their fellow financiers. Investors and insiders in the two banks were united by an affinity more powerful than politics: the class solidarity of the wealthy. Like those of its hated predecessor, the Bank of Pennsylvania's first offered stocks went for $400 each. As a group, shareholders sat at the top of Philadelphia's economic ladder. City real estate holdings provide a strong indication of the relative affluence of Bank of Pennsylvania share-holders. At the time of the bank's establishment, the median taxpayer in the city paid £35 in property taxes; on the other hand, the median Bank of Penn-sylvania stockholder had property within the city assessed for £473—more than thirteen times as much as those not holding stock. Nearly 70 percent of city-dwelling stockholders coughed up more than £100; only half that portion of the general population, 35 percent, owned enough property to be assessed such a high levy. In addition, such figures greatly understate the economic gulf between Bank of Pennsylvania stockholders and their less affluent fellow citizens, because city tax evaluations included only real estate, not the per-sonal property, commercial property, financial instruments, or property owned outside the city limits that the rich were more likely to own.[13]

The stock list included such wealthy Philadelphia merchants as Thomas Cope, Stephen Girard, Godfrey Haga, and Philip Wager, along with promi-nent Quaker City lawyers Jonathan Dickinson Sergeant and Jared Ingersoll. With few exceptions, the growth of corporate banking in the early republic did not result in a grand expansion of investment profit opportunities be-yond the already privileged. Regardless of party, early republic banks were state-sanctioned institutions used by the rich to make themselves richer us-ing methods that no elected legislature would ever undertake directly.[14]

Eventually, bank stock ownership widened, but only slightly. The compo-sition of investors and investment in early Pennsylvania banks reflected the notion that banks would yield consistent dividends without much attention from shareholders. In its initial stock offering in February 1807, the Farmers and Mechanics Bank attracted investment ranging from the 113 buyers ac-quiring three or fewer shares at a par value of $50 to the thirty investors who put in over $5,000 each, with a top initial holding of $15,250. The median holding was ten shares, or $500, a significant amount of money, and far more than the median in potentially risky ventures such as internal im-provements. The large number of big investors suggests an impression among men of capital that the bank would be a profitable venture worthy of tying up large blocks of money for an extended period of time. Especially telling, only four of the top thirty investors were on the board, suggesting that many of those men invested without the purpose or even expectation of getting special treatment when applying for loans; then again, given their resources, those big investors were the Philadelphians least likely to be pinched for cash, and most likely to be able to get it. Without the motive of insider access to credit, these investors must have seen the bank as a likely vehicle for income. Their lack of participation in the board shows their willingness to have others guard a significant portion of their wealth. Rich Philadelphians saw banks as a safe and convenient investment vehicle, one that would lend them, their families, and their class stability.[15]

Many wealthy families took advantage of bank stock as part of their strategies for economic long-term economic stability. Though a very small proportion of total investment, the number and size of stock purchases made by and for women, in trusts for children, and by charitable and social organizations indicated that many people perceived shareholding in banks as being prudent but profitable. Because minors and, to a varying degree, many women were unable or unwilling to run their own businesses (or discouraged or actively prevented from doing so), investment on their behalf was generally intended to provide for a stable income over a long period without requiring business expertise or investors' time. Some trustees were also stockholders in their own right, while others only held stock for dependents. At least one trust, consisting of sixteen Farmers and Mechanics Bank shares, belonged to a local Mason's Lodge. Out of the shares listed as originally issued by the Farmers and Mechanics Bank, 1,837, or 15.3 percent, were held by women or in trust for women or minors. Of course, some male investors may have put stocks in the names of their wives or children in order to shield assets from creditors. The size of holdings in trust almost exactly mirrored those of all investors: the median holding was ten shares, or $500.[16]

In a feat of circular reasoning, bankers touted such investments as proof of their own probity. In 1805 the board of directors of the Bank of Pennsylvania proudly claimed that "the stock of the Bank of Pennsylvania has long been considered as a most secure and provident fund, for the investment of the monies of widows, orphans, and benevolent associations, to whom the safety of their capital, and the punctual payment of its product are all important." Two years later, the Bank of North America claimed that "widows and other unmarried women, minors, and charitable institutions, hold . . . 544" shares of the institution. While bank directors were not above using hyperbole for political effect—references to helpless widows and orphans being the second refuge of a scoundrel—the bank did include many women and trusts among its stockholders. The number of shares held in trust and by women strongly indicated a widespread perception that banks offered a prudent choice for those depending upon stable long-term gains.[17]

The desire for steady income over the long haul, in turn, influenced the way insiders ran the big Philadelphia banks. Boards of directors tended to value long-term safety in their loans over the ability to stretch out available capital in an effort to maximize immediate gains. As long as the bank could provide dividends in the 7–9 percent range, bank officers eschewed lending out as much money as they possibly could, preferring to keep reserves against runs so as to promote confidence in the bank and to do their part to stabilize the money supply. Besides, banks could and did use excess capital to buy federal and local bonds that in effect yielded nearly as much as loans did anyway (although the state government later tried to curb bank investments as a percentage of overall capital in order to increase the amount available for lending). At the same time, the notorious policies of early national banks to reserve most of their loans for merchants and to be especially friendly to insiders—those on the board, their families, and business associates—certainly excluded many would-be bank customers but also operated to check credit. By definition, insiders were known quantities, people with whom the bankers had been familiar for a long time and whose businesses and expertise had been well established. They therefore appeared to be a safer bet for loans than strangers who had unfamiliar business credentials and who might not feel the same social pressure from friends and relatives to pay back loans punctually. The desires of investors and the lending policies of banks dovetailed to produce institutions with a long-term focus that could operate mostly beyond the supervision of the general population of stockholders.[18]

Indeed, the distribution of bank loans proved to be not much broader than the ownership of bank stock. Banks' opaque and ad hoc lending practices reflected their intentional exercise of power in their portioning out of credit. From its beginnings, the Bank of North America pursued a highly restrictive lending policy, ensuring that money remained mostly in the close fraternity of company founders and their associates. In its first full year of operation, the Bank of North America granted more loans to shareholders and other insiders than it did to those with no ties to the bank; those insider dealings accounted for over 56 percent of the total dollars loaned. Merchants clearly received preference over tradesmen and manufacturers and were the most active borrowers by far of any occupation. They continued to be so for the first several decades of the Bank of North America's existence. Philadelphia banks hesitated lending to manufacturers, claiming that merchants could pay back thirty- and sixty-day loans promptly, while manufacturers needed long-term loans to buy machines, build work space, and acquire raw materials. However, that reasoning is questionable, given that a great number of the short-term loans to merchants were continuously rolled over, essentially making them long-term loans, and that, once manufacturers were established, they were at least as able to generate continuous cash flow and therefore more likely to be able to pay back loans than were merchants.[19]

In addition to being generally limited to merchants, lending policy could be highly arbitrary. The personal proclivities of bank presidents often dictated lending policy, seemingly having no set parameters. Thus, bank lending was susceptible to all the abuses of any practice in which people with power are able to play favorites. True, bank boards asked for personal references when men they did not know applied for loans. But those references did not necessarily have to provide specific and detailed financial information, only their assurances as to the reliability of the potential debtor. Relia-

bility, of course, remained in the eyes of the beholder and extended well beyond financial creditworthiness to include perceived political and social
compatibility. For a banker, a creditworthy person could be identified by
"the confidence which people place in a man's integrity and punctuality, in
fulfilling his contracts, and performing his engagements," but that hardly
represented an objective set of criteria. When in 1829 Philadelphia Bank
president Robert Patterson declined an implicit invitation to join the board
of the Second Bank of the United States, he cited his comfort with his current position: "I am at home there—with uncontrolled influence." That influence extended to loan policy, where, in the presence of others who shared
his social and political preferences and in the absence of clear, objective, and
transparent credit standards, Patterson would have been inhuman had he
been a fully objective arbiter of creditworthiness. The ability to pick and
choose gave bank boards great economic power over potential borrowers.[20]

Beyond their unstated purpose to promote the upper crust's continued
wealth, state banks all fulfilled more explicit economic and financial functions.
To many in the Philadelphia area, all corporate banks were mysterious machines that created paper money and profits nearly out of thin air: one prospective stockholder wrote in wonder to Roberts Vaux, relative of longtime Bank of
Pennsylvania director George Vaux, that "dollars can be advanced ten, fifteen,
or twenty pCent by the magic of a bank charter." One observer said that as late
as the 1810s, Pennsylvanians "supposed that the mere establishment of banks
would of itself create capital, that a bare promise to pay money, was money itself." The relationship between money and banks certainly could be confusing,
but at its most basic level, Philadelphian Pelatiah Webster explained, "a BANK is
a large repository of cash, deposited under the direction of proper officers (say a
president and directors) for the purpose of establishing and supporting a great
and extensive credit." Through the selling of shares of stock upon its establishment, a bank gathered a significant pool of capital; the Bank of Pennsylvania's
original charter authorized it to raise up to $3,000,000.[21]

Once the Bank of Pennsylvania opened its doors, creditors applied for
loans. A subcommittee of the bank's board of directors reviewed loan applications twice a week. Approved borrowers then received their requested loan
in the form of banknotes, that is, currency printed by the bank, with the
bank subtracting interest up front. Because a borrower did not receive the
full sum requested, the process was known as discounting. In practical
terms, a hypothetical lucky borrower who secured a one-hundred dollar,
one-year loan at 6 percent interest (the maximum legal rate, which all banks
charged) would receive ninety-four dollars in banknotes and in return agree
to pay back his loan in specie (gold or silver coin) within twelve months.
Under most circumstances, banks backed their notes with specie: if someone
had a twenty-dollar Bank of Pennsylvania note, she could go to the bank's
office and exchange it for twenty dollars in gold or silver. Consequently,
banknotes circulated at close to face value as long as merchants and tradesmen had confidence in the bank's ability to back up the notes.

Depending upon how free or conservative a bank's board wanted to be, banks often had several times the value of their paid-in capital circulating in banknotes, because few people actually did want to redeem notes for gold on a regular basis. By lending out multiples of the cash they had on hand, bankers increased their earnings, made more credit available, and increased the money supply in ways that would not be possible otherwise. Other services less integral to banks' central mission and making little or no contribution to the bottom line included keeping money on deposit both for safekeeping and for customers to write bills of exchange (checks) against; exchanging various kinds of currencies, banknotes of other banks, and specie; and generating specialized financial instruments for use in large-scale and overseas mercantile activities. Through all these methods, but mostly through making forty-five- or sixty-day loans to individual customers, the Bank of Pennsylvania and other state banks gained most of their profit.[22]

Beyond the common corporate banking tasks of lending, issuing banknotes, and regulating the money supply, the Bank of Pennsylvania not only operated as a state bank but also served as the state's banker. In practical terms, that meant doing many of the same things for Pennsylvania's government as the bank did for private customers, but on a much grander scale. Whereas individual loans ranged from the hundreds to the thousands of dollars, as a condition of its charter the Bank of Pennsylvania was obligated to loan the state an eye-opening $500,000; subsequent legislation required smaller advances, usually in the $50,000 range. Bank of Pennsylvania notes were accepted as payment for any state taxes or fees, while the bank was to keep in its vaults any deposits from the state government as well as those from corporations such as insurance companies.[23]

These privileges and obligations proved to be a mixed blessing for the bank and for the state. Bankers preferred not to make large or long-term loans to any customer. Despite still receiving the legally mandated interest, having to offer the state government big accommodations limited lending flexibility, prevented the bank from calling in loans in troubled times, and increased the possibility of considerable danger to the institution should a really big lender default on a loan. Furthermore, the state government exacted better terms than could individual lenders: rather than receiving a discounted sum, the state treasurer withdrew the full amount and paid interest in later installments. But for the bank, other parts of the deal helped make up for these deficiencies. The state's acceptance of Bank of Pennsylvania notes ensured that the notes would continue to circulate at face value, thereby preventing the bank's effective loss of revenue through note depreciation. Also, the state's depositing of funds in Bank of Pennsylvania coffers resulted in the bank's vaults being constantly replenished, allowing it to continue discounting and bolstering public confidence in the institution. Taken together, the Bank of Pennsylvania's private business and public business fit the British mold that Bank of North America founders had modeled from.

Happy to have gained such remunerative privileges, Bank of Pennsylvania insiders such as president Samuel M. Fox were reluctant to share them. They had celebrated the breaking of the Bank of North America's monopoly, but, like all businessmen, they praised the principle of competition only when it applied to others. Consequently, they bent over backward in their efforts to prevent others from entering corporate banking. The extent to which Bank of Pennsylvania supporters sought to manipulate the unpredictable Pennsylvania legislature resulted in nearly insurmountable opposition to the incorporation of potential competitors. The Philadelphia Bank's charter application floundered in Lancaster, the erstwhile state capital, for two years, partly because of the sectional jealousies, party politics, and general suspicion of banks and moneyed institutions, but largely because the Bank of Pennsylvania lobbied strenuously against it, offering the state the astounding amount of $200,000 in cash not to charter another Philadelphia-based bank. Indeed, according to one legislator in 1803, "the memorial from the Bank of Pennsylvania" that outlined the established institution's generous proposal "had considerable effect upon the members," and he opined it would "prevent a charter to the Bank of Philadelphia [in this session]." The street went both ways: in a conversation with Jonathan Smith, the Bank of Pennsylvania's cashier, some legislators "intimated to him . . . that in case the Bank of Pennsylvania would make certain advances to the Commonwealth an extension of the Charter would be granted and the faith of the State pledged that no other Bank should be incorporated during the continuance of the Charter so extended."[24]

The political strength of the Bank of Pennsylvania combined with regional resentment toward Philadelphia banks and concerns over the proliferation of banknotes resulted in uphill battles for each new bank. Bankers used their economic and politic leverage not only against the state but also against potential competitors. Despite the eventual success of the Philadelphia Bank, Bank of Pennsylvania partisans almost succeeded in strangling the next pledge to Pennsylvania's banking fraternity, the Philadelphia-based Farmers and Mechanics Bank. Such legislative haggling convinced corporate leaders to think of the chartering process as a bothersome legislative hurdle and of the legislature as an erratic and unreliable entity.

Banking insiders used every tool at their disposal in their negotiations with elected officials. Philadelphia Bank president Joseph Tagert proved himself to be a master of such proceedings. Toward the end of the 1807–1808 session of the Pennsylvania state legislature, signs increasingly suggested that the Philadelphia Bank's friends would fail to muster a majority in favor of incorporation. Fortunately for the new bank's partisans, the state Senate's committee on banking had given the institution a good report. The bank's lobbyist, James Sharswood, wrote Tagert, suggesting they would be better off postponing a charter vote until the following session. This way, "the public may be led to suppose that . . . the lateness of the session alone prevented [the charter's] adoption," while the positive committee report and the absence of a measure preventing the bank from pursuing its operations would imply the legislature's approval. Between sessions, the bank would "be in full operation and there [could not] be a doubt but that the prudence of the Directors [would] conciliate in the public mind." However, should the bank's friends push for a charter and lose now, "our opponents," said Sharswood, especially those from districts that included Bank of Pennsylvania branches, "may take the advantage of this defeat to urge a law immediately to prevent our progress"; at the very least, Tagert and Sharswood's reapplication in the ensuing session would be severely jeopardized. Sharswood warned direly, "The victory to our opponents would be so far complete and it is but fair to presume they would not stop untill they had accomplished our final ruin." Tagert took Sharswood's advice, and together they were successful in the next legislative session (the bankers' acquiescence to loaning the state $100,000 did not hurt, either).[25]

Having a man in Harrisburg could mean even more than having someone to buttonhole legislators. When lobbyists did not do the trick, Tagert used the best leverage that bankers could have: sympathetic treatment as a quid pro quo from borrowers. John Thompson, a state legislator representing Philadelphia County, was always a friend of the Philadelphia Bank in legislative matters. And he would ask Tagert for similar treatment: when the legislator found that he was overdue to pay his notes at the bank, Thompson wrote to Tagert to "request a continuation of [his] favourable attention." From Tagert's point of view, this particular legislator was not a partner but a wholly owned subsidiary.[26]

The politics surrounding the omnibus bank bill of 1814 demonstrated the ways that various corporate interests jockeyed for position in the state legislature. By 1812, Pennsylvania had chartered only four banks, all based in Philadelphia, although the Bank of Pennsylvania was at that time operating four branch offices. Partly influenced by the dechartering of the first Bank of the United States, over the following three sessions the partisans of various associations wanting to incorporate country banks swarmed the new state capital at Harrisburg, importuning representatives to expand the banking privilege quantitatively and geographically. In 1812–1813, a bill chartering twenty-five banks passed both houses by one vote but did not have the supermajority necessary to override a gubernatorial veto; the next session legislators passed a bill for forty-one new banks, but again by a small margin. Many representatives opposed these bills individually, citing what many argued would be the inevitably ruinous expansion of paper money as well as the dilution of the value of current bank stocks in the state's portfolio. That majority, though, was a shifting one: the friends of the banks already chartered opposed the new banks as much out of fear of competition as fear of inflation, and few representatives were willing to vote for a bank in someone else's district without getting anything in return.[27]

Perhaps Pennsylvanians, especially Democratic-Republicans, had grown somewhat less uncomfortable with moneyed institutions, but, as Representative Charles Biddle noted, more than any ideological shift it was the spirit of logrolling that prevailed. "Do you vote for the bank in my county," legislators offered to their colleagues, "and I will vote for yours." The new banks' supporters continued to apply pressure. Finally, in the 1814 session, the various applicants got together to put all their banks in one bill, one that passed by so large a margin that it overrode a gubernatorial veto. Indeed, one of the bill's supporters predicted that, if the 1814 bill failed, "there is not a doubt that we shall have at least 100 banks in two years." As things turned out, most representatives did not oppose banks in general, merely other men's banks, and especially unchartered (that is, small, privately run) banks, which the bill restrained. After that act, the state legislature would not charter another new bank for decades. Certainly the Panic of 1819, which many blamed upon banks, was one reason for the end of bank proliferation, but just as important, virtually every legislative district had a strong group with a vested interest in limiting banking to those companies already chartered. While the public interest presumably formed part of the equation, corporate interests represented the crucial variable.[28]

The elaborate charter negotiations between corporate boosters and legislators were no exercise in creating quasi-public enterprise, that is, a joint cooperative venture between the state and private investors. Rather, corporate charters resulted from political horse trading on the part of mutually suspicious groups all angling to get the best deal they could. Legislators and bankers grew so leery of each other that bankers sometimes secretly engaged lobbyists to do their bidding in the statehouse: in 1824, Richard Bache wrote from the state capital in Harrisburg to William Meredith, his employer and the president of the Philadelphia Bank, "If I were to introduce the subject of Banks now to any member it would soon be known what my errand is." Rather, he was to bide his time and "hold [his] tongue and make acquaintances, unless the bank question [was] spoken of by the members."[29]

As a result of the chartering process, the state often held stock in many corporations. However, that practice did not indicate a willingness on the part of corporate boards to include the government as a meaningful partner. Pennsylvania did own shares in many banks and internal improvement companies, but a close look at the timing and circumstances of state acquisition of corporate shares suggests that this action did not constitute a true partnership. Depending upon the kind of corporation, the legislature's reasons for owning company stock belied any deep sense of common mission between corporate boosters and the state government.

Neither a boon for banks and their private investors nor a sign of government–business partnership, the state's ownership of bank stock was designed to tax bank profits so as to ensure that all Pennsylvanians would receive some benefit from the profitable opportunities offered to stockholders: what debates hinged upon was the terms of the deal. As a requirement of the Bank of Pennsylvania's first charter in 1793, the state government retained the option of investing up to an impressive $1 million in bank stock. The legislature intended to use United States bonds that the state treasury had on hand to pay for a portion of the stock; Albert Gallatin later suggested that legislators wanted to buy the stock so as not to fritter away a surplus gained as a result of the federal government's final settlement of state Revolutionary War debts. Because the state paid only par value—that is, the original issue price—for the stock, the deal allowed the state to receive more than market value for the bonds it transferred to the Bank of Pennsylvania while spending far less than market value for its new bank shares. Thus, the bank performed the valuable service of taking on the state's poorly performing assets and replacing them with an investment that was expected to yield better dividends and to appreciate quickly.[30]

The state's immediate market-value gain in the transaction, $54,187, amounted to a onetime bonus from the bank in exchange for receiving the charter. Meanwhile, the state bought the rest of its bank stock, $250,000 worth, through a loan from the bank at an annual rate of 6 percent. The state received 942 shares in exchange for its United States bonds, and 625 shares through its loan from the bank. Private subscriptions brought the total shares sold to 6,250, each worth $400. In what would become standard practice for the purchase of bank stock, the stock itself would be the collateral for the loan. Legislators held the expectation that the Bank of Pennsylvania's dividends would be similar to those of the previously chartered Bank of North America, ranging from 8–12 percent a year. The practical effect of the bonus and the stock purchase was that the state would receive 15.7 percent of all the bank's dividends up to 6 percent, and a total of 25.7 percent of all dividends above 6 percent. No cash had changed hands, but the state government received dividends on a large portion of the bank's capital.[31]

The clearest indication that legislators considered the state's bank stake as a contribution to the commonweal rather than as an encouragement to business occurred fifteen years after the Bank of Pennsylvania's painful but successful adventure. In legislative haggling over the Farmers and Mechanics Bank charter in the 1807–1808 and 1808–1809 sessions, it was the bank's opponents who were most keen on getting the state a stake in the bank. At one point the bank's lobbyist reported to cashier Joseph Tagert, "An amendment passed the Committee which will prevent our accepting a charter; this amendment is that the Bank shall allow the legislature to subscribe on the part of the State $100,000 in the stock of the bank at par." Tagert's correspondent vented his exasperation with a legislator who "opposed every favorable section and proposed all the most vexatious amendments that were attempted, and it was on his motion that the gratuity was raised to $100,000, and yet he says he is in favor of the bill!" In the end, legislators and the bankers compromised, acceding to a deal in which the bank issued the state $75,000 in shares in exchange for incorporation. The Commonwealth eventually owned stock in a number of banks, but from the bankers' point of view, state shareholding represented a regrettable cost to be paid for the opportunity to make handsome profits.[32]

In 1814, the legislature began to forgo stock purchases and instead required new banks to pay the state a certain percentage of their dividends, depending upon the individual charter. This change represented recognition on both sides that banks could afford to give up a greater share of their profits to help out the state without compromising their businesses. The new banks yielded a higher percentage of their dividends to the state than previously chartered ones. They also no longer received United States bonds that they could use to back their note issues, and as a result, gross profits were lower. The state generally took 8 percent of the dividends from the banks chartered in 1814. The percentage of their dividends paid in taxes was lower than the Bank of Pennsylvania's, but the total dividends were lower in proportion to private investment because the banks received no United States bonds from the state, even at below market value as had the Bank of Pennsylvania. From the new banks' point of view, the change was a wash at best. Thus, the legislature had streamlined the chartering process—the stock "purchases" had become increasingly convoluted—negotiating with new charter applicants an appropriate cash bonus and demanding a certain percentage of the institution's dividends for the coffers in Harrisburg. Just as corporate boosters had not given stock to the state out of the goodness of their hearts, state legislators had not insisted upon the acquisition of bank stock out of a magnanimous effort to help bankers and bank investors or because of any general desire to promote commerce: they did so strictly as a form of revenue generation, that is, as a way of taxing those institutions. By 1814 they had simply found an easier way to do so.

Ironically, competition among corporations greatly contributed to corporate insiders' common dim view of the state government. Despite corporate insiders' agreement and cooperation on many issues, the strong urge of officers in established banks to resist competition at all costs drove up the premium that new syndicates had to pay the state to get charters. In that sense, the state—and thus the community at large—profited from bank rivalries through the use of bank bonuses to pay for internal improvements and to boost the state coffers and through the steady stream of bank profits that eased the state's overall tax burden. Indeed, any concern among legislators about possibly killing the already-chartered banks laying golden eggs was assuaged by bankers' apparent willingness to part with huge sums simply to prevent the addition of newcomers in a market— the provision of credit—that clearly had plenty of room to grow. That signaled to legislators that new ventures would also be profitable. In the case of the 1814 omnibus bill, Representative Charles Biddle thought that his colleagues "must have known the bill would be against the interest of the State, by lessening the value of their stock in the other banks they had so much of their money invested in." Still, they overwhelmingly approved the measure. Maybe Biddle had honed his dim view of his fellow legislators in another milieu: he was also a longtime board member of the Bank of Pennsylvania.[33]

A major ingredient in the passage of bank charters, then, was the negotiation of the terms of taxation, an important matter for the legislature, considering that a large portion of the state's revenue came from bank dividends. On an annual basis from 1796 to 1825, banks provided the state of Pennsylvania with at least 36 percent and as much as 50 percent of its annual income. From many politicians' point of view, that income represented a comparatively painless opportunity to raise revenue while holding down constituents' property taxes. Whether they raised as much money for Pennsylvania as a state-run loan bank would have raised was open to question, but certainly corporate men were not wrong to argue that they paid a substantial sum to the state. Bank lobbyists, for their part, did not hesitate to point this out when doing so served their purposes: when one legislator threatened to exact the price of a bridge over the Susquehanna in exchange for rechartering the Philadelphia Bank in 1824, the bank's lobbyist quietly threatened that "the banks might refuse their charters and the state lose the revenue it now receives, and the Republican administration be blamed & obliged to resort to taxes to sustain itself." Luckily for both sides, the legislators did not call the bankers' bluff.[34]

Meanwhile, representatives could play the same kinds of games. One member of a legislative committee on banks, in a bid to negotiate with banks and to bolster his own political leverage, tried "to induce the Banks to propose terms" that the member could then manipulate; "indeed he conceives or wishes others to believe that he can dictate terms." From the bankers' point of view, the state's taxing of banks in exchange for incorporation amounted to a profit-draining annoyance and did not endear the legislature to dividend-conscious board members. On the contrary, the bankers' lesson from the chartering experience was that, although on occasion the legislature could be influenced, the price was steep, the bargaining treacherous, and the outcome uncertain. Better to stay clear of the state legislature whenever possible rather than open bank business to public debate and risk humiliating defeat besides.[35]

Nonetheless, the charter was, by definition, the sine qua non of incorporated banking. The Bank of Pennsylvania's charter contained some elements common to all charters, others typical of similar corporations (banks), and a few particular to its own peculiar circumstances. After a short but flowery preamble asserting that the new institution would "promote the regular, permanent, and successful operation of the finances of this state, and be productive of great benefit to trade and industry in general," the bank's founding legal document was composed of sixteen densely detailed sections and over 5,000 words. Corporate boilerplate language (typical clauses inserted into nearly all corporate charters) constituted several sections; not surprisingly, these parts of a charter had the longest heritage, harking back to medieval Europe. First, a charter defined membership: that is, what group of people actually made up the corporation being defined, in this case, anyone who bought shares of stock. At its most fundamental, a charter established the community of members as a "body politic" (the English reflecting the Latin *cors, corpis* at the root of "corporation"), with limited sovereignty to govern its own affairs. The organization could, indeed was required, to write a system of by-laws outlining its operations and general business procedures and to elect its own officers who could hire and fire employees and who oversaw the institution's routine affairs. In addition, charters provided corporations with certain basic rights and privileges in society at large. Just like a person, a corporation could sue or be sued in a court of law and could own property; it also had to abide by state and federal laws. In that sense, the corporation actually enjoyed more civil privileges than thousands of Philadelphians, including married women and all slaves. By virtue of these sections of the charter, the stockholders in the Bank of Pennsylvania would become a corporation like any other.[36]

Other parts of its originating legislation marked the new institution as a particular kind of corporation in the early republic, namely, a bank. Some sections overlapped with the previous category of pan-corporate clauses, most notably those concerning stockholders' voting rights and the composition of the board of directors. By and large, business corporations operated under the principle of one share, one vote. Not banks in the early republic. In yet another British inheritance, bank charters outlined highly graduated voting structures for the election of board members and other decisions made by the body of stockholders. Every Bank of Pennsylvania shareholder could cast one ballot for each of the first two shares owned, another for each pair up to ten, another for each four shares up to thirty, another for every six shares up to sixty, another for each eight shares to one hundred, and still another for each ten shares over one hundred; no shareholder was allowed more than thirty votes. Another typical clause limited eligibility for board membership to stockholders who were also citizens of Pennsylvania; in addition, the charter required rotation in office to prevent one group from dominating the board for too long.[37]

Other sections prescribed certain lines of business while proscribing others. The state authorized the Bank of Pennsylvania to loan money, to issue notes and bills of exchange, to accept deposits, to buy and sell specie, and to deal in some financial instruments such as particular government securities. At the same time, bank charters prohibited the Bank of Pennsylvania and its sibling institutions from buying and selling real estate or any other kinds of goods except when necessary for carrying on banking. Bankers could buy property and a building in which to do business and could purchase stationery and stamps. They could also auction off any goods or real estate that came into their hands through the seizing of collateral upon the default of errant borrowers. However, that was the limit: the bank could not set up shop to buy and sell for profit. Such language defined banks' privileges, obligations, and limits.[38]

Finally, strictures and conditions unique to the Bank of Pennsylvania revealed the many practical, political, and economic contingencies and negotiations inherent in the chartering process. Given the state of Pennsylvania's huge stake in the bank and lingering public apprehensions about banking, legislators wanted a say in how the bank was run; after all, the state would be the bank's largest stockholder. Accordingly, the charter directed each house of the legislature to appoint three members of the board of directors, meaning that publicly elected representatives chose six of the twenty-five governing members of the bank. In a carefully crafted compromise to reward representatives from outside of the Philadelphia area for their assistance, bank supporters agreed to "establish offices at Lancaster, York or Reading," on the condition that bank officers could pull the plug on such branches "if found injurious to the real interests of the corporation." To placate supporters of a loan bank, leaders of the new institution agreed to loan the state $500,000 to establish one. And in a unique sop to the particular vested interest most hostile to the new bank, legislators tucked in a provision setting aside 2,000 shares of stock for Bank of North America investors, on the condition that the Bank of North America relinquish its charter. The inclusion of this clause revealed wishful thinking at best; while many Bank of North America stockholders might have been just as content to receive their dividends regardless of which bank profits came from, certainly the older institution's leadership had no desire to give up its stranglehold over lending policy. From their point of view, better to rule in the suddenly less powerful of two banks than to serve in the other. Finally, the charter detailed the complex terms and procedures for the state's purchase of stock. Though these provisions set the Bank of Pennsylvania apart from its peers, every bank charter (even the forty-one chartered in the 1814 omnibus bill) had its share of unique birthmarks as a result of its legislative midwifery.[39]

Banks needed not only the abstraction of a charter but also the mortar and bricks of a home, and the ways bank officers had them designed and built further reflected corporate leaders' projection of power. In order to counter critics' assertions that banks were potentially flighty, bank supporters went to great lengths to present their institutions as stable pillars of the republican edifice. They did so in a variety of ways, each of which had both practical and ideological rationales. Partly as a response to public wariness and partly to attract and keep customers, bankers carefully cultivated a public image for their institutions through the most visible and durable physical manifestations of their corporations: bank buildings. When first established, banks could operate from quarters similar to merchant houses, but they soon found they needed more specialized facilities. Like mercantile operations, banks needed work space for various clerks and to store numerous account books, ledgers, and correspondence books. But the largest import-and-export mercantile businesses conducted most of their business communication through correspondence from cramped offices or through conversation in coffeehouses; banks, on the other hand, needed an open space for depositors, borrowers, and people cashing in notes. Banks also kept considerable amounts of specie and banknotes on hand, and so required strong buildings with barred windows and reinforced floors that could support and protect sizable walk-in safes. Still, bank buildings quickly transcended mere business utility. In a fast-paced society suspicious of financial chicanery, bankers paid for buildings that they intended to project an image of stability, integrity, and permanence.[40]

No one put more consideration and more money into their bank building with greater success than the officers of the Bank of Pennsylvania. In its early years, the bank's board did not buy the institution a permanent home, first renting a Freemason lodge before moving into part of Carpenters' Hall in 1798. After a robbery there resulted in the loss of $160,000, the bank's board of directors reported to stockholders in classic understatement that "the building at present occupied by the Bank is deemed insecure." In order to build "such a building as they may think sufficiently secure and convenient for the purposes of the institution," they began looking for possible sites, and soon found one on Second Street. This would be no ordinary edifice; in addition to occupying an institutional home that would be fireproof and safe from robbers, the board clearly hoped to construct a landmark proclaiming the bank's stature as a stable institution deserving the public's respect.[41]

By a lucky coincidence, B. Henry Latrobe happened to arrive in Philadelphia in the spring of 1798. Among his letters of introduction was one from Thomas Jefferson to fellow Republican Samuel M. Fox—the president of the Bank of Pennsylvania. At their first dinner, Latrobe sketched the outlines of an ambitious design that would become a model not only for banks but also for a style of architecture new to America, Greek Revival. Despite the board's protestations that "every possible care had been observed to avoid unnecessary ornament," the building, surrounding fences and guardhouses, grounds, and furnishing cost close to $230,000, almost 10 percent of the bank's total authorized capital and more than the bill for the city's first waterworks. The cost amounted to nearly four dollars for every resident of Philadelphia, then the nation's second largest city.[42]

Nonetheless, in terms of creating a lasting impression of the Bank of Pennsylvania as a solid, distinguished institution, Latrobe's elegant and distinguished building delivered considerable return on investment. At the same time, it demonstrated the institution's wealth and power. "This beautiful building is entirely of Marble and is a neat specimen of the Ionic Order," gushed Owen Biddle, publisher of a local builder's manual. The "magnificent edifice," as an English visitor to the city labeled it, boasted Ionic columns on both front and back porticoes. In yet another way that American corporations borrowed from the British, the building's elegant geometric plan took advantage of the latest European engineering innovations in vault design to create soaring interior spaces, thus impressing visitors within and without. The impressive main room combined with the extensive use of marble and the tall columns on the porches gave the intended effect of lending an air of authority and permanence to the bank. Guardhouses and a fence around the property reinforced the bank's imposing presence, especially compared with the utilitarian brick structures on either side of the building. The extent to which well-heeled foreign visitors lavished their praise on the edifice's

B. Henry Latrobe's Bank of Pennsylvania building. Note the lack of windows, the intimidating columns, the spiked fences, and the sturdy guardhouses, all designed to command respect and imply solidity and security. William Birch, Bank of Pennsylvania, South Second Street, Philadelphia c. 1800. Courtesy of The Library Company of Pennsylvania.

sophistication was no doubt matched by the lack of comfort that lower-sort Philadelphians felt approaching its intimidating, looming stone presence. By commissioning such a lavish and distinguished building, the officers of the Bank of Pennsylvania had opened another front not only on which to advance their cause of legitimizing their institution to the greater public but also to flaunt their powerful position in the economy and society. Though some later banks would try to make their structures more approachable, the Bank of Pennsylvania building clearly conveyed the corporate officers' valuing of authority over accessibility.[43]

While grand buildings could impress customers and passersby, most people came in contact with the physical manifestations of banks through far more numerous, perishable, and nearly ubiquitous artifacts: banknotes. Like the first banking premises, the first banknotes also tended to be utilitarian, with few adornments, but as with later bank buildings, bankers capitalized the printing of banknotes as an opportunity to fix positive images of their institutions in the public mind. Here, too, the practical merged with the aesthetic: the high prevalence of counterfeiting in the early republic provided the chief motivation for increasingly elaborate banknote designs and for frequent printing of new series of notes. Indeed, the problem of counterfeiting became so pronounced to bankers and customers alike that by 1832 Philadelphia had a newspaper dedicated to listing bad bills titled *Bicknell's Counterfeit Detector, and Pennsylvania Reporter of Bank Notes, Broken Banks, Stocks, &c.* To adorn their notes, bankers selected increasingly detailed images, taking advantage of advances in printing and engraving technology in their efforts to stay one step ahead of confidence men with their bogus bills. Nonetheless, they did not simply choose elaborate abstract designs. Rather, they included illustrations that promoted the impression of solidity, of economic vitality, of public service, and of civic or patriotic pride. Bankers also hoped to put distinctive images on their notes that would in some way distinguish them from their competitors. Popular cartouches included depictions of patriotic Columbia, of sturdy livestock, of jaunty merchant ships, of proud wildlife, of distinctive bank buildings, and of city landmarks. Banknotes represented the most physically widespread effort of bankers to fix positive images for their institutions in the public mind.[44]

In contrast to the presence of banknotes in so many Pennsylvanians' wallets, bankers did their best to keep at arm's length from public oversight and accountability. Despite their need for charters, law enforcement, and other favors from the state, bankers strongly abhorred any public limits on the way they ran their institutions or what kinds of decisions they might make. That virulent distaste for any form of oversight or input into corporate decision making resulted from deep-seated calculations. Pennsylvania's early-republic bifurcation between the basis of economic and political power loomed increasingly large in the mind-set of corporate insiders. Indeed, central to the motivation for founding the Bank of North America had been a desire to wrest economic policy from elected representatives as well as to establish financial institutions that would serve the business and class interests of Philadelphia's wealthiest merchants. As metropolitan merchants' grip over Pennsylvania political power slipped and those of westerners and the middling sort tightened, so did corporate insiders' disaffection from and suspicion of state government grow.

That legislators sensed insiders' unease with the state government only furthered this division. As one bank lobbyist remarked when withdrawing a proposed charter provision allowing the bank's board greater control over its relationship with the state, he did so because the clause "implie[s] too great a distrust of the legislature and giv[es] our opponents an opportunity to carp at our motives."[45] Distrust between the two parties grew to such proportions that Congressman Philemon Dickinson wrote Jonathan Smith, Bank of Pennsylvania cashier, with strange advice. "The *hostile* disposition of [the] Legislature to Pennsylvania Banks" led Dickinson to the conclusion that issuing a smaller dividend than originally intended would be "attended with many obvious advantages to the Institution"; this, despite the fact that

Banknote cartouches: Fairman, Draper, Underwood & Co., c. 1825. Courtesy of The Historical Society of Pennsylvania.

higher dividends meant more money for the state treasury. At root, beyond considerations of geography or politics, it came down to a question of class authority. Any infiltration of the lower sorts into the inner sanctums of corporate governance potentially threatened not only corporate insiders' pocketbooks but also their sense of class cohesion and superiority. To corporate men, even the most friendly of legislatures could at any moment turn into a pack of leveling hyenas, ready to raid corporate coffers in order to spread corporate wealth to the less deserving and to undermine insiders' sense of themselves as men in charge of their society.[46]

Accordingly, Bank of Pennsylvania officers and insiders vehemently resented the attendance of legislature-appointed men in the Bank's lavish, second-floor board of directors' room. They were not alone in their begrudging acquiescence to state-appointed directors. In the first negotiations for chartering the Farmers and Mechanics Bank during the 1808–1809 legislative session, the applicants' Philadelphia promoters explicitly instructed their lobbyist in Lancaster to make sure that any clauses allowing the state to appoint members to the board be struck from the bill. In the end, their efforts were rewarded. Bank of Pennsylvania leaders had not gotten off so easily, ending up with a charter that allowed the state legislature to appoint six of the twenty-five board members, three by the Senate and three by the House of Representatives. In its rechartering in the 1831 legislative session the bank's stockholder-elected officers finally managed to have the number of seats reserved for the state reduced to four. So, despite the state holding over a third of the capital of the bank, its say in internal bank affairs had been reduced to insignificance.[47]

Failing to eliminate the presence of state-appointed directors completely, bank directors succeeded in marginalizing them. Stockholders' representatives held a clear majority and excluded state appointees from membership on the all-important discount committee, the body that evaluated loan applications. In meetings of the entire board, the state's block of seats remained a distinct minority and therefore could not restrict the board or shape bank policy as long as the shareholder-elected board members kept their ranks closed. State-appointed directors therefore found themselves shut out of meaningful participation in deliberations regarding major decisions, including those—or perhaps especially those—addressing a bank's relationship with Harrisburg. Bank insiders reserved particular hostility for the few state-appointed directors who dared challenge their rule. A legislative committee found that Bank of Pennsylvania cashier Jonathan Smith had the habit of showing contempt for a particular state-appointed director "for no other avowed reason, but because that director had exercised the independence and talents requisite to discharge the duties which had been confided to him." Smith's behavior, if widespread, must certainly have cowed some men into silence. Not for another fifteen years would state-appointed directors raise their voices. In a telling 1829 incident that revealed the impotence of state directors, the Bank of Pennsylvania's shareholder-elected board members, concerned about the institution's flexibility, rejected a proposal to lend the state a significant amount of money over the loud and public protests of the publicly appointed directors. The public representatives were allowed into the boardroom, but only as spectators.[48]

Corporate leaders also increasingly resisted the state's attempts to set conditions on board elections, chafing under or simply flouting rules that limited board member tenure or dictated board member eligibility. The original charter of the Farmers and Mechanics Bank stipulated that a majority of the directors had to be either farmers or mechanics, which, given the fluid meaning of "mechanic" in the early republic, was especially vague and proved impossible to enforce. In 1817, Joseph Tagert, lifelong merchant and longtime bank president, suddenly became a "farmer," an occupation he mysteriously managed to follow despite his full-time banking duties in Philadelphia. Tagert had appealed to farmers' aspirations to get his charter through the legislature, and now he played fast and loose with the very definition of the term. When the bank received its new charter in 1824, part of the bargain included new clauses stipulating that only three-quarters of the incumbents could be reelected to the board in any given year and that no board member except the president could serve more than three years in any four-year period. This clause put the Farmers and Mechanics Bank on the same footing with the other corporate banks, which also by then had strictures requiring the rotation of directors. Nonetheless, only in 1826 and 1827 did the stockholders replace the minimum four incumbents required by law; in other years, they simply returned the full incumbent board. The board eventually sent a petition to protest term limits, weakly arguing that they had "been productive of great inconvenience to the Bank and of no sort of benefit." Corporate officers knew the letter of the law but found ways to subvert it or to get it changed.[49]

Corporate bankers and state legislators came to an implicit agreement regarding state oversight. Just as Bank of Pennsylvania insiders managed to brush aside the public's attempts to police the bank from without, legislators made banking oversight among their lowest priorities. As a condition of its charter, the bank's officials were to send the legislature an annual report with cursory figures outlining the institution's general financial condition, including its paid-in capital, debts, deposits, notes, and cash on hand; the legislature could also inspect the bank's books as long as it did not look at individual accounts. The very next year, representatives voted to relax that requirement, and so Bank of Pennsylvania officers had only to send reports upon the legislature's request. Given the general nature of the figures and a total absence of outside audit, such reports could be of some use in considering a bank's overall financial health but offered almost no insight into banking operations. In Gov. William Findlay's (no relation to William Findley) 1819 address to the legislature, he admitted that the state had neither the will nor the way to oversee banks. Despite the state's having passed a law the previous session reiterating bank charters' requirement for honoring notes with specie, numerous banks had suspended specie payments, but the laws had "not been carried into effect against any of the banks." Furthermore, referring to the practice of banks' discounting each others' notes, Findley expressed his doubt "whether any adequate remedy . . . can be expected from legislative efforts." In other words, the state left banks to their own devices.[50]

Nor did specific, targeted inquiries offer much more information. During an 1815 legislative probe into the shady dealings of Bank of Pennsylvania's Jonathan Smith, legislators strongly chided the bank's board of directors for misplaced records and terse minutes. Of course, the cashier in question was responsible for keeping track of the board's records, so perhaps the board should not have been too strongly faulted. But the longtime corporate practice of taking minutes in which "the course of conduct pursued by the minority never appears" functioned to reinforce the majority's authority by suggesting unanimity and a narrowed field of options under consideration. Such record-keeping practices left little evidence for investigation of the company majority, which was exactly the way they liked it. Despite nominal state oversight provided for in bank charters and a few other measures, in practice Pennsylvania's supervision of its corporate banks was lax at best.[51]

Bank of Pennsylvania officers further insulated themselves from public authority by transferring liability for their own misdeeds to the corporation. On September 2, 1798, a bank employee arrived early in the morning only to discover the back door open and the bank vault ajar; he summoned bank president Samuel M. Fox and cashier Jonathan Smith, who found that about $160,000 in certificates and gold had gone missing. Because the vault appeared to have been opened by an extra set of keys rather than by force, bank officers immediately accused Patrick Lyon, a highly skilled immigrant blacksmith who had recently completed work on the vault's locks; the artisan quickly and voluntarily turned himself in. After Lyon spent three months in jail, the newly profligate habits of bank-employed carpenter Isaac Davis, such as the purchase of a new carriage and suspiciously large deposits in several Philadelphia banks, led to Davis's confession and Lyon's release. Lyons felt he had been railroaded for the purpose of protecting the bank's reputation, while at the same time ruining his. In a celebrated case, Lyons sued Fox, Smith, and bank director John C. Stocker, winning a jury award of $12,000 in 1805; in the face of appeals, the case was later settled for $9,000. Offering a strong vote of confidence, Bank of Pennsylvania stockholders "conceive[d] it to be both our right and duty to support those who have acted only in a faithful execution of their trust" and decided "to appropriate the monies belonging to this institution" to pay for any eventual judgment, court costs, and legal fees. Fox, Smith, and Stocker were off the hook.[52]

The assumption of corporate responsibility for individual misdeeds set an important and profound precedent. Because they could expect the institution to pick up the tab, bank officers could now act with considerably more leeway in areas of dubious legality, knowing that they could do so with near impunity. The only cost might be to the corporation, and even that could possibly be less than might be gained through the offending behavior. Through this mechanism of corporate responsibility in the place of personal liability, corporate insiders could act with far more impunity than people in unincorporated businesses.

That said, bankers' power was not unlimited, as they occasionally found out in Pennsylvania courtrooms. Bankers were constantly concerned about their ability to collect debts and, like many Americans, often found themselves having to go to court to get debtors to pay up. Sometimes, bankers lost in court because they tripped over themselves or because their claims simply went too far even for sympathetic judges. In 1796, the Bank of North America lost a lawsuit to collect a debt when Jacob Lawerswyler, the runner for the bank, claimed that he had indeed given the debtor notice that his bill to the bank had come due. It turned out that Lawerswyler was the executor of an estate that included stock in the bank, and his testimony was thrown out because it represented a conflict of interest. No doubt the bank was reluctant to use Lawerswyler as a witness again.[53]

Nineteen years later, the Farmers and Mechanics Bank tried to exploit a small ambiguity in its charter to have its claims privileged above other ones—even those of other incorporated banks—for the purposes of collection. In other words, if someone owed money to numerous creditors, the Farmers and Mechanics Bank wanted to be the first in line. But the Supreme Court of Pennsylvania nixed the suit. Justice Jasper Yeates, seemingly shocked at "the invidious distinction contended for" by the bank's lawyers, expressed his incredulity that legislators "meant to confer the peculiar and exclusive privilege on the Farmers and Mechanics Bank, by which they would necessarily gain the most substantial advantage over the old established banks in the city." Still, by and large the courts were bankers' friends in two ways. First, they generally facilitated bank business simply by providing the legal mechanism for the arbitration of debt, and second, although they did not privilege one bank over another, they did keep banknotes on a footing with foreign bills of exchange, thus prioritizing their banknotes over just about any kind of financial instrument. Thus, while courts offered some ambiguity as to the limits of corporate banking power, they generally reified it.[54]

No one's relationship with the Bank of Pennsylvania better exemplified both the benefits and dangers of corporate banking than Mathew Carey's. Over a period of two decades, the prickly and prolix printer and political economist Carey traveled the corporate road from eager supplicant to marginalized insider to enraged whistle-blower. Born in 1760 into a well-to-do artisan family, he apprenticed as a bookseller in his native Dublin, Ireland. The young firebrand's promising Irish newspaper business ended when he ran afoul of British authorities because of his controversial pro-Catholic, anti-English writings and cartoons, so in 1784 he fled for Philadelphia, where he soon started publishing. Carey's initial success in his adopted country came from his printing transcripts of debates in the Pennsylvania General Assembly, the first time that legislative proceedings were printed verbatim in America. Like most printers of the era, Carey participated in partisan politics. Though the transplanted Irishman was a Federalist during the late 1780s, his support of the French Revolution drew him into Republican circles, and he made a clean break from his former Federalist friends in the late 1790s. Meanwhile, Carey slowly withdrew from printing in favor of publishing and bookselling. But, as with many other small business owners, Carey's enterprise remained precarious. Fortunately, in 1812, years of lobbying—and his support for Republicans—paid off when the Pennsylvania Senate voted him a seat on the Bank of Pennsylvania's board, another clear sign of banks' political nature at least through the turn of the nineteenth century. During the ensuing thirty years, Carey used his access to capital to build America's first great publishing business. In that sense, insider status at a corporation punched the ticket to Carey's success.[55]

Though Carey sat on the board for most of three decades, he became increasingly frustrated with the bank president and stockholder-elected directors, both by the closed way they ran the business and by their resistance to any form of government oversight. He first went public with his misgivings in 1817 by printing an open letter as a pamphlet. Carey chronicled a pattern of incidents in which bank president Joseph P. Norris had turned down loans to applicants apparently out of personal animosity toward Carey, simply because the publisher offered to cosign the notes. Carey came to the conclusion that "my interference in favour of any person, or any note, was sure to be prejudicial" against the applicant. Worse, just a few men held great sway over lending: "the president of the bank, on his own mere motion, without consulting the board . . . in effect hardly allowing time for the expression of assent or dissent, rejects or discounts four-fifths at least of all the notes that are offered." Nor did other state directors have any more luck than Carey: the stockholders' directors essentially reduced them to nothing more than, in Carey's withering phrase, "wig-blocks." The result was that Norris had the power to pick who would get discounts and who would not, "at his own will and pleasure." For the Bank of Pennsylvania, the corporate sphere had been reduced to one man.[56]

Carey also noted with righteous indignation that Bank of Pennsylvania insiders flouted the state's directive for the rotation of directors by marginalizing the men who entered its inner sanctum only through the electoral equivalent of a revolving door. He explained that "the letter of this clause [requiring the rotation of directors] has been complied with—but its spirit almost always violated" in a number of ways. The dominant group on the board nominated a single slate for elections, and every year managed to find "country gentlemen" whose physical distance from Philadelphia prohibited them from active participation in routine board meetings. Most of these erstwhile corporate officers showed up rarely, if at all. Unless, that is, "when, to carry some particular point, they have been summoned by express." Sniffed Carey, "So far as regards the operations of the board, or the object of the legislature in framing the clause," the annual occupants of the rotated seats might as well have been "men of straw," not because they were necessarily corrupt but because they were at worst pliable and at best nowhere to be seen. Neither they nor the state-appointed directors ever managed to coun-

Mathew Carey. In the 1840s, he had mostly given up writing political economy to concentrate on his publishing empire. So wordy and passionate that he was once asked to curtail a talk of an organization of which he was president, Carey did not shy away from controversy. John Neagle, artist (1828), and T. Henry Smith, engraver (1888). Courtesy of the Society Portrait Collection, The Historical Society of Pennsylvania.

terbalance the powerful group of directors whose motivations and directives shaped Bank of Pennsylvania policy. Bank insiders could simply write off Carey's charges as the rages of an embittered man: he had been booted off the board several years before by, in his melodramatic words, "as base an intrigue as was ever devised, & as consummate an intrigue as ever existed." While the particular circumstances (and description) of Carey's ouster may have been unique, they perfectly symbolized Bank of Pennsylvania insiders' increasingly successful campaign to gain control of their own house.[57]

Carey's most angry typescript tirade against Bank of Pennsylvania directors came off the presses in November 1829, and it revealed his sense of betrayal at the hands of men who should have better guarded a public trust. The sixty-nine-year-old writer, little more mellow than he had been as an agitating teenage firebrand, published a scathing indictment of Bank of Pennsylvania insiders' efforts to have the bank's charter renewed by the state government. He had many gripes with current management, castigating a "small body of men," only "the Cashier and two (perhaps three, but I believe not) of the directors," that dominated the bank's affairs. Carey sensed that these men shared "little or no common feeling or common interest with the citizens at large." According to Carey, because this "little oligarchy" had "procured the proxies of a great majority of the stockholders," it had the power to choose its own slate of directors that it rammed through stockholder elections. And now, Carey thundered, this *oligarchic caucus* had the arrogance "to presume *to dictate the terms on which they will condescend to accept a charter* . . . among the terms, one, which, I understand, is a *sine qua non*, is, that *the state shall relinquish the important privilege of being represented at the board of directors.*" Given his own experience in the boardroom, this prospect particularly galled him. Carey hoped the insiders would fail in their "insult to the state" because "they count largely on the ignorance or imbecility of the Legislature, or on the influence of the advocates whom they have taken wonderful pains to secure in that respectable and powerful body." Should the legislature fail, he feared that through the bank's size and its influence on other state banks and on the economy at large, this little band could "at its pleasure raise or depress the value of property, of which fluctuations wealthy capitalists are always able and ready to take advantage, to the immense injury of the middle class of society." For Carey, nothing less was at stake than the fate of the economy and the economic fairness upon which political equality was based. In his lurid pamphlet, Carey painted a prose portrait of a corporation that was in theory a partner of the state but had now run amok.[58]

In the institution's first four decades, Bank of Pennsylvania and other corporate banking insiders worked hard to build a strong corporate edifice analogous to the company's physical home. Tucked away from the public's prying eyes, the board met in its own space and on its own terms. Like the conspicuously strong safe that protected the bank's cash, specie, note dies, and other valuables, bankers followed cautious policies to inspire confidence in their ability to maintain a stable money supply and the bank's solvency. And just as the Bank of Pennsylvania closed its doors and its gates to the public after three in the afternoon, so bankers worked to limit public access to banking operations so that interaction occurred only on bankers' terms. Meanwhile, insiders at other Philadelphia-area incorporated banks, such as the Philadelphia Bank and the Farmers and Mechanics Bank of Philadelphia, employed many of the same tactics and strategies with the same goals in mind. By hook or by crook, bankers strove to establish institutions beyond the reach of the public and its elected officials. Their contemporaries in other corporations and their successors in future corporations followed these practices and precedents, further strengthening the corporate sphere.

The experience of Philadelphia's bankers differed from those in other cities or in other parts of the state or the country in the sense that to some extent each area developed its idiosyncratic banking system. Pennsylvania's "country banks" operated far differently than did their big-city corporate cousins. Many of these institutions in the Keystone State and other states worked on little paid-in capital, paid scandalously high dividends, suspended specie payments at the drop of a hat, and folded at the slightest whiff of economic trouble. New England bankers operated in an even more clubby and closed fashion than did Pennsylvania's, while New York experimented with a state-sponsored insurance system to inspire confidence in its state banks. Nonetheless, they exhibited similar ownership patterns, primarily loaned to known quantities, kept corporate government in close hands, maintained arm's-length relationships with state governments, and implicitly worked to reinforce class economic interests. Furthermore, other institutions would borrow some of the techniques that the Bank of Pennsylvania pioneered in terms of serving as bankers to state governments and opening branch offices. Early republic banks across the nation differed in the details but employed remarkably similar structures and strategies.[59]

In sum, early national corporate bankers did not become economic dictators. Not only were their resources limited—due partly to the legislature's strictures on bank capitalization and, eventually, to the policies of the second Bank of the United States—but also their competition with each other ensured that they could not fully dominate the economy the way bank leaders may have wished. Nonetheless, Philadelphia corporate banking insiders did control the largest pools of capital in Pennsylvania, wielding great influence over who would get loans, and for how much and for how long, and they did so with state approval, though not state oversight. They used their institutions for political, personal, and economic gain, both to shape the economy and to further solidify their family fortunes with stable investments that helped to establish long-term dynastic stability. By the 1830s, bankers possessed considerable influence over state and local economic policy. That said, banks were not the only corporations in the Philadelphia area; how those other corporations operated and how corporations interacted with each other are also integral parts of the story of early American corporate power.

4

INCORPORATING
THE CITY

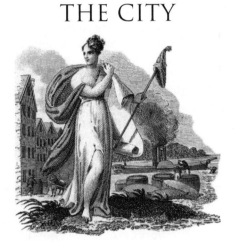

*A*fter dinner four men rode west from the settled part of Philadelphia to the end of High Street, all the way to the Schuylkill, just south of where the Middle Ferry crossed the river. Being downwind, the workman probably heard the engineer and his three friends before he saw them. B. Henry Latrobe knew all the workers on his huge project, and his companions were most likely the builder of the engine, the engine builder's business partner, and Samuel Fox, Latrobe's sponsor as president of the Bank of Pennsylvania, but more relevant on this occasion, a member of the city corporation's committee supervising the project. They probably performed any necessary introductions quickly on that frigid January evening before entering the square, two-story pumphouse on the riverbank. The four better-dressed men might have talked about the two years of work already completed or the remaining pipeline to be laid as the workman threw shovelful after shovelful of charcoal into the burner below the boiler. When the workman was done and the engine lit, the five men rode east toward the city, stopping at Centre Square. There an elegant new masonry building, comprised of a dome topping a cylinder on a box, hid well the wooden boiler and iron machinery inside. The men repeated the charcoal ritual. The tall engineer's bespectacled face must have glowed by the fire's flicker on the eve of one of his greatest professional triumphs, the completion of a project that would make his name in his adopted country. At dawn the following morning, Latrobe and city council member Thomas Cope returned to the Schuylkill pumphouse, and then back to the one at Centre Square, to turn on the pumps.[1]

That morning Philadelphia's residents woke to find water pouring out of the new street hydrants and streaming down the gutters. Amazed, they crowded around the hydrants. "Everyone must have a pull at the lever," Cope proudly noted in his diary, "and even when the water flows, many seem as if they could not believe it." People from the country who happened to be visiting the big city that day "gaped with astonishment, as at the tenth wonder of the world." Around midday, as the clouds finally broke, the mayor and the members of the two councils addressed the crowd in Centre Square, celebrating the dedication of the new waterworks that would supply clean water for drinking and cooking, for cleaning the streets, for cooling the heat in the summer, and for putting out fires all year long. Best of all, the clean water replaced the foul-smelling and foul-tasting water that many of America's best medical men believed contributed to the yellow fever epidemics that had threatened the city's survival.[2]

In contrast to the old system of private and public pumps, Philadelphia's new waterworks offered more than an efficient method to distribute larger quantities of water to a growing city, one from which nearly all residents benefited. The Centre Square works and its successors at Fairmount also provided a qualitatively different way to centralize, route, and control the flow of water throughout the city. Similarly, municipal corporate officers' administration of the technologies and financing of the waterworks represented a qualitatively new form of the distribution of power in early national Philadelphia, diffusing it in one direction and concentrating it in another. Because of its limited scale and activities, the pre-Revolutionary Philadelphia city government had little potential for use as a significant base of economic power. By contrast, the early national Philadelphia municipal corporation allowed the raising and consolidation of capital, the control over a complex and ubiquitous technology, and the civic authority that corporate officers exploited for great leverage over their neighbors within the city and its suburbs. Thus, the waterworks helped to transform Philadelphia from a preindustrial Atlantic port city into an industrial metropolis. While banks provoked far more controversy than did municipal corporations, the latter proved no less effective than the former as vehicles for the transformation of power that transcended old modes of face-to-face influence by reaching great numbers of people.[3]

In order to cope with the issue of water supply and all its attendant problems, from the late 1790s to the early 1830s the city corporation of Philadelphia slowly took on many of the characteristics of business corporations. Municipal corporations diverged from business corporations in two ways, in that their officers were publicly elected officials and in that, later in the nineteenth century, their autonomy would become increasingly eroded by state authorities. Nonetheless, like the officers of business corporations, city council members found ways to insulate their decision-making process from their constituents. In the case of the city, the use of bond issues and of a sinking fund allowed flexibility on taxes while removing crucial fiscal decisions from electoral politics. The opening of Philadelphia's first Centre Square waterworks and its eventual replacement by the spectacular Fairmount waterworks ensured Philadelphia, and soon its suburbs, a seemingly limitless supply of water for drinking, for cleanliness, for public sanitation and health, and for economic development. But, just as with the benefits of corporate banking that also entailed a consolidation of power, the waterworks came with a price. The various iterations of the waterworks cost a fortune, about $1.5 million in its first quarter century, and while all residents paid for it either directly through subscriptions or indirectly through rent or regressive property taxes, those who chose and could afford to be bondholders profited from the interest from loans for construction costs.[4]

Furthermore, while the city corporation administered the works competently and, for the most part, efficiently, corporation officials exploited citizens' dependence upon the works to consolidate legal, financial, and technological leverage over city and suburban residents. Just as the incorporation of money diffused benefits while consolidating power, so did the incorporation of the city and its resources. The city corporation exploited the technology of the waterworks to extend its economic leverage and law-making authority not only within the city limits but also well into the suburbs. As with the insiders of other corporations, Philadelphia council members could claim membership in the city's close-knit corporate fraternity—indeed, many city council members, especially those involved in administering the waterworks, had close ties to business corporations. Through its administration of the waterworks, the Philadelphia city government and especially its powerful Watering Committee had become fully ensconced in Philadelphia's corporate sphere, as personified by Joseph S. Lewis. Meanwhile, hundreds or perhaps thousands of entrepreneurs used the city-supplied water to help establish themselves and a broad middle class, as increasingly did men like Frederick Graff and other city corporation employees.

*D*uring the nation's first half century, Philadelphia increasingly required bigger infrastructure facilities, because like other cities, it was suffering from growing pains. Although the young republic's spectacular economic and population growth signaled the nation's vitality, they also brought new challenges, especially for cities. In its first decades, the United States grew at an astounding rate, doubling its population roughly every twenty-three years. Had cities merely kept pace, they would have encountered problems of scale well beyond those of American colonial cities, even the largest of which— Philadelphia—had not been much more than an overgrown town. But cities' populations grew even more spectacularly than the countrysides surrounding them. In 1790, about 33,000 people lived in New York City; by 1830, almost 215,000 people called Gotham and its new suburbs home. Philadelphia did not mushroom quite like its biggest rival but still expanded at an impressive rate over the same period, from around 44,000 to approximately 161,000 residents between the city proper and its contiguous suburbs. In turn, cities' economies became more complex and more demanding of natural resources, especially water. Meanwhile, city dwellers' household and manufacturing activities polluted what water was available; B. Henry Latrobe observed, "The inhabitants of Philadelphia drink very little water. It is too bad to be drunk." The solution for Philadelphia and for other cities required new technologies for sanitation and to distribute precious natural resources like water, bureaucracies to administer them, and fiscal devices to pay for them.[5]

Just as Philadelphia and other cities grew and changed during the republic's first decades, so did their governing bodies. In keeping with the size of their communities, most eighteenth-century American city governments exhibited little in the way of institutionalized bureaucracy. Unlike their later nineteenth-century descendants, they had no municipally funded and municipally run professionalized police forces, firefighting units, health boards, or other departments. Rather, they consisted of a small group of elected officials who passed ordinances, mediated disputes, ensured the collection of taxes, and supervised the few employees on the public payroll. For Philadelphia, those employees included a dozen constables, a few men to light and extinguish streetlamps, and market inspectors. Municipal governments did occasionally oversee construction projects such as city halls, market houses, and wharves. The Philadelphia city corporation paid for the construction of three market buildings that were the envy of other American cities, and it had also administered a project to cover over Dock Creek, a small waterway running through town that had become increasingly polluted over the course of the eighteenth century. City officials dedicated most of their energies toward the twin goals of economic promotion, mostly accomplished through the use of public property and resources for marketplaces and wharves, and market regulation in the form of inspectors of various kinds of goods for sale in the city. Philadelphia's new 1789 charter granted the corporation most of the same authority as the old one.[6]

Philadelphia's new municipal charter typified the incorporation of American cities during and immediately after the American Revolution. Between 1775 and 1789, states charted twenty-five cities and towns. These were not new settlements; rather, they were established communities gaining new governmental structures. Reflecting the Revolutionary spirit, for nearly all of these new polities, legislatures substituted elected officials in place of inherited positions, widened the franchise, and encouraged greater transparency. The reestablishment of local governments also represented an acknowledgment that, regardless of new political developments, old problems remained, in the form of enforcing order, cleaning the streets, and all the other mundane tasks necessary to keep eighteenth-century cities operating, and that these tasks could be performed only by stable city governments. Thus, while ensuring for popular participation in the selection of city officers, city charters granted municipal governments broad powers to make ordinances and enforce them.[7]

As with other cities, Philadelphia's new charter theoretically empowered officials to tackle the problem of water supply. Still, its councils did not take on the problem until the city's residents forced them to do so. Prompted by the request of a growing number of petitioners, in 1798 the city councils formed a "Joint Committee on the Subject of Bringing Water to the City" to investigate various options for supplying Philadelphia with fresh water. This committee was organized strictly for the temporary purpose of deciding what would be the best way to solve the water problem, and it explored three possible schemes that each promised to supply the city with water for drinking, cleaning, and industry: the Delaware and Schuylkill Canal and two plans for steam engine–powered waterworks, one from local inventor Oliver Evans and the other from British-trained architect and engineer B. Henry Latrobe.

The joint committee settled on the last proposal, despite their wariness of steam engines and other details of Latrobe's proposal. In some ways, Latrobe's was the most technically dubious of the three plans; a canal booster derided it as "aerial castles." Moreover, in 1802, when Evans finally gained a seat on the city's common council, he submitted a report arguing that much of the Latrobe system—already constructed—was inefficient, especially the two-engine design; the report was narrowly rejected. But after months of exasperating negotiations with the recalcitrant directors of the Delaware and Schuylkill Canal Company, the committee opined that the poorly managed canal company appeared to be more concerned with "the profits to be made by supplying the city with water" than with its obligations to the city—suspicions reinforced by the company's exorbitant demands, stipulations that seemed all the more galling because some prime movers of the company were political rivals of several joint committee members. Each of the company's proposals carried a price tag to the city of several hundred thousand dollars. The canal company offered, at various junctures, to sell the entire stock to the city at first cost (meaning that the city would pay for the company's mistakes) and for the city to pay annual rent or make a onetime payment for the water at fairly exorbitant rates. The City Corporation and the Delaware and Schuylkill Canal Company negotiated for much of 1798 and 1799, to no avail.[8]

The canal was out, leaving the two steam-engine proposals. Unlike Evans, who had recently campaigned against the incumbent council and would again in future elections, Latrobe had no political ambitions. Furthermore, three promises of Latrobe's design proved crucial to its adoption: a pipe system that would distribute the water into more areas of the city, discounted water piped directly into investors' homes, and, perhaps most important, the inclusion of public hydrants, which made the water available for free to the entire population. Lastly, in a city undergoing an image crisis, Latrobe's suggestion to sheathe the upper engine in a graceful pumphouse, giving it the appearance of a temple of republican technology, provided an elegant landmark. It may not have been the most reliable or cheapest technology available, but it was the one that best accorded with the committee's politics, interests, and ambitions for the city.[9]

In Latrobe's plan, a seawall reaching into the east side of Schuylkill River guided water into a small basin. By the bank, a large steam engine—with a forty-inch cylinder, far larger than any yet made in America, and so powerful that the city leased its excess power to its builder—pumped water through a four-foot-six-inch-wide, seven-foot-high tunnel from below the river's waterline to Centre Square, so called because it was in the middle of Penn's plan for the city, although then still at the western outskirts of city settlement. There, a smaller engine—at thirty-two inches, still to be the third largest in the country—pumped water from the conduit to an aboveground reservoir, basically a short water tower. That Latrobe would think of using steam engines was not surprising given his background. As a well-read engineer, he knew that steam engines had first been designed to pump water out of mines, and his design showed striking similarities to a waterworks in Chelsea, not far from his boyhood London home. Once in the aboveground reservoir, the water flowed by gravity through wooden mains down the major streets, and residents got water from public hydrants or by building a connector at their own expense from the main to their property. The most aesthetically attractive part of the plan was the pumphouse in Centre Square, a beautiful, geometric structure: a box (containing the engine, fuel, parts, and tools) fronted by Greek columns and topped by a dome (containing the upper reservoir). Excess steam escaped in a plume from the top of the dome. The plan impressed many Philadelphians as a sophisticated example of the application of the latest technology to one of their direst needs.[10]

As much as they were pleased by the practical results, Philadelphians also appreciated Latrobe's skillful camouflaging of the engine's machinery in the graceful pumphouse, which became the centerpiece of a beautiful park. Before the pumphouse, Centre Square had been half wilderness, a mostly untended field. Philadelphians had yet to build upon areas west of the first seven or so blocks that hugged the Delaware River. Serving as an unofficial park on the outskirts of town, its only official function was as a venue for public hangings. But with the addition of the masonry pumphouse, it quickly became recognized as the city's prettiest site. A road ringed the square, connecting with several poplar-lined walkways cutting across swaths of open grass. In 1809, the city commissioned native sculptor William Rush to create a wooden fountain called "The Nymph of the Schuylkill." Allegedly modeled after the daughter of a member of the Watering Committee, the fountain became the pride of Philadelphians. In person and in the many prints produced of them, the pumphouse and the surrounding square allowed Philadelphians to believe that the new technologies of the nineteenth century could be harnessed in beautiful, bucolic, artistic ways that belied the changes in their city and society that they may have found more disturbing.[11]

Latrobe's Centre Square pumphouse, called by locals "the pepper pot" because of its distinctive shape, a cylinder mounted on a box. "The Water Works, in Centre Square Philadelphia," W. Birch & Son, 1800. Courtesy of The Library Company of Philadelphia.

The waterworks fulfilled another, more subtle need: at the turn of the nineteenth century, Philadelphia faced a series of crises that threatened the validity of the boast that their city was, in the words of Abigail Adams, "the *metropolis* of America, as these Proud Phylidelphians [had] publickly named it." Although Philadelphia's commerce and population both grew in absolute numbers during the 1790s, New York City had succeeded the Quaker City as the country's largest and busiest metropolis. Meanwhile, Baltimore's spectacular growth meant increased competition for the resources and markets of the Delaware Valley. Economic threats to Philadelphia's preeminence paled next to the blows it had received from the two governments to which it owed allegiance. In 1799, Pennsylvania had removed its seat of government from Philadelphia's State House—not called Independence Hall until Lafayette's triumphant return in 1824—to Lancaster, and eventually to Harrisburg in 1811. Even more depressing, the federal government relocated to its new permanent capital on the banks of the Potomac in 1800. Both losses came as the result of politics beyond the control of the city: for Pennsylvania, animosity toward eastern interests and the desire to have a more central capital, and for the United States, the implicit deal between Jefferson and Hamilton over the capital and the national bank. Having lost both its renters, the State House suddenly grew silent; the legislature let its second story to Charles Willson Peale for free for use as a museum. Still a location for occasional public ceremony, the State House stood merely as a sullen reminder of Philadelphia's reduced political stature.[12]

The waterworks and its elegant, Greek Doric pumphouse restored Philadelphians' faltered confidence. If Philadelphia could no longer be the political or the financial capital, it could lead the nation in manufacturing and technology. When the first Philadelphia waterworks were built, residents instantly seized upon the graceful, pepperbox-shaped building as the thing to see for visitors. Philadelphians faced the incoming century with the waterworks as a sign that their city would continue its role as one of the great cities of America. In 1820, Philadelphian Thomas Cope could visit the now much-larger and more prosperous New York City and still remark in his diary that he was "continually reminded of the advantages which Philada. enjoys, over that thriving city, in the article of water." All the city's urban competitors—Baltimore, Boston, New York, and Pittsburgh—sought advice from Philadelphia when they began work on their systems in the 1820s and 1830s. The waterworks brought with it another benefit: the triumphant demonstration of steam technology in America. The success of the engine immediately established Philadelphia as the nation's leader in steam technology and heavy manufacturing.[13]

As the center of steam technology, the City of Brotherly Love immediately attracted engineers from America and abroad. Even before the engines were completed, James Smallman, the chief workman at engine builder Nicholas Roosevelt's plant in Passaic, New Jersey, moved to Philadelphia to set up shop. Oliver Evans, a Delaware native who had arrived in Philadelphia the year before, transferred his shop to a larger building at Market Street and Ninth Avenue to begin building steam engines to exploit the new demand. The waterworks so impressed the city that in 1804 it hired Evans to design a steam-powered dredging machine; the result was his "oruktor amphibolos," which not only dredged but could propel itself on land as well. Daniel Large, an English engineer, migrated to Philadelphia in 1807 to build engines. To compete, the next year Evans constructed his famous Mars Works, thereby making his reputation as "the American Watt." Between the two shops, Philadelphia became the first American city to have facilities dedicated to the regular building of steam engines. Philadelphia technophile printer Thomas Fessenden bragged that "there is no part of the world in proportion to its population, where a greater number of ingenious mechanicks may be found than in Philadelphia and its immediate vicinity," explaining that "steam engines with all their various improvements are built and applied, beneficially to the most usefull purposes."[14]

Those purposes were sundry. Roosevelt's rolling and splitting mill soon faced competition; by 1819, at least three breweries in Philadelphia used stationary steam engines; and by the 1820s, several steam sawmills were hard at work. Oliver Evans produced engines for steamboats and for the United States Mint. In 1830, Philadelphia mechanics became the first in the nation to build a steam locomotive. Of the 174 steam engines in use in Philadelphia in 1838, including 27 in engine and machine making, 19 in bleaching, dying, and printing cloth, 16 in ironworks, and 10 in sawmills, at least 133 had been built within the city limits. In 1875, the chief engineer of the Philadelphia Water Department credited the waterworks with launching "the pre-eminence which this city has always enjoyed in the construction of machinery."[15]

Despite the pumphouse's elegant shape, its steam-powered contents proved unreliable. Latrobe's engines were inefficient, partly as a result of their design and partly because of the inexperience of the builders, who had never even seen one and had not rolled plate with those kinds of specifications before. They were dangerous, too; in 1801, a pair of workmen suffocated when working on the boiler chamber, the first of several fatal accidents over the following decade. The Watering Committee replaced the lower engine in 1808, and in 1813 scrapped both engines for a single, high-pressure one from Oliver Evans situated farther north on the Schuylkill, in an area soon to be renamed Fairmount. That engine, too, was replaced in 1819. Like its predecessors, the new one was not only unreliable but also expensive to run, drawing about $30,000 in maintenance and fuel from the city coffers annually. Two years later, the city threw a dam across the river at Fairmount, finally harnessing the free power of the river. Above the dam, the city built the gorgeous Fairmount works; with gardens added in the 1830s, it became one of the most celebrated and pictured spots in antebellum America and, indeed, was pictured far and wide in Europe as well.[16]

In sum, the initial decision for Latrobe's steam-powered system over the Delaware and Schuylkill Canal was motivated not by a desire to innovate but largely by nontechnical considerations and held significant political consequences for Philadelphia. It meant that the water supply system would be run by the city. The joint committee became the Watering Committee, a de facto permanent body. Alone among subcommittees of the city councils, the Watering Committee gained control over a separate budget, authority to enter into contracts, and the ability to hire and fire its own employees. As city councilmen, members of the Watering Committee were elected officials; nonetheless, they possessed far more influence and economic leverage than the entire city government had before the construction of the first waterworks. In effect, the Watering Committee became a government-within-a-government, collecting its own taxes in the form of water rents and making overtly political decisions about city development as it decreed where new water mains would go and when. It issued its own printed annual reports and kept its own records separately from the city councils'. It owned land, paid its own bills, and ran a growing bureaucracy, running up substantial debts in doing so.

Like business corporations, Philadelphia's municipal corporation required the election of corporate officers, and of course the city's elections were much more open than were business corporations' shareholder elections. In some years, city council elections featured hot partisan contests and, occasionally, considerable turnover. The city's corporate business elite and its political elite were not coequal. Many elected officials pandered to the people in ways that other corporate men found vulgar and distasteful. For their part, many corporate insiders held little but contempt for Robert Wharton, who sat as Philadelphia mayor for almost a dozen one-year terms over a quarter century, culminating with nearly continuous service from 1815 to 1824. One descendent of Philadelphia's corporate elite later referred to him as "an uneducated, rough man . . . very pompous in his manners" and repeated a contemporary poem accusing Wharton of being overly impressed with his own popularity with free blacks and white working men.[17]

Nonetheless, the membership of the Watering Committee in particular showed remarkable stability and was nearly always led by men with deep connections to business corporations. The man behind the initial push for Philadelphia's waterworks was Samuel Fox, erstwhile president of the Bank of Pennsylvania. Longtime Watering Committee member merchant James Vanuxem served on the boards of the Delaware and Schuylkill Navigation Company and several other Philadelphia-area internal improvements and insurance corporations; similarly, Joseph Watson shared time on the Watering Committee, as president of the Union Canal Company, and as a board member of the Schuylkill Navigation Company and the Lehigh Coal and Navigation Company. Joseph S. Lewis moved from the presidency of the Watering Committee to the presidency of the Schuylkill Navigation Company, crossing paths with his Watering Committee presidential successor, John P. Wetherill. Thus, even though the city's economic elite did not dominate the city's affairs the way its colonial predecessor did, in the decades of the early republic a few of its members still exerted great influence in city governance.

Influence was one thing, but willingness to pay for it was another. Despite overwhelming public support for a better supply of fresh water, the city government at first struggled mightily to finance the waterworks. Because of the fear of future yellow fever epidemics, the city councils certainly had a mandate to spend some public money to improve the city's water supply; indeed, one joint council report argued that the specter of yellow fever "rendered a copious supply of more wholesome water, in the estimation of many, indispensable to the health and preservation of the city." However, politicians that they were, council members wanted to avoid large tax hikes. In 1799, the total city budget amounted to $72,397.18, of which $56,000 was to come from tax revenue and the remainder from relatively fixed-income sources such as rental of corporate properties, licensing fees, and fines. The Latrobe plan that the city councils finally selected carried an original estimate of $127,000—the councils were a little less optimistic, allocating $150,000—all to be spent on construction in the space of one year. To raise that sort of money through local taxes would mean nearly quadrupling them, an economically unwise and politically suicidal solution.[18]

From their initial negotiations with the Delaware and Schuylkill Canal Company through their construction of the works at Fairmount in 1819, the councils attempted to raise money in ways besides taxing the electorate or restructuring taxes to fund the works all in one fiscal year. The universally preferred budget management method has always been to spend someone else's money with no strings attached, and indeed, the men running the Corporation of the City of Philadelphia certainly tried their best to do so. With hope in their hearts, in 1797 members of the city councils appealed to the Pennsylvania General Assembly for direct aid. Not surprisingly, no funds were forthcoming from a legislature that had recently relocated Pennsylvania's seat of government away from Philadelphia because of sectional jealousy and general rural uneasiness with the big city. The General Assembly also rejected the city corporation's pleas for another politically painless solution (from local politicians' point of view, that is), the right to receive taxes on all auctions taking place in the city, the revenue from which currently went into state coffers. Indeed, the legislature had just spurned a request from the City Corporation to grant auction duties to contribute to the construction of a bridge across the Schuylkill, too. And although some institutions raised money successfully through state-sanctioned lotteries, none did so on a great scale, so the city councils could easily rule out that possibility as an effective way to collect capital. The Corporation of Philadelphia was forced to look for new methods to gather enough capital to build its waterworks.[19]

Not wanting to risk further epidemics, the city councils resorted to the fund-raising method that had met with such success for the federal government: the issuance of interest-bearing bonds. The councils proposed to sell 1,500 bonds, each for $100, to cover the estimated $150,000 in construction costs for the waterworks. They would be sold as subscriptions: buyers were to pay ten dollars at the time of purchase, and thirty dollars in each of three subsequent payments scheduled over the next six months. Once paid up, subscribers received 6 percent annual interest in semiannual payments, in other words, two payments a year of three dollars each. In addition, subscribers' houses would be hooked up to the city water for three years free of the usual five-dollar annual charge, increasing the bond's annual yield for the first three years to a substantial 11 percent. The council members calculated that the impressive interest rate would be more than enough to attract significant investment.[20]

They were wrong. The city's unsuccessful attempts to fill all, or even most, of the 1,500 subscriptions demonstrated the novelty and fragility of complex municipal finance in the early republic. The city councils only managed to sell around $73,000 of the $150,000 dollar issue. They partly blamed the weather: the weeks following the passage of the ordinance had been cold and snowy, preventing the commissioners from making the rounds in their neighborhoods as thoroughly as was hoped. Still, despite fervent appeals to the financial community—bankers and insurance company insiders—and door-to-door canvasses, the city's seemingly attractive offer fell short.[21]

The city's biggest obstacle was its inability to convince investors of its long-term prospects of honoring its loans. Federal bonds sold well because investors had confidence in the national government's ability to collect taxes and so felt assured that the government would have the necessary cash flow to pay interest on the bonds. However, the yellow fever epidemics had coincided with Philadelphia's local summertime tax collection efforts, and the city corporation had encountered great difficulties collecting its entire assessments during the 1790s. In the ordinance authorizing the bonds, the councils admitted that "though there is reason to hope a liberal aid will be granted by the legislature, towards enabling the city to complete this important work . . . the speedy accomplishment thereof appears to require the immediate exertions and resources of the citizens of Philadelphia." Given that they had unsuccessfully appealed for state money before with the lobbying assistance of the Delaware and Schuylkill Canal Company, the chance that they would get any money over the company's objections was slim indeed. However, the councils hoped that invoking the General Assembly would give potential investors confidence that the state might back the city's ability to make good on its loans.[22]

The city's deficiencies in revenue collection at first discouraged potential investors in municipal bonds. Motivation for investment in Philadelphia city bonds shifted over the course of the first two decades of the nineteenth century. The people and organizations buying bonds in the first issue of 1801 and 1802 invested either out of civic duty or because of a potential increase in property values, much like internal improvement investors. Most bondholders purchased only one bond, many of them doubtless doing so because of the combined inducement of interest and the free water subscription for the first three years. Institutional investors certainly hoped for gains, but they also bought bonds because the successful completion and operation of the waterworks could contribute to their respective missions. The Insurance Company of Pennsylvania bought twenty of the one-hundred dollar bonds, and the Mutual Assurance Company bought thirty. Each most likely expected the waterworks to greatly enhance the city's ability to fight fires. The Pennsylvania Hospital purchased another ten, both because of the medical consensus that fresh water would make the city's residents healthier and more resistant to yellow fever and because the hospital was extremely water-intensive. It would become the waterworks' second largest consumer, behind the city almshouse. Although some investors bought multiple bonds, most seemed to be content with buying one to do their part in keeping the city pleasant and livable.[23]

That said, the prevailing tax structure that generated the revenue for most of the waterworks, its maintenance, and interest on bonds placed a proportionately higher burden on the city's poorer residents than its rich ones. Philadelphia primarily gained its revenue through annual real estate taxes, but that was not the only possibility conceived of or even in practice in the early republic. Property tax assessments in Boston and New York City at the time included real estate and personal property—that is, not only on the land and buildings that all people paid to the city (in Pennsylvania, renters generally paid property tax directly) but also on the silver, carriages, furniture, stocks, bonds, and other financial instruments of the well-to-do. In 1806, a few city council members proposed revising Philadelphia's tax code, offering an ordinance explicitly arguing that the one in place "imposes a tax on certain specified property . . . essentially necessary, particularly to the most industrious and poorer class of citizens and exempts from taxation, articles of luxury and that species of property usually possessed by the most wealthy." Furthermore, the proponents specifically tied a change in taxes to the municipal corporation's ability to afford "improvement to the city," such as extending the waterworks, enlarging the markets, and other such projects. The measure narrowly made it through the select council, which had approved the bill with many revisions, but the common council soundly rejected it in a vote cutting across party lines. Until the waterworks' rents income finally exceeded the ongoing costs of the waterworks in the late 1810s, the public hydrants may have seemed free to poor Philadelphians, but part of the ultimate cost (and interest on it being paid to bondholders) was still coming out of their pocketbooks.[24]

Philadelphia municipal officials found another way to tap the resources of the wealthy, albeit by offering not only services but also monetary returns. The terms of the first round of water subscriptions included both a 6 percent annual return on investment for the one-hundred-dollar certificates and a free private hook-up to city water for three years. For the city to sell these long-term bonds—the first issue actually had no stated maturation date—the councils had to come up with a way of paying down the debt or at least of paying the interest into the indefinite future. In 1807, after struggling to fill out their third bond issue, they turned to a financial device that had first been suggested nearly a decade before, had been all the rage in British financial circles from the 1760s on, and become popular in the United States in the 1790s: the sinking fund. The city corporation would contribute a given amount every year into an account set aside specifically to pay off the debt. This sum would be an appropriation in the annual budget just like those for salaries, paving the streets, and fuel for public buildings. The money in the fund could then be used to pay off current interest, gaining returns through investment in state or federal bonds, or buying back city bonds until the corporation owned them all, at which point the debt could be retired. The city councils quickly found that the existence of the sinking fund gave potential bondholders much greater confidence in the corporation's ability to redeem bond issues. Prudent administration of the sinking fund could also give the city the financial security to attract investment in city bonds and to pay off city debts.[25]

After the city councils' establishment of the sinking fund, the corporation had little trouble selling bonds. Declaring their intent that "the reduction and payment of the debt due from the city of Philadelphia should be effected as speedily as circumstances will permit," in 1807 the councils passed an ordinance allocating $5,000 a year from the income of the corporate estates—city-owned buildings, wharves, market space, and real estate leased on an annual basis—to be put in a "'sinking fund,' to be applied to the purchase and redemption of the several species of stock, constituting the funded debt of the city." Eventually, the city sold bonds above par and put the premiums into the sinking fund, for example, for the loans of 1819 and 1820. Demand for stable investment proved so strong that from 1821 to early 1822 (on the heels of the Panic of 1819) the city managed to sell bonds bearing 5 percent interest rather than 6 percent, allowing it to refinance much of its outstanding debt at the lower percentage.[26]

At first, the councils passed an ordinance stipulating that the money in the sinking fund could be invested only in federal bonds, although they later relaxed that requirement to allow the fund managers to buy stock in local internal improvements, thereby investing in the community at the same time as paying down the debt. The councils increased the annual appropriation from the corporate estates to the sinking fund to $7,000 in 1811 and then to $8,000 in 1816. Once the annual operations of the waterworks exceeded routine costs, the councils began to set $4,000 aside every year from the water rents, too, increasing that amount to $10,000 and eventually to $14,000. From time to time the councils added stock from investments in local projects such as the Schuylkill Permanent Bridge Company and the Schuylkill Navigation Company, as well as premiums (that is, any amount paid above par) on the sale of the municipal bonds. When interest rates fell slightly in the early 1820s, the city consolidated much of its debt by selling a total of $535,000 in bonds at 5 percent annual interest to pay off earlier debts contracted at 6 percent. The fund grew from its modest establishment in 1807 to one of the largest single pools of assets in the Philadelphia area by the late 1820s, reaching a value of $383,266.88 in March 1830.[27]

The use of a sinking fund revealed two assumptions on the part of the men who ran Philadelphia's city councils. The first was that the councils would have the political discipline to make significant appropriations to the fund on a regular basis while not raiding it for purposes other than debt reduction. This premise held true. From its inception in 1807 through 1830, every disbursement made from the sinking fund went either to the purchase of financial instruments for the purpose of income or toward the acquisition of city bonds to retire the debt. The second assumption behind the sinking fund was that the corporation's revenue base would continue to increase at a rate that equaled or exceeded the growth in the corporation's routine costs. In other words, as long as the city's economy grew faster than the cost of governing it did, the councils could afford to pay off the interest on their loans without resorting to higher taxes with potentially adverse economic (and electoral) effects.

Over the years, councils would fudge the difference. While the city grew, its debts grew even faster: Philadelphia's per capita debt rose from $6.70 in 1810 to $25.39 in 1835. As early as 1807, a city council subcommittee argued against higher taxes, claiming that the increased tax burden resulting from the cost of the waterworks had been "very injurious by lowering the value of real estates, and discouraging improvements" (clearly economic effects that the real-estate owners and businessmen on the council felt more than common people, who probably appreciated the lower rents that came with lower real-estate values). The subcommittee believed that loans to be paid off by future revenue made more sense, because "the benefits arising from the water works are of a permanent nature, and the income from that source likely to increase." The committee suggested that the most "expedient" course would be "to raise by tax no more than the sum necessary for the usual expences of the year, and that the moneys necessary to pay for . . . permanent improvements, ought to be borrowed." Here, too, the councils proved prescient: Philadelphia's economy and its waterworks revenue expanded fast enough to accommodate the cost of government and government services without necessitating significant tax hikes. The sinking fund became an efficient tool in the city councils' finances, and it no longer struggled to find capital.[28]

For the city councils, bondholders became the best kind of partners in their building of Philadelphia: investors who footed the bill with no questions asked. Although taxpayers were willing to pay for a budget that included incrementally larger appropriations into a sinking fund—payment for debts already contracted—they were loath to approve big new expenditures or to support unexpected costs. Bondholders were much less fickle than taxpayers as a source of immediate funding for large capital projects and for overruns and annual expenditures. They did not demand efficiency, responsibility, or even competence—merely their interest payments twice yearly. They invested in city bonds for some of the same reasons that they invested in banks or insurance companies: precisely because they desired steady profits and did not want to spend the time and energy necessary for other potentially profitable pursuits. After the Panic of 1819, which showed that banks could lose money or even go under, the stability of municipal bonds made them even more attractive. Meanwhile, bondholders' lack of energy suited the politicians on the city councils, especially the common council, whose members stood for reelection annually; through the sinking fund and city bond issues, the corporation shifted the burden of financial scrutiny of its affairs from the electorate to people one of whose preconditions for investment was the option of ignoring the details of the corporation's finances altogether.

Despite their discipline in refraining from raiding the sinking fund directly for routine costs, the city councils did use the sinking fund and the city budget in creative ways to lessen the immediate tax burden and to pay for potentially controversial projects. The success of the sinking fund device in liquidating debt and assuring potential bond buyers of the security of their investment offered unexpected flexibility to the councils in dealing with cost overruns and other costly contingencies. From 1805 on, the city councils borrowed money by issuing interest-bearing bonds nearly every year and sometimes several times in a year for a variety of purposes. They took out loans to pay for other capital improvements to the city, such as the construction of culverts and markets. They issued bonds to pay for emergencies, such as to build fortifications to defend the city in the War of 1812 or to make up for budgetary shortfalls. They even sold bonds to buy the old statehouse, soon to be called Liberty Hall, from the state government. The city councils also issued bonds to fund improvements to the waterworks. To expand the pipe distribution system, the councils authorized another $70,000 in bond issues in 1818. The following year the city began its efforts to expand the waterworks at Fairmount, trading Josiah White and Joseph Gillingham $150,000 in city bonds for land and water rights at the Falls (in addition to issuing bonds worth the $200,000 earmarked for construction). White interpreted the bonds-for-land swap to be politically possible specifically because of the use of bonds rather than tax moneys. Incumbents could point to their acquisition of lands to expand the waterworks while temporarily holding down taxes by spreading the cost of improvements over many years.[29]

On at least one occasion, the councils used the sinking fund to absorb directly a budgetary shortfall. In late 1824, the city councils found that the corporation needed approximately $26,000 to provide for unexpected costs in a variety of categories and voted to authorize a bond issue for that amount. A week later, the sinking fund committee pointed out that the fund had $19,315.77 in cash on hand, and the committee could sell enough of its federal bonds to make up the difference to buy the entire issue, a proposal soon approved. In this particular incident, the account for the ensuing year's tax fund was charged, meaning that the money would still have to be accounted for out of taxes somehow. This case is a particularly clear example of an unstated purpose for which the councils used the sinking fund: to put off indefinitely the consequences of tough financial decisions. For the members of the common council, who were up for reelection annually, postponing budgetary crises essentially meant avoiding them altogether, because the sitting council would not be blamed for problems inherited from the previous session. The loss of a council seat because of budget problems was not an idle threat: in 1802, Democrat-Republicans swept the incumbent Federalists out of the councils largely by blaming the officeholders for cost overruns on the waterworks and the taxes that those extra expenditures necessitated. Wise use of the sinking fund gave the city councils the wherewithal to spend tomorrow's money today rather than raise taxes, relieving politicians on the council of the politically heavy burdens of unpopular tax hikes or cuts in services. They could cut up their revenue pie and eat it too, as long as municipal levies brought in enough dough to bake a bigger one the following year.[30]

The ability to float bonds either for budget overruns or for potentially unpopular projects insulated the city councils from making controversial budgeting decisions because it allowed them to postpone cutting services, raising taxes, or answering to the electorate for particular appropriations that might be objectionable. This is not to say that the city councils demonstrably mis-led the public about how much the corporation was spending or on what projects. Indeed, skillful manipulation of the sinking fund allowed the cor-poration a welcome flexibility to pay for unforeseen expenses and for water-works-related construction without raising taxes sharply in any given year, surely a benefit to administrators and taxpayers alike. However, any time the councils felt pressure on the corporation's bottom line, they could simply is-sue bonds that investors willingly snapped up. The cost associated with the bonds would be transferred to the sinking fund and therefore out of the year-to-year, potentially contentious process of deciding upon appropria-tions. The annual appropriation to the sinking fund amounted to a discre-tionary fund for the councils to build or to spend: the overruns and the building projects they funded only appeared in the annual appropriations under the rubric of the sinking fund. No one would be willing to oppose council incumbents on a political platform suggesting that the corporation should not pay its bills—especially if he ever expected to get a loan from any Philadelphia-based bank, several of which held large blocks of city bonds.[31]

The move into the black allowed the City of Philadelphia to act as a medium for an exchange of financial power over the course of the early decades of the nineteenth century. Through its flexibility and its potential for being manipulated, the sinking fund increasingly fulfilled a political role beyond that of a convenient financial device: its use allowed the city coun-cils to make significant financial decisions regarding the corporation in ways that limited public scrutiny of city council policy. Noninvesting residents benefited from the best citywide waterworks in America and stable tax rates, at least as long as the city's economy grew. Meanwhile, the sinking fund pro-vided investors with city bonds, an extremely safe vehicle for capital apprecia-tion. Through their use of the sinking fund, the Philadelphia councils had the freedom to spend what they wanted, when they wanted, with a minimum of public input. On the one hand, the investment benefits of corporations were distributed widely among the wealthiest quarter of the population. By the late 1820s, thousands of Philadelphia residents owned city bonds. Through buying these financial instruments, they were investing in their own futures as well as in the future of the city. On the other hand, the average taxpayer, too, got something: a better regional transportation network and a citywide freshwater supply system with little cost in terms of increased state taxes. The state had contributed none of the expenses for the waterworks: bond investors had put in the lion's share of the principal. In terms of city taxes, as long as Philadelphia continued to grow, the increased taxpayer base and those who used the water-works most intensively would pay off the interest and eventually much of the principal for building the waterworks.

Despite such benefits, the users, taxpayers, and smaller investors did not get something for nothing. Rather, the floating of public debt amounted to a shell game that merely hid the unpleasantly high costs of infrastructure proj-ects necessary to the economic and urban development vision of corporate promoters. The waterworks provided the city a necessary service for its continued success but disproportionately rewarded those who had the wherewithal to buy municipal bonds. Meanwhile, everyone's taxes paid for the interest support and the maintenance of the sinking fund that paid off bond-owners, through a regressive tax system that levied real estate (which landlords passed on to renters) but not the silver, the stocks, the furniture, the ships, the country houses, and land speculations of the wealthy. The waterworks not only redistributed water but also redistributed wealth as well. The individuals in control of capital had devised institutions and methods that guaranteed their ability to skim off the cream of economic development.

Indeed, through their gathering of capital, through their lending and investment, and through their use of city funds, corporate captains' use of money yielded the same results as their use of technology: the diffusion of some benefits alongside the consolidation of important resources. Complicating the Revolutionary promise of popular governance (especially during the late 1770s), the general public ceded much control of financial affairs and the institutions that administered them to a small group of men who would direct Philadelphia's economic growth. These men, on the city councils or on the boards of various corporations year after year, determined the routes and capacities of the navigations and the city water mains as well as what to charge consumers. They made decisions involving hundreds of thousands of dollars—huge sums at the time—with little input from the electorate or, in the case of business corporations, any public authority. For the public, the price of cheap access to water, transportation, and credit was the loss of control over the corporations responsible for those technologies and services.

The waterworks also allowed an unprecedented concentration of money for a locally controlled project, with all the economic leverage and political patronage that such concentration entailed. Philadelphia newspapers abounded with Watering Committee advertisements calling for bids on thousands of feet of lumber, on bushels of coal, on carpentry work, on masonry work, and on tunneling work, giving it tremendous potential for political patronage. The amount of money the Watering Committee had at its disposal for such contracts began high and grew astronomically. Latrobe's original estimate for his waterworks was $127,000 for construction, not including maintenance. According to Watering Committee calculations, the total cost as of October 12, 1801, was $220,310.55; as of November 1, 1803, $296,604.34; a year later, $336,830.99; and five years after that, $482,212.55.[32]

And that was just the beginning. In any given year, from the first acceptance of the Latrobe proposal in 1799 through 1825, the construction, maintenance, and financing of Philadelphia's water supply system commanded a huge portion of the city government's energies and resources, measured either in total dollars or as a percentage of city expenditures. Over that period, the city pumped nearly half of all its resources into the waterworks; every year, the city councils poured more money into the waterworks than for any other city service or project, even more than for fortifications during the War of 1812. Often, the waterworks constituted over half of all city spending. Only twice in that time did the waterworks cost less than 30 percent of the city's outlays (1809 and 1811, at 27.4% and 25.3%, respectively); in nine different years, the waterworks constituted over half of all city spending, reaching over 60 percent four times. By the 1820s, the Fairmount waterworks supplied water reliably to Philadelphia and several of its suburbs, and the Watering Committee decided how and where every penny was spent.[33]

Alone among subcommittees of the city councils, the Watering Committee had a separate budget, authority to enter into contracts, and the ability to hire and fire its own employees. In 1822, the city passed an ordinance giving the Watering Committee its own rent collectors, separate from city tax collectors; thus, the Watering Committee now possessed almost total control over its own cash flow. It issued its own printed annual reports and kept its own records separate from the city councils'. It owned land, paid its own bills, and ran a growing bureaucracy, running up substantial debts in doing so. The Watering Committee commanded a large part of Philadelphia's budget, the surest sign of bureaucratic and political power. With its hands on hundreds of thousands of municipal dollars in building and maintenance of the nation's first grand municipal infrastructure project, the Watering Committee had become the behemoth of Philadelphia politics.[34]

CITY CORPORATION OF PHILADELPHIA
TOTAL EXPENDITURES, 1799–1825

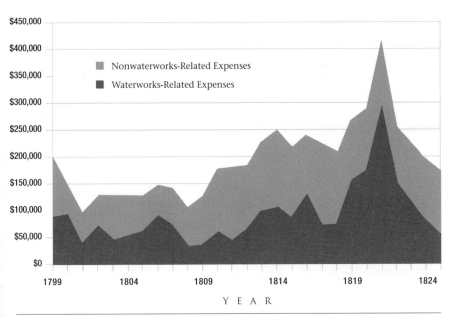

Sources: *Accounts of the Corporation...* (1799–1827); *Report of the Watering Committee...* (1803–1825); General Accounts, Corporation of Philadelphia, vols. 3-5, Philadelphia City Archives. For further information regarding the sources and methodology of these calculations, consult the Essay on Sources and Methodology found at the end of this volume.

The waterworks' centrality in the market and diffusion of reward distinguished it from previous economic ventures, especially municipal ones, in the United States that could not diffuse benefits on the same scale. The Centre Square works reached an unprecedented financial and geographic scale, far surpassing the most productive mills and the grandest plantations. Upon completion in 1802, the waterworks served about a quarter of Philadelphia's approximately 43,000 residents; by 1830, the Fairmount Works provided all of the water for Philadelphia's population of 80,000, and perhaps half for the additional 87,000 in nearby suburbs, a total of approximately 123,000 people. Undoubtedly, those people benefited from the fresh, cool water, and the city was far better off with its spectacular water system than it would have been had it struggled with more wells and pumps. Nonetheless, with benefits came dependence, and regardless of the ends to which the city councils used their leverage over that dependence, the fact remained that the Watering Committee gained indirect influence over Philadelphia residents.[35]

Control over distribution contributed significantly to the Watering Committee's power. The construction of Latrobe's main-and-pipe system as opposed to the aboveground gutters proposed by the canal company resulted in greater income, authority, and responsibility for the city government. The pipe system required hookups to use, either to public hydrants or private ferrules (pipes connecting mains to delivery systems) to houses and businesses. Therefore, any person or neighborhood wanting water could obtain it only through the Watering Committee. When the system became operational in 1801, the city passed an ordinance setting residential water permits at five dollars a year and charging "brewers, sugar-refiners, hatters, soap-boilers, inn-keepers, dyers, curriers, and others, who will require the water for other purposes than the supply of their private-dwelling houses" rates proportional to the amount of water to be consumed. A few wealthy residents were so anxious to get Schuylkill water that they advanced the city interest-free loans to have mains installed on their block. All sorts of businesses signed up, including ones like distillers, whose work was water-intensive, and banks, whose officers wanted the running water for prestige and convenience. Some firms paid as much as $80 for the privilege. The largest customer, year after year, was the almshouse, for the enormous sum of $100 proving that even charities had to pay their share. The Watering Committee could not charge firefighting companies, because they used the public hydrants; however, as of 1812, private fire companies had to apply to the Watering Committee for permits to test or clean their engines and hoses. Three years later, the Watering Committee gained control over the annual $2,000 disbursement to fire companies that helped them defray their equipment costs.[36]

In more physical terms, the Watering Committee also contended with making sure the water flowed as regularly as the revenue did. Administration of the waterworks entailed the enactment and enforcement of a series of measures for "regulating the distribution of Schuylkill water," first in 1801, then in 1806, twice in 1809, and again in 1818 and 1821. Measures to solve specific, practical problems included ordinances specifying size and length of hookups, materials, and stopcocks, all of which had to be installed according to the Watering Committee's exacting standards. For instance, an 1809 law specified that private hookups for city water include a stopcock attached "at the distance of twelve inches from the gutter to prevent accidents from the leakage of said pipe." The enactment and enforcement of such ordinances ensured that individual irresponsibility, incompetence, or malfeasance on the part of a few residents would not endanger everyone's supply of water; in that sense, such laws were the necessary consequence of such a large, complex system to which so many people had access. The sum of these laws, however, amounted to more than their individual parts: they represented an unprecedented degree of the city corporation's administrative control over its residents. Anyone in Philadelphia wanting Schuylkill water had to lobby the Watering Committee to have a main put in, pay a Watering Committee rent collector, and hire a Watering Committee–appointed plumber to install a hookup according to Watering Committee specifications. This became a routinized and thus less arbitrary process, but the Watering Committee's authority became reinforced every time it happened. Through technological necessity, the Watering Committee parlayed its control over water distribution into many arenas of the city's operation.[37]

To protect the waterworks, the Watering Committee eventually constructed a considerable body of ordinances that targeted a range of behaviors, many dangerous but others not. In 1801, the city councils passed a law imposing fines plus costs of repair and recovery for intentionally breaking pipes or mains. As the councils gained experience with the system and some residents found new ways to abuse it, the city added fines for "soaking, or rinsing . . . manufactured" goods, opening hydrants unnecessarily, and tapping into a main without permission, the last carrying a hefty $20 penalty. City officials took enforcement to heart, as one William Eaton found out in 1815 when he received a summons from the mayor because of "a Complaint having been made that [he] permitted the Hydrant water to waste from [his] enclosure contrary to the Ordinance." Eventually, Philadelphians could incur legal punishments for not using strong enough stopcocks, for not covering them properly, for using someone else's water, for not using licensed plumbers, and for not having pipes at the right depth, among a host of other petty offenses. The continuous operation of the waterworks necessitated such measures, lest the laziness or incompetence of a few bad apples ruin the water system upon which everyone depended.[38]

But yet another ordinance allowed city constables to slap a fine on "idle and disorderly persons . . . in practice of collecting about the hydrants . . . and wasting water." A bunch of ne'er-do-wells hanging about open hydrants on summer nights looked like a public nuisance to the good and proper members of the city council. Some type of control was necessary for efficient operation of the works and for public safety: improper installations made repair difficult and caused leaks that not only wasted water but also resulted in mud in the summer and treacherous ice in the winter. The specificity of the ordinances eased enforcement problems and allowed for consistent penalties for given offenses. Still, though all Philadelphians could seek legal reparation from others who damaged their property, just the Watering Company had the power not only to recover the cost of replacement but also to exact a heavy fine. In sum, the Watering Committee held great power over Philadelphians.[39]

Nonetheless, the city corporation gained such leverage only because so many other people saw the waterworks as essential to their own aspirations. The waterworks and the centralized bureaucracy that ran it were neither the result of nor resulted in merely a power play by the municipal government or a few well-placed city officials. Rather, the waterworks and its encumbrances came about and grew because fresh water was, as the city councils pointed out, "an object so much desired by . . . fellow citizens." In the first couple of years after the building of the works, few subscribed for the fresh water, but as the system of mains snaked its way into the city's neighborhoods, more and more people signed up for water in their homes. Residents began petitioning the Watering Committee to put mains down their streets so that they could get hooked up.[40]

Those who could afford to receive the fresh, cool Schuylkill water pumped into their homes gained convenience, prestige, and privacy in exchange for their water rent. By 1828, Philadelphia houses built in the "usual convenient style" boasted a "bath house, water closet &c. and abundant supply of Schuylkill water in every room, even to the garret"; the "luxurious water right is purchased of the corporation at the small price of eight dollars a year." Once hooked, residents abandoned their old wells, never to return to them. Soon, the convenience of running water became a marker of middle-class attainment, and voters consistently supported extensions to the works. By the late 1820s, suburbs Spring Garden, the Northern Liberties, and Southwark bought their water from the Corporation of the City, falling into the orbit of the city that would incorporate them in 1854. The ability of certain blocks or people in those areas to get their own water signaled their growing ability to distance themselves from those below them, a critical juncture in forming class identity in nineteenth-century America.[41]

The waterworks offered more than an opportunity to establish or show off family status. For many in the City of Brotherly Love, the resources expended on the waterworks seemed well spent, for the waterworks were a great source of municipal pride. Philadelphians boasted of their waterworks, first the pumphouse in Centre Square and eventually the fabulous Fairmount Works. If at the dawn of the nineteenth century Philadelphia could no longer be America's political or financial capital, it could still lead the new nation in manufacturing and technology. Within a few years, exclaimed one city dweller, "Philadelphians were more proud of the water works than of Independence Hall. They said one might as well visit London without viewing Westminster Abbey as come to Philadelphia and not see the water works." When Englishman Cyril Thornton visited in 1833, Quaker City residents pestered him "a dozen times a day" to see the waterworks; he "was told that [he] positively must visit them; that they were unrivalled in the world." Residents faced the nineteenth century with the waterworks as a sign that Philadelphia would continue its role as one of the great cities of America. First the Centre Square works and then especially the Fairmount works and its surrounding gardens appeared in dozens of engravings and lithographs at home and abroad. The waterworks gave residents the satisfaction of living in the self-proclaimed "Metropolis of America" in exchange for the huge sums spent on the works and the centralized authority that came with it.[42]

That centralization extended well beyond the city's limits. As fast as the city of Philadelphia proper was growing, its suburbs gained population at an even higher rate. As with any adolescent, Philadelphia's growing pains involved learning how to control and coordinate its extremities, in this case the residents and governments of neighboring communities that bordered the city. In 1819, the Watering Committee began planning to replace its steam-powered waterworks with a cheaper, more reliable water-power system; it also saw the new works as a way to make money for the city and extend its administrative influence over the suburbs through the sale of surplus water. A Watering Committee report pointed out that "the ability it affords of supplying the districts, and thereby adding materially to the income of the City, will . . . justify the expenditure" on the new system. The city soon built its fabulous Fairmount waterworks. By the mid-1820s, water rent revenue from the suburbs exceeded the costs of routine maintenance and the waterworks' distribution to the sinking fund, that is, the cost of building the works. Plus, suburbs paid to install their own mains. In effect, the suburbs footed the bill not only for much of the waterworks' ongoing maintenance costs but also for more than their portion of the debt service on initial construction costs, with the extra money going into Philadelphia's general revenue fund. Thus, the suburbs paid at least their share of initial cost and upkeep as well as for Philadelphia city services from which they received little or no benefit.[43]

While control over water pricing gave Philadelphia leverage over its neighbors, the regulation of that water proved to be an even more insidious form of conscious municipal manipulation. True, the suburbs received many of the same benefits of the waterworks as did city residents. That said, Schuylkill water also came with the price of giving the Watering Committee great leverage over suburban municipal administration. Clauses of Philadelphia's 1827 contract with neighboring Spring Garden baldly demonstrated Spring Garden's subordination. The suburb was to receive water only if Philadelphia had enough for its own needs; Spring Garden water rent books and assessments had to be approved by the Watering Committee; Philadelphia charged Spring Garden residents 50 percent more than its own residents for private water; Spring Garden had to enact all the same ordinances as Philadelphia had relating to the distribution and wasting of water; and, most crucially, the Watering Committee could shut off the suburb's water if Spring Garden did not pay rent or if its pipes were not properly maintained. This final stipulation, giving Watering Committee employees the authority to shut off Spring Garden's water, provided the Watering Committee with the most leverage by rendering Spring Garden vulnerable to municipal blackmail. Such contracts provided the Watering Committee with more than control over Philadelphia suburbs' water; the technology of water supply gave the Watering Committee influence over suburban administration, tax collection, and legislation—leverage that increasingly rankled those communities before they were incorporated into the city in 1854. The Watering Committee definitely demonstrated the potentially centralizing effects of the technology it administered.[44]

Through manipulating that technology, the Watering Committee had great power to create winners and losers in the Philadelphia area. Because of the immense cost involved in constructing a network of water supply, the waterworks did not supply the entire city from the very beginning. Rather, the Watering Committee directed the construction of water mains to neighborhoods, then installed branches going down individual streets, and finally allowed individual property owners to connect to the new pipes. Not surprisingly, the Watering Committee made sure to send pipes down the streets of Philadelphia's best neighborhoods first, without much prompting from ward residents. Others were not so lucky. Some blocks of residents made numerous appeals before getting action, while brewer Frederick Gaul had to grovel in the form of a petition to the select council before action was finally taken to run a pipe down Callowhill Street between Second and Third Streets, an area full of workshops and housing for tradesmen but just outside the city limits. Many Philadelphians caught lower-paying but steady jobs as plumbing inspectors, clerks, and maintenance workers; John Gotwalt was able to draw a salary and find rent-free housing for his family when he wangled a patronage job from the Watering Committee as a toll taker. Gotwalt and other corporate employees could avoid the constant danger of chronic or intermittent unemployment that most Philadelphia-area workers faced. Regular pay offered stability for them and for their families. The point here is not that Philadelphians were universally worse off, far from it; rather, that through the waterworks and its administration the men on the Watering Company had a great deal of say over who would benefit most and who least from the Fairmount works.[45]

A look at one of those influential men and another who benefited puts the waterworks in more human terms. No one's fortunes became more intertwined with the Philadelphia waterworks than Frederick Graff's, whose life began with the nation's, whose career was bracketed by the beginning of the Centre Square works at one end and the recognition of the Fairmount works as a national urban model at the other, and whose position within the municipal corporation showed the possibilities and limits of continued class tensions within corporate life. The son of a middling Philadelphia master carpenter, Graff was born in 1775 in the house where, the following spring, Thomas Jefferson boarded while attending the Continental Congress and composing the Declaration of Independence. Trained in the same trade as his father, the young man hurt his leg on a job in the late 1790s but put his draftsman's skills to work when Latrobe hired him as an assistant during the construction of the first waterworks. In 1805, the Watering Committee selected Graff to become superintendent of the works, a position he held until his death in 1847. In between, he designed the steam-powered works at Fairmount and the later water-powered facilities there as well as the beautiful buildings that housed them, accomplishments that led several dozen other cities to hire him to consult upon or design their own water supply systems. Like thousands of others in the Philadelphia region, Graff parlayed his corporate work and corporate connections into a secure livelihood and a respectable living. Furthermore, his son Frederick, Jr., succeeded him as superintendent of the works and became a national authority on water systems in his own right. Still, despite those accomplishments, there remained a clear class distinction between him and the men on the councils.

Graff used his position at the waterworks to gain something that became possible in America only with the growth of corporations in the early republic: a steady, well-paying job with a stable institution that could guarantee virtual lifetime employment. Shortly after his appointment as superintendent of the waterworks, he began courting one Judith Sweyer. In successfully proposing marriage to his sweetheart, Graff assuaged her fears of economic insecurity by proclaiming that, while he had no independent fortune, he had confidence in his abilities, pointing out that "my situation in life is that of a dependancy upon my industry for a genteel livelihood, which . . . I shall always be able to make." Livelihood and industry, definitely: the waterworks clearly would be a permanent installation, and one that demanded his constant attention. The waterworks always required maintenance, labor, and supplies. In addition, fairly common mechanical problems could beckon at any moment. As a newlywed, Graff complained to his bride of receiving "marching orders to attend my old plague the Engine" that prevented him from visiting her. Such problems never fully abated. Broken boilers, burst pipes, or busted waterwheels could occur at any moment, sometimes requiring Graff to leave home in the middle of the night and work frantically nearly nonstop for days at a time. Even in 1824, once the more reliable water-powered works at Fairmount had been completed, Graff complained that "being so much engaged settling my accounts and paying the men keeps me at work both night and day." But if the work was hard, it was also steady, as was Graff's salary. And when he died, Frederick Graff, Jr., succeeded him in the position of superintendent of the waterworks. The Graff family could depend upon employment beyond the whims of individual employers or the uncertainties of the market.[46]

Frederick Graff looking more youthful than his twenty-eight years, posed in front of the Centre Square waterworks of which he had recently become superintendent. James Peale, c. 1804. Courtesy of The Historical Society of Pennsylvania Collection, at the Atwater Kent Museum of Philadelphia.

Despite his success, Graff understood that his ability and standing as an engineer for the waterworks formed the foundation upon which his middle-class identity rested, and his ambiguous relationship with the Watering Committee ensured that his sense of attainment and accomplishment was never fully secure. Perhaps it had to do partly with a sense of insecurity concerning his professional attainment; in 1811, when planning the steam-powered works at Fairmount, the Watering Committee hired John Davis of Baltimore to help Graff, because it wanted "the assistance of an experienced engineer." And the committee members were right. Even seven years later, Graff's written queries to English hydraulic engineers demonstrated an ignorance of basic mathematical principles in fluid dynamics surprising in the superintendent of such a major waterworks but perhaps to be expected from one with no formal engineering training; Graff's transatlantic colleague graciously offered that "the local knowledge of this gentleman [Graff] must give him such advantages" but continued on to correct many of Graff's assumptions. Only after decades of service to Philadelphia and of consulting with other American cities would he finally receive greater professional respect from the men on the councils.[47]

Furthermore, the tone in Graff's correspondence with the Watering Committee always bespoke a mutual sense of differing status that went far beyond the distinction between employer and employee. His 1827 letter to mayor Joseph Watson revealed Graff's sense of being beholden to the city government. He had moved to the northwest section of the city specifically "for the convenience of the Public work," but a tavern across the street attracted a clientele that clearly offended his family's bourgeois sensibilities. Graff wailed that the tavern was "a recepticle for all the loose women of the city" and grumbled that "regular dances are held twice a week which occasions a collection of the most vulgar class of men and boys that the city affords, rioting, breaking windows &c. is regularly carried on to an excess beyond conception." But he did not circulate a petition among his neighbors, because of his "particular engagement on the waterworks," presumably to avoid the appearance of agitating against his city council superiors. He begged Watson to refuse the tavern a new permit or Graff would have to move his "much distressed" wife and three daughters.[48]

Meanwhile, Graff was only half kidding when he privately referred to the men on the Watering Committee as "my masters." And the Watering Committee returned the favor. Upon Graff's death, after over forty years of his faithful service to the city, the Watering Committee passed a resolution praising "the personal worth of Mr. Graff and of his eminent abilities as a public functionary," his "fervent zeal," and "the great practical science which he ever manifested in [the waterworks'] management," but most of all applauding "the gentlemanly courtesy which characterized his official intercourse with the members of the Committee," or, in other words, the deference he showed to his corporate superiors. Corporations allowed for new middle-class attainment while corporate men used their institutional status to reinforce class lines.[49]

If Graff represented the rise of the middle-class corporate man, then Joseph S. Lewis personified the integration of the city corporation's Watering Committee into the corporate sphere. A descendant of early Pennsylvania settlers, by the time Lewis was born in 1778 his father, Mordecai, had already established himself as a successful merchant. Mordecai Lewis engaged in the China trade as well as transatlantic commerce, and through Thomas Willing eventually did considerable business with the House of Baring. An early director of the Bank of North America, the Insurance Company of North America, and the United States Insurance Company, Mordecai Lewis held a seat for several years in the City Corporation's common council during the early 1790s. He also served as a longtime treasurer of the Pennsylvania Hospital. Typical of the second and succeeding generations of Philadelphia's corporate elite, Joseph S. Lewis found the skids to corporate positions already greased by his father's many connections and, indeed, became involved in many of the same institutions. The son followed the father on the board of the Bank of North America and as treasurer of the Pennsylvania Hospital. Also like his father, Joseph S. Lewis moved easily between business corporations and the city government. First elected to the common council in 1806, he gained reelection most years until 1824; he spent the last six years of his council tenure as the powerful chairman of the Watering Committee, during which time he presided over the construction of the grand Fairmount Waterworks.[50]

If the Philadelphia corporate community was a web, Joseph S. Lewis was at its center. At various points, he held seats on the boards of the Bank of North America, the Delaware and Schuylkill and Susquehanna and Schuylkill Canal companies, and the Philadelphia Insurance Company, and he ended his long corporate career as president both of the Pennsylvania Contributionship for Insuring Houses from Loss by Fire and the Schuylkill Navigation Company. His brother, Samuel, sat as a director of the Marine Insurance Company. Lewis's ties went beyond the boardroom: he served as executor or trustee of many colleagues' estates and was friendly with other corporate bigwigs, such as James C. Fisher, Robert Wharton, and James Vaux.[51]

Lewis further exemplified the corporate elite in his ability to profit personally from his board connections. As part of a huge package to bail out the struggling Schuylkill Navigation Company in 1824, Lewis subscribed for $10,000. He was not alone; Joseph Norris, a Bank of Pennsylvania director, subscribed for $15,000 and Henry Nixon of the Bank of North America subscribed for $8,000. He was only taking after Stephen Girard's example; after having served on a Schuylkill Navigation Company board subcommittee that recommended acquiring a loan, Girard engrossed the whole loan for himself for the astounding sum of $230,850. These men could avail themselves of such a good investment opportunity because of their insider status. In addition, because they knew that through their ties to financial institutions, they could afford to tie up capital for long periods without the fear of insolvency, should one run short of cash, he could always take out a loan from the company on whose board he served. They were also using their corporate links to aid companies in which they owned stock privately or stood to gain in increased property values upon the completion of the various improvements.[52]

The actions of Joseph S. Lewis and others on the Watering Committee suggest that Philadelphia's corporate men understood perfectly the power dynamics at work with the Philadelphia water supply system. The waterworks not only functioned as a medium for the concentration of water in reservoirs and its redistribution throughout the city and its suburbs but also did so in the realm of technological, economic, financial, and legal power. Certainly Philadelphia and suburban citizens benefited in innumerable ways from the waterworks. At the same time, the ability of the waterworks to distribute such benefits, combined with the corporate form, gave Watering Committee members a large amount of control over a vital resource upon which so many residents depended.

The city councils' actions and strategies in running the waterworks demonstrated that, regardless of their election by the public at large, council members found ways to exploit technology and to isolate certain kinds of financial and operational decisions from public debate no less effectively than their business corporation brethren. However, their power was not nefarious, complete, or dictatorial in the city, nor was it in the suburbs. In fact, in 1832 council members lamented that Spring Garden officials refused to allow Kensington to route Fairmount water through Spring Garden; despite "a common interest," councilors complained, "the City cannot control either" district. That would be partly remedied in the coming decades, when, in 1854, all of Philadelphia County would be consolidated under a new city corporate government. Just as the waterworks would be a model of municipal waterworks and other American urban infrastructure projects, so would Philadelphia's consolidation presage the larger city governments of the late nineteenth century. Because of the waterworks, the corporate community had extended its reach throughout the city and the suburbs. And with the incorporation of internal navigations, that influence would extend far beyond metropolitan limits.[53]

5

◆ INCORPORATING ◆
THE COUNTRYSIDE

*T*he water taunted them. Just a mile beyond the settled parts of the Philadelphia, the Schuylkill River ran swiftly on its course from deep in eastern Pennsylvania on its way to the Atlantic Ocean. Though in 1680 William Penn had envisioned the City of Brotherly Love stretching from the Delaware on the east to the Schuylkill on the west, by the late eighteenth century the city remained mostly huddled on the waterway named for Lord De La Warr rather than the one the Dutch had called "hidden creek." Philadelphians knew that success in their commercial rivalries with New York and Baltimore hinged on a race to gain the commerce of the Ohio River and the Great Lakes region; the Schuylkill represented a potential waterway into Philadelphia's hinterland and perhaps to the west, if only it could be made navigable. The opening of New York State's Erie Canal in 1825 intensified their anxiety because, while it showed what was technologically possible, it now made New York City that much more fearsome a competitor.[1]

Furthermore, with the surrounding forests increasingly denuded, city residents found themselves in an energy crisis despite the tantalizing quantity of coal that lay seemingly for the taking in the upper Schuylkill River Valley, if only there were a way to get it to market. They also knew that there was coal available in the Lehigh River Valley, though that seemed even more remote. But when the wind came in from the northwest, Philadelphians could hear the roar of water coming through the Falls of the Schuylkill, a couple of miles upstream from the city. It was not actually a full waterfall; it was more a series of rocks and boulders over which the water rushed. Nonetheless, it and other rough areas along the length of the river prevented any water-borne traffic but flatboats whose owners were willing to brave rapids to take country goods downstream, and upstream navigation was simply impossible. And the Lehigh River, which flowed into the Delaware upstream of Philadelphia, was even more rough than the Schuylkill.

What made the issue of the Schuylkill River, the Lehigh River, and artificial waterways even more pressing was that all America, it seemed, also wanted to get to market and thereby more closely connect city and country, part of the greater process of the economic integration of the nation, with all that the process entailed. Philadelphians did not want to be left behind, because the transportation improvements built in the early republic allowed the movement of people, goods, and information cheaper and faster than colonial Americans ever imagined possible. These advances resulted in more than simply increased economic activity; they also set in motion a self-reinforcing cycle of economic changes that had profound social repercussions. When rural families found that they could buy goods like clothing that they used to produce themselves, or when they realized that they could sell perishable goods in bulk to nearby cities, they rearranged their labor patterns, leading to new household roles and arrangements. Similarly, when city artisans saw that they could distribute goods cheaply to the countryside, they innovated ways to harness power in factories or rearrange labor into putting-out systems, thus greatly affecting the American workplace. Every new transportation project led to the creation of new cities and to the decline of former boomtowns, contributing to Americans' sometimes bewildering penchant for mobility while breaking the sometimes comforting small-town isolation of many communities.[2]

The establishment of corporate internal improvements led to another effect of this integrating process: changes in the geography of power that such close connections would bring. In the first decades of the nineteenth century, Philadelphians finally harnessed the Schuylkill River. A business corporation, the Schuylkill Navigation Company, supervised the construction and maintenance of a string of canals and river improvements stretching 108 miles upstream. Officers of another business corporation, the Lehigh Coal and Navigation Company, administered an even more challenging forty-six-mile project along the rugged Lehigh River. Combined with other corporate-administered canals, these two navigations formed part of an internal navigation network spanning thousands of square miles of Philadelphia's hinterlands. Just as the city waterworks affected more than the flow of water, internal improvement projects changed far more than the physical landscape. The decisions behind their construction and administration held long-term consequences for nearly the entire population of eastern Pennsylvania.

Because improved transportation was integral to the city and the region's economic growth, Philadelphians and their countryside neighbors used the Schuylkill and Lehigh navigations to remake contours of economic and political power in the region. A new corporate elite eclipsed old established families, while engineers, superintendents, tradesmen, boat owners, and contractors found new niches in a growing middle class. Laborers, mechanics, and small farmers found themselves finally free from the dominance of local bigwigs only to discover themselves even more under the thumb of corporate officers. All of them demonstrated the countless ways that area residents carved their niche in society through their newfound access to markets, but such changes could also be greatly unsettling. The ability to participate successfully in the growing economy gave strivers the opportunity to distance themselves from other social groups. In early nineteenth-century America, the use of internal navigations allowed workers to become less beholden politically to local patrons by taking advantage of the quick transportation along the river to turn their own labor into a marketable commodity.[3]

In short, a great number of people exploited the Schuylkill and Lehigh navigations to establish a distance from workers, while both groups used such technologies to help themselves break free of the political and social power of the local grandees. The bonus for the proprietors of such ventures, beyond their profits, was the ability to engage those who made the exchange in a growing cycle of even more subtle, and yet in other ways more profound, dependence. Schuylkill and Lehigh company insiders used the facilities they built to project power across space on a scale far greater than their gentry predecessors, as the residents of Manayunk discovered and Josiah White exploited. Some forms of power were diffused toward the many, while others were concentrated by the few. Technologies like canals and river navigations served as a prism, refracting the wavelengths of America's market revolution to distribute its benefits among a large spectrum of the population in one direction while in the other focusing its power for a select few.[4]

While city merchants and country farmers certainly welcomed the opportunities better transportation could create, an increasing demand for energy prompted the project that would render the Schuylkill and Lehigh rivers navigable. The rivers' waters began their journey in the hills of northeastern Pennsylvania, hills rich with a resource of great potential value: coal. Throughout the eighteenth century, Pennsylvania settlers and passers-through had noted the ready availability of the black mineral in the colony's mountainous central region, though they made few sustained efforts to get it to market. Like most urban and even many rural Americans, by the turn of the nineteenth century Philadelphians cast far and wide for power sources. Philadelphians had long supplemented their supply of firewood and charcoal that had been floated down the Schuylkill or Delaware with bituminous or "soft" coal shipped from Britain and Virginia, because its use as ballast kept it affordable. However, during the War of 1812, with the British blockading the coast, coal from either the old country or the Old Dominion became unavailable. Although the cost of fuel dropped when the war ended, the demand for energy grew faster than the population. As one city resident observed, "the rapid disappearance of wood from all the streams connected with Philadelphia" continued apace, resulting in ever-rising fuel prices. Philadelphians continued to seek cheaper sources of energy.[5]

The long-term solution to Philadelphia's energy shortage was a technological innovation typical for its combination of conscious intent and random luck, one that could "afford a supply of fuel to the capital, not only indispensably required at this period of distressing want, occasioned by the interdiction and destruction of the coasting trade, but commensurate with its utmost demands for centuries to come." It was anthracite coal. Inventor and entrepreneur Josiah White's promotion of anthracite held huge implications for Pennsylvania's industrial future. White ran a wire-pulling plant on the east bank of the Schuylkill, just north of the city, on lands at the Falls of the Schuylkill. He had heard of a kind of "hard" or "stone" coal available from up the Schuylkill, and he knew that Frederick Graff, the superintendent of the waterworks, had tried to use it in 1808 to no avail; this Watering Committee failure remained on humiliating public display, the unburned rocks used to gravel paths around the waterworks' central pumphouse in Philadelphia's Centre Square.[6]

The problem was simple: no one could get the stuff to light. When people had tried to burn it, they gave it lots of air, as they did with the bituminous coal that they purchased from Virginia or England. White bought some and his workmen tried and tried, one day finally slamming the door of the furnace shut in frustration and knocking off for supper. Had the coal been the bituminous variety that the men were used to, closing the door would have put it out. When one man came back, having forgotten his coat, he found the furnace red-hot and called back his coworkers. They proceeded through four runs of iron before the furnace finally cooled. Pennsylvania's anthracite, it turned out, had different properties than bituminous coal: anthracite required little oxygen to burn but much heat in order to ignite fully. White immediately realized that this different kind of coal, anthracite coal, could solve Philadelphia's fuel dilemma, and he quickly set out to find a way to transport large quantities of it to the city.[7]

White faced physical, financial, and political barriers, but he was not to be deterred. The closest anthracite fields lay many miles up the unnavigable Schuylkill; White could not afford to undertake the project on his own, and he would have to pilot his proposal through the state legislature. Undaunted—perhaps naively so—White rounded up a stable of investors who lobbied the Pennsylvania legislature to charter the Schuylkill Navigation Company. Its purpose was to render navigable the length of the Schuylkill River that stretched from the coalfields in sparsely settled central eastern Pennsylvania through Reading and on to Philadelphia before it flowed lazily into the Delaware River. However, the Schuylkill Navigation Company had problems acquiring a charter, because a board member of the Union Canal Company held a General Assembly seat for Philadelphia County. The Union Canal Company, a successor to the assets of several failed canal efforts, had gotten a charter in 1811 to build a canal connecting the Susquehanna to the Schuylkill around Reading. Led by William Duane, the state representative from Philadelphia, Union Canal Company investors considered the Schuylkill Navigation a potential competitor and opposed White's efforts to get a charter. Only in the next session, when Schuylkill Navigation Company backer Cadwalader Evans, Jr., replaced Duane did the charter pass. White and his backers finally got their charter.[8]

Of course, the Schuylkill Navigation Company was not the only or even the most notable American internal improvement begun as part of the post–War of 1812 economic boom. That honor belonged to New York State's Grand Western Canal, later known as the Erie Canal. Administered by a state-appointed canal commission, that great project was financed through the sale of bonds backed by a property tax on lands within twenty-five miles of the canal and by toll revenue. When finished, it stretched 363 miles, from the far eastern shores of Lake Erie to the Hudson River, thus connecting the Great Lakes area with New York City. That effort prompted Philadelphians and Baltimoreans to redouble their efforts to better transportation to their hinterlands. The Erie Canal would inspire state-sponsored efforts such as Pennsylvania's Main Line system, begun in 1825, and Ohio's later internal improvement network. Meanwhile, the Boston men who formed the companies to develop the Lowell textile mills in the late 1810s also invested in corporations to gain control of the waterpower upon which their factories depended and to better transportation between Boston and its surrounding areas. Americans experimented with two basic models of organizing their internal improvement efforts, through state commissions or by corporation. And while many of the economic effects of the two different types of administration were the same, they also exhibited crucial differences. State-run projects tended to be well funded and thus constructed fairly quickly, while corporate ones often struggled at first and sometimes languished for years. More crucially, projects overseen by state governments remained accountable and responsive to the public, while corporate men put their own interests first.

Like other corporate internal navigation boosters, Schuylkill Navigation Company supporters soon found that raising money proved even more difficult than securing a charter. Early internal improvement companies' rosy predictions of profits did little to sway potential investors, so internal improvement boosters had much more difficulty raising cash than did corporate banks. As tireless Philadelphia supporter of internal improvement Charles Paleske observed, a successful project "requires a large capital, a fixed, unalterable plan, regular and constant superintendance, and great economy," but few internal improvement projects boasted such characteristics. Subscription was the most typical form of soliciting investment for internal improvement: individuals gave a low deposit—usually five or ten dollars—and signed an agreement with the company to pay additional installments. Some companies set a particular schedule for subsequent payments, many called for payments whenever the company needed additional funds, while still others practiced a combination of the two. Raising money through subscriptions proved popular because it did not require investors to put up much money initially in projects unlikely to deliver immediate returns (or, as was the norm with internal improvements, ever), nor did it require sending in a large sum at any one time. Furthermore, despite a legal obligation to pay the company in full, subscribers always had the option of reneging on their contracts. Subscriptions potentially appealed both to the money-savvy and to a broader swath of the population.[9]

Unfortunately for early canal companies, the subscription system often failed to raise the requisite capital. Despite canal boosters' impassioned appeals to "the confidence and patriotic exertions of the Citizens of Pennsylvania," investors let their subscriptions lapse for a variety of reasons that ranged from personal, family, or business-related financial straits to a growing, well-warranted lack of confidence in the completion of the projects. Company officials repeatedly tried to coax lapsed investors to complete their subscriptions, both offering the carrot of full shares and waving the stick of legal action. But despite companies having the right to sue their subscribers for nonpayment, the cost and trouble of doing so might not justify the effort, and such action might alienate potential new investors.[10]

Canal boosters also tried to raise money by running state-sanctioned lotteries, a common device for early republic states to allow churches, hospitals, and other public-minded institutions to raise money from high-risk, high-reward investors. That they expected lotteries to be more successful than subscriptions for generating capital demonstrated the general public's skepticism toward internal improvement as an investment: ticket buyers apparently considered random luck to be more likely to succeed than company management. In 1795, the General Assembly granted the Delaware and Schuylkill and the Susquehanna and Schuylkill companies the privilege to raise $400,000 by lottery; it also gave them exclusive lottery rights in Pennsylvania. The lottery offered substantial prizes in cash and in company stock, with the grand prize valued at $100,000.[11]

Unfortunately, the companies' efforts to raise money through lotteries became as futile as their subscription travails. Legislators could not resist the pleas of bridge companies, religious congregations, and libraries to conduct their own lotteries; combined with out-of-state lotteries, the companies faced stiff competition for the legal gambling dollar. Difficulties in selling tickets, however, did not exempt companies from having to award prizes, and corporate officers got embroiled in lawsuits over disputed prize payments, diverting the companies' money and attention away from construction. One pamphleteer later suggested that the companies netted only $50,000 in their lotteries, although an insider more familiar with company finances admitted that "the lotteries heretofore granted to the canal companies, have actually involved them in debt." Lotteries, then, did not provide a viable solution for the financial woes of inland navigation companies.[12]

The need for subscriptions and for lotteries persisted because even the most successful of these initial ventures—for example, the Middlesex Canal in Massachusetts—were poor direct investments. Before the canal-building craze of the 1810s and 1820s, Americans had gone through a turnpike mania in the 1790s. The most famous of the 1790s turnpikes, and the one that set off a turnpike-building frenzy throughout the nation in its first decade of operation, was the Philadelphia and Lancaster Turnpike. With an initial cost of $465,000 and with yearly maintenance and wages costing around $8,000, the company generally issued annual dividends from 2 to 6 percent for its first three decades. Given that the contemporary standard for investment was 6 percent annual return, profits averaging a third of that widely accepted figure did not provide the main impetus for the stampede to build turnpike roads that occurred in the years following the completion of the Philadelphia and Lancaster Turnpike. Indeed, thirty years later one investor complained about the high costs of maintenance and calculated that since 1796, the shares had yielded an annual return of 3.69 percent a share, hardly the best of investments. Any turnpike investment, considered purely on its own, was effectively a losing proposition.[13]

However, the Philadelphia and Lancaster Turnpike showed Americans that a well-constructed and regularly maintained toll road could cover its costs on a regular basis while significantly lowering the cost of overland transport, and that became enough to trigger a nationwide turnpike mania. Turnpike boosters rarely harbored sober, realistic expectations to get rich from the roadway. But as landowners or merchants, they had other possibilities in mind. Like other internal improvement boosters, they hoped that lower transportation costs would result in better business opportunities and increased property values in the communities through which the project traveled. In Pennsylvania in particular, they also invested out of a sense of boosterism, to promote local economies. Investment in turnpikes remained predominantly local, because it made sense only in conjunction with other area investments, whether economic or sentimental.[14]

Whether early canal boosters expected to make money on their favored projects is hard to divine, but the financial struggles of two of the Schuylkill Navigation Company's predecessors, the Delaware and Schuylkill Canal Company and the Schuylkill and Susquehanna Navigation Company, suggest that the few overly optimistic investors who might have hoped for direct profits were quickly disillusioned. Chartered in early April 1792, the Delaware and Schuylkill Canal Company had sold its full allotment of 2,000 subscriptions by the end of May, a sign that the project held great promise. The shares were widely distributed: 1,124 different individuals had bought in, none holding more than three shares. First on the list were Robert Morris and John Nicholson, each signing for only one share. According to its charter, individuals were allowed to buy one share on the first day of the offering, another two shares on the second day, up to three shares on the third day, and as many as available thereafter.[15]

Even given the possibility that the project sold out in two days—thus explaining the maximum holding of three shares—the reluctance of men such as Morris and Nicholson to buy more shares suggests that they did not think that the project would be profitable. Considering their experience with the founding of the Bank of North America, shares of which skyrocketed in price immediately after its initial stock sale, Morris and Nicholson most likely believed that the canal would not be a financial success. As officers of the doomed project later admitted, "capitalists . . . of course prefer that mode of employing their money, which secures to them an immediate and a certain profit." Some people doubtless overestimated the profit potential of early projects: the Schuylkill and Susquehanna Company shares were so popular that the company was oversubscribed, and the board had to assign shares by lottery. Schuylkill and Susquehanna shares were widely distributed too, with the vast majority of investors holding only one or two shares. Even if no one invested large sums, at least the projects elicited widespread if not deep investor enthusiasm.[16]

However, difficulties in retaining an engineer, choosing routes, buying out or compensating property owners, and lining up contractors for construction plagued both companies—not to mention inefficiencies resulting from company insiders' greed. When French tourist the duc de la Rochefoucauld-Liancourt passed through Pennsylvania in April 1795 he counted only fifty men working on the Delaware and Schuylkill Canal; he foresaw "little chance of success." The Frenchman observed that the canal had been routed through hard-to-cut marble and porous sand on one side of the river rather than the solid ground on the other bank, because "much to the interest of the directors of the company, that the canal should pass through its estates, they were deaf to every other proposal." That allegation was more than rumor. The board had approved numerous land deals to its members, exactly the kind of transactions likely to occur in an institution with no public oversight. Robert Morris was one of the worst offenders; the company agreed to pay him a significant sum for his Hill Farm tract of land in 1795. Since the company's charter three years before, its workers had managed to cut only three miles from the Norristown end and an equal distance from the southern terminus. At the same time, a decreasing number of the subscribers continued to cough up the installments on their subscriptions.[17]

The companies' directors found themselves caught in a vicious cycle: they had trouble covering construction costs because subscribers did not pay installments, and subscribers did not want to make payments on projects that did not make adequate progress. The companies' boards of managers repeatedly warned that "suits will be commenced . . . [against] every person in solvent circumstances . . . indebted to this Corporation." Like internal improvement companies throughout the United States, including New York State's Western Inland Lock Company, a predecessor to the Erie Canal, the two Philadelphia-area projects' troubles lasted longer than their investors' patience. By 1810, of the original 1,000 subscriptions to the Susquehanna and

Schuylkill Navigation Company, 867 had been forfeited back to the company because investors had let their subscriptions lapse; the Delaware and Schuylkill Canal Navigation Company fared slightly better, with 464 out of the original 1,000 subscriptions totally paid in. Few investors were faithful or optimistic enough to continue throwing good money after bad. By the late 1790s, efforts on these two potentially pioneering efforts had petered out.[18]

Internal navigation companies rarely found themselves the darlings of investors, nor did they enjoy overwhelming success in their efforts to get support from the state government. While the Schuylkill Navigation Company downstream terminus would be in the heavily populated Philadelphia area, its upstream end would be as near as possible to the coalfields of eastern Pennsylvania. That is to say, once beyond Reading in fairly prosperous Berks County, its farthest upriver reaches ran through territory sparsely settled in the 1810s and early 1820s, dotted with occasional villages and with farms that barely generated enough cash to pay taxes. At least the Schuylkill Navigation would pass through Reading and eventually have the Union Canal as a feeder. That was barely enough to convince the state legislature to purchase $100,000 in Schuylkill Navigation Company stock after the Panic of 1819, more a measure intended to create temporary employment than a grand commitment to the project's completion. With that exception, however, direct state investment in Philadelphia-region corporate canals ended. Inland navigation company officials would have to find private sources of investment.

Despite the willingness of boosters from cash-strapped internal improvement companies to ask the legislature for money, the state usually provided only a small fraction of those ventures' overall capital. Rather, it provided a boost, a financial stopgap while companies scrambled to attract more private investment and to finish construction so that they could generate their own cash flow from tolls; in this, Pennsylvania's policy was typical of early republic state policy toward corporate internal improvements. State investment in Pennsylvania paled next to private investment in turnpikes, bridges, and internal navigations. Even when the legislature granted companies large sums, they were only a fraction of the total cost of construction. According to a Pennsylvania Senate report, as of 1822 the state had invested $1,861,542 in turnpike stock, compared to $4,158,347 in private investment; $382,000 in bridges, compared to $1,629,200 in private investment; and $130,000 in internal navigation companies, compared to $1,416,510 in private investment. Overall, then, the state provided 31 percent of turnpike funding, 19 percent of bridge funding, and a mere 8 percent of internal navigation funding—and that was just before the explosion in spending by the Schuylkill Navigation Company and the Lehigh Coal and Navigation Company, both built almost entirely with private money. The corporate figures for private investment were most likely inflated: in some cases, they represented reported subscriptions, rather than actual money paid in. Nonetheless, the state was not involved in every corporate enterprise. It was only bailing out the ones whose proponents had the political wherewithal to cobble together an omnibus bill for public aid.[19]

Pennsylvania generally did not put up the bulk of the money for internal improvements, especially for those most likely to succeed. Private investors supplied all $465,00 for the Philadelphia and Lancaster Turnpike, all $285,000 for the Germantown and Perkiomen Turnpike, all $300,000 for the Schuylkill Permanent Bridge, and all but $100,000 of the nearly $2,000,000 for the Schuylkill Navigation Company, each among the period's most expensive and the Philadelphia area's most used improvements. The larger the corporation, the less its supporters asked of the Pennsylvania legislature, and the more fiercely it guarded its financial independence from public authorities.[20]

Ironically, the state's unwillingness either to build its own improvements or to fund business corporations adequately resulted in the control of projects being consolidated in fewer hands—exactly the kind of centralized power most American critics of government abhorred. The Schuylkill Navigation Company began in 1815 with a roster of investors closely resembling those of previous projects. The average investment in the Schuylkill Navigation Company was just over $350, with a maximum single holding of $2,500. But the chronic shortage of cash on the part of the Schuylkill Navigation Company in the late 1810s and early 1820s gave potential large investors a strong position in dictating terms to boards of managers of struggling projects, further concentrating control of the institutions. Those investors used their leverage to protect their money in a variety of ways, each of which placed their rights and privileges ahead of earlier stockholders and lenders. In 1817, the Schuylkill Navigation Company board bent to the demands of large investors when it became clear that there would not be broad interest in a new stock issue. "From the backwardness of the people to come forward and make further additions," the board reported, "it appears not probable that much progress can soon be made therein." Board members weighed the offer of "a number of monied men . . . to subscribe large amounts on condition that such subscriptions shall not be binding on them unless the full amount of five thousand shares now wanting shall be fully made up and subscribed." In the end, the board voted to accept the rich men's offer, having no other alternatives to raise the needed sums.[21]

Wily Stephen Girard found another way to use investment at a critical time to gain a significant stake in a struggling company. Having immigrated to America from France as a young man in the 1780s, Girard had used international connections, a gambler's acumen, and his knack for driving hard bargains to become Philadelphia's and perhaps the nation's richest man. In 1823, the Schuylkill Navigation Company ran out of cash and projected needing another several hundred thousand dollars to finish the waterway. The board of managers had already exhausted the usual methods of raising funds: no more would be forthcoming from the state, and company officers despaired of selling yet more stock to an unenthusiastic public. Accordingly, the company board negotiated a series of loans from the ever-adroit Girard amounting to a total of $230,850, an incredible sum for one individual to be able to offer. The final agreement was structured first as a mortgage on the entire navigation paying

Girard 6 percent interest annually; however, he reserved the option to convert any value of the loan into company stock at par value.[22]

Girard had exacted fabulous terms that nearly guaranteed him a profit at the expense of previous investors, regardless of the company's ultimate fate. Should the Schuylkill Navigation Company go bankrupt, Girard would own all its land and its water rights, whose value far exceeded the amount he had put in. Should the company be successful and issue big dividends, he could convert his loan into stock at par—well below the market price—and then either sell the stock at a handsome profit or collect the dividends. Somewhere in the middle—that is, were the navigation to be finished but be only marginally profitable—Girard could sit back and receive the interest due on the loan. Girard had found a way to ensure that he would profit in any given scenario, while previous stockholders could be hurt in several ways: loan payments or dividend payments to Girard would cut into their dividend payments; and if the project failed, Girard would be the beneficiary of their investment. The ability to lend a large sum at a particularly vulnerable moment for the company gave Girard the chance to dictate favorable terms and to have a considerable say in company affairs because he also retained the option of calling in his loan. Through his use of capital, one man virtually owned the Schuylkill River.

By 1819, financial troubles and technical reverses convinced impatient investors to force founder Josiah White from the company, but work continued. Schuylkill Navigation Company officials and canal laborers overcame a host of obstacles. They dug canals to bypass falls and rapids; they used hammers or gunpowder to eliminate impediments such as rocks and tree stumps; they built dams to alleviate shallows; and they designed reinforced locks and especially strong dams to negotiate spring freshets. When the project was fully completed in the late 1820s, the Schuylkill Navigation Company's board of managers boasted of its impressive statistics: it ran 108 miles, 62 of them by canals that skirted falls, rapids, and shallows, and the other 46 by channels and pools in the river, all having towpaths, and included 120 locks and 65 lock keeper's houses. Company officials estimated traveling speed along the navigation to be four miles per hour through the pools and channels and three through the canals. For the first time, barges filled with goods could travel the length of the Schuylkill.[23]

The company acquired its first license to charge tolls before the spring season in 1819, and a trickle of coal and other goods found its way down the river that spring and summer. The navigation was for the most part completed by 1825, the year the anthracite coal market took off, carrying the corporation's fortunes with it. That season, the company took in $20,123.91 in tolls and in rents for company real estate, almost six times the previous year's total, and four years later, the Schuylkill Navigation Company declared its first dividend, paying $3.50 a share in profits. Company stock reflected its newfound success. Before 1825, the company had been unable to unload shares at the original price of fifty dollars; after traffic began in earnest, they fetched around seventy-five dollars on the open market.[24]

EASTERN
PENNSYLVANIA
in
1830

—— Schuylkill Navigation

– – Lehigh Navigation

•••••• Union Canal

•–•–• Delaware & Hudson
Canal

NEW YORK

N

SUSQUEHANNA

WAYNE

Honesdale

Lackawaxen R.

Scranton

PIKE

LYCOMING

Wilkes-Barre

LUZERNE

Delaware R.

COLUMBIA

Susquehanna R.

NORTHAMPTON

Mauch Chunk

PENNSYLVANIA

Lehigh R.

Easton

NEW JERSEY

UNION Sunbury

NORTHUM
-BERLAND

Pottsville

SCHUYLKILL

Allentown

LEHIGH

DAUPHIN

BERKS

LEBANON

Reading

Lebanon

MONTGOMERY

Trenton

Schuylkill R.

Harrisburg

Middletown

LANCASTER

Manayunk

PHILADELPHIA

Lancaster

BUCKS

CHESTER

PHILADELPHIA

DELAWARE

Camden

Susquehanna R.

York

Chester

YORK

Wilmington

DEL.

0   20
Miles

MARYLAND

The completion of the Schuylkill Navigation along with the Union Canal that fed into it marked the beginning of the economic explosion of the Schuylkill River Valley. Real estate values rose, both because the company purchased many parcels for canals and tollhouses and because farmlands, mines, and mills along the river became more profitable now that residents could transport their goods more cheaply. Although the overseas demand for wheat dropped at the end of the War of 1812, Schuylkill Valley residents used the navigation to specialize in more marketable crops and to better exploit the miles and miles of coal beneath them. They began sending not only huge quantities of anthracite downstream but also enormous amounts of all sorts of goods extracted from the ground. In 1827, for example, 31,630 tons of coal, 1,472 tons of limestone, 526 tons of iron ore, 678 tons of marble, and 6,078 tons of building stone floated down the Schuylkill, accompanied by traditional agricultural products, including 31,436 barrels of flour, 24,244 bushels of wheat, 12,951 bushels of corn, 1,643 bushels of rye, 6,151 bushels of flaxseed, and ample quantities of other commodities, such as apples, eggs, live hogs, soap, nuts, glue, whiskey, tallow, bark, and even rags. Such increased market production enabled upriver residents to afford the cornucopia of goods flowing up the navigation. These included regular household products such as china and cloth, foreign comestibles like sugar and Madeira, and even the oceanic delicacy of fresh sea bass. If the Schuylkill navigation allowed residents to wet their feet in the market, a good many of them dove in headfirst.[25]

The Schuylkill navigation did more than simply facilitate the easy transport of goods: its construction and use allowed Philadelphians and their hinterland neighbors to create new ebbs and flows of political and economic power. The waterway allowed the consolidation of control over precious resources crucial to the city and region. Much to the growing frustration of local nabobs all along the Schuylkill River Valley, a handful of Philadelphia men running a private corporation gained increasing economic and legal leverage over hinterland residents, especially the millers and landowners along the river's banks. This process repeated itself along all the artificial waterways feeding Philadelphia's growing markets. Thousands of other opportunists in the city and the country also seized the chances made available because of ongoing construction and maintenance, cheap transportation, and administration of the corporation that ran the navigation. These manufacturers, merchants, farmers, engineers, superintendents, boat owners, contractors, miners, and others joined the ranks of the middle class. Philadelphians used the economic opportunities offered by the navigation to remake their social and political worlds.

So many people gained—or lost—through the Schuylkill navigation because it acted as an engine of a profound economic and social transformation in the Philadelphia region during the early decades of the nineteenth century. It was at the nexus of a great portion of the area's economic activity. Transportation improvements on the local, regional, and sectional scales helped accelerate economic growth. More than links with other domestic markets or international trade, changes within the region drove this grand economic expansion. Beginning in the 1810s, the economic landscape of Philadelphia and its surrounding hinterlands—western and southern New Jersey, eastern Pennsylvania, and much of Delaware—began to change considerably. Towns sprouted on the Schuylkill and the Lehigh rivers when the mining of anthracite began in earnest. The increased use of coal laid the foundation for the development of the United States' first heavy industry, the manufacture of high-pressure stationary steam engines, in the Philadelphia area during the second quarter of the nineteenth century. Closer to the city, Manayunk and Spring Garden became manufacturing centers whose production rivaled their more famous cousins such as Lowell, Lynn, and Paterson. Meanwhile, farmers in the surrounding countryside began to specialize in particular crops for sale to the growing population of the city, deviating from their past practices of sending surpluses of general farm produce to more local markets. Philadelphia slowly shifted from an emphasis on foreign commerce to manufacturing products that it could sell in exchange for its hinterlands' growing bounty, and so began to look as much inland as it had toward the Atlantic in the previous century. Exploiting the increasing productivity of the countryside looked like the way to prosperity in the early nineteenth century, and Philadelphians desperately wanted their share of the loot.[26]

This process of regional integration was but one scene in the larger play of economic growth and increased market participation in the early republic. As in any epic drama, some characters exited the stage in triumph at the expense of others who remained strewn on the stage floor. Both producers and consumers began to concentrate more intensely upon products for sale in the nearest metropolis and to use the new income to buy even more factory-made goods. Internal improvements paved the way to prosperity by more tightly linking hinterland and metropolitan production. A group of local farmers typified the attitude toward new canals and turnpikes, being "fully convinced of their utillity by so greatly facillitating the conveyance of the produce of their Farms to Market, and . . . desirous that a participation of those Benefits, may be further extended." In a time when the great optimism for economic advancement was matched only by the fear of being left behind, Philadelphians nearly fell over themselves in their rush to accept improvements on almost any terms. Because economic development in the Schuylkill River Valley depended upon the navigation, the Schuylkill Navigation Company, in its ability to determine toll rates for various commodities, modulate the volume of traffic, change the route of the navigation, and modify the width of the waterway, held huge influence over local economies along the 108 miles of the improved river's banks.[27]

The Schuylkill navigation's centralizing phenomenon resulted from the effects of its serving as a nexus of the region's exploding economy. The navigation formed a hub of constant interaction between controllers and the customers who employed these technologies in countless ways. Philadelphia residents heated their houses and fueled their furnaces with coal that had been shipped down the navigation and used the Schuylkill navigation to sell their finished goods in upriver markets; similarly, hinterland farmers, miners, lumberjacks, and tradesmen sold their products downriver and bought wares from workshops in Philadelphia and beyond. In essence, the navigation produced nothing tangible. Rather, it provided constant occasion for Philadelphia and Schuylkill Valley residents to exchange opportunities in return for the tolls the navigation company demanded. The navigation sprinkled benefits to thousands of residents in the broad geographic area it affected. Not only did stockholders prosper; others also could use the technologies for their own ends. Furthermore, people used them constantly, rather than making a single purchase or interaction.[28]

These two qualities, diffusion of reward and continuity of exchange, made internal improvements qualitatively unique in terms of their increasing centrality to the growth of the market exchange economy in the early republic. Because of their strategic location at the center of social and economic activities, technologies like internal improvements could be exploited by their controllers (investors or administrators) and their users in fundamentally different ways, ways that have deep political and social implications not measured or properly defined in economic theory. The Philadelphia region's economy expanded in terms of productivity and per capita income as well as the increasing pervasiveness of market participation and behavior. The use of technologies like the Philadelphia waterworks and internal navigations allowed people to enter the market more fully and to become more productive once engaged in it. New market participants found that nexus technologies soon became indispensable to their engagement with the economy, and the people who controlled such projects thus placed themselves in positions of great leverage over the market activities of others.[29]

The Schuylkill navigation's centrality in the market and diffusion of reward distinguished this and other internal navigation projects from previous economic ventures in the United States that could not diffuse benefits on the same scale. Its monopoly reached unprecedented scale in terms of numbers and space, far surpassing the most productive mills and the grandest plantations. The Schuylkill navigation became the lifeblood of economies all along the river: Pottsville, Port Carbon, Schuylkill Haven, Hamburg, Reading, Pottstown, Phoenixville, Norristown, Conshohocken, Manayunk, and western Philadelphia. By 1830, about 325,000 people lived within fifteen miles of the navigation; the men who controlled it touched a great many people. Because so many people used it, the navigation also allowed an unprecedented concentration of money, with all the leverage that such concentration entailed. The Schuylkill Navigation Company also had tremendous sums of money to throw around, because the navigation's construction involved a huge infusion of cash into the region in the form of wages and the purchase of construction materials such as lumber, stone, and lime. Through 1826, the Schuylkill Navigation Company had spent over $1.8 million on improving the river. By a stipulation in its charter, the company deposited its operating funds at the Farmers Bank of Reading, a local lending institution that became a company fiefdom. From a trickle in 1818, the goods going up and down the river turned into a flood in the late 1820s: tolls increased almost every year well into the 1830s, reaching a high of $604,190 in 1837. With their hands on hundreds of thousands of dollars, Schuylkill Navigation Company insiders had vast resources available for patronage.[30]

Corporate internal improvements also exhibited great potential for extending power across space on an unprecedented scale. Older merchant and farmer elites usually limited their power to certain neighborhoods or groups in the case of a city, or at most two or three adjoining counties in the hinterland. Their leverage emanated from their ability to spread credit around and through their social standing, neither of which reached beyond a few hundred people. Even the largest of manufacturers in the early republic employed at most a couple hundred workers. The Schuylkill Navigation Company's board of managers made decisions affecting perhaps most of the people living within twenty miles of their navigation—an area of 2,000 square miles—for the Schuylkill was now their connection to markets regional and beyond. Prospective stockholders were not the only boosters for the Schuylkill Navigation Company; the thousands of people whose businesses or jobs depended on the canalized river formed a powerful constituency in favor of such policies.

Internal improvement company officials knew how to use their projects to get out the vote in order to further company interests. Boat operators, merchants, farmers, and contractors often supported internal improvement companies when they lobbied for laws that would give them better terms in eminent domain suits or that would impose harsh penalties for those convicted of sabotage on canals. Struggling to gain financing, company officials circulated printed petitions in Philadelphia pointing out that "in anticipation of its great utility, the lands on the sides of the river . . . have vastly increased in value," and that "the large expenditures on it, have circulated great sums of money among the towns and villages on its banks." Soon afterward, ten petitions, bearing hundreds of signatures, arrived at the statehouse as if out of thin air.[31]

Sometimes even the threat of voter mobilization could be enough to get what company officers wanted. Because both the Schuylkill Navigation and the Fairmount works required the Schuylkill's waters for their operations, the Watering Committee and the Schuylkill Navigation Company sometimes clashed over who owned the rights to the Schuylkill's water, waterpower, and banks. In 1824, as part of a series of complicated agreements between the city and the company, the Watering Committee supervised the construction of a dam and a canal, both of which would be owned by the company. The company and the Watering Committee bickered over the materials, design, route, and specifications—in short, just about everything they could find to disagree about. One controversy concerned the building of an expensive retaining wall, for which the city would foot the bill. Company officials sent a letter to Joseph S. Lewis, erstwhile president of the Watering Committee, that concluded by reminding him that if the dam and canal were not well made, "the Board of Managers do not think it necessary to add any thing more to enduce the Watering Committee whose constituents are so deeply interested in the navigation of the Schuylkill to order the walls to be immediately made." In other words, if the city corporation continued to drag its feet, the company would bring its case to the council members' "deeply interested" constituents—the Philadelphia voters—in the next election. The wall was soon finished according to Schuylkill Navigation Company specifications. The board of managers had used its leverage well.[32]

Technology proved central to the economic and legal leverage that the Schuylkill Navigation Company gained over other people and groups. Internal navigations turned out to be far more fragile than their natural cousins. Accordingly, the Schuylkill Navigation Company board, in cooperation with boards of other companies, prevailed upon the legislature to enact laws regulating the size of boats, their speed, and boatmen's use of various kinds of poles to navigate through the locks. Such measures were necessary to ensure the navigation's efficient operation and thus were in the interest not only of the company but also of its customers. Regardless of its benefits, though, the implementation of these regulations through corporate officers rather than state auspices afforded company officials the authority to make inspections of boats, boatmen, and cargo. The Schuylkill Navigation Company held sway over water traffic.

In the most glaring cases of market leverage, internal improvement company backers lobbied for and benefited from laws to criminalize what they defined as unauthorized use of the projects they controlled. For example, Schuylkill Navigation Company officials gained the authority to have local sheriffs arrest those who interfered with the navigation. In 1826, the Pennsylvania legislature passed a law that imposed fines and even jail sentences for bringing animals not used for towing on company towpaths, for going too slow or too fast, or for blocking or damaging the navigation, among other petty offenses. That measure even gave the navigation company the authority to enforce speed limits at its own discretion: boatmen could be fined $20 for going above the plodding speed of four miles per hour. However, the Schuylkill Navigation Company could grant permission to exceed that rate, essentially giving company officers the privilege to enforce state law as they saw fit. Petty vandalism and annoying behavior now could be quashed or at least more easily discouraged through fines and arrests. Such ordinances did more than merely ease maintenance and save water. By criminalizing unauthorized use, Schuylkill Navigation Company officers could and did use the force of the state to establish and defend their position as arbiter of transportation policy.[33]

Other technological features also allowed the company officers to compel the state to interpose between themselves and their customers and other citizens. Several clauses in the Schuylkill Navigation Company's charter—a rather typical early nineteenth-century canal charter—addressed the contentious issue of "damages." "Damages" encompassed any cost to landowners whose property had been injured by the company, including flooding from the dammed river, crops trampled by workmen, and construction detritus. Pennsylvania granted the company the right to put its constructions anywhere along the river, that is, on anyone's property, and to pay the damage done, taking into account not only the cost of replacement but also "the advantages which may be derived to such owner or owners by the navigation"— "advantages" being defined as increased property value. This definition of advantage represented a hidden subsidy to the navigation company: offsetting the legally retrievable cost of damages with increased real estate market value meant that company workmen and officials could cause substantial harm to properties along the navigation without having to pay for them. This policy was established by the legislature and enforced in the courts.[34]

In other words, the state legislature decided to prioritize the region's economic development over local property rights—certainly a reasonable decision that led to economic growth. But just as with the state's technologically oriented regulations relating to internal improvements, the new definition of damages also privileged corporations as opposed to other economic actors. As one landowner lamented, "the law allows a claim for compensation; but what compensation will make whole my farm cut in two, and the loss of my stock? None, I fear, that a jury will be disposed to give." The question of damages pitted the interests of those who used a navigation, represented by the company that owned and operated it, against the interests of the people who lived directly along it. In 1822, Southwark residents petitioned against a canal from the Delaware to the Schuylkill cutting through their neighborhood, because it would be "destructive to the best interests of your Memorialists." Pointing out the "inconvenience and destruction to public and private property, in making a Canal through a thickly settled district," they further wrote that they were "fearful [that] any attempt to recover damages by the tedious and expensive process of law, will not compensate the sufferers for the injuries they will thus sustain." Although many people benefited from the extension of inland navigations, those who lived along the routes testified that canals and river navigations were a decidedly mixed blessing. The legislature intended to foster economic growth, but the legislation also resulted in the navigation companies gaining an economic advantage over other participants in the marketplace.[35]

Schuylkill Navigation Company officers' increased influence was not limited to their relationships with neighboring property owners. Anyone, including boatmen, teamsters, or local residents, who in some way injured the navigation had to pay twice the damages, as well as the company's cost in recovering them. The company also determined the cost of damages to the navigation, while a six-member, theoretically impartial panel decided upon damages to landholders. In 1821, company backers managed to have the legislature amend its charter so that the company could appeal any decision on damages to a panel from any county in the state; whoever lost the appeal would pay for all court and travel costs—a risk most plaintiffs against the company could ill afford. Thus, in their confrontations, Schuylkill Navigation Company officials held all the cards compared to their opponents: the offset cost of "improvement" (regardless of whether landholders wanted a navigation in their backyards), a lower burden of proof, double damages, potentially friendly appeals panels, and the risk of high court costs. On the one hand, such clauses protected the economic lifeblood of the entire region. On the other, the Schuylkill Navigation Company's board of managers gained leverage to bully its less powerful neighbors. The company's legalized monopoly over water rights interposed the state between economic actors, namely, the Schuylkill Navigation Company on one side, its customers and other citizens on the other. In all of these examples, the ability of those who controlled nexus technologies to impose their interests through the use of the state against all comers testified to the ways that use of such projects subtly changed the construction of power in early nineteenth-century America.[36]

Schuylkill Navigation Company insiders continued to gain influence over communities along the river's banks because so many other people perceived internal improvements as essential to their own aspirations. Some came to enjoy middle-class attainments through their own exploitation of canals. Engineers like Ariel Cooley, Lewis Wernwag, and Loammi Baldwin drafted careers out of designing canals, navigations, and bridges. Their work depended upon getting contracts, but those contracts paid handsomely. Others found more stable pursuits within the institutional structure of projects that required constant maintenance. Thomas Oakes collected steady pay as the Schuylkill Navigation Company superintendent until his death in 1823. Regular pay offered stability for corporate employees and their families. Philadelphia craftsmen used the navigation to transform the port city into the machine in the garden of eastern Pennsylvania. Small tradesmen and large manufacturers alike took advantage of the navigation's cheap transportation, to buy the materials they needed. The flood of anthracite catalyzed Philadelphia's development into a national center for the manufacture of steam engines and heavy machinery.[37]

As "valuable as [the coal trade] is, there is yet another source for the augmentation of the business," the Schuylkill Navigation Company's board of managers told its stockholders. Although more coal traveled downstream than any other product, a host of other commodities floated down to Philadelphia for use in the city's workshops and building trades. Canal companies boasted about "*iron, coal, lead, zinc, marble* of great beauty . . . many sorts of *lime stone* including that with which hydraulic or Roman cement is made, *soap stone, sand stone,* for ornamental buildings, *granite* for flag pavements and curb-stones." Company reports enumerated the commodities transported by type and by quantity, thus providing manifests of intraregional commerce and production. Coal, of course, topped these lists, but lumber, stone, limestone, iron, iron blooms, iron ore, nails, and sawed marble also went down to Philadelphia in significant quantities. The cheap availability of these commodities in large quantities contributed significantly to the ability of Philadelphia craftsmen and manufacturers to step up production, especially in the crucial iron-working trades that produced the tools and engines necessary to so many of the city's and region's manufacturing enterprises. The downstream traffic from the Schuylkill Navigation and other internal improvement projects also provided a great deal of the materials for Philadelphia's building trades that provided the growing city's new warehouses, offices, workshops, and housing stock.[38]

Just as the hinterland provided raw materials, the growing population of the city and the region formed an ever-greater market for local tradesmen and manufacturers. "The increase in the return [ascending] trade has exceeded that of the descending navigation, and forms a source of revenue not much calculated upon at an early stage of our work," the Schuylkill Canal Company board cheerfully reported to stockholders in 1827. What was more, the navigation promised "to be of great importance; for as the population of the country bordering on the Navigation increases, their demand of supplies must also increase." Heavy with ore, grain, and minerals, downstream traffic on all the inland navigations in the Philadelphia region exceeded upstream traffic by weight, but the return traffic of finished goods and foreign luxuries was of greater value. Quaker City industry gained at least as much from the canal and river navigations as did the people who lived along their banks.[39]

The Schuylkill Navigation brought ways to distribute a greater quantity of goods into the hinterland, spurring commerce and market production all along the Schuylkill. Fertilized by navigation commerce, warehouses and taverns sprouted in towns such as Reading, Schuylkill Haven, Mt. Carbon, and Pottsville. Here again, the company's control of the economy complemented increased general prosperity. Such gains could be wonderful, such as the joy of eating fresh sea bass 100 miles inland, "which had such an effect upon the visages of our mountaineers that it would have been a fit subject for the pencil of a Hogarth to imitate." They could also be troubling, because of the increased mobility—physical and social—endemic of any quickly growing community, whether in northeastern Pennsylvania or along the Erie Canal. However, all of them demonstrated the countless ways that area residents took advantage of the access to markets to carve their niche in society. The ability to participate successfully in the market gave many the opportunity to distance themselves from other social groups. In exchange, the Schuylkill Navigation Company not only collected tolls but also subtly exercised great influence over regional development.[40]

Inland navigations also offered another source of energy for manufacturing besides coal: waterpower. Among the corporations in the Philadelphia region, the Schuylkill Navigation Company had the largest stake in the promotion of waterpower both because of its proximity to the city and because, of all the projects, in the Schuylkill River it had by far the most reliable source of constant flow pressure. Even before the founding of the company, mills dotted the river's banks in such places as Norristown, Reading, and Mill Creek, and the first petitioners for incorporation to improve the river for navigation asked for the right to rent or sell the river's power, a right that the General Assembly granted to the Schuylkill Navigation Company in its charter. The City Corporation of Philadelphia soon became the company's largest single customer. In agreements signed from 1819 through 1824, the company leased to the city corporation enough water to supply the city waterworks along with the power necessary to raise it to a reservoir in exchange for a payment of $26,000 and an arrangement by which the city would maintain the company's installations through city property. The city government, in turn, quickly set out to sublet the excess power from the river once the waterworks were properly supplied. The Philadelphia councils put "disposal of water power for manufactories" as a primary reason for purchasing the waterpower, because of the "facilities thereby afforded to a branch of industry deserving of encouragement, as a means of employing a vast number of our people, and of increasing the wealth" of Philadelphia. The municipal corporation and the navigation company had thus become partners in their efforts to foster industrial growth.[41]

In short, a great number of people exploited the navigation to establish a distance from workers, while both groups used such technologies to help themselves break free of the political and social power of the local gentry. The bonus for the proprietors of such ventures, beyond their profits, was the ability to engage those who made the exchange in a growing cycle of even more subtle, and yet in other ways more profound, dependence. Owners used nexus technologies to project power across space on a scale far greater than had their gentry predecessors. Some forms of power were diffused toward the many, while others were concentrated by the few.

However, the changes brought about through the use of canals and waterworks did not shower benefits on everyone—far from it. Those who did the physical work of laying pipes, digging trenches, pouring cement, and shoveling coal ended up at best with little to show for their backbreaking toil building and maintaining engines, mains, and waterways. At worst, they lost life or limb, sometimes as a direct result of company policies: in 1821 the Schuylkill Navigation Company president Cadwalader Evans, Jr., regretted that "a poor man was drowned in one of the locks" because of their shoddy construction. Often, workers found themselves in dire straits. Internal improvement corporations were often short on cash; at more than one point during construction of the navigation, Evans admitted that "the hands are starving, and must disperse if nothing is done soon." And thousands of workers in coal mines, textile mills, forges, and other new forms of employment managed to make ends meet but had few opportunities for advancement and found the new economic order alienating. Like the locks along the navigation, nexus technologies lifted some boats and lowered others.[42]

Canal workers and property owners along the route suffered together and separately. As Samuel Breck astutely pointed out, "these works are for the publick benefit . . . altho' to the great detriment of individuals." In 1799, B. Henry Latrobe recalled from his experience in England that having land along canal routes "exposes it to the depredations of boatmen . . . often in want of fruit and poultry and fence-rails for fireing"; a farmer could also expect "the destruction of his meadows, the inconvenience, and also to buy insurance from depredations." American farmers found the same to be true. Samuel Breck constantly complained that "the men employed on the towing path in front of my lawn . . . take stones & earth wherever they choose, and knock down trees without ceremony." He hoped for "a day of Reckoning." For some living along internal navigations, that day of reckoning came far too soon: residents found conditions "very mortal along the Canal, & within the range of it." In contrast to the formerly free-flowing river, the navigation's still waters bred sickness, "no doubt owing to . . . scum upon the surface" that "has caused a very humid atmosphere, together with the stagnant water in many places." Certainly the property owners suffered less than the boys and men who dug the navigation and towed the boats along it, but few were pleased by the results.[43]

Still others found that the economic opportunities presented by the Schuylkill Navigation Company and other corporations passed them by entirely. Some were literally bypassed: the innkeepers on roads less taken and the millers who saw their millraces slow to a trickle. For a great many more, the increased flow of economic activity did nothing to wash away social dams holding back economic advancement. Though Philadelphia's African Americans built the nation's most vibrant free black community and formed their own middle class, they did not share proportionately in the prosperity of their neighbors, being shut out from bank credit, from many manufacturing jobs, from corporate boardrooms, and from elected office. Irish and, to some extent, German immigrants gained slightly more success, but not before their rage and frustration boiled over into vicious 1830s and 1840s riots that targeted blacks as their closest economic competitors. And while a few women did find entrepreneurial success in the City of Brotherly Love, the most notable way for women to benefit economically from the waterworks or the canals was through the relatively stable income that investments in them provided—that is, for those already prosperous enough to buy stocks. Notwithstanding the economic growth associated with the navigation, members of these groups still found themselves working hard to swim upstream.[44]

While many people could not take advantage of the technology of the navigations, other people would not, and resisted the extension of corporate power in a variety of ways. These battles almost always ended up in the courts, whose role in the expansion of corporate power was as complex as that of legislatures. On the one hand, the general legal philosophical trend during this period encouraged the growth represented by corporations over the traditional economic activities generally pursued by landowners. Judges on higher courts often leaned toward corporations, but, not surprisingly, local courts—and especially local juries—tended to give sympathetic hearings to property owners. Despite the increasingly corporation-friendly definition of damages, some landowners received generous settlements for encroachments on or damages to their lands. Jurors could be neighbors who perceived that the corporation had deep pockets, and traditional jurisprudence leaned toward compensation when property was essentially being given up involuntarily. Internal navigation officials constantly complained that they were being fleeced by country bumpkins that they nonetheless often held in little regard. Corporate boards and their lawyers preferred to avoid court by "settl[ing] with those they think have sustained damages and who are not in their opinion extravagant in their demands." Of course, local juries still had to take into account the rise in property values because of a canal, corporate lawyers tended to be more learned in the law than local practitioners, and court actions could not stop a canal from being built. Still, successful suits against internal navigation companies demonstrated that corporate power had its limits.[45]

A headstrong few tried to stop navigations completely, or at least to reroute them. In 1794, nine Lebanon, Pennsylvania, property holders tried to block the Schuylkill and Susquehanna Canal from going through their property. The Schuylkill and Susquehanna Navigation Company officials then proceeded to take the men to court, but the resourceful group connived with the county sheriff and jury to award them damages large enough to force the company to change routes; ringleader Michael Diffebach vowed "that the canal should never pass through his lands." But, as would so often be the case in such disputes, what local jurors gave, metropolitan judges could take away. When the Pennsylvania Supreme Court heard the case, the justices found that, contrary to earlier claims by the backcountry cabal, company officials had made a reasonable effort to come to terms with the Lebanon men before taking legal action, and that further negotiations would most likely only result in the officials having to "experience insult." They found for the corporation. Using the courts worked for property holders who wanted reasonable (and sometimes even unreasonable) compensation, but they still had no choice but to accept a navigation going through their land.[46]

And that could involve inconvenience and dislocation beyond the value of what corporations could or would compensate, as judges sometimes acknowledged. In 1818, a new Schuylkill Navigation Company dam backed up the river near Mill Creek, which flowed into the river at Lower Merion, about a dozen miles upstream of Philadelphia. As a consequence, James Thoburn's sawmill and cotton spinning operations lost their waterpower, and his meadow was flooded. He sued the company not only for the immediate cost of his machinery and buildings but also for the business he would lose now that milling on his property would no longer be possible. As usual with damages suits, lower courts sympathized with Thoburn, but the state Supreme Court did not. Company lawyers complained that Thoburn did not have the status to sue in the first place, because he had mortgaged the land, but justices latched onto the issue of just compensation. The justices agreed with the judge who presided over the case in Montgomery County, who had instructed the jury that they could take into account only the damages incurred at the time (offsetting them, of course, by the increased value of the land now that it bordered the navigation).[47]

Thus, the court would not consider either future damages, that is, how the land might have been productive had it not been flooded, nor would it consider any value that it could not put a dollar value on, or, as they put it, "for injuries done to his feelings." As one judge reasoned, if the dam had resulted in the destruction of a tree, a property owner could recover only the value of the trees, not "the imaginary value it set upon it, because it was inestimably dear to him as having been planted by his deceased father, or because, in that grove, he had formed those tender attachments, which had united him to his partner for life." And Pennsylvanians learned the lesson. When a Philadelphia-based syndicate floated the idea of a corporate canal across Southwark (the community directly south of Philadelphia) connecting the Delaware and the Schuylkill, local property owners petitioned against it. They argued that "from the experience of your memorialists, they are fearful any attempt to recover damages by the tedious and expensive process of law, will not compensate the sufferers for the injuries they will thus sustain." Among the possible "injuries," they listed "inconvenience and destruction to private property" such as breaking up streets and "cutting through vegetable gardens," as well a deadly rise in "those dreadful Fall and Bilious Fevers which has swept, as with a pestilence, of some of the fairest portions of our country." Such was the price of progress that courts and corporations would only value in money.[48]

At best, if an entire community got together, it could at least negotiate, though rarely from a position of strength. The impact of nexus technologies proved enormous, integrating Philadelphia's hinterland into the web of metropolitan corporate power. While corporate officers had access to great pools of capital and could route their navigations where they liked (physics and geography permitting), hinterland landowners' assets and influence were place-bound and thus at the mercy of corporate city men. The result was that some of the best-organized opposition to internal improvement companies still played into corporate men's hands by accepting the premise that the navigation was desirable at almost any cost. So the landowners of Reading discovered in 1827, when they realized that Union Canal Company officials intended to route their project to flow into the Schuylkill Navigation downstream of Reading rather than in town, thereby threatening the small city's position as a growing hinterland trans-shipment center. Reading residents complained that the new route would "avoid Reading altogether and thereby deprive the citizens of any chance of navigation, the river, or the canal," which they feared "would be productive of the most fatal consequences to their town."[49]

Convinced that having the intersection there would "not only promote the public interest, but *enduce in the highest degree to the growth and prosperity of the town of Reading,*" local citizens held a series of town meetings and engaged in negotiations with legislators, local landowners, and representatives of both the Union Canal Company and the Schuylkill Navigation Company. Negotiations dragged on nearly four years, pushed back the completion of the Union Canal, and frustrated Schuylkill Canal Company officers, who complained of the "great source of interruption and delay" for the Schuylkill navigation "caused by the nature of the limestone formation over which it pass[ed]." The Reading citizens won, but at a cost: they agreed to drop several pending lawsuits against both corporations and not to sue in the future for property damages. In effect, by giving up some of the value of their lands adjoining the navigations, Reading residents subsidized the construction and future costs of the navigations. The episode showed the ways that even the leaders of united hinterland communities found themselves economically subordinate to metropolitan-based corporate officers.[50]

Perhaps no place demonstrated the transformative potential of the Schuylkill navigation more than sleepy Roxborough's becoming bustling Manayunk. For nearly a hundred years, four local clans—the Livezeys, Robesons, Rittenhouses, and Leverings—had dominated the small community of Roxborough, a half-dozen miles north of Philadelphia. The Levering family held the most land, while the other three ran highly profitable gristmills supplying flour for the city and for markets overseas. Because these four clans rented to or employed the majority of the population, they expected and received the community's social and political deference. In 1816, Schuylkill Navigation Company officials optimistically estimated the waterpower above Roxborough—to which the company now owned the rights—sufficient to "turn day and night, about one hundred and forty overshot mill wheels." When the company bought land along the river's banks and laid it out to be the town of Manayunk, the Leverings managed to get the route of the main road through Roxborough changed to accommodate future mills. But in 1819 the navigation company built a millrace and rented the waterpower to wealthy Philadelphia merchants associated with the board, men such as J. J. Borie and Jerome Keating.[51]

Within seven years, where once had stood a dozen buildings, there now existed what one travel guide called "a large manufacturing village"; a Philadelphian estimated that "the town, composed of more than an hundred houses, is still encreasing." The next year, one local characterized it as "one of the greatest manufacturing establishments in the vicinity of Philadelphia." Indeed, by the 1830s it had become one of the nation's foremost textile-manufacturing districts. The local families did not suffer financially: their lands appreciated considerably, and they now had an even closer market for their flour and produce. But in their little community, they were pushed aside by the big money of the new cotton manufacturers. Textile mill owners built houses in Manayunk but did their banking, trading, and socializing in Philadelphia. Meanwhile, neither the thousands of textile workers in the instant manufacturing center nor the new middle-class managers who supervised them had much reason to respect the old families the way local residents had; it was the new factory owners that workers targeted when they protested "all the injustice we suffer from an overbearing aristocracy." The nexus technology of the navigation had facilitated the reordering of society in a new industrial Philadelphia metropolis.[52]

The phenomenon of nexus technology seems to form a tantalizing paradox. As Philadelphian William Duane pointed out, the development of large infrastructure projects like internal navigations possessed the potential of heralding a new order of democracy based on increased access to markets, energy, information, or natural resources. That said, it just as easily could have led to authoritarianism based on centralized control of crucial resources. Similarly, the creation of a market economy—made possible by transportation improvements—both stimulated greater mass participation in politics and precipitated greater consolidation of political and economic power. As it turned out, the concomitant diffusion and consolidation of power was not as contradictory as it might seem. What the examination of nexus technologies reveals is that these apparent paradoxes were in fact the complementary developments that such projects entailed. Nexus technologies acted as media for a few to concentrate political and economic power in exchange for the many's ability to use them to pursue their own agenda.[53]

The story of Josiah White and the Lehigh Coal and Navigation Company demonstrated the extent of the consolidating possibilities of corporate internal navigations. Over his career, White evolved from someone interested in corporations only for the purpose of organizing internal transportation to a man who used a corporation's economic leverage to dominate the entire Lehigh River Valley. In his use of rhetoric, exploitation of technology, and even raising of capital, White came to exemplify corporate power and the corporate sphere. Josiah White was born of Quaker stock in Mount Laurel, New Jersey, in 1781. He worked hard, lived frugally, tried to set a positive example, and even in his diary claimed to consider the public interest as much as his own. After an apprenticeship with a Philadelphia ironmonger, he went into the hardware business for himself and managed to beat by two years his boyhood goal of comfortable retirement at age thirty. Soon bored, he underwent a personal transformation from merchant to manufacturer, deciding to get into the wire-pulling business, buying land at the Falls of the Schuylkill. There he built an ironworks, managed to dam the river—a feat which many had thought to be impossible—and even constructed a wire bridge across the broad waterway, yet had trouble making money.

White's high fuel costs inspired him to hatch his plan for the Schuylkill Navigation Company. But the moneyed men of the company forced him out when he and a partner pressed them to open the navigation despite the company's not yet having state authorization to charge tolls. His humiliation was complete when he argued that the board's intransigence would lead to coal competition from the Lehigh River Valley: members of the board "laughed at our pretended Rivalship from the Lehigh, & thus ended our last intercourse with them on the subject of using their navigation."[54]

But White remained determined and set his sights on the Lehigh River, a fast-flowing and rocky waterway running from the coalfields to the Delaware River some sixty miles above Philadelphia. White's travails in his quest for funding for the Lehigh Navigation and Coal Company demonstrated the closed nature but great power of the corporate elite. Initial reactions to White's capital-raising efforts ranged from passive encouragement to outright rudeness. Joshua Longstreth made an appointment, "but he was gone next door to a party to have some fun"; Jacob Ridgway "treated the project & ourselves with much Contempt"; John Rogers "hoped we would do well"; John Stille "proceeded to Read his news paper, & he was so mutch engaged at Reading the chit chat, occurences of the day, that he had no time to bid us good night." It looked like White had struck out.[55]

Not to be defeated, White appealed to Jacob Shoemaker, who had been a founding director of the Bank of Philadelphia and actuary of the Pennsylvania Company for Insuring Lives and Granting Annuities. Shoemaker told White that in exchange "for 20 shares of stock he agreed to give . . . his weight and influence to get [the] Stock subscribed." Shoemaker quickly enlisted corporate cronies Condy Raguet, James Spence, and John Stoddart for $10,000 stakes. According to White, "the Balance of the stock was then fill'd in about 24 hours." In 1821 Lehigh Canal and Coal Company officers adopted a British financial stratagem when they began issuing preferred stock. Pioneered in Britain, these methods of raising capital were replicated nearly identically in America. Josiah White and Erskine Hazard, who jointly held $150,000 in stock and by far the largest stake in the company (over 30% of it), agreed to accept a lower priority on dividends for that block of stock. In other words, should the company make a profit, all the other stockholders—old and new—would get to share the dividends first, and White and Hazard would get a share of the profits only once everyone else had received a reasonable return. New investors could now take advantage of the company's straits to demand better terms. White had accessed the capital of the corporate elite, who in turn had consolidated its stake in a major waterway.[56]

Between 1822 and 1833, White's Lehigh Coal and Navigation Company became wildly successful and grew to be the most powerful entity in the Lehigh River Valley. Despite the contempt shown by the Schuylkill Navigation Company board, the Lehigh navigation beat its older sibling to market, shipping coal down the Lehigh in 1820. The company paid its first dividends to preferred investors in January 1822, its first dividends to regular investors that June, and its first dividends to White and Hazard a year and a half later; in 1826, all the stock was put on equal footing. Just like the Schuylkill Navigation Company, the Lehigh Coal and Navigation Company generated revenue from leasing waterpower and from tolls on lumber, iron, and especially coal: 365 tons the first season, 1,073 the next, 2,240 the year after that, and reaching the

Josiah White, mechanic-turned-entrepreneur-turned-corporate leader, in the 1840s. A. Newsam, artist, P. S. Duval & Sons, Philadelphia, engravers. Courtesy of The Historical Society of Pennsylvania.

amazing total of 123,000 tons of anthracite in 1833. Furthermore, unlike the Schuylkill firm, the Lehigh corporation had the additional privilege of being able to own and develop land, and so made even more of its profits on coal mining and developing town plots in South Easton, White Haven, Mauch Chunk, and Nesquihoning, all on company property. Josiah White's personal project had quickly become a big player in eastern Pennsylvania.[57]

That growth translated into power. When challenged by would-be competitors, White fought back in the papers and in the legislature by testifying just how great an influence—in his mind, a positive influence—the Lehigh Coal and Navigation Company had over the economy of Mauch Chunk, its principal depot on the river, and the areas through which the navigation flowed. He countered his opponents by claiming that when the company began construction, the area was a "wilderness" with fewer than ten families living within a dozen miles of the river landing. Now, though, "10,000 citizens are interested materially" in the continued success of the navigation. Having access to great pools of Philadelphia capital and considerable cash flow from toll and coal revenue, the company had expended close to $2.2 million in the area.[58]

Everyone in the region, White suggested, owed the company a great deal of thanks, and he was not shy to trumpet his interpretation of his corporation's accomplishments. He pointed out that his firm had "supported a population in and near Mauch Chunk, for a number of years, exceeding 1,500 souls." It employed over 500 people, "whose annual savings exceed $30,000 per year, which is put out to interest, or invested in lands or in trade." Echoing the refrains of bankers, White boasted that company shares were held in "a considerable portion by the working class—the widow and the orphan." In sum, he estimated that "10,000 souls are . . . supported . . . by the outlays of this concern, or injured by the long suspension of dividends." Even "pine forest owners," White claimed, owed the company thanks, "for raising and keeping up the value of the lumber" that before the navigation's construction was "not to be considered worth stealing, owing to the expense that would attend getting it to market." White's arguments were a paean to the company's diffusion of economic benefits.[59]

The company's critics cited the same statistics but offered a much less rosy interpretation of their consequences. In December 1832 a convention of angry Lehigh Valley residents met in Luzerne County to consider how to counteract "the monopoly . . . exercised by the Lehigh Coal and Navigation Company" and "the oppressive conduct of said company towards their fellow-citizens." These complainants argued that "the investment of near three millions of dollars" and "the great number of men under their control" resulted in "the immense influence the managers of that company now possess," and they feared "the advancing power of this mamoth institution." They pointed out that the company had kept up the price of tolls so as to make the cost of transporting coal prohibitive to its rivals. Also, despite the company's initial commitment to clear the Lehigh all the way to Nesquihoning, it had stopped a mile and a half short, because "their town of Mauch Chunk would cease to be the head of the navigation, and the old Lehigh landing, the property of others, would then occupy and possess the advantages of that enviable situation." By doing so, the company had "severely injured the owners of forests of valuable lumber," countering White's claim. Every place White saw benevolent growth, his opponents sensed malevolent dominance. In short, "the mass of the population ha[d] become either directly or indirectly dependent upon [the Company]," and had to "submit to great pecuniary sacrifices, or lend assistance to the perpetuity of their present power, and the advancement of their plans of prospective agrandizement."[60]

Though a talented inventor and indefatigable worker, White demonstrated his greatest abilities in exploiting people's economic ambitions in order to further his. In 1824, White had lobbied the state legislature for permission to run a steamboat navigation along the Delaware. White printed up petitions and sent them to friends in the region, asking them "to complete them and send them on to Erskine Hazard in Harrisburg or to [their] members as [they thought] best." He suggested pointing out to potential signatories that "every settler on either of the branches of the Susquehanna would have an interest in this improvement to the navigation." Soon after, a number of petitions covered with signatures arrived in Harrisburg. When White needed support in the legislature, he often wrote to Lewis Coryell, a New Hope sawmill owner who supplied wood for canal construction. "Please give us [your] accustomed activity in procuring signings to our Petition," White instructed Coryell, "& send by the bearer and retain a subscription paper to be sent on with what more thee can add to . . . Harrisburg." During the late 1820s, the Lehigh Coal and Navigation Company successfully lobbied the state to build a navigation along the Delaware River from where it met the Lehigh down to Philadelphia. The company's board of managers did not exaggerate much when it pointed out to the Pennsylvania legislators that its proposed "improvement of the Delaware must be a matter of deep interest to nearly one half of the population of this state and of New-York." White understood how to hitch his neighbors' ambitions to his own corporate wagon.[61]

Those arguments also worked very effectively to keep the legislature in White's corner but out of his hair. In 1835, he published extracts from an 1834 Pennsylvania Senate committee nominally charged with looking into the operation of coal industry. The committee had been formed at the behest of "a convention of delegates, representing several of the northern counties interested in the navigation of the Lehigh, asking an investigation of the grounds of complaint against the Lehigh coal and navigation company." Nonetheless, the committee defended the company. Declaring that the navigation was "admitted to be the best in the United States," the committee denied any wrongdoing on the part of the company, arguing that "whether they have adopted a wise or erroneous policy, which, by grasping after large tolls, may prevent them from receiving any, is a question between them and the stockholders." In other words, company officials, not the public, had the authority to decide what tolls would be charged on a river that previously had been legally defined as a public highway, open to all. That the committee so firmly backed the Lehigh Coal and Navigation Company confirmed the corporation's growing political clout. That said, the company's clout did not sit well with the White's detractors, some of whom began to resent that company officers "had carefully concealed" their motives in lobbying the statehouse, and so "had obtained an unjustifiable advantage over those who forwarded their enterprise."[62]

Despite the impressive leverage that White could bring to bear in the legislature, such influence paled compared to the company's power over the town of Mauch Chunk, a community built to become a corporate fiefdom. Nothing more than a hardscrabble landing on the Lehigh River in the 1820s, it was chosen by White as the loading entrepôt closest to the company's mines. By 1829, the company had paid for a hotel, a mill, a pair of iron furnaces, a store, a wheelwright's shop, and a school, among the more than 120 business and residential buildings its workers had constructed. The town that White built was no less "benevolent" than those constructed at Lowell, Massachusetts, in the same period. In keeping with his Quaker heritage,

White abolished the sale of hard liquor, kept a close eye on the one tavern—company-owned—and fired alcoholics and those accused of abuse or neglect either toward their families or to animals. He even set up a medical service for employees at a low annual pay-in cost, perhaps the first company-run health maintenance organization.

But in Mauch Chunk, too, there were two sides to the story. One visiting journalist observed that "stricter obligations are here prescribed and observed than could be enforced by the state." Other observers agreed, noting that the town and its surrounding area "presents a singular spectacle in the midst of republican Pennsylvania, of a dominion unknown to the laws." Owning all of Mauch Chunk, company officials had restricted immigration to the town and required not only the tavern keeper but also all others following a trade there to obtain a company license—even the shoemaker. Although local citizens did send their duly elected representatives to Harrisburg and Washington and were free to discuss economic, social, and political affairs at the local tavern, Josiah White's Lehigh Coal and Navigation Company was their true ruler. Even the region's most successful men understood that their fortunes were tied to mining and railroad corporations run from Philadelphia or New York. By the early 1830s, the corporate sphere dwarfed the public sphere in Mauch Chunk, Pennsylvania, and it would continue to for the rest of the century.[63]

Not all internal improvement corporations carried such weight or enabled their officers to throw it around like the Schuylkill Navigation Company or the Lehigh Coal and Navigation Company. In fact, most probably lost money, so their construction was essentially financed by a voluntary tax on those both able and willing to subscribe to stock with the assumption that doing so would lead to better market opportunities and higher real estate prices. Furthermore, most of those would be locally owned and run and would eventually fall into disrepair over the course of the nineteenth century as railroad technology became increasingly competitive on a cost basis. Most users of these navigations paid only for upkeep (in the form of tolls), while reaping many of the same benefits as did users of profitable operations like the Schuylkill and Lehigh navigations. Nonetheless, successful internal improvement corporation officers pioneered the methods that railroad executives would later use to the same effects. And although like navigations, most railroad corporations would not profit; unlike navigations, railroads could be connected and subsumed into larger systems that would consolidate metropolitan control over hinterland access to goods and markets.[64]

While both corporate and state-run early national internal improvements shared many of the same economic effects, they held differing consequences for distribution of economic power. Regardless of who ran them, major canals had the effect of allowing for a wider distribution of raw materials and finished goods, for intensified market participation, and for greater specialization on the part of farmers, artisans, and manufacturers. Just as Pottsville miners enjoyed their sea bass that had been shipped up the

Schuylkill navigation, Batavia residents reveled in the upstate-New-York availability of Long Island oysters shipped along the Erie Canal. Just as the Schuylkill Navigation Company promoted the use of waterpower for textile manufacturing at Manayunk, the various corporations promoted the use of waterpower for textile manufacturing on the Charles and the Merrimack rivers. In all these cases, whether prompted by corporate leaders or canal commissioners, state legislatures engaged in debates, and state courts wrangled with cases that pitted economic growth and the authority of canal administrators against property owners and traditional property rights, shippers against residents, and outsiders against locals.[65]

The main difference between corporate endeavors and their state-run equivalents lay in the increased economic power and authority that incorporation conferred on private citizens. The areas of upstate New York through which the Erie Canal traveled would not be economically dominated by New York City capitalists for many decades. But in both Pennsylvania and Massachusetts, urban capitalists in Philadelphia and Boston, respectively, gained great economic power over their hinterlands from the 1820s on. Citizens with grievances concerning the Erie Canal brought their complaints to a canal board appointed by their elected officials, but the people of Manayunk and Mauch Chunk had no such recourse against the depredations and dominance of the Schuylkill and Lehigh navigation companies. Philadelphia men had used corporations to extend their economic influence to the city's hinterlands. That would only continue with their later investment in railroads.

By the 1830s, Philadelphians no longer heard the steady dull roar of the Falls of the Schuylkill, through which water now flowed lazily; the Schuylkill had been tamed. Rather, they and other people living along the 108 miles of the navigation heard a more varied, more lively cacophony of boatmen, toll takers, laborers, passengers, merchants, brokers, buyers, and sellers. Similarly, the docks at Mauch Chunk became a beehive of daily activity. These sounds evidenced both the economic integration of the Schuylkill and the Lehigh river valleys into Philadelphia's corporate world and man's mastery over nature. From the turn of the nineteenth century on, nexus technologies like canals and river navigations constantly facilitated exchanges, leading to myriad opportunities for regional residents and to impressive economic growth. More than connections with other regions, transportation improvements of the Philadelphia region led to its transformation into a complex, primed, productive, integrated economic machine, with an ever-growing selection of ever-cheaper goods.

While many benefited from this process, the men who ran the institutions that facilitated it gained great sway over the entire region, in effect leveraging their position in the region's integration to further their own interests. Because anyone wanting to participate in the market between Philadelphia and the Lehigh or Schuylkill valley sections of its hinterland needed to transport their goods down the navigations, the two companies gained money and political clout from every sale up or down the rivers.

Previously, patrons had dictated those exchanges for their clients; now, municipal bodies or private companies used technologies such as the waterworks or canals to affect the terms of economic interactions. Those who controlled nexus technologies gained influence, but, as the term *exchange* implies, the technologies' users gained something as well. Schuylkill and Lehigh company officials used their waterway to centralize one kind of power while diffusing another. Along with banking corporations and municipal corporations, internal improvement corporations allowed for the exercise of unique facets of corporate power. When corporate men worked to coordinate their efforts, their influence would be greater still.[66]

CREATING A
CORPORATE SPHERE

*P*ennsylvanians had two choices in the 1820 gubernatorial election, Republican William Findlay and Federalist Joseph Heister. Neither hailed from Philadelphia. Furthermore, for the first time, party leaders did not choose the candidates in a closed caucus; rather, delegates came from around the state to attend nominating conventions to choose their partisan standard-bearers. Certainly it seemed as though the political power of elite insiders had most emphatically come to an end in the Keystone State, replaced by the open pageantry of the politics of the common (white) man. But just as Philadelphia corporate insiders worked to build individual institutions such as corporate banks, the city's municipal corporation, and corporate internal improvements, they also reached out across corporate lines, both socially and professionally, to reinforce their economic leverage in ways beyond electoral politics.[1]

In a typical gathering that summer of 1820, ten Philadelphia men got together for dinner. Many of the men had known each other for decades. A wealthy bunch, they included a doctor, a federal judge, two lawyers, a merchant, and several men who considered themselves "gentlemen." While the men may have gossiped, they also could have had quite a bit of legitimate business to talk over. George Vaux, the president of the city's select council, might have consulted with Joseph S. Lewis, select council member and president of the councils' Watering Committee, or he may have turned to state legislator William Lehman, himself a former member of the common council; together, they could have discussed a legal issue with William Rawle, often kept on retainer by the city, or with Richard Peters, longtime federal judge. Then their conversation could have turned to internal improvement. Vaux was also president of the Susquehanna & Tioga Turnpike Road Company, Peters the president of the Schuylkill Permanent Bridge Company, and William Lehman the superintendent of the Union Canal Company. Banking also might have been a fruitful topic, with directors of the Bank of Pennsylvania, the Bank of North America, the second Bank of the United States, and a major stockholder in the Farmers and Mechanics Bank all in attendance.[2]

American politics in general and Pennsylvania politics in particular entered a new era of egalitarianism, public pomp, and party organizing during the 1810s and 1820s, a sure sign that Philadelphia corporate men no longer held much sway over state-level electoral politics. In an age with an increasingly broad franchise and when appearing to be rural and rough-hewn could be exploited as political assets, no group would seem to be more strangely and ironically marginalized than silk-stockinged men whose primary exertions consisted of walking from fancy Philadelphia townhouses to bank offices and riding between the nation's second-largest city and their suburban country seats. Their retreat from competition at the ballot box was gradual but inexorable; the days when someone like Robert Morris could be a main figure in both politics and business corporations was nearly a memory. Furthermore, some wealthy Philadelphians completely withdrew from the pursuit of power, preferring to tend to the family fortunes and various cultural pursuits. Still, as the convivial August dinner demonstrated, the city's corporate men neither had become irreparably fractured as an elite nor had given up on power, and they showed in their private writings and in their professional conduct their desire to stamp their own sense of order within and among corporations that they found so lacking in electoral politics.[3]

The corporate elite in Philadelphia coalesced in the 1810s and 1820s. Through social, family, and business connections, a small group of men—no more than 300—came to hold the reins both of Philadelphia's Watering Committee and of the business corporations that together drove the city's and the region's economy. Because of the partisan composition of the first banking corporations, business rivalries, and limited natural resources, the corporate scene was always to some extent an arena of competition. However, by the 1810s the establishment of numerous banks, insurance companies, and internal improvement companies led a close and increasingly interconnected community of corporate insiders to mute political differences in favor of emphasizing common business and class interests. The evolving composition of Philadelphia's corporate elite reflected changes in the area's economic complexion. Though the first generation of corporate men had made their money mostly through trade, many of their sons and nephews used family money to move into manufacturing pursuits.

Furthermore, despite hitting their own common stride, corporate men often found themselves marching to a different drummer than the state legislature. Finding their views, interests, and personal political influence increasingly pushed aside from the rough-and-tumble of Pennsylvania politics, corporate officers and their friends endeavored to carve out a realm beyond the reach of what they considered grasping politicians and hidden from the eyes of a justifiably suspicious electorate. To do that, they developed an administrative and legal framework within which to control and to run their various projects. In that vein, corporate leaders pursued two interrelated goals. First, board members and other insiders worked to make corporations independent from the Pennsylvania state government. Second, corporate boards created structures to administer their tasks within the corporation and to coordinate policies between corporations. Their success in doing so allowed a small corporate oligarchy of several hundred men to have great influence over economic regulation and development in the Philadelphia area, to put themselves in position to reap disproportionately the rewards of that growth, and to use their leverage to further their greater class, economic, and policy goals. In nearly all cases, they worked together and separately to pursue a common agenda that emphasized extensive urban growth, privileging the wealthy over the poor, the city over the country, insularity over transparency, and elite policy making over democratic rule. Some of this elite, like the Wurts brothers, exploited their connections to the utmost of their ability, while others, like Samuel Breck, meticulously used the corporate sphere to bolster and reinforce their own sense of social and economic elitism. Together, these men and a couple hundred others carved out a separate, corporate sphere of activity.

The Philadelphia corporate sphere began with the Bank of North America but expanded to include insurance companies, internal improvement companies, and the city government. The generation that founded Philadelphia's first corporations had lived to see the incorporation of rival institutions in banking and insurance; the next generation of corporate officers found ways to bridge the political chasms between corporations to ensure their mutual success. The ebb and flow of politics gave men of various political persuasions the chance to join the corporate fraternity. The Bank of North America remained a Federalist stronghold beyond the 1790s. Republicans, meanwhile, had managed to push the Bank of Pennsylvania's charter through the legislature in 1793. With the arrival of the Philadelphia Bank in 1803 and the Farmers and Mechanics Bank in 1809, and a handful of others in 1814 (Bank of the Northern Liberties, Commercial Bank of Pennsylvania, Mechanics Bank of the City and County of Philadelphia, and the Schuylkill Bank), the club was complete. All the banks charged the same interest—6 percent annually—and offered the same services for a city in which the number of potential borrowers far outweighed the capacity for loans. Rather than engage in internecine fighting, bankers realized that they had common business interests: their desire to escape state regulation, their suspicion of country banks, and their fear of counterfeiters. Furthermore, as wealthy businessmen, they had common class interests that transcended political partisanship. The establishment of potentially rival business corporations in Philadelphia did not result in the ruinous competition that the partisans of previously chartered institutions had direly prophesied. Quite the opposite. The inclusion of seemingly disparate political groups into the corporate community effectively co-opted the most potent opposition to such institutions as the Bank of North America. From about 1810 onward, corporations endured a period of comparative political stability.

The composition of the City Corporation's councils followed a similar path as that of corporate banks. In the first election in 1789, Federalists gained twenty-two of the thirty-three available offices, including the new mayoralty, captured by Samuel Powel. Because it was elected on an annual basis, the common council functioned like a weathervane of the city's political winds. The select council was formed in 1796, and its members sat for three-year terms, thus lending a bit more continuity and stability. Still, in the few times that parties changed majority, there could be considerable council turnover. Regardless of party affiliation, though, there were always a few council members who moved within the same circles as insiders of other corporations. Furthermore, men from both sides of the aisle rubbed shoulders with other corporate insiders, especially as the number of banks and internal improvement companies expanded to include partisans of all political stripes.[4]

Direct overlap between business corporation boards and the councils was limited by some companies' charters, especially those of banks that explicitly forbade bank directors from holding political office. Nonetheless, the city's elected officials counted among the corporate elite. Longtime common council member Henry Drinker had been part of Morris's Society for Improvement of Roads and Inland Navigation in the state of Pennsylvania efforts and would later serve on several corporate boards, as would the son of common council member Benjamin Chew. Joseph Watson served as alderman and on each council at different points in the late 1810s and early 1820s; he also sat on the boards of several internal improvement companies. That integration, overall, decreased with time, as the business elite for the most part retreated from politics, though not completely, as some men continued to sit on corporate boards and on the city councils. At any time, as many as a third of council members had connections with banks or insurance companies. There was still enough interconnection for corporate insiders' concerns to be addressed in city councils: in the bitterly contested city elections of 1833, only one man gained nomination from both parties, Joshua Lippincott, who was a longtime director of the Schuylkill Navigation Company. For Philadelphia's corporate men, class interest trumped political partisanship.[5]

That class solidarity became increasingly clear with the maturation of the second generation of corporate insiders, a cohort less anxious about the fate of the republic but with an even keener interest in encouraging Philadelphia's growth than their predecessors'. It included men like Samuel Wetherill, Jr., the son of a prominent local paint-and-dye manufacturer, who pioneered the manufacture of white lead and mined much of his ore in the Schuylkill Valley; and Joshua Gilpin, a Delaware paper mill owner. Their interests often contradicted those of their merchant predecessors (and, for that matter, contemporary merchants, too), on a number of issues ranging from tariffs to credit policy. These men wasted little time worrying about the fragility of the nation but gave much thought to Philadelphia's economic prospects and how to push the city in directions that would ensure their own fortunes as well as their community's. Like many Philadelphians, they argued that the city's future lay in economic expansion inland rather than toward the Atlantic and that manufacturing would form a crucial component of that growth.[6]

The members of this second corporate generation appeared to have few doubts about the strength of the federal union, and even fewer hesitations about making a buck when they could, but many new ideas about how that money could be made. While some of these men were public-minded, others exploited the new corporate possibilities on a scale that might have shocked earlier generations. Maurice (1783–1854), William (1788–1858), and John (1792–1861) Wurts were born in Flanders, New Jersey. As a teenager, Maurice apprenticed to a dry-goods merchant in Philadelphia, and in 1810 William came to the big city to join his older brother as a partner in their own dry-goods business; John arrived two years later to clerk in a law firm. During the War of 1812, the Wurtses realized that whoever could bring an inexpensive, local source of energy to the market would make a pretty penny indeed. In 1814, William found anthracite in the far northeastern corner of the state, near the Lackawaxen River in what would eventually become Carbondale, Pennsylvania. After several false starts, in 1822 they began their mining activities in earnest. Their employee laborers extracted over a ton of the black stones, sledded them to the Lackawaxen River, and then rafted them down the Lackawaxen and the Delaware to Philadelphia. Meanwhile, the Wurtses' careers progressed in lockstep: John got elected to the Pennsylvania General Assembly, Maurice moved to New York, where he made valuable contacts in the financial community, including banker Philip Hone, and William's dry-goods business flourished in Philadelphia.

The Wurtses' ultimate achievement served as a fitting capstone to four decades of manipulation of corporation connections, often to the detriment of competitors and the public. Together, the Wurts brothers masterminded the organization, chartering, and financing of the Delaware and Hudson Canal, designed to bring coal from the northern anthracite field to the Delaware River and from there downriver to Philadelphia and by canal to the Hudson River and thence New York City. If the public interest entered their minds during the chartering process in the Pennsylvania legislature, they made no mention of it in their letters to each other during the 1823 and 1824 legislative sessions. Because the Delaware and Hudson Canal Company would own mines in addition to the navigation, John successfully campaigned in the legislature for a rate of toll that the brothers calculated would be low enough to be acceptable to the legislature but high enough for the company—which, unlike its competitors, would not have to pay tolls on its own coal—to acquire a virtual lock on anthracite shipped along its route to the lucrative New York City market. In addition, the company's charter, unlike otherwise similar ones, would never have to be renewed. "Tho' apparently for 20 years," John gloated in a letter to Maurice, "it is in fact a perpetual grant, at such a rate of toll as makes it a complete monopoly." The Wurts brothers considered the legislature in particular and the public in general as entities to be negotiated with at best and fooled if necessary. They showed no reluctance to use underhanded tactics on fellow investors, either. The Wurtses, in their frank and ruthless pursuit of their own interests in the corporate arena, presaged the nineteenth-century phenomenon of the robber baron.[7]

While the Wurts family portrait indicates change from corporate founders like Bingham and Willing, a moving picture of Philadelphia's corporate community might seem to move not much faster than a snapshot. The composition of corporate boards embodied stability, with most of the incumbents getting returned to their seats year after year. From the Farmers and Mechanics Bank's 1807 inception until 1830, its board had an annual 90 percent retention rate, most often losing only one incumbent and never more than four of the thirteen members from the previous year. Even this low rate of change exaggerated turnover, because some board members left only to return a year or two later. Internal improvement company board turnover could be high in the first few years of operation but generally settled into the same pattern as did financial corporations. Beginning in 1815, the Schuylkill Navigation Company returned twelve or more of its fourteen board members in every election but one during its first fifteen years of operation. In 1817, nine of the fourteen incumbents retained their seats, still retaining a strong majority of incumbents. With rare exceptions, board members held their seats until they retired from all business pursuits or until they died. Incumbent board members even outlasted the direst company crises and general economic downturns. The Farmers and Mechanics Bank returned most of its directors every year, despite the normal vicissitudes of banking and the upheavals of the Panic of 1819. Notwithstanding chronic money problems before the late 1820s, the Schuylkill Navigation Company did the same. Regardless of companies' fortunes on the unpredictable economic seas of the early republic, they kept the same hands at the tiller year in and year out.[8]

Boards' continuity of composition, combined with the longevity of many seat holders, demonstrated the degree to which a small group of men could dominate Philadelphia-based corporations. To some extent, board membership was self-selected: the vast majority of stockholders invested in corporations precisely to be able to reap steady profits while minimizing their own active involvement in business affairs, and perhaps few were willing and able to spend the time to sit on a company board. Incumbent directors handpicked new members when a seat came open, and sometimes a man leaving the board could anoint his successor. Even annual stockholders' meetings generally did not attract a majority of the investors. Widespread stockholder lethargy contributed to the ability of men with energy and connections to get on the board, and once there, to stay in as long as they wanted. Stockholders threw out few board members, but a number of board minute entries declared feelings of sympathy for the families of members who died in office. By then, of course, even unrelated board members may have felt like family to each other, having gathered together so many times over a period of years or even decades. And like family, they were quick to defend their common interests and to fight for common goals.

If one corporate board could be considered as a large nuclear family, then they all belonged to the same exclusive and cohesive Philadelphia clan. The interlocking of corporate boards resulted in a small community of men dominating Philadelphia-area companies. Although most banks had articles in their charter that forbade the holding of seats on other bank boards, insurance and internal improvement company charters had no such strictures prohibiting the holding of seats on the boards of potential competitors, and none of the charters addressed the question of holding seats on the boards of businesses that would not compete directly with the company in question. As a result, the same men got on the boards of multiple corporations, allowing intercorporation communication and cooperation. From the very beginning of Philadelphia corporations, the men who sat on the boards of the canal companies were often bank or insurance company directors as well. At any given time from 1800 to 1830, about a quarter of the men sitting on the boards of Philadelphia-based corporations held seats for multiple corporations. Some sat on many at once, men such as Jacob Downing, who in 1814 sat on the boards of the Bank of North America, the Lancaster and Philadelphia Turnpike Company, the Schuylkill Permanent Bridge Company, and the Pennsylvania Contributionship for Insuring Houses from Loss by Fire.[9]

In addition, at least a sixth of the men had relatives sitting on boards of other companies. John Nixon served as president of the Bank of North America from 1793 to 1808, and his son Henry served as a director from 1804 until the 1830s; the younger Nixon also sat on the Insurance Company of Pennsylvania's board from 1804 to at least 1830, the Ridge Turnpike Company's board in the late 1810s, and the Lancaster Schuylkill Bridge Company's board in the early 1820s. Brothers Robert and Jesse Waln shared a merchant business. Jesse Waln held seats on the boards of the Insurance Company of Pennsylvania and the Germantown and Perkiomen Turnpike, while his brother Robert held seats at various times on the boards of the American Insurance Company, the Bank of North America, and the Philadelphia Insurance Company. Their cousin Jacob was also a board member of the American Insurance Company, the Bank of North America, and the Insurance Company of North America. Relative William Waln also helped to direct the Bank of North America and the Philadelphia Insurance Company. Whether for inland navigation companies or other corporations, blood was thicker than water.[10]

Many board members had close business associates as officers in various corporations. Henry Drinker, the cashier of the Bank of North America from 1805 to 1821 and an early director of the Schuylkill and Susquehanna Navigation Company, speculated in lands together with Samuel W. Fisher, a director of the Germantown and Perkiomen Turnpike Company from 1805 to 1814 and the president of the Insurance Company of North America until 1805, when he became president of the Philadelphia Insurance Company, an office he held for over a decade. Both Manuel Eyre, longtime director of the Delaware Insurance Company of Pennsylvania, the American Fire Insurance Company, the Schuylkill Navigation Company, and second Bank of the United States, and Abraham Kintzing, who at various times sat on the boards of the Pennsylvania Insurance Company, the Schuylkill Permanent Bridge Company, and the Bank of North America through the 1810s, had apprenticed together for merchant Henry Pratt in the late 1790s. Pratt, who took Kintzing into his firm as a partner, later sat on the boards of both the first and second Banks of the United States, the Commercial Bank, the Insurance Company of Pennsylvania, the Insurance Company of North America, the Bustleton and Smithfield Road Company, and the Philadelphia and Lancaster Turnpike Company. Joseph Evans and John Welsh not only sat together on the boards of the Philadelphia Bank and the Delaware Insurance Company of Pennsylvania: Welsh took Evans into his firm, and Evans married Welsh's wife's younger sister. Whether through birth, brides, or business, the men on Philadelphia boards were bound together in myriad ways.[11]

This interconnection meant that men who individually or through familial or business ties represented their concerns in multiple companies held more than a third of the seats of Philadelphia corporations. In 1821, for example, Schuylkill Navigation Company president Cadwalader Evans, Jr., also sat on the board of the Bank of the United States; he was a former board member of the Delaware and Schuylkill Canal Company, and his father still held a seat on board of the Pennsylvania Company for Insuring Lives and Granting Annuities. Evans also had friendly personal and business dealings with Henry Drinker, the cashier of the Bank of North America, and Joseph Ball, a former president and current director of the Union Insurance Company. Three other members of the Schuylkill Navigation Company's board of managers also sat on the board of at least one insurance company, and a fourth had a brother on the boards of two insurance companies and the Bank of Pennsylvania. This core of men who sat on several boards or who had families or associates on various boards formed the nucleus of influence and opinion guiding Philadelphia's growth.[12]

That influence extended to the City Corporation of Philadelphia and often concentrated in the Watering Committee. For the city's first bond issue to raise funds for the waterworks, the city councils named commissioners to sell the instruments. Eight of the twelve men listed moved in corporate circles, including notables Jacob Shoemaker, Edward Tilghman, and John Inskeep. Many men alternated between sitting on the city councils and sitting on corporate boards. James Vanuxem, for example, who served on the Watering Committee for several years of its first decade and as its president in 1806, sat on the boards of the Union Insurance Company, the American Fire Insurance Company, the Germantown Turnpike, and the Delaware and Schuylkill Canal Company. Some families had connections in both the city councils and corporate boards: Jacob Shoemaker's brother Abraham sat on the city councils off and on from 1801 to the early 1820s. Samuel Wetherill would become head of the Watering Committee in 1824, once Joseph S. Lewis left that position to assume the presidency of the Schuylkill Navigation Company.[13]

Others extended their influence even further: during Cadwalader Evans's tenure as Schuylkill Navigation Company president, he also sat for several years in the Pennsylvania legislature. Robert Waln, on the boards at various times of the Bank of North America, the Philadelphia Insurance Company, the American Insurance Company, and the Insurance Company of North America, not only held a seat on Philadelphia's common council in the early 1790s and select council in the early 1810s but also was elected to the Pennsylvania House of Representatives for two terms in the 1790s and the United States House of Representatives in 1798. John Sergeant, counsel for and board member of the Schuylkill Navigation Company, the Union Canal Company, the second Bank of the United States, the American Fire Insurance Company, and the Pennsylvania Company for Insuring Lives and Granting Annuities, gained a seat in the Pennsylvania House of Representatives and sat on its Roads and Inland Navigation Committee for the 1807–1808 term before serving four consecutive terms in the United States House of Representatives, beginning in 1815, and being Henry Clay's running mate in the 1832 presidential election. The Philadelphia corporate community was both connected well and well connected.[14]

The interconnection of corporate boards had a number of consequences for Philadelphia's corporate community and its behavior, exhibited in a number of ways. The most obvious was the possibility for corporations to work together to set prices or policies, as Philadelphia banks eventually did. Another was simply the communication of business information and the diffusion of business techniques: by sitting on various boards, men learned what was going on in a variety of businesses and could transfer one corporation's techniques to another. The connection between financial firms—banks and internal improvement companies—and other kinds of corporations, including the municipal corporation and internal improvement corporations, allowed for cash-poor firms to have access to capital and for creditor corporations to monitor the behavior of their debtors. Finally, the close interlocking of corporate boards provided for a sense of community and common economic and business interests among the economic elite, one that in many instances could transcend intercorporate competition or political differences.[15]

Philadelphia's corporate men made sure to keep their projects in familiar and trusted hands. At first, corporate boards did their best to administer their projects on their own, often depending upon one or a small number of their members to do most of the work. Internal improvement companies in particular usually relied upon their presidents to do much of the necessary work to keep the business going through the construction phase and beyond. The deciding factor in who would hold ultimate power over a given internal improvement usually hinged upon that most basic of business principles: capital. Erskine Hazard, the son of Schuylkill Permanent Bridge Company board member Ebenezer Hazard, teamed with Josiah White to supervise the construction and much of the early administration and financing of the Lehigh Coal and Navigation Company. White had mechanical talent and drive in abundance, and Hazard great meticulousness, but at the time neither possessed subtle political sensibilities or the deft financial touch that White would later demonstrate. Compounding their problems—or perhaps symbolizing them—neither White nor Hazard got elected for many years to the board of the company they had founded. White and Hazard's company started as a three-man undertaking (the third, George Hauto, turned out to be a confidence man who, upon being discovered, was subsequently bought out by the other two). Eventually it gained a large infusion of capital from big investors. Having great sums invested, these later entrants demanded control over the management of their funds. They did not worry over precise technical details: they could pay White and Hazard to oversee construction while keeping the overall direction of the company in their own hands.

Other company boards were more explicit about choosing men with expertise in account books rather than mechanical diagrams. The Schuylkill Navigation Company's board of managers chose a new president in 1825, and the selection process included an explicit admission that their decision was informed by a desire to pursue class interests rather than a need to guarantee technical competence. With Cadwalader Evans, Jr.'s, resignation from the presidency, the company's board of managers looked for a replacement. Evans had divided his energies among many pursuits and projects, but now that the project was substantially operational the board wanted someone who would work full-time for the company. They first considered hiring an engineering expert, but competent engineers were in short supply, and furthermore the navigation's impending completion somewhat obviated their need for a full-time engineer. They also thought about employing a superintendent for the works, admitting "It is possible that such an officer may be found necessary, as well as inferior superintendents, limited to portions of the line over which they should maintain a continual personal inspection."[16]

The main concern of the Schuylkill Navigation Company board members was not with minor technical matters or everyday operations. Rather, "the capital invested is large, the navigation is of great and increasing importance," reasoned the managers, "and the public have in various ways an interest in preserving its activity and usefulness, which, no less than the interest of the Stockholders, calls for continued & even increased watchfulness and care." In other words, they feared that improper management of the Navigation might give "occasion to great public complaint" with concomitant political consequences along with raising their own ire. Besides the assumption that an engineer might not be politically adept, the objection to hiring an engineer to run the company would be that "his inferiority of station . . . would prevent him from having the needful freedom in communicating with the Board, and from having the requisite weight and authority in his intercourse with others." Insiders wanted an executive who could deal with public pressures, but even more, a peer who would defend the board's interests as if they were his own. So they picked one of their own, to the unanimous affirmation of stockholders: Joseph S. Lewis, who had helped negotiate the company's $230,000 loan from Stephen Girard, served on the boards of various insurance companies and had been president of Philadelphia's Watering Committee. The selection of Lewis signified the board's desire that the company put its strategic economic and political goals ahead of its technological tactics in building and maintaining the waterway.[17]

Banks, too, kept important leadership positions in familiar and trusted hands. While internal improvement companies often required the services of an engineer, each banks had its own specialist, a cashier. The cashier oversaw account keeping—a major task for banks with hundreds of active customers—the issuing of notes, and routine bookkeeping; supervised the clerks and other employees; and made day-to-day management decisions. A close circle of men dominated these positions, both by necessity and by board preference. Nobody in Philadelphia had run a full-fledged corporate bank before their founding, and the city's most accomplished businessmen were the best at keeping track of complicated financial projects. Even those who worked their way up the ranks did so through family and professional connections, joining the corporate oligarchy as they climbed the corporate ladder. Quintin Campbell, a Scottish orphan who had immigrated to America as a cabin boy, served as a clerk for Levi Hollingsworth and became a virtual member of the powerful Hollingsworth flour merchant clan. His patron secured him a job as a clerk with the Bank of Pennsylvania; in 1804 he became the first teller for the Philadelphia Bank and, when cashier Joseph Todd died, replaced him and kept the position well into the 1830s. Toward the end of his long career, Campbell also sat on the boards of other companies, confirming his induction into the corporate elite. Once ensconced as cashier, men tended to stay for a long time, lending stability to the institution while ensuring that both the pecuniary and social interests of the board remained primary.[18]

Like all families, the corporate community found ways to take care of its own. This meant not only bringing in sons and sons-in-law as clerks and colleagues; also a safety net was provided for those who might otherwise tumble back into the mass of Philadelphia society. Despite banks' nominal forty-five- or sixty-day note limit, bank boards routinely rolled over loans to insiders, essentially carrying them over until they got their hands on some cash. As one of their investments, insurance companies granted mortgages; more than a few of these went to insiders' friends and families. And boards protected community members who went astray. In 1823, a clerk admitted to having pilfered $1,100 from the Schuylkill Bank. Cashier Hoseah Levis explained to bank president William Meredith that he had pledged everyone in the bank to secrecy about the entire affair, so as "to be able to preserve in a degree the feelings of a large & respectable family—and [the clerk] the degradation of being looked upon as a common felon" (while for most common felons, no doubt, stealing $1,100 was beyond their wildest dreams). Of course, Levis acted to protect more than one man's reputation; he also feared "that a circumstance of this kind, and at this moment, being made public would jeopardize the reputation of the Institution." Regardless of the motivation for keeping the debacle confidential, the result was that a wayward son with family connections received far more lenient treatment than even the most petty of thieves. When it came to issues of class, the corporate men kept their solidarity.[19]

No matter how cohesive, all communities endure conflict. Despite their many connections and a common general social and economic outlook, members of Philadelphia's corporate elite sniped over strategy, dickered over details, and wrestled for resources. Divisions in the corporate elite tended to be the most bitter when they occurred within a single corporation. Most such battles remained in the boardroom, but the messier ones spilled out into more public squabbling. The 1811 merging of the Schuylkill and Susquehanna Navigation Company and the Delaware and Schuylkill Canal Company into the Union Canal Company set off an open and acrimonious contest between the original stockholders who had sold out to salvage what they could of their initial investment and new stockholders whose shares suddenly held value. In the late 1810s, a rancorous debate split the Lehigh Navigation and Coal Company in two. Many investors considered the corporation's rights to the Lehigh River to be its best asset; they calculated that tolls on the navigation and the leasing of waterpower to millers would yield a steady flow of dividends. Other stockholders thought the heavy investment in the navigation to be a financial albatross but expected the company's real estate in coal country would lead to a bonanza. When both sets of shareholders came to their senses and realized that neither venture would be profitable on its own, they reorganized into the Lehigh Coal and Navigation Company, in 1821. While the existence of such conflicts demonstrated that the corporate elite and even the boards of individual companies were far from monolithic, they also showed the limits of corporate disagreements in that the debates were over the tactics of the bottom line rather than the strategies of control over resources and capital. On those more fundamental issues, Philadelphia's corporate insiders closed ranks.[20]

Samuel Breck personified the common class outlook of the corporate elite. The son of a grand Boston merchant—also named Samuel Breck—he had the great good fortune to have picked his relatives carefully. After spending the early 1780s attending a French military academy, in 1792 he followed his father to Philadelphia, to which the elder man had recently moved, ostensibly to escape the high Boston taxes but more likely to take advantage of the better business climate in the Quaker City. The senior Breck quickly joined the board of the Bank of the United States. Staked with $10,000 in family money as a twenty-year-old, Breck speculated a bit before settling into stable investments in stock and real estate. Breck sat on the boards of the Union Canal Company, the Lancaster Schuylkill Permanent Bridge Company, and the Schuylkill Bank, often attending board meetings and stockholder meetings. He also entered politics, and his terms in the Pennsylvania House of Representatives in the late 1810s proved to be an apprenticeship for his service as a representative in the 18th Congress. He would return to Harrisburg as a state senator from 1832 to 1834. The long-lived Breck remained a prominent member of the corporate elite nearly until his death in 1862.[21]

Even more than his professional attainments, Breck's daily calendar, ambitions, and prejudices gave a social face to Philadelphia's corporateers. In 1795, he married Jane Ross, the daughter of Bank of Pennsylvania director John Ross. Two years later, they settled in Sweetbriar, an estate he had built on the west side of the Schuylkill River. "It is a fine stone house," he happily recorded, "fifty-three feet long, thirty-eight broad, and three stories high, having out-buildings of every kind suitable for elegance and comfort." The grounds, too, staked his claim as a member of Philadelphia's social elite. Visitors to the estate could admire "the prospect," which "consist[ed] of a river . . . of a beautiful sloping lawn, terminating at that river . . . of side-screen woods; of gardens, greenhouse, etc." And unlike the Anglophiles of the previous generation, Breck was unafraid to adorn his villa and grounds with Italian and French decor. Breck's choice to live across the river from the city not only demonstrated his wealth and social attainment; it also effectively marked his retirement from everyday commercial activity.[22]

Still, Breck remained busy following his investments, educating and doting on his only daughter, and dining with his peers. In his diary he noted a social scene populated with other corporate men, often dining together after board meetings. A typical party at Sweetbriar included among its number bank president William Meredith, Schuylkill Permanent Bridge Company president (and neighbor) Richard Peters, and nearly a quorum for a Union Canal Company board meeting; had all the invitees been able to attend, there would have been at least one board member there of each of seventeen Philadelphia-area corporations. The elite who dined together stuck together. As he took care of his friends, so he made sure to take care of his family. In 1821, Breck turned down a request that he run for state Senate, preferring to attend to "the education of [his] daughter." In his solidarity with other corporate men, in his graduating to a life of leisure, in his continuing of his family fortune, and even in his conviction that manufacturing was Philadelphia's future, Breck exemplified the second generation of the city's corporate elite.[23]

Just as Breck and his colleagues defined themselves by the houses they built and the company they kept, they did their best to separate themselves from working Philadelphians not only socially but also through the use of corporate investments and corporate power. The second-generation corporate elite raged against the lack of deference paid them and when possible used corporate connections to reestablish what they deemed to be the proper order of things. Despite having almost nothing but kind words for his corporate compatriots, Breck looked askance at those he considered below himself on the social ladder. He constantly disparaged his employees, grumbling that "fickleness, drunkenness, and not infrequently insolence, mark the character of our domestics." The "insolence," clearly, bothered Breck the most; in 1822, he complained bitterly about the "vile calumnies . . . propagated too by men to whom I have paid thousands of dollars for work and always treated with civility and kindness." He found "the preponderance of Democracy" in his district simply intolerable. At the same time, Breck's position in the corporate elite allowed him access to authorities and legal stratagems unavailable to most residents, and he was all too willing to use them to put his inferiors in their places. After a near-accident on the Schuylkill Permanent Bridge in 1820, he approached friend, neighbor, company president, and federal judge Richard Peters in a vindictive effort "to prosecute a hackney coach-man, who put the lives of two respectable citizens in jeopardy, by rash driving." Breck explained that "an example, now and then, keeps those people in order." In more ways than financial and political, corporate men used their institutions to bolster their dominance over the city and its environs.[24]

They continued that dominance, generation after generation, even as the city changed. Beginning in the 1810s, Philadelphians began transforming their city from the self-proclaimed "Metropolis of America" to the proud "Workshop of America." Although the city remained a coastal and oceanic entrepôt, it increasingly functioned as a manufacturing center, with local shops producing lead, iron, soap, textiles, hats, steam engines, and a host of other finished goods. Manufacturers and tradesmen then sold most of these goods within the region, sometimes directly through their own networks but more often with the help of distributors. In the first decade of the nineteenth century, Quaker City manufacturers exported products worth $505,774, five times the value in goods that they had produced the decade before. After the disruption of the War of 1812 and the Panic of 1819, production once again skyrocketed: Philadelphia exported over a $1 million from 1825 to 1829, twice the value in goods that they had in the entire decade at century's opening. The composition of the third generation of the corporate elite reflected Philadelphia's newfound manufacturing muscle. Samuel Breck used his connections with Manayunk manufacturers J. J. Borie and Marks Richards to help two of his nephews enter manufacturing, rather than mercantile pursuits. His encouragements in that direction typified the transformation of the city as well as a corporate elite entering its third generation.[25]

The social consolidation of Philadelphia's corporate elite helped drive the social cohesion of the Quaker City's upper crust. This stratification process had begun nearly the instant William Penn set foot in the capital of his new colony. Over the course of the eighteenth century, fewer and fewer Philadelphians controlled more and more of the wealth of the city. Even before independence, the richest twentieth of Philadelphia's population owned over half the city's wealth. However, over the next half century, corporations contributed not only to the stability of the very rich but also to the engrossing of most property in the hands of the well-to-do: by the 1830s, the bottom three-fifths of the population owned less than 1 percent of the assessed residences of the city. That is not to say that Philadelphia's corporate community and its social elite were one, but that there was considerable overlap. Furthermore, even the members of Philadelphia's social elite who did not participate in corporate affairs nearly all profited from corporate investments, as lists of stockholders suggest. Men like Samuel Breck came to expect that corporations would simply be another tool by which they could set themselves apart from their less fortunate neighbors.[26]

Perhaps to compensate for their lack of control over and deference from their less well-heeled neighbors, Philadelphia's corporate leaders strove to create an orderly corporate sphere. By marking off their own arena for debating and administering Philadelphia-area corporations, corporate officers defined a space sequestered from state officials, from public debate, and even from the agitation of stockholders. On the one hand, they were at least nominally subject to state authority, and the Corporation of Philadelphia was a publicly elected government. Many of their proceedings were technically matters of public record, though corporate officers kept terse minutes and made records public only when doing so would show their institutions in a positive light on a very narrow, particular issue. Corporate men conducted their business in an environment that the close circle of corporate officers and their friends attempted to put beyond the realm of the public. Shareholders elected corporate board members in meetings limited to those owning stock, and even those proceedings represented little more than an affirmation of incumbent board members or their chosen successors. Once chosen, directors made decisions regarding the region's economic future behind closed doors. They directed their many employees, from lawyers and lobbyists to lock keepers and laborers, to do their bidding. In addition, they had economic leverage over many people not in their employ and decided among themselves how to use that leverage. By the second quarter of the nineteenth century, corporate activities formed a sphere of social interaction unto themselves.

Charters and corporate bylaws became the prime vehicle for defining the corporate sphere within a given corporation. Charters could be written or amended only through an act of the legislature; thus theoretically, they were the product of legislators (although they were largely composed by applicants). However, corporate board members and insiders wrote all of a company's bylaws, constituting a corporation's internal code of operation. This set of rules outlined the roles of officers and the internal procedures of the organization. In practice, corporate boosters wrote most of their own charters, and charters and bylaws overlapped considerably, especially regarding the voting privileges of stockholders, for which legislators often insisted upon graduated plans in efforts to keep larger stockholders from dominating elections and votes. Taken together, charters and bylaws provided the legal and procedural structure for regulating the corporate sphere. The progression of intracorporate codes from the 1790s to the 1830s demonstrated that the corporate sphere became a place with its own peculiar modes of conduct both for the municipal corporation of Philadelphia and for business corporations. Like so many other features of Philadelphia-area corporations, these strictures followed British precedent; they also developed in ways that limited popular access to the corporate decision-making process and concentrated policy making to a small number of insiders. Various rules governing stockholder voting, the election of board members, and meeting protocols began with eligibility of stockholders to vote and continued through the particularities of board member conduct. Considered as one body of rules, they clearly demonstrated corporate leaders' efforts to solidify their control over their institutions while establishing a corporate culture to their liking.[27]

Though certainly thankful for investors, corporate officers did their best to limit stockholder involvement in management decisions. One way to insulate the board from stockholders was to limit stockholder participation. Business corporations' charters all called for at least one annual stockholders' meeting, and most required two weeks' public notice in several newspapers; some also delineated what day that would take place and where. The initial intention of such laws was to ensure access to meetings for all stockholders. Nonetheless, some company boards even enacted rules that, whatever their design or motivation, clearly limited the participation and influence of the body of stockholders. In 1823, the Schuylkill Navigation Company amended its bylaws to allow the board of directors to call a stockholders' meeting at only five days' notice, rather than the thirty days previously required. The intent may have been to allow the board to consult with the stockholders on a timelier basis. However, for an enterprise administering an unfinished internal improvement project stretching through 108 miles of occasionally rugged country, five days was not enough for people far up the river to receive notice, make arrangements, and travel downriver to Philadelphia. If travel were that easy, no navigation would have been needed in the first place. Thus, the change essentially limited stockholder participation in potentially important emergency meetings to Philadelphia-area investors. Those Philadelphia stockholders would be more likely to sympathize with the Philadelphia-dominated board in potentially controversial votes over the allocation of resources to the upper or lower section of the navigation. Through a seemingly innocuous bylaw change, the Schuylkill Navigation Company board consolidated its control over the company.[28]

A similar shift occurred in the area of stockholder voting, in which board members and associated large stockholders did their best to limit oversight from within as well as from outside the company. Despite their apparent design to put large and small shareholders on an equal footing, corporate structures minimized the influence of all but the largest, most active, and most vocal stockholders. Almost every charter included a system of graduated stockholder voting for both director elections and changes in company by-laws—that is, the internal rules for the company's operations as written by the stockholders and the board—a practice directly derived from British precedent. The Lehigh Coal and Navigation Company's 1822 charter granted one vote for any number of shares owned up to ten; another for each ten if holding between ten and one hundred shares; one more vote for each twenty shares up to five hundred; and three more votes for every one hundred shares above that. Banks tended to have the most circumscribed voting rules: the 1809 Farmers and Mechanics Bank charter allowed each stockholder one vote for each of the first two shares owned, another vote for every pair of shares up to ten owned, a vote for every four shares between ten and thirty owned, a vote for every six shares between thirty and sixty owned, a vote for every eight shares up to one hundred owned, and a vote for every ten shares owned over one hundred. No stockholder was allowed to have more than thirty votes. Though graduated voting rights had been designed to minimize the influence of large stockholders, they also helped to ensure that control of the company stayed in the same hands. With most small stockholders staying home rather than attending stockholders' meetings, only those diehard shareholders from the company's founding tended to vote, resulting in the same men being returned to the board year after year.[29]

Corporate insiders had varying attitudes toward the use of proxies, that is, the practice of allowing stockholders to authorize an agent to cast their votes in elections and other shareholder ballots. Proxy voting tended to favor insiders who could amass large blocs of stockholder votes. Accordingly, the initial draft of the Bank of North America's charter allowed stockholders to appoint proxies. The plan generally worked, sometimes to an alarming degree. The elder Samuel Breck's proxy rights in the first Bank of the United States allegedly "were so numerous, that for many years he had the agency of a majority of the stockholders, and by consequence the whole control of the Election." Still, his son claimed that "never was power lodged in safer hands. Never was a bank better administered, or wound up more easily and satisfactorily." Other corporate insiders looked more skeptically at proxies. When Farmers and Mechanics Bank founder Joseph Tagert haggled with the legislature over that company's first charter, he instructed his agent in Harrisburg to "strike out all about proxies" in the bill. He considered all the possibilities: local stockholders "ought to attend elections personally," but "if they do not feel sufficiently interested in the choice of directors their shares ought not to be made use of for the purposes of intrigue." Those stockholders living farther away, he argued, "cannot be sufficiently acquainted with their fellow stockholders, to give an opinion on the merits of the different candidates unless they come to the place of election in which case they will be entitled to vote." By combining reason with self-interest, Tagert made sure that he and his cronies would control the bank for decades to come. Corporate men differed on particular tactics but agreed upon the basic principle of stable, secure insider control.[30]

The inclusion of such clauses in many company bylaws as well as corporate charters suggests that they reflected the intentions of corporate founders and of the board of directors as much as those of cautious or perhaps hostile legislators. Though welcomed by legislators as apparent attempts to limit the influence of large capital, these measures had the collateral effect of securing control of the corporation for the founding group. Small shareholders rarely worried over who ran the company or how, desiring rather what they had invested for: the building of the internal improvement or the issuing of dividends. For their part, corporate board members and their associates cared greatly that their command of the company remain unthreatened. Because stockholding in most corporations was broad, low turnout at annual and even emergency stockholders' meetings ensured that board members and their friends could muster enough votes to quell any potential investor rebellion. Thus, the rules against proxy voting and the exchange of stock for voting purposes immediately before stockholder meetings functioned to prevent outsiders buying stock in the short term or acquiring proxies in order to change the company's management or direction. In short, they kept the affairs of the company in the same hands that had founded it.[31]

In addition to constructing corporate bylaws intended to limit stockholder input, corporate leaders occasionally used the courts to take action against stockholders, though, as with their legislative dealings, such initiatives met with mixed results. By 1803, the board of the Delaware and Schuylkill Canal Navigation had lost its patience with recalcitrant stockholders who had fallen behind in their subscriptions. The company's charter gave officers two options to hold shareholders' feet to the fire: one was to sue for the value of the unmade installments plus legal interest (at that time, mandated to be 6% a year), the other was to declare the shares forfeited and be free to resell the shares. Obviously, given the state of the company, the prospect of trying to sell shares did not offer much promise, so the company's board proceeded to file lawsuits. The move signaled the desperation of company managers willing to pay legal costs, alienate shareholders, and distract themselves from the business of completing projects long overdue, underfinanced, and overbudget. William Sansom had failed to keep up with installments both for the five shares he had bought directly during the initial subscription drive and for the fifteen shares he had subsequently bought from others. Rather than throw good money after bad, he directed his lawyers to argue that he could choose to forfeit the shares (the cheapest way out of what he undoubtedly perceived as a money pit). In a Solomonic decision, the Supreme Court of Pennsylvania split the difference: it ordered Sansom to pay up for the shares that he had originally bought but released him from further obligation on the ones he later picked up. The court had upheld the authority of the company and its charter while limiting stockholder exposure.[32]

Given the unpredictability of courts and legislatures, corporate officers worked to achieve better order over venues that they could control. Insiders not only kept the corporate arena insulated from many stockholders and the public but also shaped conduct within the corporate sphere in ways that limited wide-ranging discussion. Corporate bylaws delineated a code of behavior, especially in the context of board meetings. Generally, the rules governing such meetings resembled pared-down versions of parliamentary rules: the president called the meeting to order, recognized speakers, and brought matters to a vote. The councils governing the Corporation of Philadelphia worked to streamline their operation while curtailing discussion and stifling dissent. In their 1803 bylaws, the common council prohibited any member from "speak[ing] more than twice on a given issue" without a majority vote, but motions to adjourn were always in order, resulting in an atmosphere in which dissent could be swept away in a rush to the door. Such strictures were far from unique; neighboring suburban governments operated under similar rules.[33]

Of course, if even council members suffered to be gagged on occasion, the public was less lucky. A 1796 amendment to the city charter commanded that "the doors of the respective halls of the said Select and common councils shall be open, for the admission of all peaceable and orderly persons, who shall be desirous of being present at the discussion of any bye-laws, ordinances, rules or regulations, for the welfare and good government of the city." But at least in the perception of common council members, not all people who wanted to attend council meetings constrained themselves to "peaceable and orderly" conduct: in 1802, the common council denounced the habit of "certin evil disposed persons" who "made it a practice to attend in the lobby of this council & to behave in a noisy, indecent manner," and ordered the constable to be present at future meetings "for the purpose of preserving order." Perhaps the councilors were protecting themselves from the catcalls and jeers of tipsy interlopers, but they certainly also availed themselves of their authority to use force to silence the voices of potential opponents.[34]

For both the city councils and business corporations, the corporate sphere had a common code of behavior alien to contentious legislatures, raucous taverns, bustling coffeehouses, or quiet homes. Rather, the corporate sphere was an ordered space for insiders to discuss the strategy, tactics, and operations of their institutions. Just as the city corporation did, bank and canal corporate boards passed bylaws that limited board debate to a minimum. They too required the president to call a meeting to order, set strict two-comment quotas on individual topics, and offered common rituals of seconding motions and majority rule. This priority on efficiency could also potentially lead to sloppiness. Bank boards decided weekly upon "discounts"; that is, they examined applications to decide who would receive loans and for how much. Despite the care that such operations required, one dissenting board member complained that "cases have occurred of the discounts of a Bank being done in 25, 30, and 35 minutes," arguing that "such despatch is utterly incompatible with a sound or correct procedure." But as long as no one objected, business moved quickly. At least the municipal corporation recorded yea and nay votes in the required minutes; the clerks of business corporations saved ink, paper, and their wrists by only mentioning whether boards passed a measure, rejected it, or tabled it for another day, giving curious stockholders the impression that most decisions were unanimous. The lone theoretical exception to such practices were instances in which a banking board voted to pay stockholder dividends that cut into the bank's initial capital; because the practice was illegal and board members endorsing such actions could be held liable, charters provided for dissenters' names to be noted in the minutes. But in early republic Philadelphia, that rarely happened, if ever.[35]

Ideally, board meetings were solemn affairs, but the reality differed widely. The specificity of some corporate bylaws suggests that some boards resembled a social occasion rather than a meeting of hardened businessmen. Not only did the Bank of Philadelphia's bylaws forbid members from interrupting each other or the chair, it also explicitly directed them to "avoid all private conversation." Those men who violated the code put their positions at risk. In 1822, a few Schuylkill Bank directors successfully purged John Horner from his seat, because of "his coarse and overbearing behaviour at the board." Horner did not appear on another board until his election to the common council in 1829, where, presumably, his colleagues never summoned the constable to kick him out among the riffraff; his movement from the business corporate sphere into more popular politics seemed emblematic of the growing rift between corporate culture and political culture. The increasingly elaborate rules for discussion demonstrated the need for such deliberative bodies to make decisions quickly, with a minimum of dickering and debate. After all, the men who sat on boards and councils had other affairs that demanded their attention, and without some ability to obtain consensus or closure, meetings could have taken all day. Limiting debate was more than a practical measure: it ensured a minimum of controversy. Corporate officers could thus provide a united institutional front.[36]

Corporate men also did their best to coordinate efforts across corporations. Company officers engaged in two general modes of intercorporate cooperation: one to regulate the economy, the other to promote economic growth. Once chartered, Philadelphia's corporate bankers had little to compete over. Their charters stipulated that they could charge no more than 6 percent interest, by which they all abided; they all offered similar services and their notes were discounted at similar rates in the city and beyond; and they all had more potential customers than, in aggregate, corporate banks could accommodate. However the city banks faced common threats, especially the comparatively inflationary policies followed by incorporated country banks. Accordingly, Philadelphia bank officers cooperated to regulate their own behavior and thus collectively to set local money supply and currency policy. Internal improvement companies competed with each other in some areas (different toll rates for coal shipping, for example, could have the effect of stimulating more mining activity and thus more business on one or the other navigation) but behaved sympathetically in others. Nonetheless, nearly all officers in Philadelphia's corporate world—both business corporations and the municipal corporation—shared an interest in particular kinds of economic growth, especially those related to increased commerce, so they cooperated to foster that goal. Of course, regulation and promotion could overlap considerably. A central assumption of regulating the money supply was that stable currency and a regular supply of credit could help banking customers and thus lead to increased economic activity. Conversely, corporate leaders assumed that the Philadelphia region's economic expansion would also contribute to economic, social, and political stability. But these two general patterns involved different motivations and took on distinctly different forms.

Bank officials did not need to interlock their directories to coordinate their regulatory activities. Most direct communication between banks began on an ad hoc basis. Depending upon the situation, representatives of bank boards met to hash out mutual solutions to common problems. In reaction to an 1810 specie shortage partly resulting from the impending close of the first Bank of the United States, Farmers and Mechanics Bank board members suggested that "some understanding ought to take place respecting the intercourse between the different Banks in the present Crisis," and they approached the boards of other banks to suggest a conference on the matter. That meeting resulted in an agreement among Philadelphia banks "for mutual support, and a free communication of sentiments, to constitute the respective cashiers a Confidential Committee." The attendees resolved "to confer together, and enter into such regulations, & make such arrangements, as may appear to them, best calculated for the general good on the present peculiar & interesting occasion." Thus began a pattern of more routine interbank coordination.[37]

Eventually, the largest Philadelphia-based chartered banks held joint meetings, usually sending their cashiers as representatives. These men gathered at the behest of any one of their number in regard to particular issues that might require the cooperation of banks across the city. One such set of meetings took place in 1814 at the suggestion of Henry Drinker, the Bank of North America's cashier, after the legislature chartered forty-one new banks. He wrote to the boards of the city's three other established chartered banks, the Bank of Pennsylvania, the Philadelphia Bank, and the Farmers and Mechanics Bank, proposing that they adopt a joint policy on the acceptance of these new banks' notes. Ultimately, the group decided, for the time being, to accept the notes only of those banks in Philadelphia city or county and, for the satellite branches of the Bank of Pennsylvania and the Philadelphia Bank, to accept only notes from banks in the same location as the branch. Later they took such notes but discounted them heavily (that is, paid fewer than one hundred cents on the dollar for them). On another occasion, the same group agreed not to issue or accept any note with a face value under five dollars, despite the state's vacillation over its restrictions on low-denomination issues (the legislature forbade and then allowed the issuing of notes below five dollars at least twice between 1814 and 1820). The prohibition on interlocking directories did not inhibit the big Philadelphia banks from acting in concert on issues that affected them collectively.[38]

The coordination of bank policies showed the extent to which Philadelphia corporate associates extended the corporate sphere, extralegally controlling banking and monetary policies for the Philadelphia region and indeed for the entire state. Their decision to accept only the notes of some rather than all of the banks chartered in 1814 revealed that bank directors held far more sway over money policy than did public authorities. The big-city bank directors argued that they were doing their best to keep the money supply at safe levels, thus limiting inflation and the chance of a run—a point they would bring up during the Panic of 1819, which many observers blamed upon the excessive issues of the forty-one banks chartered five years earlier, with some reason. As for the issuing of notes below five dollars, Philadelphia bankers provided the discipline that elected representatives and some of the poorly run country banks could not. Certainly, some kind of financial regulation was necessary, and the legislature's sporadic, occasionally strict but invariably toothless measures proved inadequate. If the government would not or could not rein in the excessive printing of banknotes, with its inherent danger for the entire economy, at least Philadelphia bankers claimed to have tried their utmost to give Pennsylvania's economy a solid foundation while providing capital for growth. Nonetheless, no matter how much the banks' collusion may have been motivated by the desire to follow sound financial policy, it also reflected the clout of the Philadelphia banking community and its ability and willingness to use that power.[39]

There was only one problem: Philadelphia bankers eventually engaged in the same deflationary practices as country banks, and in defiance of stipulations of their own charters. Of all corporate banks' obligations, the one unanimously agreed upon required banks to honor their notes by paying the bearer the equivalent amount in gold or silver (known as specie payments). Otherwise, the prevailing wisdom went, a corporate banking charter became a license to print money that eventually no one would be willing to take. But Philadelphia's corporate banks fell into a vulnerable position in 1813. Unincorporated banker Stephen Girard presented over $1.1 million in their notes and demanded specie, in retaliation for their ongoing hostility. The next year, with the economic crisis of the War of 1812 escalating and specie scarce, there was nearly a nationwide run on the banks. Like their counterparts in Baltimore and New York City, Philadelphia's bankers decided to suspend specie payments in the late summer of 1814, although in a rare public meeting, Philadelphia's corporate bankers pledged to restore specie payments at the end of the conflict. The value of Philadelphia banknotes quickly plummeted to about 85 percent of what they had bought before. Had specie payments been resumed with the restoration of peace, the suspension might have been regarded as a regrettable necessity of wartime. But even in February 1817, with the postwar economic recovery in full swing, Philadelphia corporate bankers only "nominally" announced the resumption of specie payments, "sensible that their power over the community was so great" that no one would dare demand specie, as a later (toothless) legislative investigative committee charged. Accordingly, banknotes continued to circulate at about 80 percent of their nominal value.[40]

Philadelphia's corporate bankers had extralegally enacted their own private debt relief program. By not honoring their notes, they essentially defaulted upon their implied contract with the public, leaving noteholders to swallow the difference between the dollar values printed on cash and the actual value those notes commanded in the marketplace. Furthermore, by no longer having to demand specie from lenders to back future loans, bankers now could extend preferential treatment to inside borrowers who had fallen on hard times. They had announced resumption of specie payments only in response to antibank petitions to the legislature, but, with the bankers' public assurance of resumption, the House committee on banks backed off, and the banks were not held to their pledge. Suspension was an ironic act for the merchants serving as corporate bank directors. Just two years later, they would blame the Panic of 1819 on farmers and consumers who in the previous years had lived beyond their means, and would oppose legislative measures to relieve poorer people's debts in that economic crisis. Through their financial might, corporate bank officers managed to save themselves and their institutions—in direct defiance of the charters under which they operated—while criticizing their fellow citizens for the same financial sins that the bankers themselves had committed, namely, letting the optimism of good economic times go to their heads. The difference between the corporate bankers and other economic actors is that through their combined capital, banking insiders had the wherewithal to engage in questionable, partial, and even illegal business practices, knowing that there would be fewer consequences for them than other Pennsylvanians might face.[41]

While bankers worked together to protect their own interests, the officers in nearly all Philadelphia-based corporations cooperated to pursue policies that primarily promoted extensive economic growth, that is, growth through increased commerce, though within a system ostensibly fair but that favored those already with access to capital and transportation. Indeed, prevailing economic thought presumed that economies must either grow or decline, and, given Philadelphia's competition with Baltimore and New York, standing still did not seem like a viable option. Corporate insiders understood that such growth would have the collateral effects of helping mercantile firms' hinterland and export business, offering new markets for local manufacturers, and providing opportunities for local real estate speculation. Accordingly, Philadelphia corporate officers made sure to see that internal improvements had the resources that corporate men deemed necessary for the city's economic expansion and thus future viability. Rather than through common meetings, though, as bankers did to coordinate activities, economic promotion generally occurred through informal contacts between particular institutions.[42]

The interconnection of boards allowed the corporate community to allocate funds from money-rich corporations to cash-poor internal improvement projects. The Schuylkill Navigation Company in particular benefited from such coordination. In August 1817, Pennsylvania Company for Insuring Lives and Granting Annuities board member Cadwalader Evans, Sr., convinced his colleagues to approve purchasing thirty shares in the navigation company, notwithstanding that it was far riskier than the usual insurance company investment. Evans could at least vouch for the quality of the navigation company's management, because his son and namesake was the president. In 1821, William Boyd convinced the Pennsylvania Company for Insuring Lives and Granting Annuities to invest $20,000 in the Union Canal Company. It was no coincidence: Boyd was on the boards of both companies. Three years later, the Schuylkill Navigation Company's board of managers authorized a $180,000 loan negotiated from a group of bankers, insurance company officers, and the organizations they represented, who subscribed on the condition that they would hold a mortgage (subject to the prior claims of financier Stephen Girard) and that they would be obligated to pay in only if the entire subscription were filled. Investors included the American Marine Insurance Company, subscribing for $5,000, and the Marine Assurance Company, subscribing for $10,000. The city government, too, lent a hand when it could, primarily by investing money from its sinking fund in internal improvement company stocks. In this way, the corporate community supported local economic development by funding internal improvement projects for which they may not have expected any direct returns.[43]

Sometimes, Philadelphia corporate officers managed to manipulate their relationship with the state government to further local promotional aims. Eager to renew their charter in 1823, Philadelphia Bank partisans considered several offers to the legislature in exchange for reincorporation. Eventually, they negotiated for the bank to make a one-time purchase of $100,000 in the Chesapeake and Delaware Canal Company rather than the bank giving its own stock or a cash bonus to the state. Legislators could justify the deal by pointing out that the bank paid for its new charter by supporting an important internal improvement. Compared to earlier charters, though, the legislature had come away with relatively little. Rather than holding out for cash to relieve the immediate tax burden or bank shares to ease the long-term tax burden, representatives settled for a transfer of wealth from one corporation to another. The men on the boards of the bank and the canal company had used the chartering process to get something both wanted: in the bank's case, a low price for the charter, and in the canal company's case, a useful infusion of cash. In essence, these men saved the bank from paying the state a bonus, because they might have made the same transaction anyway, even had the state required a cash bonus for the bank charter. George Gillaspy, one of the Philadelphia Bank's founding members, sat on the Chesapeake and Delaware Canal Company's board of managers and at least three men currently or formerly on the bank's board had family ties to men on the canal board. They easily could have gotten the bank to buy the shares. The state's endorsement made the exchange easier, because now the bank's board did not even have to justify to stockholders its investment in the struggling canal company. By coordinating their lobbying efforts, the two boards had paid less to the state and had done an end run around the bank's stockholders while transferring funds from a company that easily attracted investment—the bank—to one that had more trouble doing so. In the process, Philadelphia corporate insiders found ways to promote internal improvement.[44]

Corporate officers had a purpose behind those deals beyond convenience and business shrewdness: they also followed an agenda designed to promote Philadelphia's economic expansion in a way that fit their view of urban capitalist economic growth, and when push came to shove, they had to decide between competing priorities. During 1832–33, Philadelphia's corporate insiders had to make such a choice. Given the limited resources of the Schuylkill River's waters, what was more important, increasing the traffic capacity of the Schuylkill Navigation or ensuring a steady and adequate supply of water to the city, its suburbs, and their residents? Leaders of the Schuylkill Navigation Company and the Philadelphia municipal corporation eventually came to an arrangement that favored the former, thereby guaranteeing an increase in value of navigation company stock, commercial real estate on the river's banks, and other investments in the Schuylkill River Valley at the expense of water supply to the city's suburbs, which would lose their water first should there be a shortage and where none of the company directors lived. For a dozen years, the officers in particular worked together in impressive efforts to share and exploit the waters of the Schuylkill River both to supply the city with water and to increase the city's reach into the hinterlands. And even when the two companies eventually conflicted, they did so in a way that kept their dispute primarily within the corporate sphere rather than spiraling into an affair that could damage them both.

Watering Committee and Schuylkill Navigation Company insiders began their relationship in 1819. The Watering Committee bought land at the Falls of the Schuylkill, a rocky stretch of water upstream of the city. This purchase and the subsequent construction of the Fairmount Waterworks and Reservoir at the site required the cooperation of the Schuylkill Navigation Company. The city would be diverting large quantities of Schuylkill water both for the new reservoir and for the new works to pump the water. The navigation company, for its part, wanted to ensure that it would be able to collect tolls and retain enough water for the locks to be operable. Accordingly, the two corporations arranged a complex series of deals from 1819 to 1824 that provided for the city to build and maintain a lock navigation around the dam according to Schuylkill Navigation Company specifications. The navigation was on city property. All tolls went to the Schuylkill Navigation Company, as did a one-time payment of $26,000 that helped the cash-strapped concern complete construction elsewhere. In return, the city retained all the rights to the actual water of the Schuylkill not required for the navigation, a big concern for the growing metropolis. The solution gave both parties what they wanted: for the navigation company, cash and a proper facility at no cost; for the city, a guaranteed supply of fresh water; and for both sets of corporate men, conditions for future economic growth.[45]

The agreement turned out to be short-lived because the Schuylkill Navigation Company succeeded beyond even the company's grandest expectations. In 1824, a pamphlet writer optimistically estimated the navigation's annual downstream capacity at around 540,000 tons—and that assumed traffic 24 hours a day, 250 days a year. None of these figures was realistic, given the inevitable delays because of weather, canal repairs, and other unforeseen circumstances; a more likely figure would be around 350,000 tons. In the following years, the company continued to widen particular bottlenecks so as to increase capacity. But by 1832, traffic volume reaching an amazing 327,921 tons, with no limits in sight. Accordingly, in 1832 the company began building a second set of locks at the navigation's busiest points along the lower part of the navigation, putting in eight new locks alongside the original ones in order to double capacity. On October 2, citing "the very great increase of trade along the Schuylkill," company officials informed the Watering Committee that they intended to do the same at Fairmount, the location of the city-built and city-owned locks. The new lock would be dug right at the location of the current lock tender's house—John Gotwalt's home was a perk of his employment with the city. On December 8, 1832, Joseph S. Lewis, the president of the Schuylkill Navigation Company, wrote to Gotwalt instructing him to vacate the premises so that the navigation company could build the new locks. The company wanted to be ready for even greater profits, beginning with the 1833 season.[46]

That the Schuylkill Navigation Company came into conflict with the city corporation of Philadelphia over the building of the new locks demonstrated many of the ways that the two corporations had grown in importance to the city and, indeed, to the region's economy. Company supporters claimed with some justification that the "navigation . . . has, in its results nearly doubled the population of city, extended its borders even beyond William Penn's ambitious framework, caused the banks of the fair Schuylkill to teem with life from its highest sources to its very mouth." The increase in availability of anthracite did more than benefit coal-mining areas: it contributed directly to the establishment of Philadelphia as a capital of steam-engine production in the 1820s and 1830s. Succeeding early steam pioneer Oliver Evans, men like Matthias Baldwin and William Norris began making steam engines for locomotives, establishing Philadelphia as perhaps the world's premier city for the manufacture of railroad engines. The building of those steam engines required great quantities of steel, metal requiring such high heat to work that anthracite became the fuel of choice for steel mills.[47]

While the availability of coal allowed the production of heavy machinery sent all over the world, the value of products sent up the navigation actually exceeded the value of those coming downstream. On an annual basis from

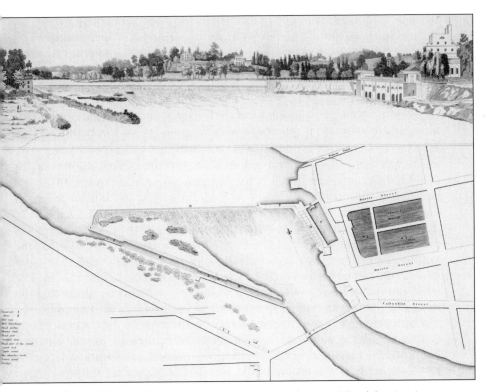

Above, an image of the Schuylkill River looking north from the middle of the river just west of Philadelphia, and below, a schematic of the river improvements there. Each shows the Schuylkill Navigation canal on the left, the dam across the river in the center, and on the right the Fairmount waterworks. T. Birch, Philadelphia c. 1830. Courtesy of The Library Company of Philadelphia.

1831 to 1835, about $4,000,000 worth of goods made their way south and east along the Schuylkill toward Philadelphia, but over $6,000,000 in value traveled north and west into the hinterland, away from the city. Given that Philadelphia County's population in 1830 approached 200,000 people, the Schuylkill Navigation Company alone accounted for approximately $50 per person every year in regional trade coming to and from the metropolis. The company's board asserted that "the additional work at Fair Mount has become so essential to the accommodation of the increasing trade on the river, that without it the navigation will be much impeded." According to their terms, the city's commerce could grow only if the navigation could be expanded at high traffic points, especially at Fairmount.[48]

But the silver lining of economic growth came accompanied by a dark cloud of increased demand. Though of course in favor of greater commerce, the Watering Committee had legitimate concerns that the operation of a second set of locks at Fairmount might threaten the city's flow of water and, for that matter, water revenue. The city's growth, the extension of the waterworks into the suburbs, and greater per capita water use had resulted in the expansion of the waterworks and its administration. The first plan for the waterworks had been based on an expected need of one million gallons a day, a figure quickly increased by half during the construction of the engines; the contract for the engines stipulated a total capacity of up to three million gallons daily. By late 1811, the Watering Committee decided to build two new reservoirs, each with a one-million-gallon capacity. Six years later, peak needs approached two million gallons daily, but the narrow wooden mains could handle only half that. Complaints that summer led to the 1818 construction of wider iron water mains capable of delivering five million gallons in a twenty-four-hour period. Within a year, the Watering Committee was already planning the Fairmount works, with its projected ability to supply up to ten million gallons daily, and by 1825 it was supplying four million gallons on the hottest summer days. By the early 1830s, demand was so high that during dry spells in the summer the level of the Schuylkill dropped far enough that the city could not draw water from it without violating its contract to ensure that the navigation had enough water to operate. The water used by an additional lock had the potential to lower the reservoir even further.[49]

That increasing supply of water flowed to all districts within the city limits and to the neighboring suburbs of Spring Garden, the Northern Liberties, and Southwark. It also resulted in a great deal of money for the city coffers. In 1826, for the first time, water rents exceeded direct outlays spent maintaining the waterworks; in 1827 the city gained a $4,800 surplus, and revenues had continued growing quickly. Furthermore, the Watering Committee controlled water policy not only for the city but also for the metropolitan area, and its members perceived the building of another set of locks as a short-term threat to the performance of the waterworks and as a long-term threat to the city's public health and continued growth. John P. Wetherill, chairman of the Watering Committee, wrote to Joseph S. Lewis, "granting facilities to the increasing coal trade" should be matched with "corresponding facilities . . . to meet the increasing demand for water power arising from the rapid growth of the City and the neighbouring districts." The navigation and the waterworks truly were at the nexus of economic activity and urban development.[50]

The ways that the Schuylkill Navigation Company officials went about building the new locks demonstrated the company's use of its financial, ideological, and technological leverage, over even the Watering Committee. After so many lean years during construction, the company had become rich. Issuing its first dividends in 1829, the company could afford to expand in 1832 because it was flush with cash. The company also had the legal authority to build more or less whatever it wanted in connection with the navigation of the river as well as to invoke the power of local law enforcement against anyone who opposed it. When Lewis's letters to the Watering Committee did not result in Gotwalt's voluntary removal from the toll keeper's house, he called William Simpson, a Philadelphia County sheriff, to evict Gotwalt. In order to do so, Lewis invoked the 1826 measure that various canal companies had helped push through the state legislature that included a clause allowing canal companies to call local constables to remove "refractory" toll keepers from company premises. Corporate boosters had been able to get that clause passed as part of a litany of infractions that could slow traffic along the navigation—impediments to the technology that the company had built. Beyond having the money to build and the authority to destroy, company officials could rely on the paid manpower and the loyalty that came with employment. When Simpson came to evict Gotwalt, the sheriff was accompanied by a score of burly Schuylkill Navigation Company employees. In financial terms, in legal terms, and in technological terms, the Schuylkill Navigation Company held a great many cards in its hand, even compared to a city corporation governing over 80,000 people.[51]

The arguments that Lewis and company lawyers put forth to defend their action to construct another lock conveyed their sense that the Schuylkill Navigation Company controlled the river. Responding to a Watering Committee offer to negotiate a solution acceptable to both parties, Lewis denied that "the alterations in the use of [Schuylkill water] at Fair Mount, are such as makes it proper for them to communicate those alterations to the City Councils for their approbation." Lewis flatly stated that the navigation company "Board [did] not suppose that the right to use the water and water power of the river for the purposes of navigation to the extent that they may deem necessary, is subject to any question." Later, company lawyers would argue that even if the company had wanted to sell water rights to the city, the original charter did not authorize the selling of those rights if doing so impeded the navigation of the river as determined by the company—notwithstanding that the city's purchase of water rights beyond what the company used at the time was clearly the purpose of the 1824 agreement costing the city $26,000. Before the incorporation of the company, the Schuylkill River, like all waterways, was legally a public highway. In late 1832 and early 1833, the Schuylkill Navigation Company successfully asserted its ownership of the river and its right to use it in perpetuity, and could arrest anyone who interfered with that right. The Schuylkill River had once been a public highway, but by the 1830s it was wholly owned by the Schuylkill Navigation Company.[52]

The intimacy of the corporate community also played a part in the Schuylkill Navigation Company's successful building of its new locks at Fairmount. When Lewis wrote to Watering Committee chairman Wetherill, it was with a certain degree of familiarity. The two men typified the degree of interconnection between and among Philadelphia corporations. John P. Wetherill's brother Samuel closely linked Lewis, Wetherill, and the two corporations. Joseph Lewis and Samuel Wetherill served on the board of the Schuylkill and Susquehanna Canal Company from 1807 to 1811. Separately,

Samuel Wetherill had served on the boards of the Bank of Pennsylvania, the Schuylkill Bank, the second Bank of the United States, the Germantown Turnpike, and the Union Insurance Company—and, in 1823, the Schuylkill Navigation Company. In addition to Lewis's many corporate appointments, he had not only served on the city councils but also was chairman of the Watering Committee from the late 1810s well into the 1820s, negotiating the 1819 and 1824 agreements on behalf of the Watering Committee. Through all the letter writing, Wetherill did not take the step of filing suit to halt company construction. Despite his letters of protestation about the company's actions, Wetherill and the rest of the Watering Committee never actually did anything that would stop the Schuylkill Navigation Company from completing its expansion. Long after the construction was over, the city corporation sent a halfhearted petition of protest to the legislature in April—too close to adjournment for legislative action—and finally filed suit in June. In asserting their control over the river, Philadelphia's corporate men had shown that they were in charge of the Quaker City's economic development.

The denouement of the affair showed how even in conflict, corporate men used their power to protect their institutions through the limiting of public debate. Although they disagreed, corporate insiders did their best to bury the controversy, both because Schuylkill Navigation Company officials did not want that sort of trouble and because the Watering Committee had long boasted members from both parties. Accordingly, the big issue in the city elections of 1832 was the city councils' administration of the considerable fortune that Stephen Girard had left to the city several years before. Leaders in neither party wanted to bring up the Watering Committee–Schuylkill Navigation Company dispute as an election issue. Their common interests far outweighed public concern regarding, in one pamphleteer's words, the city's "most cherished improvement, its most important security against pestilence, its only safeguard against conflagration, its best source of revenue, [and] the object of its honest pride." Such protests fell on deaf ears. As one anonymous, enraged Philadelphian noted, "only one vote was given against the Watering Committee" during its confrontation with the Schuylkill Navigation Company, "and that vote was given by JOSHUA LIPPINCOTT, Esq." Lippincott no doubt felt safe to vote that way, knowing which direction the political wind was blowing; his seat on the council remained so secure that he became the only man chosen by party bigwigs to run on both tickets for the next city elections. And that was not the only position that the man safely held: Lippincott was a longtime director of none other than the Schuylkill Navigation Company, a seat he continued to hold for several more years. Lippincott knew as well as anyone that a full-blown political controversy involving the Watering Committee and the Schuylkill Navigation Company would benefit neither and possibly endanger both, and he no doubt did his utmost to ensure that the corporate sphere would be preserved.[53]

By creating that corporate sphere, the Philadelphia associates placed themselves at the forefront of the formation of a new corporate class in and across the industrial cities of America. Despite the passage of a federal constitution that clearly reinforced elite political and economic interests, perhaps the rise of a coherent, national economic elite could not have been possible during the first half century after the Revolution. Although at times they might support particular policies, the economic interests and social norms of eastern, southern, and western merchants, planters, manufacturers, lawyers, and politicians precluded any such unity. They may not even have shared snobbery, given that each looked upon the other's values and lifestyles with less respect than disdain. But Philadelphia's corporate men could look at the rising elites of Boston, New York, Baltimore, Pittsburgh, and other big cities and probably see much that looked familiar. In these and in other, smaller cities, small groups of men founded banks, transportation companies, and other corporations, and often worked hand-in-glove with officials in municipal corporations. Despite differences of background, religion, and party affiliation, when it came to local and regional economic policies they found much in common: a suspicion of popular government at the state level, a desire for limited credit expansion that benefited those of their class, and a vision of economic growth that privileged cities over hinterlands, insiders over outsiders, and the already wealthy over those less fortunate.[54]

At the same time, Philadelphia's corporate leaders were not running a malevolent oligarchy silently trampling the rights and will of the people, all for a small thrill and an extra half cent on the dollar. Through their creation of a corporate sphere, they fulfilled a variety of functions that state and local governments sometimes could not or would not perform. Corporations provided a framework to mobilize credit for economic development, raise funds for internal improvements, pursue rational money-supply policies, and provide a safety net for struggling projects. In husbanding Philadelphia's economic expansion from the 1790s to 1830, the city's corporate business elite kept the city's economic and population growth on a pace exceeded only by New York and Baltimore, both of which had already been growing faster in the 1780s and had better harbors and easier geographical access to their hinterlands. By three of the most important economic measures—real wages, productivity, and population—Philadelphia's economy in 1830 vastly outperformed its 1790 predecessor. At the same time, corporate men touted and promoted economic expansion while eliding the more vexing and troubling questions of the social consequences of that growth and how it was distributed.[55]

Still, the Philadelphia associates proceeded largely on their own and preferably with as little public input and comment as possible, and while the whole city grew, company partners profited disproportionately from economic expansion and regional economic integration. From the 1790s to the 1830s, the concentration of wealth, status, and influence among a small number of elite families in Philadelphia became increasingly pronounced, and the ways that corporations were administered in terms of credit policies and land and resource allocation certainly played a large part in that consolidation. While Manayunk manufacturers profited from their access to raw materials and inland markets, the workers in their factories suffered from increasingly poor working conditions and eternally low wages. Board members did not duck the responsibilities that came with their influence, but they minimized the burdens when they could and were not reluctant to grab the rewards when opportunity called. The corporate associates had built a corporate sphere in Philadelphia.[56]

milling, and ironworking that contributed to the Philadelphia region's becoming an industrial powerhouse. Tocqueville arrived at the moment when Philadelphia made the transition from being the late eighteenth-century "Metropolis of America" to the "Workshop of America" in the second third of the nineteenth century. The availability of cheap transportation, inexpensive clean water, and credit made that evolution and expansion possible.[1]

Despite this economic explosion, U.S. democratic politics and political culture impressed Tocqueville most and became the subject of his instantly famous and long-enduring work, *Democracy in America*. Tocqueville found that the social leveling instinct of the majority of the population and the structure of government combined with nearly universal white male suffrage had led to a strong and stable democratic state that nonetheless held the potential for tyranny of the majority. Not surprisingly, he first entertained such thoughts in the Pennsylvania portion of his American sojourn. From its first settlement, Pennsylvania's ever-widening mosaic of geographic, ethnic, religious, and geographic diversity had ensured a colorfully fractured political picture, but two things that an increasingly large electoral majority could agree upon were a resistance to elites and an aversion to increased taxes, both of which many Pennsylvanians still associated with the danger of centralized authority. Similarly, Tocqueville abhorred centralized power as a medium for majority despotism. But he distinguished between "governmental" centralization, by which he meant a single authority in each state to make the laws, and "administrative" centralization, that is, bureaucracies that ran large sectors of the economy or society. Tocqueville argued that "only the first exists in America, the second being unknown." Furthermore, he wrote that the rule of the majority had marginalized a resentful and brooding American upper class whose members had been thrust "almost entirely outside politics" and, as a result, become an impotent elite. Despite getting so many things right, here he fired slightly off the mark.[2]

The young Frenchman had not traveled to Mauch Chunk, not struggled to secure a bank loan, nor had he paid high suburban water rents to subsidize Philadelphia property taxes. Without such experiences, Tocqueville had not been exposed to corporate power. That said, he had observed the disdain that members of the corporate elite held for their fellow citizens. In a conversation with Roberts Vaux, a former Philadelphia common council member and brother to Bank of Pennsylvania director George Vaux, the Philadelphian confessed to him, "I have never approved of the system of universal voting rights; in very truth it hands over the governing power to the most passionate and least enlightened classes of society." Vaux would have preferred a Senate "chosen by the large property-holders." Such attitudes differed little from those manifested by Bank of Pennsylvania president Joseph Norris's behavior toward Mathew Carey; Norris "never [treated] in this manner those whom he consider[ed] his equals." Josiah White's stern rules governing behavior in Mauch Chunk were no less condescending, nor was the Watering Committee's treatment of Frederick Graff. Tocqueville certainly detected the existence of elites. He noted that "the wealthy classes . . . form, within the state, a private society with its own tastes and enjoyments," though by that he meant elite society and not necessarily an American corporate elite. Little did Tocqueville realize that corporate men had also formed, within the state, their own space from which to project great influence over Philadelphia and indeed much of Pennsylvania.[3]

Tocqueville's inability to detect Philadelphia's corporate sphere despite his lengthy, detailed, and perceptive study of American society and politics testified to the success and demonstrated the limits of Philadelphia's corporate elite. Merely in the Quaker City, seven banks, a half-dozen canals and river navigations, as many turnpikes, a dozen insurance corporations, even the municipal corporation—the corporate sphere rendered all these powerful, highly capitalized, sometimes labor-intensive institutions nearly invisible to even the most acute observer of popular politics, precisely because Tocqueville did not participate in the American economy. And that anonymity was exactly what corporate men wanted. They desired not only to be able to run their businesses as they saw fit; they also hoped to be able to project influence over the direction of economic growth and to have sway over how the fruits of that growth would be distributed without much notice by the public. They knew such clout would elude them in electoral politics, and so they found other ways to channel what assets they did have— money, technological and legal expertise, and financial savvy—to cut a significant slice of economic control out of the public sphere. And once those elements of economic policy had been removed from the hands of public officials, the ideology of liberalism that corporate men championed made putting it back in nearly impossible.

Perhaps the reasons for Tocqueville's failure sheds light on the difficulties historians have faced regarding the transformation in the geography and structure of economic power in the early national North. Until the Revolution, the connections between wealth and governance simply could not be missed. Members of economic elites dominated nearly every colonial government, and Pennsylvania was no exception. An observer ignorant of eighteenth-century Anglo-American sartorial customs who watched governors' councils and colonial legislatures might have confused lace ruffles and silver buckles for a uniform of office. The proof was in the legislative pudding: electoral districts that overrepresented established eastern counties compared to growing backcountry areas, land-distribution policies that favored the wealthy and well connected, and laws that privileged property over labor typified policy at the colonial level. Until the Civil War, that dominance of government by economic elites continued in the South, where the planter gentry ruled over their plantations, their counties, and their state governments, always conscious to subordinate all policy issues to the continuance of what some northerners derisively labeled the "slaveocracy," and it was easy to spot both for contemporaries and for later scholars. But in the North, especially in Philadelphia during the first few decades of the republic, the elite seem to have made more money but beat a political retreat, grumbling to their townhouses, banished from government, and garnering little respect from their neighbors. Both Tocqueville and many historians have confused this decline in social and political authority with a general lack of power.[4]

Just like Tocqueville, historians have recognized the many ways that the early republic seemed to be the era of the common (white) man, whose stridency in American politics and culture seemed to indicate that the United States had become an egalitarian polity, devoid of whatever deferential, hierarchical characteristics the former British colonies had exhibited. Strengthening that trend of the diffusion and devolution of political power, the federal government remained a fairly small operation whose presence in most people's lives remained limited to the operations of the local post office. Scholars debate the extent to which state-level institutions mediated among various interests, but in the main arenas of political and legal contestation, state legislatures and courts sometimes found ways to protect everyday people from the predations of their wealthier or more aggressive neighbors as well as from the ravages of the marketplace. At the same time, the burgeoning of a self-conscious middle class appeared to show that the incipient capitalism of the early republic served to mitigate the power of elites while providing more opportunity for those at the lower rungs of the social and economic ladder. Combined, these trends would seem to suggest that the American Revolution and the revolutionary settlement had succeeded not only in establishing independence from Britain but also in breaking the power of the old elite and putting it in the hands of common people at the local level.[5]

Furthermore, Philadelphia's corporate leaders were far from omnipotent, nor was the corporate form universally adopted. One particularly large segment of the Philadelphia economy—the building trades—operated mostly without resorting to bank credit. Philadelphia's property laws allowed for a ground-rents ownership structure that enabled master carpenters to build on speculation, thus obviating the need for bank loans, though developers also did take out mortgages and loans from merchants. Many other urban entrepreneurs also flourished without going to the banks for credit; innkeepers, tanners, and brewers did not rank highly among the groups that procured loans from corporate banks, though the perseverant and lucky operators in all those trades certainly profited and found ways to expand their operations. The city's largest manufacturing industry, the textile trade, showed that Philadelphia entrepreneurs could produce not only for a local but even for a national market without bank credit, again often leaning on the mercantile community for capital. In addition, when Pennsylvania passed its general manufacturing and incorporations laws in the late 1840s and early 1850s, few groups took advantage of general incorporation, and Philadelphia's textile manufacturers in particular continued to prefer partnerships over corporations to organize their enterprises, notwithstanding their competition with the incorporated mills of Lowell. Beyond Philadelphia, Pennsylvania's sponsoring of the Main Line project showed that the state was indeed capable of large-scale projects, even if public officials did make a poor bet with their combination canal and inclined-plane system rather than opting for a railroad. And while the city corporation grew, it became in some ways more firmly under the thumb of state government than in earlier decades.[6]

In addition to these limits to the effects of early republic corporations, Andrew Jackson's war against the second Bank of the United States further obscured to historians the lasting sources of the growing role of corporations and corporate power in American life. Jackson's rhetoric and bearing implied to many of his followers (and later students of the Jackson presidency) that his attack on the bank constituted no less than an epochal struggle against entrenched economic elites that threatened to dominate the nation's nascent democracy, and his ultimately successful campaign was blessed by having the perfect foil in bank president and urbane Philadelphia patrician Nicholas Biddle. Both historians and contemporaries have seized on the fact that in declawing and eventually destroying the "bank monster," Jackson eliminated the only early republic corporation of national scope, one whose directors wielded the clout to affect national money supply and credit policies and did not hesitate to use it to force local banking institutions to adjust their practices accordingly. At the same time, early national and scholarly observers acknowledged that Jackson's actions greatly benefited the "pet banks" that now received federal deposits and no longer had Biddle and his cronies looking over their shoulders. While Jackson certainly exaggerated the bank's power and its effects (some of which actually helped the economy by preventing state banks from running amok), he was not wrong in saying that it was an undemocratic institution that, if abused, could wield dangerous political and social influence. But in defeating the bank, Jackson did not eliminate corporate power, nor did he aim to. Rather, he reinforced the power of state corporate banks, especially the "pet banks" that clearly benefited from and contributed to the Democratic Party political machine—thus, he weakened one corporate elite by strengthening others. Jackson's killing of the "monster" merely ensured that its corporate cousins would thrive at the state level.[7]

Thrive they did. While there would continue to be resistance to individual corporations and their actions, no strong and lasting movement emerged to challenge the principle of incorporation itself. In Pennsylvania, the legislature's willingness to grant incorporation to business continued to accelerate, as it did in other states. From 1780 to 1800, it incorporated 22 companies; from 1800 to 1830, 428 companies; in the 1830s, another 420; 431 in the 1840s; and a generous 1,041 in the 1850s. And many of the later ones were enacted after the state passed a series of general incorporation laws that allowed various kinds of manufacturing and mining firms to incorporate through a state-run bureaucratic process rather than only through legislative acts, a measure that made the adoption of the corporation irreversible, if it had not been so already. While acts of incorporation could still raise partisan hackles, politicians nearly always found ways to make deals across the aisles in Pennsylvania and elsewhere. And as it went in legislatures, so it did with other forms of resistance to corporations. Though they might use slightly different rhetoric when fighting corporations rather than partnerships, textile workers and miners concentrated mainly on the terms of their oppression rather than on the legal and institutional form of their oppressors. They understood that, while their immediate situations might be negotiable, the stamping out of a now nearly ubiquitous institution was not.[8]

Just as corporations seemed to sprout everywhere in the middle decades of the nineteenth century, the growth of the corporate power in early national Philadelphia spread across the nation, overlapping with similar efforts based in New York, Boston, and Baltimore. Though New England's banking system, through which that region's money supply and credit facilities were far more tightly controlled by corporate officers than were Pennsylvania's, remained peculiar to that region, most of the country eventually adopted the more diffused, multibank, crazy-quilt system more typical of the Keystone State and its Empire State neighbor. Although not all states would have a more or less official state bank like the Bank of Pennsylvania, institutions in other states followed the Bank of Pennsylvania's lead in a number of respects that would be recognizable to Americans for over a century: the establishment of branches in remote areas that would follow the central institution's policies and thus subordinate localities to metropolitan priorities, the coordination among banks for considering money supply and clearing each other's notes, and even stately buildings with grand columns that became an immediately recognizable trademark of established urban banks.[9]

Philadelphia and its city corporation also provided a template for other urban communities, from the city's layout to its administration of public works. The Centre Square works and later the Fairmount works led over a dozen other cities to consult or employ Latrobe and later Graff to design their own city water systems. Such projects formed part of a pattern among American city governments in the nineteenth century. Not only waterworks but also street lighting, gas distribution, and waste disposal projects became increasingly common as American cities grew larger and as their citizens demanded the latest technological answers to the physical challenges of urban life. Many cities used methods similar to Philadelphia's to finance and administer these expensive new services and installations, resorting to bonds and sinking funds and often controlling large pools of capital. Largely because of the costs and administration of the waterworks, all of Philadelphia County was incorporated into the City Corporation of Philadelphia in 1854, creating the largest single municipal district in the country at that time and serving as a template for the incorporation of other large cities, including New York's later absorption of its outer boroughs.[10]

In terms of internal improvement and corporate power, states adopted a variety of combinations of public works and corporate projects before overextensions in state systems and the Panic of 1837 put so many states in financial trouble; after that, the reluctance of legislators to adopt new projects, combined with the increased adoption of railroads and the availability of financing from Boston, New York, Philadelphia, and Baltimore, led to business corporations' domination of American transportation from the 1840s onward. The process had begun in New England at much the same time as it had in Philadelphia, though Philadelphians pushed the trend to its logical conclusion. In 1846, Thomas P. Cope, a corporate insider who near the beginning of his long career had been on the city corporation committee overseeing the construction of the city's first waterworks, helped establish the Pennsylvania Rail Road Company. And the intercorporate cooperation to facilitate growth continued: the Philadelphia city corporation bought 50,000 shares of Pennsylvania Rail Road Company stock. Eleven years later, the Pennsylvania Rail Road Company purchased the state of Pennsylvania's bankrupt Main Line system for the bargain price of $10,000,000, a fraction of the original cost. The company's charter and bylaws held remarkable similarities to 1820s and 1830s railroad charters, which in turn had been patterned after canal charters, just as early railroad finance methods followed their earlier counterparts. After the Civil War, the Pennsylvania Railroad Company become the world's largest business corporation, a position it held for thirty years. Philadelphia corporate men numbered among the foremost architects of the blueprint for the American urban corporate consolidation of money and power.[11]

Philadelphia's corporate elite also helped to establish a national trend. The combination of business corporation and municipal corporation investment instruments provided middle- and especially upper-class families a vehicle for the establishment of stable family lines. This cushioning from the extremely volatile world of mercantile enterprise allowed many Philadelphia families to ride their early-republic prosperity well into the twentieth century. And just as the corporate community started, with overlap between the old social elite and new economic strivers, so would Philadelphia's upper crust, with every generation co-opting new, economically successful members whose children and grandchildren could be fully accepted into Philadelphia high society. In other cities, such as Pittsburgh, Boston, and New York, corporate elites also remained flexible enough to welcome a few new members, and they used corporations as economic tools to increase their economic power and bolster their social standing. That said, while the process of elite class formation continued hand-in-hand with the process of the establishment of the business corporate elite, in Philadelphia and elsewhere these elites increasingly withdrew from electoral politics even at the municipal level, and indeed they would later rail against the popular politics of urban ward heeling. Eventually in some cities corporate businessmen found other ways to extend influence over city development, especially where business corporations provided water, gas, and eventually, electricity, or services such as garbage disposal. Corporate men and corporate power were here to stay in Philadelphia and in America.[12]

The making of Philadelphia's corporate sphere demonstrates a strong counterpoint to interpretations of the early republican North as a time and place of great promise, fostering broad social and economic fluidity and bereft of a strong economic elite. In fact, the Philadelphia corporate elite constituted one of the many local, cooperative economic elites that historians continue to find the more that they have looked for them; furthermore, significant quantitative evidence indicates that, during the nation's first half century, the gap between the haves and the have-nots continued to widen. But the complementary processes of concentration and diffusion that led to the development of the corporate sphere also contradict the interpretation that the rise of both capitalism and increased democracy was somehow paradoxical. The men who founded and administered Philadelphia-area corporations did more than help make the market revolution and increased political democratization possible through money supply, credit, transportation, and city services. They also built a bridge between a colonial period of economic power advanced through government domination by elites, deference, and personal fortunes, to the antebellum period and beyond, when metropolitan economic elites leveraged corporate institutions, finance, technologies, and ideology to project power through space in a democratic republic.[13]

Furthermore, consideration of Philadelphia's corporate elite in relation to other elites of the period suggests a more complicated view of elites than previously argued. Most analyses of early national elites have either focused on small, geographically bounded elites in the North or the planter elite in the South, nearly all arguing against a cohesive, national-level elite. The study of Philadelphia's corporate elite shows that we might think of many elites rather than one elite. Philadelphia's corporate elite overlapped with its social elite and, over the decades of the early republic, decreasingly with the city's political elite. Nearby Manayunk's manufacturing elite also intersected with Philadelphia's corporate elite but was clearly economically subordinate to it, as were Reading's most prosperous and prominent citizens (though one of them, Joseph Heister, clearly was more politically powerful than any member of any Philadelphia group). Meanwhile, Philadelphia's black elite developed separately but just as self-consciously. Accordingly, we should begin to think of many elites intersecting at some points but not at others. They can also be measured in terms of scale and scalability: that is, while local proprietary manufacturing elites could be dominant at certain geographic or social scales (for example, the textile oligarchy in Rockdale, Pennsylvania), the use of corporations allowed Philadelphia corporate men to project their power through space and extend their influence over more people.[14]

The story of Philadelphia corporations raises additional questions beyond the scope of this study. Clearly, Americans in many other cities also adopted and developed corporations. That the corporate form, methods of corporate consolidation, and the culture of the corporate sphere would be replicated by subsequent generations of Philadelphians offers little surprise, but these patterns would also show up in other American cities, whether in railroad

administration, banking, or municipal governance. Did this convergence occur because of intercity connections that functioned to diffuse information,
like Thomas Willing's correspondence with early New England bankers or
the Wurts brothers' operations in both Philadelphia and New York City?
Given the increase in the availability of economic information and growing
interurban ties, it probably did. Did corporate men in the early United States
all work from the same British blueprints, merely working out slightly different details in different American cities? Chances are that men in cities other
than Philadelphia had access to and made use of the same sources of information as did their Quaker City counterparts. Was there something distinctive about the conditions of the early American republic—as opposed to
other nations—that made some of its residents more predisposed to the political and economic potential of the corporate form? The combination of
British heritage and republican revolution may have made the U.S. experience with corporations unique, distinguishing it from the postcolonial societies of other empires and from British Commonwealth states such as
Canada and Australia that underwent evolutionary rather than revolutionary change. More study of corporate communities and the corporate sphere
in other cities and in other nations, and especially the connections among
them, will be required to offer any definitive answers.[15]

One thing is clear: by establishing business corporations and intertwining
them with the municipal corporation, Philadelphia's corporate men established a self-sustaining system that placed elite economic interests at the
head of the urban economic agenda, one with great ramifications to the current day. Business corporations became powerful institutions whose main
goal was to make money, and their officers generally assumed that the best
way to pursue that goal was through promoting policies that furthered economic growth on their terms (corporate profit) at the expense of other considerations (distribution of wealth, quality of life, etc.). Urban officials have
often accepted this agenda either implicitly or explicitly, and scholars have
found that the extent to which cities have adopted this urban growth regime
has been reflected in the strength and exclusivity of local economic elites
but not in increased employment, thus suggesting that the fruits of such
growth have been far from equitably distributed.[16]

Nonetheless, the early national Philadelphia model demonstrates the
strong connection between the development of corporations and the establishment not only of urban elites but also of an urban (and later suburban)
middle class. The corporate mills at Lowell provided an example for the development of instant industrial corporate capitalism in an isolated area, one
that would be followed by the establishment of corporate towns from the
mines of Colorado to the factories of Homestead. But, like the Massachusetts
corporate mill towns, these later corporate fiefdoms never developed much
of a middle class, never offering the economic space or supporting the local infrastructure in ways that supported much in the way of other entrepreneurial activities. Conversely, Philadelphia's corporate elite, by pursuing

urban growth policies, provided the facilities for entrepreneurial artisans to fill economic niches unavailable in places like the factory towns of the Merrimack River Valley. Over the course of the nineteenth century, Philadelphia became home to a smaller-scale textile industry featuring smaller-scale shops that were running well into the twentieth century, long after most Massachusetts mills had fallen silent. Other Philadelphia artisans helped make the city a national center for the design and manufacture of steam engines. This pattern of smaller-scale urban manufacturing alongside corporate manufacturing could be seen in almost any city of the nation. American historians have pondered the question of the origins of its middle class; American corporations helped make that middle class possible.[17]

Historians have also considered the meaning of early corporations, and especially their implications for our understanding of the American Revolution. Rather than either the result of brilliant Yankee ingenuity or a revolutionary adaptation of an ancient institution, American corporations resulted from the wholesale adoption of a contemporary British legal and organizational form. Thus, while the tinkering with corporate charters may have intrigued Americans in their newfound interest in constitutions, they did not have to look to corporations in the first place: the structure of incorporation was far less innovative than more long-standing American-pioneered institutions like land banks and public internal improvement commissions.[18]

Rather, the debate over and the results of the adoption of corporations shed light on two facets of the American Revolution and its aftermath. First, the struggle over corporations demonstrated the multivalent meanings of the revolution. For early corporate founders, especially those so in touch with British developments, corporations represented the chance to establish British-style institutions denied them by imperial authorities, while for many opponents, political independence also meant establishing a new nation based on newfound American principles and institutions. In other words, the battles over corporations revealed fault lines between those interested primarily in being able to exercise their own authority and those whose Revolutionary fervor was based more on nascent American nationalism. The use of corporations to set economic policy fit with Revolutionary republican ideals of representative rule by an ostensibly disinterested natural aristocracy, but it fundamentally clashed with those who conceived of the Revolution in more egalitarian terms, that is, the fault line between those adopting an English-style republican ideology and those with a more radical view of ideal human relations. In their professions as merchants, the founders of corporations generally supported a more liberal view of the relationship between the state and the economy, yet, as their critics noted, they championed corporations that at best allowed some economic actors advantages over others in the marketplace and at worst included state-mandated monopolies or cartels. Thus, corporate men wanted state privileges while rejecting an activist state. As much as the debates over slavery in the early republic, the battles over corporations reveal that Americans held many different views—even often inherently contradictory ones—concerning what they had revolted for and what their new republic was all about.

The second facet of the American Revolution that the story of early corporations reveals is that the use of corporations should be considered an integral part of the Revolutionary settlement. To look only at the structure of the state and federal constitutions and the first political battles and parties of the new nation provides us with an incomplete picture of the distribution of power. The shaping of new institutions—political or social—inherently reflects prevailing differences in power among the various groups involved. Corporations numbered among the new governing institutions of the early republic, right at the intersection between policy and power. The inclusion of corporations and their growing strength show a nation becoming far less egalitarian than only analyses of political developments would indicate. That insight proves even more crucial to our understanding of the 1820s and 1830s, when many states expanded the franchise while continuing to charter corporations that entrenched local and metropolitan elites' control over issues that previously had been under the purview of public officials. In short, the study of early corporations reveals a far less radical long-term Revolutionary settlement than previously argued, one that allowed greater political participation while further entrenching the power of economic elites.[19]

The nation's first corporate founders established more than ad hoc solutions to Philadelphia's problems: they were founding an enduring and perhaps permanent institutional structure that allowed them and their successors to generate and enforce economic policy every bit as far-reaching as legislation and jurisprudence, often in lock-step with governmental policy. Indeed, given that corporations were—and are—authorized through act of government, they can be said to be part of the U.S. governmental apparatus no less than legislatures. Economic historians whose main questions have concerned economic efficiency have noted how nineteenth-century corporate officers worked toward both vertical and horizontal integration, that is, the ways that these men (and they were exclusively men) organized large swaths of the economy in order to control the entire production of products from the harvesting of natural resources to the delivery of the final product, or to gain a monopoly on the production and sale of a given commodity or service. They did improve efficiency, raise production, invent new technologies, and make goods and services available cheaply and more broadly than any eighteenth-century person could have ever imagined. That said, corporate officers increasingly made decisions and promoted policies that affected the nation and its citizens every bit as much as governors and senators, sometimes more so. Whether it was bananas from planting in Central America all the way to local grocery stores, oil from Pennsylvania wells through refining and to local gas stations, or the building, supplying, and running of vast railroad networks, corporate leaders worked in tandem with government to mobilize millions of workers, to allocate natural resources, and to enforce an order both at home and abroad to make such large-scale efforts both possible and profitable. Thus, for better or for worse, in terms of how the nation would be (and is) run, corporate pioneers should be counted as American founders no less than the politicians who conceived and implemented the first federal, state, and local governments.[20]

Furthermore, early corporate behavior may provide the best answer to one of the most puzzling conundrums in U.S. history, namely, the strong and apparent hostility America's corporate community has had and continues to have for its state and national governments. Although some captains of industry and lions of Wall Street have enjoyed cozy relationships with various policy makers at different times, from the White House to the mayor's mansion and from the Department of Defense to the municipal dump, by and large American company officers have long held very dim views concerning the role of the state in the economy in general and its relationship to corporations in particular. This attitude seems especially bizarre considering that, despite some notable exceptions such as antitrust legislation and the Taft-Hartley Act, American government at all levels has historically been congenial in innumerable ways to corporate interests. Consider the countless corporate concessions, such as land grants, tax abatements, research subsidies, access to federal lands, foreign-policy support, liability protection, bailouts, authorization for airwaves, and corporate-friendly copyright, patent, and trademark law. Furthermore, the state and national governments have greatly shielded American corporations from all kinds of economic uncertainties. Although American business leaders' ire toward popular government has varied by industry and by individual and has waxed and waned, often in rhythm with swings in the political pendulum or stages in the business cycle, it goes back to the earliest days of the republic.[21]

Robert Morris, James Wilson, and their associates planted the first seeds of corporate America as a direct response to what they perceived as a hostile political environment during and after the American Revolution. Over the following fifty years, their commercial heirs made sure that the germinating corporate sphere grew firm and extensive roots. And while the resulting plants have grown and changed nearly beyond recognition, they still contain the kernels of suspicion of popular government that continue to bear fruit over two centuries later. Philadelphia's corporate leaders did not name and certainly did not tout the corporate sphere that they brought into being in the opening decades of the republic, but eventually American corporate officers would embrace and defend the later concept of an even greater "private sector" as an alternative to what they perceived as the excesses, inefficiencies, and irrationality of popular government, especially in its relationship to the free market. Even demographically, twentieth-century corporate boards, which continued to be overwhelmingly white and male, increasingly diverged from their political counterparts. Thus, the businessmen of the American Revolution and the early republic bestowed two conflicting legacies: a corporate structure that has played so great a part in the United

States' economic success, and a corporate ethos still at war with the greatest American Revolutionary achievement, representative popular government.[22]

In keeping with this hostility toward the people's representatives, after the 1820s the leaders of each kind of corporation, by their use of finance, technology, and ideology, continued in their efforts to limit the level of public scrutiny and input over corporate affairs. Municipal officials at least remained accountable to the electorate, but beginning in the 1850s business leaders increasingly espoused economic liberalism as their mantra to be repeated whenever public officials dared to question the motives or actions of business corporations— notwithstanding the willingness for corporate officers and investors to lobby for land grants, tax abatements, subsidies, legislative barriers to potential competition, and other governmental favors. According to this philosophy, not only was the government less capable of regulating the economy than the "invisible hand" of the marketplace, but also it had no right to try.

As the evolution of corporations in Philadelphia indicates, economic liberalism served as a justification for structures already established by 1830. In the Revolutionary period, no one questioned the primacy of civil authorities in political and economic matters, because everyone understood the two to be inextricably connected. With the ensuing establishment of a corporate sphere, business corporation boosters created the self-serving illusion that many fundamental economic issues lay beyond the proper bailiwick of elected officials. After the Civil War, corporate leaders would even make the case that the government existed to serve them, convincing governors and presidents to do the corporations' bidding by using government troops in the corporations' private battles against their own employees. When corporate leaders did so, they cited what they called a right to free enterprise, but carefully avoided making reference to the Spirit of '76.

Today, the era of fledgling state banks, internal navigations, and steam-powered waterworks may seem distant, but its legacy of corporate power continues. This book opened with a vignette of barges traveling at the wondrous speed of four miles per hour during Reading's public celebration of Schuylkill Navigation Company's corporate-owned waterway, marking a new era of economic possibilities for the town and economic influence for the corporation's officers. But that event was not so different from ceremonies we see today, when mayors and governors cut the ribbons on new corporate facilities. Some of these are paid for by private investors, face ruthless market competition, and are central to the nation's economic production. Others, like professional sports stadiums used a dozen times a year and defense plants producing weapons for threats that do not exist, represent public investments in corporate ventures of dubious value to the wider community. And we can still see, in the many other ways that corporate officers work to promote their particular vision of economic growth through city halls, statehouses, and the federal government, that despite a one-person, one-vote political system, corporate insiders clearly continue to wield economic power greatly disproportionate to their numbers.

To contemporary Americans, then, this tale of corporate consolidation in Philadelphia may seem familiar, with reverberations in current trends. The American economy continues to be a dynamo of growth and vitality. Corporate officers in big cities still find ways to offer more services and produce more products, at the same time extending their influence over both the cities where they live and smaller outlying communities in innumerable economic, political, and social ways. Corporations still serve as convenient legal and financial structures to provide for economic activities and thus economic growth but still distribute those benefits in a grossly inequitable manner. The mixed legacy of Joseph S. Lewis and Josiah White still lives in the United States, a society unparalleled in its capacity for economic and technological development but often plagued by the public's inability to brook the power of corporate officers whose greatest interests are putting the bottom line in the black and themselves in the clear. These developments were not inevitable. They are the result of choices people made in Philadelphia then and continue to make today.

METHODOLOGY
AND SOURCES

$\mathcal{I}$n several sections in this book, I have drawn conclusions based on data gathering and interpretation that bear further explanation, specifically corporate stockholding and bondholding, the interlocking of corporate boards, and the role of spending on the waterworks in the City Corporation of Philadelphia's expenditures from 1799 to 1825.

The gathering of data concerning stock and waterworks bond ownership entailed constructing databases from published lists of stockholders, corporate manuscript stockholder lists, or dividend payout ledgers. I entered these into a database consisting of 4,736 records, each noting the stockholder's name, the date purchased or recorded, the number of stocks, and the par value. To consider the wealth and occupations of stockholders compared to the general population, I compared the data I had compiled with data generously provided to me in spreadsheet form by Billy G. Smith that included an extensive sampling of the Philadelphia municipal tax rolls from 1789 and 1798.

The data concerning the interlocking of Philadelphia corporate boards involved intensive data gathering and manipulation. Covering the 1780s through the early 1830s, most of the data came from listings of board members and council members in Philadelphia directories, generally issued on an annual basis, especially from the 1810s on. Other sources included newspapers and the manuscript minute books and election returns of various corporations, including the Philadelphia City Corporation, the Farmers and Mechanics Bank, the Schuylkill Navigation Company, and the Bank of Pennsylvania. These were listed in two databases, one of 7,283 records listing business corporation board members; the other, 1,339 city council members. Each record included first and last name, year, and title. These were then sorted by year and by name, with duplicate last names flagged to indicate potential board links. I considered men to be related when they had the same last name, not counting those so common, such as Smith, that were less likely to be related, while adding in links to men that I knew to be related from other sources, including diaries and published accounts of Philadelphia society and the merchant and corporate community in particular. The number of interlocks thus generated is very likely underrepresentative, because of the great number of men with business or families ties who had different last names but shared interests, and whose ties I did not come across in my research.

To examine how the Philadelphia councils allocated their funds, I compiled spreadsheets of all the city's budgets and expenditures from 1799 to 1825. To do so, I consulted council publications, including periodic pamphlets on city budgets and city expenditures (these were sometimes printed annually, though by the late 1810s on a four-year basis), as well as some of the councils' manuscript sources at the Philadelphia City Archives. Exact, complete data were available for all years except 1804, for which the surviving data are incomplete. For 1804, I used the extant data while interpolating between 1803 and 1805 for the unavailable information. To determine which costs were related to the waterworks, I identified all payments expressly dedicated to the waterworks as well as ancillary costs that I determined were directly related to waterworks construction or maintenance. This latter category included paving over pipes, construction of pipes, machinery for pipe boring, the purchase of land and water rights for the Fairmount works, and debt service on waterworks construction (as designated by the councils and as an estimated portion of overall debt service). From this total, I subtracted waterworks income deposited in the sinking fund, including both water rent and sale of old or excess materials. Not included are funds for old pumps and wells not connected to the central water supply system, interest on city loans taken out because of cash-flow problems induced by payments for the waterworks, or the opportunity cost on investment in the waterworks. Thus, the water expenditures as illustrated in the chart in Chapter 4 and noted in the text are, if anything, probably lower than the actual costs of the waterworks borne by the city corporation.

PRIMARY SOURCES

By their nature, institutions keep a good deal of documentation, so any history of corporations necessitates mining the printed and manuscript documents generated by corporate officers. While doing my research, I always kept in mind that the originators of these documents promulgated and, sometimes, disseminated them not for future historians but for themselves and their perceived contemporary audiences. I was careful to collect and consider the information presented; to interrogate the terms of its presentation; and to note what was elided, avoided, or left unmentioned. I found that the documents seldom addressed motive, that is, why people did what they did. While I took the rhetoric quite seriously, I also decided that, when considering individuals' motivations, I privileged their actions over their words.

Many corporations left extensive paper trails. The City Corporation of Philadelphia regularly published reports concerning its finances; in addition, every several years a series of publishers produced editions of all city ordinances passed since the previous such publication. The city councils occasionally published reports on various topics. The Watering Committee in particular eventually published annual reports as well as issued specific reports, for example, the decision to expand the Fairmount works and a booklet including the contracts necessary to purchase the land for this project. Both the city councils and the Watering Committee left extensive minutes and other records, most of which reside in the Philadelphia City Archives, though the Philadelphia Water Department still retains some of the latter's records.

Business corporate records have been more scattered. Most corporations published pamphlets containing their charter and bylaws, and many eventually published reports on a regular basis. For Philadelphia-area institutions, most of these reports are available either at the Library Company of Philadelphia or at the Hagley Museum and Library. Such sources included the printed reports of the Schuylkill Navigation Company, the Bank of Pennsylvania, the Union Canal Company, the Farmers and Mechanics Bank, and the Philadelphia Bank. In addition, many of these corporations' internal records—depending upon the institution, minutes of board and stockholder meetings, lists of stockholders, letterbooks, and account books—reside at the Hagley, the Historical Society of Pennsylvania, or the Pennsylvania State Archives. For records concerning British corporations, especially canal companies, the best United States site is the Huntington Library.

Institutions may gain their own momentum, yet they are still composed of individuals who make choices; early Philadelphia corporations were no exception. In my attempt to flesh out the people involved with these corporations, I consulted a range of published and manuscript sources. Some of the actors' papers have been edited and published in various forms. The correspondence, journals, and drawings of Benjamin Henry Latrobe, for example, are available in numerous works. Published autobiographies or diaries include those of Charles Biddle, Josiah White, William Findley, and James Allen. Valuable manuscript sources included the Graff Family Papers, the Breck Collection, and the Mathew Carey Section of the Edward Carey Gardiner Papers, all at the Historical Society of Pennsylvania. Carey also left a considerable body of books and pamphlets.

SECONDARY SOURCES

The interpretations in this book lie at the intersection of several related avenues of historical thought—general ones on corporations and states' relationship to them, on banking and internal improvement, on urban development in the new nation, on the early national economy, on early American political economy, and on early national elites, as well as more specific ones relating to Philadelphia and Pennsylvania. In addition, my ideas have been informed by more theoretical works concerning power, elites, and corporations not previously applied to the issue of the origins of American corporations and corporate power.

Strangely, not many historians have directly addressed why Americans so readily adopted the corporate form. Oscar and Mary Handlin, in 1945, argued that Massachusetts used the corporation, which was an earlier British construct, as a way to empower the community to achieve public purposes, rather than as an avenue for capitalists. A later work that espouses this general view but emphasizes American invention over British precedent is Ronald E. Seavoy's *The Origins of the American Business Corporation, 1784–1855*. Pauline Maier, too, saw the corporation as a uniquely American, republican adaptation of a "moribund" British institution, although Ron Harris has convincingly demonstrated that the British were quite active in the use and development of corporations during the eighteenth century, in *Industrializing English Law*.

Turning to American public finance before the Revolution, a number of scholars have considered American and Pennsylvanian efforts, nearly all of them emphasizing the high degree of American innovation in coping with colonial economic conditions within a restrictive British imperial system. The main debate has concerned the level of success in dealing with issues of money supply, with the consensus moving from interpretations of inadequacy (based on a bias against paper money) to one of general adequacy. Theodore Thayer, in 1953, offered a general treatment of land banks; for the Pennsylvania case, see Mary M. Schweitzer's *Custom and Contract*. Richard Sylla provided a brief survey of colonial currency experimentation; for Pennsylvania in particular, see John J. McCusker's *Money and Exchange in Europe and America, 1600–1775*. The most extended overview of currency and finance spanning colonial British America and the early national period is *American Public Finance and Financial Services, 1700–1815,* by Edwin J. Perkins.

The historiography on the relation of corporations to the state has a long heritage. The literature began by espousing a mostly laissez-faire interpretation of early American governance. Major early works include Guy S. Callender, "The Early Transportation and Banking Enterprises of the States in Relation to the Growth of Corporations," and Joseph S. Davis, *Essays in the Earlier History of American Corporations*. The commonwealth school of the 1940s and beyond—perhaps an inheritor of eighteenth-century republican ideology—assumed the existence of one common good and the desire for governments to regulate, but also held suspicion of governmental corruption and power. This general trend of thought was developed in Oscar Handlin and Mary Flug Handlin's *Commonwealth* and Louis Hartz's *Economic Policy and Democratic Thought: Pennsylvania, 1776–1860*. It was later modified by Cater Goodrich and his students to consider government encouragement of business in terms of a "state-in, state-out" model, rather than extended involvement, in works such as Goodrich, ed., *The Government and the Economy* and "Internal Improvements Reconsidered."

Over the past two decades, most scholars have moved to a more nuanced array of positions acknowledging both the encouragement and regulation of business. Furthermore, they also treat corporate officers as actors in their own right, and often at odds with the state. Sean Patrick Adams, comparing Virginia to Pennsylvania, argued that state activity was crucial to economic development, while John D. Majewski, comparing the same two states, focused more on local actors. L. Ray Gunn found that New York State increasingly abdicated its role in economic oversight; John Lauritz Larson argued the same for the federal government; his *Internal Improvement* is the most important synthesis of literature on internal improvements, public and corporate.

The role of the courts in the development of capitalism in the early republic has taken a different path than the consideration of legislation and legislative intent. In the 1970s, scholars James W. Hurst and Morton J. Horwitz, among others, examining federal and state higher courts, emphasized judges' sympathy toward corporations and economic growth. More recently Tony A. Freyer, William J. Novak, and Peter Karsten have moved toward citing the ways that judges, especially in lower courts, protected smaller consumers and producers against larger capitalist enterprise.

Historians have generally identified the rise of corporate power with industrialization during the mid-nineteenth century and after. The most influential interpretations of the rise of American corporations are Thomas C. Cochran and William Miller, *The Age of Enterprise,* which put the rise of corporations in the greater context of late nineteenth-century America, and Alfred Chandler, *The Visible Hand,* which argued that corporations grew vertically as a way for managers to better mitigate market forces. More recently, Martin J. Sklar, Olivier Zunz, and William G. Roy have provided sensitive, sociologically informed treatments of corporate power later in the nineteenth century that nonetheless give the early republic short shrift. David B. Sicilia provided an excellent overview in "Industrialization and the Rise of Corporations, 1860–1900."

Of course, much of the study of corporations has been the province of economic historians, who often are interested in past phenomena's applicability to contemporary economic issues. Until the 1970s, just as with considerations of colonial currency, nearly all economic studies of early American banking concerned the issue of money supply; Richard E. Sylla's "American Banking and Growth in the Nineteenth Century" serves as a good survey. While greatly contested, still the most prominent work concerning the intersection of banking and states is Bray Hammond's *Banks and Politics in America.* In recent decades, economists Naomi Lamoreaux, Robert E. Wright, and Howard Bodenhorn have increasingly examined banks' role in terms of economic growth, focusing mostly on credit. Richard Sylla provides an analysis of unincorporated banking in "Forgotten Men of Money: Private Bankers in Early U.S. History." Like Hammond, Susan Hoffman considers more of the political than the economic ramifications of banking in *Politics and Banking.*

Major questions in the historiography of the economic role of internal improvements have included the issues of who invested in internal improvements, whether investments in internal improvements that did not make direct profits pay off adequately in other ways, and the extent to which internal improvement networks primarily result in growth fueled by intraregional or by extraregional trade. The trailblazing work connecting internal improvements to national economic growth was George Rogers Taylor, *The Transportation Revolution,* echoed by contributors to Goodrich's edited volume *Canals and American Economic Development.* However, Diane Lindstrom demonstrated that internal improvements generally contributed most to intra-regional growth.

The two major interpretations of the transformation of the American city during this period are Jon Teaford, *The Municipal Revolution in America* and Hendrik Hartog, *Public Property and Private Power.* These two authors argued that the eighteenth-century American municipal corporation performed essentially regulatory (in terms of regulating markets and prices) and promotional functions, though Teaford emphasized the former while Hartog emphasized the latter, focusing on the use of public property to encourage various kinds of enterprise. Leonard P. Curry provided an impressive analysis of the changes in American urban administration—and its connections to other corporations—in *The Corporate City.* Other major works include those by Sam Bass Warner, Jr. (whose work skips the early republic), Charles R. Adrian, Martin Schiesl, and Eric H. Monkkonen.

The literature concerning early American ideology is vast, and indeed republicanism in particular has probably gotten attention out of proportion to its importance compared to other competing ideologies. The seminal works include Bernard Bailyn, *The Ideological Origins of the American Revolution;* Gordon S. Wood, *The Creation of the American Republic, 1776–1787;* and Drew McCoy, *The Elusive Republic.* Daniel T. Rogers offered a useful summary in "Republicanism: Career of a Concept." For an interpretation of these ideas in the context of Pennsylvania, see Douglas M. Arnold's *A Republican Revolution.*

The roots of liberal ideology and the moral economy have recently garnered more attention. Albert O. Hirschman provided perhaps the definitive analysis of the origins of arguments relating to the role of interest in eighteenth-century political-economic thought; Cathy D. Matson and Peter S. Onuf presented a more specific analysis of American political economy in *A Union of Interests.* Joyce Appleby's essay "Liberalism and the American Revolution" is also valuable. Peter Linebaugh and Marcus Rediker outlined an Atlantic world moral economy in *The Many-Headed Hydra;* for the Pennsylvania context, consult the articles by Ronald Schultz and Terry Bouton.

Historians have looked particularly at Philadelphia's elites, spurred by E. Digby Baltzell's sociological study *Philadelphia Gentlemen* despite the fact that he extrapolated backward from the 1940s, and thus his findings were not representative of the early national period. Contradicting Baltzell's argument that the elite retreated from city politics, Thomas M. Doerflinger provides the most complete account of Philadelphia merchants in *A Vigorous Spirit of Enterprise.* For the most extensive treatment of the Philadelphia elite in the late eighteenth century, see Robert J. Gough's dissertation. Important studies that consider other elites with similar ambitions include those by Robert F.

Dalzell, Jr., and David Hancock. Yet the "elite"—particularly on the national level—eluded Philip H. Burch, Jr., and other scholars, as demonstrated by Sven Beckert, and Gary J. Kornbith and John M. Murrin.

Historians have produced copious scholarship on Pennsylvania and Philadelphia, generally agreeing that Philadelphia's city government was closed and elite-dominated during the colonial period, as Judith Diamondstone demonstrated. Richard Alan Ryerson, Eric Foner, and Gary Nash emphasized the extent to which Philadelphia and its politics became increasingly fractured by class during and after the American Revolution. Tom W. Smith compiled what is still the best overall construction of Philadelphia society in this period, while Robert Gough considered economic elites and Billy G. Smith examined the role of Philadelphia's poor. George David Rappaport offers a structural discussion that includes a discussion of the founding of the Bank of North America, in *Stability and Change in Revolutionary Pennsylvania.*

Philip Scranton has forcefully argued that nineteenth-century Philadelphia grew as a manufacturing center primarily through entrepreneurs' use of partnerships, in *Proprietary Capitalism.* His arguments have been extended and affirmed by studies of entrepreneurs in particular trades by Rosalind Remer, Donna J. Rilling, and Kathleen M. Catalano.

Pennsylvania politics has attracted significant scholarly attention, reaching consensus that colonial Pennsylvania politics were dominated by two elite factions, while early Quaker State politics' most significant trends were toward class, sectional, and party strife. For the most recent interpretation of colonial Pennsylvania politics and political culture, see Richard R. Beeman's *The Varieties of Political Experience in Eighteenth-Century America.* Another recent study, Andrew Shankman's *Crucible of American Democracy,* considers in particular the intersection between politics, ideology, and economic development in Pennsylvania. James H. Hutson offered an extended treatment in *Pennsylvania Politics.* Sanford Wilson Higginbotham's *The Keystone in the Democratic Arch,* James A. Kehl's *Ill Feeling in the Era of Good Feelings,* and Philip Shriver Klein's *Pennsylvania Politics, 1817–1832,* continue to be foundational works.

The idea of a "market revolution" occurring during the early nineteenth century has recently captivated historians of the period, becoming the reigning interpretive paradigm. Charles Sellers noted the contradiction between democratization and increased inequality in the definitive work on the subject, *The Market Revolution,* while Gordon Wood argued for a less ambiguous egalitarianism in *Radicalism of the American Revolution.* Contributors to the following volumes explore other facets of the "market revolution": Paul A. Gilje, ed., *Wages of Independence;* Scott C. Martin, ed., *Cultural Change and the Market Revolution in America;* and Eric Foner, ed., *The New American History, Revised and Expanded.* Of all the scholarship on this subject, perhaps the most interesting concerns the ambiguous meanings and social effects of the economic changes. The most relevant work in this area, concerning internal improvements, is Carol Sheriff's *The Artificial River.*

In addition to considering these various historiographies, I reexamine in this work changes in the nature of power and who wielded it. Philosopher Terence Ball identified three kinds of power: realist, communicative, and deconstructive. This study focuses mostly, though far from exclusively, upon realist power, a more traditional definition of power associated with personal relations. Jack Knight explored the ways that social and political institutions are shaped by prevailing power relationships; the modes of power he delineated were evident in early corporate leaders' relationship to the general public, to other economic actors, and to the state government.

The primary locus of corporate power was corporate boards and their intersection. Various scholars, most notably Davita Silfen Glasberg, G. F. Davis, Robert Gogel and Thomas Koenig, and James D. Westphal, Marc-David L. Seidel, and Katherine J. Stewart, have investigated interlocking corporate directories. Mark S. Mizruchi discussed interlocks as a vehicle for class cohesion in *The Structure of Corporate Political Action*. For a comprehensive and insightful overview of the scholarship on corporate interlocks, see Mizruchi's "What Do Corporate Interlocks Do?" and Walter A. Friedman and Richard S. Tedlow's "Statistical Portraits of American Business Elites."

The interlocks became even more powerful when integrated with city governance, as happened in early national Philadelphia. Harvey Molotch outlined the original theoretical underpinnings of the "urban growth regime"; Alan Harding reviewed discussion of the idea and its critics in "Elite Theory and Growth Machines." There is considerable evidence that the urban growth agenda leads to increased economic inequality, according to Larry Lyon, Lawrence G. Felice, M. Ray Perryman, and E. Stephen in "Community Power and Population Increase." The idea that urban elites sometimes exercise power by ensuring that potential policy threats are headed off before they reach the stage of decision originated with Peter Bachrach and Morton S. Baratz in "Two Faces of Power."

NOTES

ABBREVIATIONS

BPA	Bank of Pennsylvania
BHR	*Business History Review*
CCP	City Corporation of Philadelphia
CPA	Commonwealth of Pennsylvania
HML	Hagley Museum and Library
HSP	Historical Society of Pennsylvania
JAH	*Journal of American History*
JEH	*Journal of Economic History*
JER	*Journal of the Early Republic*
PH	*Pennsylvania History*
PMHB	*Pennsylvania Magazine of History and Biography*
PSA	Pennsylvania State Archives
PCA	Philadelphia City Archives
SNC	Schuylkill Navigation Company
UCC	Union Canal Company
WMQ	*William and Mary Quarterly*

INTRODUCTION

1. SNC, *Report . . . to the Stockholders. January 2, 1826* (Philadelphia: Lydia R. Bailey, 1826). Frederick Graff to Judith Graff, July 6, 1824, Graff Family Papers, HSP; *Reading Gazetteer* as quoted in J. Bennett Nolan, *The Schuylkill* (New Brunswick: Rutgers University Press, 1951), 84. Frederick Graff to Judith Graff, July 6, 1824, Graff Family Papers, HSP.

2. The SNC board of managers included Cadwalader Evans, Jr., Manuel Eyre, Thomas Firth, Thomas Harper, George Holstein, John Hoskins, Joshua Lippincott, Samuel Mifflin, Caspar Morris, Lindzey Nicholson, Jonas Preston, Richard Randolph, George Thompson, and Charles Watson. As of 1825, this group was still on the board;

only two were not listed in the Philadelphia directory published that year. Minutes, Board of Managers, SNC, Roll 1, October 7, 1815–January 5, 1846, PSA; Thomas Wilson, *The Philadelphia Directory* (Philadelphia: John Bioren, 1825).

3. Alan Taylor, *William Cooper's Town: Power and Persuasion on the Frontier of the Early American Republic* (New York: Vintage Books, 1995); Joyce Appleby, *Inheriting the Revolution: The First Generation of Americans* (Cambridge: Harvard University Press, 2000); Daniel Feller, *The Jacksonian Promise: America, 1815–1840* (Baltimore: Johns Hopkins University Press, 1995).

4. Gordon Wood, *The Radicalism of the American Revolution* (New York: Vintage Books, 1992); Gordon Wood, "The Enemy Is Us: Democratic Capitalism in the Early Republic," *JER* 16, no. 2 (1996): 293–308; Charles Sellers, *The Market Revolution: Jacksonian America, 1815–1846* (New York: Oxford University Press, 1991); Harry L. Watson, *Liberty and Power: The Politics of Jacksonian America* (New York: Hill & Wang, 1990).

5. Richard D. Brown, *Modernization: The Transformation of American Life, 1600–1865* (New York: Hill & Wang, 1976). Jon Butler, *Becoming America: The Revolution before 1776* (Cambridge: Harvard University Press, 2000); L. Ray Gunn, *The Decline of Authority: Public Economic Policy and Political Development in New York, 1800–1860* (Ithaca: Cornell University Press, 1988).

6. Ronald E. Seavoy, *The Origins of the American Business Corporation, 1784–1855: Broadening the Concept of Public Service during Industrialization* (Westport, CT: Greenwood Press, 1982); Oscar Handlin and Mary Flug Handlin, "Origins of the American Business Corporation," *JEH* 5 (May 1945): 22.

7. Joseph P. Davis, "Charters for American Business Corporations in the Eighteenth Century," *Publications of the American Statistical Association* 15, no. 116 (Dec. 1916): 426–35; Ron Harris, *Industrializing English Law: Entrepreneurship and Business Organization, 1720–1844* (New York: Cambridge University Press, 2000).

8. Andrew Shankman, *Crucible of American Democracy: The Struggle to Fuse Egalitarianism & Capitalism in Jeffersonian Pennsylvania* (Lawrence: University Press of Kansas, 2004).

9. Terence Ball, "New Faces of Power," in *Rethinking Power,* ed. Thomas Wartenburg, 14–31 (Albany: State University of New York, 1992); Jack Knight, *Institutions and Social Conflict* (New York: Cambridge University Press, 1992), 41–42.

10. Thomas C. Cochran and William Miller, *The Age of Enterprise: A Social History of Industrial America* (New York: The Macmillan Company, 1942); Alfred Chandler, *The Visible Hand: The Managerial Revolution in American Business* (Cambridge: Belknap Press, 1977).

11. Philip Scranton, *Proprietary Capitalism: The Textile Manufacture at Philadelphia, 1800–1885* (New York: Cambridge University Press, 1983); Rosalind Remer, *Printers and Men of Capital: Philadelphia Book Publishers in the New Republic* (Philadelphia: University of Pennsylvania Press, 1996); Donna J. Rilling, *Making Houses, Crafting Capitalism: Builders in Philadelphia, 1790–1850* (Philadelphia: University of Pennsylvania Press, 2001); Kathleen M. Catalano, "Cabinetmaking in Philadelphia, 1820–1840: Transition from Craft to Industry," in *American Furniture and Its Makers,* ed. Ian M. G. Quimby, 81–138, Winterthur Portfolio, vol. 13 (Chicago: Published for the Henry Francis du Pont Winterthur Museum by the University of Chicago Press, 1979).

12. Robert J. Gough, "Towards a Theory of Class and Social Conflict: A Social History of Wealthy Philadelphians, 1775 and 1800" (PhD diss., University of Pennsylvania, 1977); E. Digby Baltzell, *Philadelphia Gentlemen: The Making of a National Upper Class* (New York: Free Press, 1958).

13. David B. Sicilia, "Industrialization and the Rise of Corporations, 1860–1900," in *A Companion to 19th-Century America,* ed. William L. Barney, 139–51 (Malden, MA: Blackwell, 2001).

14. Guy S. Callender, "The Early Transportation and Banking Enterprises of the States in Relation to the Growth of Corporations," *Quarterly Journal of Economics* 17 (Nov. 1902): 111–62; Joseph S. Davis, *Essays in the Earlier History of American Corporations,* 2 vols. (Cambridge: Harvard University Press, 1917); Oscar Handlin and Mary Flug Han-

dlin, *Commonwealth: A Study of the Role of Government in the American Economy* (Cambridge: Harvard University Press, 1947); Louis Hartz, *Economic Policy and Democratic Thought: Pennsylvania, 1776–1860* (Cambridge: Harvard University Press, 1948); Carter Goodrich, *Government Promotion of American Canals and Railroads, 1800–1890* (New York: Columbia University Press, 1960); James W. Hurst, *The Legitimacy of the Business Corporation in the Law of the United States, 1780–1970* (Charlottesville: University Press of Virginia, 1970); Carter Goodrich, "Internal Improvements Reconsidered," *JEH* 30 (June 1970): 289–311; Morton J. Horwitz, *The Transformation of American Law, 1780–1860* (Cambridge: Harvard University Press, 1977); Seavoy, *Origins;* Gunn, *Decline;* and Pauline Maier, "The Revolutionary Origins of the American Corporation," *WMQ,* 3rd ser., 50 (1993): 51–84.

15. Jon Teaford, *The Municipal Revolution in America: The Origins of Modern Urban Government, 1650–1825* (Chicago: University of Chicago Press, 1975); Hendrik Hartog, *Public Property and Private Power: The Corporation of the City of New York in American Law, 1730–1870* (Chapel Hill: University of North Carolina Press, 1983).

16. J. Van Fenstermaker, *The Development of American Commercial Banking, 1782–1837* (Kent, OH: Kent State University, 1965); Naomi Lamoreaux, *Insider Lending: Banks, Personal Connections, and Economic Development in Industrial New England* (New York: Cambridge University Press, 1994); Robert E. Wright, *Origins of Commercial Banking in America, 1750–1800* (New York: Rowman & Littlefield, 2001); Howard Bodenhorn, *State Banking in Early America: A New Economic History* (New York: Oxford University Press, 2003); George Rogers Taylor, *The Transportation Revolution* (New York: Harper & Row, 1951); Carter Goodrich, ed., *Canals and American Economic Development* (New York: Columbia University Press, 1961); Diane Lindstrom, *Economic Development in the Philadelphia Region, 1810–1850* (New York: Columbia University Press, 1978); Ronald E. Shaw, *Canals for a Nation: The Canal Era in the United States, 1790–1860* (Lexington: University Press of Kentucky, 1990); John D. Majewski, *A House Dividing: Economic Development in Pennsylvania and Virginia before the Civil War* (New York: Cambridge University Press, 2000); Martin J. Sklar, *The Corporate Reconstruction of American Capitalism, 1890–1916: The Market, the Law, and Politics* (New York: Cambridge University Press, 1987); Olivier Zunz, *Making America Corporate, 1870–1920* (Chicago: University of Chicago Press, 1990); and William G. Roy, *Socializing Capital: The Rise of the Large Industrial Corporation in America* (Princeton: Princeton University Press, 1997).

17. Theodore Steinberg, *Nature Incorporated: Industrialization and the Waters of New England* (New York: Cambridge University Press, 1991), 99–165. Vera Shlakman coined the term "Boston Associates" in *The Economic History of a Factory Town: A Study of Chicopee, Massachusetts* (Northampton: Smith College Press, 1935); Dalzell, *Enterprising Elite;* François Weil, "Capitalism and Industrialization in New England, 1815–1845," *JAH* 84, no. 4 (Mar. 1998): 1334–54.

18. Scranton, *Proprietary Capitalism;* Remer, *Printers;* Rilling, *Building Houses* and "Sylvan Enterprise and the Philadelphia Hinterland, 1790–1840," *Pennsylvania History* 67 (Apr. 2000): 194–217.

1—ESTABLISHING CORPORATIONS

1. Benjamin Franklin, *The Interest of Great Britain Considered* . . . (London: Printed for T. Becket, 1761).

2. François Jean, marquis de Chastellux, *Travels in North America* . . . (New York: [s.n.], 1828), 179; J.-P. Brissot de Warville, *New Travels in the United States of America: Performed in the Year 1788* (Dublin: W. Corbet, 1792).

3. Isaac Weld, *Travels through the United States and the Provinces of Upper and Lower Canada, during the Years 1795, 1796, and 1797* (London: John Stockdale, 1799), 3.

4. Chastellux, *Travels in North America,* 161; Gary B. Nash, *Urban Crucible: Social Change, Political Consciousness, and the Origins of the American Revolution* (Cambridge: Harvard University Press, 1979), 325, 395.

5. Frederick B. Tolles, *Meeting House and Counting House: The Quaker Merchants of Colonial Philadelphia, 1682–1763* (Chapel Hill: University of North Carolina Press, 1948); Thomas M. Doerflinger, *A Vigorous Spirit of Enterprise: Merchants and Economic Development in Revolutionary Philadelphia* (Chapel Hill: University of North Carolina Press, 1986); Gough, "Towards a Theory."

6. Anon., *Order of Procession, in Honor of the Establishment of the Constitution of the United States . . .* (Philadelphia: Printed by Hall and Sellers, [1788]). Gary B. Nash, *Forging Freedom: The Formation of Philadelphia's Black Community, 1720–1840* (Cambridge: Harvard University Press, 1988), 38; Nash, *Urban Crucible*, 312–25; Billy G. Smith, *The "Lower Sort": Philadelphia's Laboring People, 1750–1800* (Ithaca, NY: Cornell University Press, 1990).

7. Richard R. Beeman, *The Varieties of Political Experience in Eighteenth-Century America* (Philadelphia: University of Pennsylvania Press, 2004), 204–42, 270; James H. Hutson, *Pennsylvania Politics, 1746–1770: The Movement for Royal Government and Its Consequences* (Princeton: Princeton University Press, 1972); Teaford, *Municipal Revolution*, 57.

8. Gary J. Kornblith and John M. Murrin, "The Dilemmas of Ruling Elites in Revolutionary America," in *Ruling America: A History of Wealth and Power in a Democracy*, ed. Steve Fraser and Gary Gerstle, 27–63 (Cambridge: Harvard University Press, 2005), 27–63. Merrill Jensen, *The Founding of a Nation: A History of the American Revolution, 1763–1776* (New York: Oxford University Press, 1968); Robert Gough, "Can a Rich Man Favor Revolution? The Case of Philadelphia in 1776," *PH* 48, no. 3 (July 1981): 235–50.

9. Richard Alan Ryerson, *The Revolution Is Now Begun: The Radical Committees of Philadelphia, 1765–1776* (Philadelphia: University of Pennsylvania Press, 1978), 183, 186; Eric Foner, *Tom Paine and Revolutionary America* (New York: Oxford University Press, 1976), 107–44; Charles S. Olton, *Artisans for Independence: Philadelphia Mechanics and the American Revolution* (Syracuse, NY: Syracuse University Press, 1975); Nash, *Urban Crucible*, 339–86; Harry M. Tinkcom, "The Revolutionary City, 1765–1783," in *Philadelphia: A 300–Year History*, ed. Russell B. Weigley, 109–54 (New York: Norton, 1982); and Gough, "Can a Rich Man," 235–50.

10. Edward Countryman, *The American Revolution*, 2nd ed. (New York: Hill & Wang, 2003), 125–28, 163–65.

11. Robert L. Brunhouse, *The Counter-Revolution in Pennsylvania, 1776–1790* (New York: Octagon Books, 1971 [1942]); James Allen, "Diary of James Allen, Esq. of Philadelphia, Counsellor-at-Law, 1770–1778," *PMHB* 9 (1885): 196.

12. Chastellux, *Travels in North America*, 180, 181.

13. Kenneth Roberts and Anna M. Roberts, ed., *Moreau de St. Méry's American Journey, 1793–1798* (Garden City, NY: Doubleday, 1947), 262–63.

14. Chastellux, *Travels in North America*, 67, 76, 109, 180.

15. Sam Bass Warner, Jr., *The Private City: Philadelphia in Three Periods of Its Growth* (Philadelphia: University of Pennsylvania Press, 1968), 3–22; Teaford, *Municipal Revolution*, 56–58.

16. Shaw Livermore, *Early American Land Companies: Their Influence on Corporate Development* (New York: Commonwealth Fund, 1939); Philip Scranton, *Proprietary Capitalism;* Naomi R. Lamoreaux, "Constructing Firms: Partnerships and Alternative Contractual Arrangements in Early Nineteenth-Century American Business," *Business and Economic History* 24 (Winter 1995): 43–71.

17. George Winthrop Geib, "A History of Philadelphia, 1776–1789" (PhD diss., University of Wisconsin, 1969), 220–43; Teaford, *Municipal Revolution*, 56–58; Donald R. Adams, Jr., *Finance and Enterprise in Early America: A Study of Stephen Girard's Bank, 1812–1831* (Philadelphia: University of Pennsylvania Press, 1978).

18. Richard Sylla, "Monetary Innovation in America," *JEH* 42, no. 1 (March 1982): 21–30; John J. McCusker, *Money and Exchange in Europe and America, 1600–1775: A Handbook* (Chapel Hill: University of North Carolina Press, 1978), 175–88; Edwin J. Perkins, *American Public Finance and Financial Services, 1700–1815* (Columbus: Ohio State University Press, 1994), 29–55; Elmus Wicker, "Colonial Monetary Standards Contrasted: Evidence from the Seven Years' War," *JEH* 45 (Dec. 1985): 869–84; as quoted in E. James Fer-

guson, *The Power of the Purse: A History of American Public Finance, 1776–1790* (Chapel Hill: University of North Carolina Press, 1961), 3; Anne Bezanson, *Prices and Inflation during the American Revolution* (Philadelphia: University of Pennsylvania Press, 1951), 345; Charles W. Calomoris, "Institutional Failure, Monetary Scarcity, and the Depreciation of the Continental," *JEH* 48, no. 1 (Mar. 1988): 47–68.

19. Theodore Thayer, "The Land Bank System in the American Colonies," *JEH* 13, no. 2, (Spring 1953): 145–59; Mary M. Schweitzer, *Custom and Contract: Household, Government, and the Economy in Colonial Pennsylvania* (New York: Columbia University Press, 1987), 115–68; Mary M. Schweitzer, "State-Issued Currency and the Ratification of the U.S. Constitution," *JEH* 49, no. 2 (June 1989): 311–22; CPA, *Report of the Senate, Appointed to Enquire into the Extent and Causes of the Present General Distress* (Lancaster: Pennsylvania Senate, 1820), 12; Leslie Brock, *The Currency of the American Colonies, 1700–1764: A Study in Colonial Finance and Imperial Relations* (New York: Arno Press, 1975).

20. Robert McCulloch, *The Pennsylvania Main Line Canal* (York, PA: American Canal and Transportation Center, 1976); Bernard Bailyn, *Ideological Origins of the American Revolution* (Cambridge: Belknap Press, 1967), 146–60; Gordon S. Wood, *Creation of the American Republic* (Chapel Hill: University of North Carolina Press, 1969), 28–36; Charles G. Paleske, *Observations on the Application for a Law to Incorporate "The Union Canal Company" Respectfully Submitted to the Members of Both Houses of the Legislature of Pennsylvania* (Philadelphia: Duane, 1808), 5.

21. Judith Marion Diamondstone, "The Philadelphia Corporation, 1701–1776" (PhD diss., University of Pennsylvania, 1969); Michael McMahon, "'Publick Service' versus 'Mans Properties': Dock Creek and the Origins of Urban Technology in Eighteenth-Century Philadelphia," in *Early American Technology: Making and Doing Things from the Colonial Era to 1850*, ed. Judith McGaw, 114–47 (Chapel Hill: University of North Carolina Press, 1994); Geib, "History," 67–68, 155–64.

22. B. L. Anderson and P. L. Cottrell, *Money and Banking in England: The Development of the Banking System, 1694–1914* (London: David & Charles, 1974); Richard Roberts and David Kynaston, *The Bank of England: Money, Power and Influence, 1694–1994* (New York: Oxford University Press, 1995); Henry Hamilton, *An Economic History of Scotland in the Eighteenth Century* (Oxford: Clarendon Press, 1963); Richard Saville, *Bank of Scotland: A History, 1695–1995* (Edinburgh: Edinburgh University Press, 1996), 1–278; Charles W. Munn, *The Scottish Provincial Banking Companies, 1747–1864* (Edinburgh: John Donald Publishers, 1981); John Phillips, *A General History of Inland Navigation . . . with Considerations on Those Projected* (London: I. and J. Taylor, 1792); Joseph Priestley, *Historical Account of the Navigable Rivers, Canals and Railways throughout Great Britain* (London: n.p., 1831); Broadside, House File, 17th Session-1, 1793–1794 (Canal and Navigation Companies, Roads, Turnpikes) Pennsylvania General Assembly, Records of General Assembly, Record Group 7, PSA; Ron Harris, *Industrializing English Law: Entrepreneurship and Business Organization, 1720–1844* (New York: Cambridge University Press, 2000).

23. "Appendix: Stockholders' Liability" in Perkins, *American Public Finance*, 373–76.

24. Richard Godbeer, *Sexual Revolution in Early America* (Baltimore: Johns Hopkins University Press, 2002), 327–28; Smith, *"Lower Sort,"* 7–39.

25. Gough, "Towards a Theory," 671–701.

26. Foner, *Tom Paine*, 145–82; Geib, *History*, 91–134; Hubertis Cummings, "Robert Morris and the Episode of the Polacre 'Victorious,'" *PMHB* 70, no. 3 (July 1946): 239–57.

27. John K. Alexander, "The Fort Wilson Incident of 1779: A Case Study of the Revolutionary Crowd," *WMQ*, 3rd ser., vol. 31, no. 4 (Oct. 1974): 589–612.

28. Alexander Hamilton to Robert Morris, April 30, 1781. E. James Ferguson, ed., *The Papers of Robert Morris, 1781–1784*, vol. 1 (Pittsburgh: University of Pittsburgh Press 1973), 31–32.

29. Bodenhorn, *State Banking*, 125–26; Wright, *Origins*, 60–61; Perkins, *American Public Finance*, 106–36; George David Rappaport, *Stability and Change in Revolutionary Pennsylvania: Banking, Politics, and Social Structure* (University Park: Pennsylvania State University Press, 1996), 137–222.

30. Geib, "History," 286–87; CCP, *The Ordinances of the City of Philadelphia* . . . (Philadelphia: Zachariah Poulson, Jr., 1798), 21.

31. CCP, *Ordinances of the City* (1798), 21–44, 59; Teaford, *Municipal Revolution,* 64–78.

32. Teaford, *Municipal Revolution;* Hartog, *Public Property;* J. H. Powell, *Bring Out Your Dead: The Great Yellow Fever Plague in Philadelphia in 1793* (Philadelphia: University of Pennsylvania Press, 1993); William Currie, *Memoirs of the Yellow Fever* . . . (Philadelphia: John Bioren, 1798).

33. *Address of the Committee of the Delaware and Schuylkill Canal Company, to the Committees of the Senate and House of Representatives on the Memorial of Said Company* (Philadelphia: John Ormrod, 1799); George Edward Reed, ed., *Papers of the Governors,* vol. 4, Pennsylvania Archives, no. 4 (Harrisburg: Commonwealth of Pennsylvania, 1900), 267; Nelson Manfred Blake, *Water for the Cities: A History of the Urban Water Supply Problem in the United States* (Syracuse, NY: Syracuse University, 1956), 26–44.

34. Paleske, *Observations,* 7; "A Proposal and Plan for Carrying into Immediate Execution the Improvement of Roads and Inland Navigation," reproduced in William Smith, *An Historical Account of the Rise, Progress and Present State of the Canal Navigation in Pennsylvania* . . . (Philadelphia, 1795), 17–20.

35. January 24, 1812, *Poulson's Daily Advertiser.*

36. "List of the Stockholders Who Have Completed Shares in the Delaware & Schuylkill Canal Navigation," 1807, HSP Miscellaneous Collection, HSP.

37. Alexander Hamilton to Timothy Pickering, April 20, 1781, in *The Papers of Alexander Hamilton,* vol. 2: 1779–1781, ed. Harold C. Syrett and Jacob E. Cooke, 595 (New York: Columbia University Press, 1961), also see editors' note, 596. Hamilton most likely encountered them during his days as a clerk on Nevis, and certainly consulted the *Universal Dictionary* in 1775.

38. Joseph Dorfman, introduction to Malachy Postlethwayt, *The Universal Dictionary of Trade and Commerce* (New York: A. M. Kelly, 1971), 7; *Catalogue of the Books, Belonging to the Library Company of Philadelphia* . . . (Philadelphia: Bartram & Reynolds, 1787); *The First Booklist of the Library of Congress* (Washington, DC: Library of Congress, 1981); Wyndham Beawes, *Lex Mercatoria Rediviva: or, the Merchant's Directory, Being a Complete Guide to All Men in Business,* 2nd ed. (London: R. Baldwin, 1761); "Banks and Banking," Postlethwayt, *Universal.*

39. Joseph Hume Francis, *History of the Bank of England* (Chicago: Euclid, 1888), 58–63; William Robert Scott, *The Constitution and Finance of English, Scottish and Irish Joint-Stock Companies to 1720,* vol. 3 (New York: Peter Smith, 1951), 253–56; BPA, *Charters, Laws, and By-Laws, of the Bank of Pennsylvania* (Philadelphia: Clark & Raser, 1830), 2–21; "Act of Parliament for Erecting a Bank in Scotland Edinburgh, July 17, 1695," Appendix 1, Saville, *Bank of Scotland,* 819–25; *Remarks on Money, and the Bank Paper of the United States: Together with a Review of Governor Snyder's Objections to the Bank Bill Passed by Two of the Legislative Branches of the State of Pennsylvania, at Their Session of 1812–1813* (Philadelphia: n.p., 1814), 14, 15.

40. Data compiled from Davis, "Charters," 433, and Priestley, *Historical Account.*

41. Smith, *Historical Account,* 1; Charles Vallancey, *A Treatise on Inland Navigation* . . . (Dublin: George and Alexander Ewing, 1763), 4. Which source Smith quoted from is open to question. The full passage originally appeared as part of the entry for James Brindley in Andrew Kippis, *Biographia Britannica: or, the Lives of the Most Eminent Persons Who Have Flourished in Great Britain and Ireland,* vol. 2, 2nd ed. (London: W. and A. Strahan, 1780), 591–604. This work, in turn, contains long quotes from [James Brindley], *The History of Inland Navigations, Particularly those of the Duke of Bridgewater* . . . , 2nd ed. (London: T. Lowndes, 1769); Phillips, *General History;* Richard Whitworth, *The Advantages of Inland Navigation* . . . (London: R. Baldwin, 1766).

42. Whitworth, *Advantages,* 17–24.

43. George Heberton Evans, Jr., *British Corporation Finance, 1775–1850: A Study of Preference Shares* (Baltimore: Johns Hopkins University Press, 1936), 11–25; Smith, *Historical Account,* 23–44; Maier, "Revolutionary Origins," 77–78; Rochdale Canal Company,

Bill for Making and Maintaining a Navigable Canal from the Calder Navigation . . . ([London]: n.p., 1792); Richard D. Brown, *Knowledge Is Power: The Diffusion of Information in Early America, 1700–1865* (New York: Oxford University Press, 1989), 110–31.

44. Mathew Carey, ed., *Debates and Proceedings of the General Assembly of Pennsylvania, on the Memorials Praying a Repeal or Suspension of the Law Annulling the Charter of the Bank* (Philadelphia: n.p., 1786), 21; Saul Cornell, "Aristocracy Assailed: The Ideology of Backcountry Anti-Federalism," *JAH* 76, no. 4 (Mar. 1990): 1148–72.

45. John Wilson to Joseph Pemberton, February 24, 1782, Pemberton Papers, HSP; Wood, *Creation*, 471–518; Cathy Matson and Peter Onuf, *A Union of Interests: Political and Economic Thought in Revolutionary America* (Lawrence: University Press of Kansas, 1990).

46. Robert C. Alberts, *The Golden Voyage: The Life and Times of William Bingham, 1752–1804* (Boston: Houghton-Mifflin, 1969), 17; Stock transfer book, Phoenix Insurance Company, HSP Miscellaneous Collection, Box 12-A, HSP; Stock subscription book, SNC, Miscellaneous Records, Manuscript Group 110, PSA; Stock subscription book, 1809, Pennsylvania Company for Insuring Lives and Granting Annuities, Accession #1476, HML; Robert E. Wright, "Thomas Willing (1731–1832): Philadelphia Financier and Forgotten Family Founder," *PH* 63, no. 4 (Autumn 1996): 525–60.

47. Alberts, *Golden Voyage*, 17, 207; William Bingham to Richard Price, December 1, 1786, as quoted in Alberts, *Golden Voyage*, 173.

48. Robert Morris and Benjamin Franklin to William Bingham, September 21, 1776, Robert Morris Collection, Huntington Library. Bingham's library included many works with relevant information regarding British corporations; these included Blackstone's *Commentaries*, Parliamentary Papers, Smith's *Wealth of Nations*, several of Hume's works, the *Parliamentary Register* from 1774 to 1798, *Parliamentary Debates* from 1668–1744, *Debates of the House of Commons*, debates in the Irish House of Commons, Sheffield's *Commerce of the American States*, Mortimer's *Dictionary*, Whitworth's *Trade of Great-Britain*, fourteen volumes of pamphlets and other assorted pamphlets, broadsides, and ephemera. *Catalogue of Books . . . at the late Mansion House of William Bingham, Esquire, deceased* ([Philadelphia]: n.p., 1805); Henry Wansey, *The Journals of an Excursion to the United States of North America, in the Summer of 1794* (Salisbury: J. Easton., 1796), ch. 1; Ralph Hidy, *The House of Baring in American Trade and Finance: English Merchant Bankers at Work, 1763–1861* (Cambridge: Harvard University Press, 1949), 29.

49. Joseph Mortimer Levering, *A History of Bethlehem, Pennsylvania, 1741–1892* (Bethlehem: Times, 1903), 160; Talbot Hamlin, *Benjamin Henry Latrobe* (New York: Oxford University Press, 1955), 16; Robert Scott Burn, *The Steam Engine: Its History and Mechanism . . .* , 7th ed. (London: J. Ogden and Co., n.d.) 33.

50. Edward C. Carter II, ed., *The Virginia Journals of Benjamin Henry Latrobe, 1795–1798* (New Haven: Yale University Press, 1977), vol. 1, 185, 3; vol. 2, 341; Benjamin Henry Latrobe, *View of the Practicability and Means of Supplying the City of Philadelphia with Wholesome Water. . . .* (Philadelphia: Zachariah Poulson, Jr., 1799).

51. Edward C. Carter II, "The Engineer as Agent of Technological Transfer: The American Career of Benjamin Henry Latrobe," in *Benjamin Henry Latrobe and Moncure Robinson: The Engineer as Agent of Technological Transfer,* ed. Barbara E. Benson, 11–32 (Greenville, DE: Eleutherian Mills Historical Library, 1975); Eliza Cope Harrison, ed., *Philadelphia Merchant: The Diary of Thomas P. Cope* (South Bend, IN: Gateway Editions, 1978), 60, 80; Eleanor Maass, "A Public Watchdog: Thomas Pym Cope and the Philadelphia Waterworks," *Proceedings of the American Philosophical Society* 125 (Apr. 1981): 135–54; Hamlin, *Latrobe*, 165; Edward C. Carter II, *Benjamin Henry Latrobe and Public Works: Professionalism, Private Interest, and Public Policy in the Age of Jefferson* (Washington, DC: Public Works Historical Society, 1976); Warner, *The Private City*, 80–82.

52. John Wilson to Joseph Pemberton, January 12, 1782, Pemberton Papers, HSP; Mark Prager & Co. to James St. Ferrall, Philadelphia, February 9, 1797, Prager Letterbook, HSP, as quoted in Robert E. Wright, "Bank Ownership and Lending Patterns in New York and Pennsylvania, 1781–1831," *BHR* 73 (Spring 1999): 42; Perkins, *American Public Finance*, 260.

53. Tom W. Smith estimated the average personal wealth per decedent in Philadelphia in 1791 to be between $604 and $660. Tom W. Smith, "The Dawn of the Urban-Industrial Age: The Social Structure of Philadelphia, 1790–1830" (PhD diss., University of Chicago, 1980), 69.

54. Seavoy, *Origins*, x–xii; Richard Sylla, John B. Legler, and John J. Wallis, "Banks and State Public Finance in the New Republic: The United States, 1790–1860," *JEH* 47 (June 1987): 391–403; Gerry Stoker, "Regime Theory and Urban Politics," in *Theories of Urban Politics*, ed. David Judge, Gerry Stoker, and Harold Wolman, 54–71 (Thousand Oaks, CA: Sage, 1995).

55. Joseph P. Davis, "Charters for American Business Corporations in the Eighteenth Century," *Publications of the American Statistical Association* 15, no. 116 (Dec. 1916): 434–35.

56. Shankman, *Crucible;* Thomas Paine, *Dissertations on Government, on the Affairs of the Bank, and Paper-Money* (Philadelphia: Charles Cist, 1786).

2—INCORPORATING THE OPPOSITION

1. Anon., *Remarks on a Pamphlet, Entitled, "Considerations on the Bank of North-America"* (Philadelphia: John Steele, 1785), 8.

2. Hartz, *Economic Policy,* 69–79.

3. Cathy Matson, "Capitalizing Hope: Economic Thought and the Early National Economy," *JER* 16, no. 2 (Summer 1996): 273–92.

4. Seavoy, *Origins*, xii; Gunn, *Decline,* 143; Maier, "Revolutionary Origins."

5. Bailyn, *Ideological Origins;* Drew McCoy, *The Elusive Republic: Political Economy in Jeffersonian America* (Chapel Hill: University of North Carolina Press, 1980); Wood, *Creation;* Douglas M. Arnold, *A Republican Revolution: Ideology and Politics in Pennsylvania, 1776–1790* (New York: Garland, 1989); Albert O. Hirschman, *The Passions and the Interests: Political Arguments for Capitalism before Its Triumph* (Princeton: Princeton University Press, 1977); Matson and Onuf, *Union;* Joyce Appleby, *Capitalism and a New Social Order: The Republican Vision of the 1790s* (New York: New York University Press, 1984), 140–60; E. P. Thompson, "The Moral Economy of the English Crowd in the Eighteenth Century," *Past and Present,* 50 (Feb. 1971): 76–136; Foner, *Paine,* 145–82; Ronald Schultz, "The Small-Producer Tradition and the Moral Origins of Artisan Radicalism in Philadelphia 1720–1810," *Past and Present,* no. 127 (May 1990): 84–116; Peter Linebaugh and Marcus Rediker, *The Many-Headed Hydra: Sailors, Slaves, Commoners and the Hidden History of the Revolutionary Atlantic* (Boston: Beacon Press, 2000); Terry Bouton, "A Road Closed: Rural Insurgency in Post-Independence Pennsylvania," *JAH* 87 (Dec. 2000): 855–87.

6. See Hartz, *Economic Policy;* Handlin and Handlin, *Commonwealth;* Harry N. Scheiber, "Government and the Economy: Studies of the 'Commonwealth' Policy in Nineteenth-Century America," *Journal of Interdisciplinary History* 3 (Summer 1972): 135–51; Seavoy, *Origins,* 255–74; James Karmel, "The Market Moment: Banking and Politics in Jeffersonian Pennsylvania, 1810–1815," *PH* 70, no. 1 (Winter 2003): 55–80.

7. Edward Coke, as quoted in *The Oxford Essential Quotations Dictionary* (American ed.) (Berkley Books, 1998), Oxford Reference Online, Oxford University Press, accessed September 3, 2003, <http://www.oxfordreference.com/views/ENTRY.html?subview=Main& entry=t92.002943>; Lord Thurlow, as quoted in ibid., accessed September 3, 2003, <http://www.oxfordreference.com/views/ENTRY.html?subview=Main&entry=t92.000745>; Anon., *Remarks,* 11; [William Barton], *The True Interest of the United States, and Particularly of Pennsylvania . . . with Some Observations on the Subject of a Bank, on Agriculture, Manufactures and Commerce* (Philadelphia: Charles Cist, 1786), 22; February 7, 1833, *Philadelphia Pennsylvanian.*

8. Petition to Pennsylvania House of Representatives [1800?], House File, 24th Session-1, 1799–1800 (Canal and Navigation Companies, Roads, Turnpikes), Pennsylvania General Assembly, Records of General Assembly, Record Group 7, PSA; McCoy, *Elusive Republic.*

9. *Aurora General Advertiser,* January 1, 1796, as quoted in Schultz, "Small-Producer Tradition," 109.

10. Broadside, House File, 17th Session-1, 1793–94 (Canal and Navigation Companies, Roads, Turnpikes) Pennsylvania General Assembly, Records of General Assembly, Record Group 7, PSA; Petition to Pennsylvania House of Representatives [1800?], House File, 24th Session-1, 1799–1800 (Canal and Navigation Companies, Roads, Turnpikes), Pennsylvania General Assembly, Records of General Assembly, Record Group 7, PSA; Anon., *An Address to the Assembly of Pennsylvania, on the Abolition of the Bank of North-America* (Philadelphia: Robert Aitken, 1785), 5; Nash, *Urban Crucible;* Smith, *"Lower Sort,"* 7–39.

11. Smith, *"Lower Sort,"* 100, 109, 120, 121; Wright, "Bank Ownership," 40–60; Majewski, *House Dividing,* 37–58.

12. Anon., *Address . . . Abolition,* 5; Doerflinger, *Vigorous Spirit,* 304; Wright, "Bank Ownership," 40–60; Thayer, "Land Bank System," 155.

13. Wright, "Bank Ownership," 40–60; Minutes of the Directors, BPA, Reading Branch, November 7, 1810, HSP.

14. Charles Biddle, *Autobiography of Charles Biddle, Vice-President of the Supreme Executive Council of Pennsylvania, 1745–1821* (Philadelphia: E. Claxton and Company, 1883), 142; James A. Kehl, *Ill Feeling in the Era of Good Feeling: Western Pennsylvania Political Battles, 1815–1825* (Pittsburgh: University of Pittsburgh Press, 1956); Kenneth Keller, *Rural Politics and the Collapse of Pennsylvania Federalism* (Philadelphia: American Philosophical Society, 1982).

15. Karmel, "Market Moment."

16. Robert D. Arbuckle, *Pennsylvania Speculator and Patriot: The Entrepreneurial John Nicholson, 1757–1800* (University Park: Pennsylvania State University Press, 1975); July 1, 1789, *Pennsylvania Packet,* as quoted in Arbuckle, *Pennsylvania Speculator,* 46.

17. John Nicholson to George Meade, June 1, 1793, as quoted in Arbuckle, *Pennsylvania Speculator,* 50; Robert E. Wright, "Artisans, Banks, Credit, and the Election of 1800," *PMHB* 132, no. 3 (1998): 211–40.

18. James Karmel, "Banking on the People: Banks, Politics, and Market Evolution in Early National Pennsylvania, 1781–1824" (PhD diss., University of Buffalo, 1999), 52–55, 62–64, 112.

19. John Caldwell, *William Findley from West of the Mountains: A Politician in Pennsylvania, 1783–1791* (Gig Harbor, WA: Red Apple, 2000), 20; William Findley, "William Findley of Westmoreland, PA., Author of 'History of the Insurrection in the Western Counties of Pennsylvania.'—An Autobiographical Letter," *PMHB* 5, no. 1 (1881): 446.

20. *Pennsylvania Packet and Daily Advertiser,* August 30, 1786, quoted in Teaford, *Municipal Revolution,* 68; William Findley, "Autobiographical Letter," 444.

21. Carey, *Debates,* 65; Wood, *Radicalism,* 256–58.

22. James Wilson to George Washington, December 31, 1791, as quoted in Mark David Hall, *The Political and Legal Philosophy of James Wilson, 1742–1798* (Columbia: University of Missouri Press, 1997), 30; Charles Page Smith, *James Wilson: Founding Father, 1742–1798* (Chapel Hill: University of North Carolina Press, 1956).

23. James Wilson, *Considerations on the Bank of North-America* (Philadelphia: Hall & Sellers, 1785), 19–24.

24. Smith, *Historical Account,* iii, 3, 23.

25. Address of Governor Simon Snyder to the Legislature, December 5, 1811, in *Pennsylvania Archives,* 4th ser., ed. George Edward Reed, 752 (Harrisburg: State of Pennsylvania, 1900); UCC, *Report . . . of the Union Canal Company, of Pennsylvania . . . to the Legislature of the State of Pennsylvania, at Their Session 1812–13* (Philadelphia: John Binns, 1812), 9; CCP, *Report of the Watering Committee, on the Disposal of the Surplus Water Power of the River Schuylkill, and the Construction of a Canal between the Schuylkill and Delaware* (Philadelphia: Councils of the Corporation of Philadelphia, 1825), 12.

26. Hirschman, *Passions;* Matson and Onuf, *Union of Interests.*

27. Bouton, "A Road Closed"; Thomas Slaughter, *The Whiskey Rebellion: Frontier Epilogue to the American Revolution* (New York: Oxford University Press, 1987); Paul Moyer, "Wild Yankees: Settlement, Conflict, and Localism along Pennsylvania's Northeast Frontier, 1760–1820" (PhD diss., College of William and Mary, 1999).

28. [Albert Gallatin], *Report of the Secretary of the Treasury, on the Subject of Public Roads and Canals; Made in Pursuance of a Resolution of Senate, of March 2, 1807, April 12, 1808* (Washington: R. C. Weightman, 1808), 8; Robert Fulton to Albert Gallatin, December 8, 1807, as quoted in Gallatin, *Report*, 123; UCC, *Report of the President and Managers of the Union Canal Company . . .* (Philadelphia: John Bioren, 1818), 3.

29. *Report on Roads, Bridges and Canals, Read in the Senate, March 23, 1822* (Harrisburg: C. Mowry, 1822), 18.

30. Robert Morris to Thomas Mifflin, November 26, 1793, and Report from the judges of the court of common pleas of Dauphin county respecting some disturbances in the neighbourhood of the Schuylkill and Susquehanna Canal, February 24, 1794, Secretary of the Commonwealth, Internal Improvements File, Canal & Navigation Companies, Schuylkill & Susquehanna Canal & Lock Navigation Company, PSA.

31. Citizens of Philadelphia, Petition to Pennsylvania General Assembly, House File, 49th Session-1, 1824–1825, Folder 5, Pennsylvania General Assembly, Records of General Assembly, Record Group 7, PSA.

32. Paleske, 2, 3; *Aurora General Advertiser* (Philadelphia), January 15, 1812.

33. UCC, *Memorial . . . 1812–1813*, 8.

34. Population of 111,210 in 1810 from University of Virginia Geospatial and Statistical Data Center, *United States Historical Census Data Browser*, 1998, University of Virginia, accessed August 14, 2003, <http://fisher.lib.virginia.edu/census>.

35. John M. Taylor to Charles G. Paleske, February 28, 1809, Gordon Chambers Collection, HSP.

36. William Crawford Armor, *The Lives of the Governors of Pennsylvania . . . from 1609 to 1872* (Philadelphia: J. K. Simon, 1872), 308–24; Jurgen Heideking, "Simon Snyder," in *American National Biography*, vol. 20, ed. John A. Garraty and Mark C. Carnes, 350–51 (New York: Oxford University Press, 1999); Petition, Mar. 4, 1793, House File, 17th Session-1, 1792–1793 (Bridges, Streams, Roads), Records of General Assembly, Record Group 7, PSA.

37. George Edward Reed, ed., *Pennsylvania Archives*, fourth series, vol. 4 (Harrisburg: State of Pennsylvania, 1900), 805–9, 836.

38. The statistics cited here were compiled from CPA, *Proceedings and Debates of the Convention . . . 1837* (Harrisburg: Packer, Barrett, and Parke, 1837), 212–27; and William Miller, "A Note on the Business Corporations in Pennsylvania, 1800–1860," *Quarterly Journal of Economics* 55 (Nov. 1940): 150–60.

39. Karmel, "Market Moment," 55–80; Herbert Ershkowitz and William G. Shade, "Consensus or Conflict? Political Behavior in the State Legislatures during the Jacksonian Era," *JAH* 58, no. 3 (Dec. 1971): 591–621.

40. Sean Patrick Adams, *Old Dominion, Industrial Commonwealth: Coal, Politics, and Economy in Antebellum America* (Baltimore: Johns Hopkins University Press, 2004), 157–65; Clifton K. Yearley, *Enterprise and Anthracite: Economics and Democracy in Schuylkill County, 1820–1875* (Baltimore: Johns Hopkins University Press, 1961), 80–81.

41. March 3, 1833, *United States Gazette* (Philadelphia).

42. Anon., *A Shot from a Backwoods-Marksman, Most Respectfully Addressed to the People of the Commonwealth of Pennsylvania, by Their Humble Servant, a Shinglemaker* ([Philadelphia]: n.p., 1832); Yearley, *Enterprise*, 81–89; George Taylor, *Effect of Incorporated Coal Companies upon the Anthracite Coal Trade in Pennsylvania* (Pottsville, PA: Benjamin Bannan, 1833), 9, as quoted in Hartz, *Economic Policy*, 60.

43. Adams, *Old Dominion*, 162–63.

44. Hartz, *Economic Policy*, 58–62.

45. Tony A. Freyer, *Producers versus Capitalists: Constitutional Conflict in Antebellum*

America (Charlottesville: University Press of Virginia, 1994); John Lauritz Larson, *Internal Improvement: National Public Works and the Promise of Popular Government in the Early United States* (Chapel Hill: University of North Carolina Press, 2001).

46. List of subscribers, Thomas Willing Balch, *The Philadelphia Assemblies* (Philadelphia: Allen, Lane, and Scott, 1916), 98–99; Baltzell, *Philadelphia Gentlemen*, 70–106.

47. Gunn, *Decline of Authority*, 99–143; Maier, "Revolutionary Origins," 51–84.

3—INCORPORATING MONEY

1. Anon., *To the Senate . . . The Memorial of the Subscribers, Inhabitants of the Borough of Pittsburgh, and Its Vicinity* (Pittsburgh: n.p., 1810).

2. CPA, *Report of the Senate . . . General Distress*, 2–3; Murray N. Rothbard, *The Panic of 1819: Reactions and Policy* (New York: Columbia University Press, 1962); Robert M. Blackson, "Pennsylvania Banks and the Panic of 1819: A Reinterpretation," *JER* 9, no. 3 (Autumn 1989): 335–58.

3. Mary Schweitzer, "State-Issued Currency," 311–22; United States Constitution, Article I, Section 10.

4. Hartz labeled corporations in which the state had a stake as "mixed enterprise." Hartz, *Economic Policy*, 82–128; Seavoy, *Origins*, 256–59.

5. Redlich, *Molding of American Banking: Men and Ideas* (New York: Johnson Reprint Corp., 1968), 2:60–84; Richard Sylla, "Forgotten Men of Money: Private Bankers in Early U.S. History," *JEH* 36, no. 1 (Mar. 1976): 173–88.

6. Lamoreaux, *Insider Lending;* Howard Bodenhorn, *State Banking;* Rilling, *Building Houses*, 45–51; Adams, *Finance and Enterprise;* Elva C. Tooker, "A Merchant Turns to Money-Lending in Philadelphia," *Bulletin of the Business Historical Society* 2, no. 3 (June 1946): 71–85.

7. Bruce H. Mann, *Republic of Debtors: Bankruptcy in the Age of American Independence* (Cambridge: Harvard University Press, 2002); Edward J. Balleisen, *Navigating Failure: Bankruptcy and Commercial Society in Antebellum America* (Chapel Hill: University of North Carolina Press, 2001).

8. Bray Hammond, *Banks and Politics in America, from the Revolution to the Civil War* (Princeton: Princeton University Press, 1957); Susan Hoffman, *Politics and Banking: Ideas, Public Policy, and the Creation of Financial Institutions* (Baltimore: Johns Hopkins University Press, 2001), 2–70.

9. Anon., "Proposals for Establishing Another Bank in the City of Philadelphia, by the Name of the Bank of Pennsylvania" ([Philadelphia]: n.p., 1784).

10. Richard G. Miller, *Philadelphia—The Federalist City: A Study of Urban Politics, 1789–1801* (Port Washington, NY: Kennikat Press, 1976), 17; Thomas Wistar to Caspar Wistar, May 15, 1784, Leach Collection, HSP.

11. Anon., *Address . . . Abolition*, 10; Pelatiah Webster, as quoted in Anna Jacobson Schwartz, "The Beginning of Competitive Banking in Philadelphia, 1782–1809," *Journal of Political Economy* 55, no. 5 (Oct. 1947): 417–21.

12. Karmel, "Banking," 39–51; Anon., "Proposals . . . Bank of Pennsylvania"; BPA, "List of Stockholders in the Bank of Pennsylvania" ([Philadelphia]: E. Oswald, [1790]); Martin S. Pernick, "Politics, Parties, and Pestilence: Epidemic Yellow Fever in Philadelphia and the Rise of the First Party System," *WMQ*, 3rd ser., 29 (Oct. 1972): 559–86.

13. Biddle, *Autobiography*, 245; statistics generated by comparing the BPA, "List . . . Pennsylvania" (1790) with an 80% sampling of the 1789 Philadelphia assessment; the latter data were graciously provided to the author by Billy G. Smith; Mathew Carey, *Cursory Reflections on the System of Taxation . . .* (Philadelphia: Mathew Cary, 1806).

14. BPA, "List . . . Pennsylvania" (1790).

15. These statistics and the ones that follow regarding the stockholders of the Farmers and Mechanics Bank were compiled and calculated from Corporate Series, vol. 8, Stock Ledger, Farmers and Mechanics National Bank, Accession 1658, HML; Wright, "Bank Ownership," 40–60; Hurst, *Legitimacy*, 26.

16. Of the original issue of 12,000 shares, 11,970 are accounted for in the list of original stockholders; the 1,837 are taken as a percentage of 11,970 in the list. Corporate Series, vol. 8, Stock Ledger, Farmers and Mechanics National Bank, Accession 1658, HML.

17. BPA, *To the Senate . . . the Memorial of the President and Directors of the Bank of Pennsylvania* (Philadelphia: n.p., [1805]), 2; *To the Senate . . . the Memorial of the President and Directors of the Bank of North America . . . Founded on the Representation given by the Stock Books of the Bank of North America . . .* ([Philadelphia: 1807]).

18. Perkins, *American Public Finance*, 266–81; Donald R. Adams, Jr., "Portfolio Management and Profitability in Early-Nineteenth-Century Banking," *BHR* 52, no. 1 (Spring 1978): 61–79; Wright, "Bank Ownership," 40–60.

19. Rappaport, *Stability*, 234; Doerflinger, *Vigorous Spirit*, 305; Wright, "Artisans," 233; Robert E. Wright, *The Wealth of Nations Rediscovered: Integration and Expansion in American Financial Markets, 1780–1850* (New York: Cambridge University Press, 2002), 193–211.

20. Wright, "Bank Ownership," 40–60; Pelatiah Webster, *An Essay on Credit: In Which the Doctrine of Bank, Is Considered, and Some Remarks Are Made on the Present State of the Bank of North America* (Philadelphia: Eleazer Oswald, 1786), 3; Robert B. Patterson to General Bernard, December 25, 1829, Robert Patterson Papers, HSP.

21. Samuel Emlen to Roberts Vaux, March 16, 1813, Vaux Papers, HSP; CPA, *Report of the Senate . . . General Distress*, 5; Webster, *Essay*, 9.

22. BPA, *Charters . . . Bank of Pennsylvania*, 41; BPA, *Laws of the Bank of Pennsylvania* (Philadelphia: John Binns, 1811), 13; McCusker, *Money and Exchange*, 19.

23. BPA, *Charters . . . Bank of Pennsylvania*, 17, 18.

24. Stephen N. Winslow, *Biographies of Successful Philadelphia Merchants* (Philadelphia: James K. Simon, 1864), 167; Joseph Reed to Paul Beck, December 30, 1803, McAllister Collection, HSP; February 3, 1804, Minutes of the Stockholders of the BPA, 1793–1842, HSP.

25. James Sharswood to Joseph Tagert, March 13, 1807, Historical Records, Box 1, 1807–1820, Accession 1658, Farmers and Mechanics National Bank Collection, HML.

26. John Thompson to Joseph Tagert, March 9, 1809, Historical Records, Box 1, 1807–1820, Accession 1658, Farmers and Mechanics National Bank Collection, HML.

27. Karmel, "Market Moment," 55–80; CPA, *Report of the Senate . . . General Distress*, 6.

28. Biddle, *Autobiography*, 344; Thomas Burnside to William Norris, March 10, 1814, Gratz Collection, HSP; Karmel, "Market Moment," 55–80; Shankman, *Crucible*, 173–224.

29. Hartz, *Economic Policy*, 83–128; Richard Bache to William Meredith, January 1, 1824, Meredith Papers, HSP.

30. Sylla, Legler, and Wallis, "Banks," 391–403; John Joseph Wallis, Richard E. Sylla, and John B. Legler, "The Interaction of Taxation and Regulation in Nineteenth-Century Banking," in *The Regulated Economy: A Historical Approach to Political Economy*, ed. Claudia Goldin and Gary D. Libecap, 129 (Chicago: University of Chicago Press, 1994).

31. BPA, *To the Senate . . . Bank of Pennsylvania*, 6.

32. Joseph Clay to Joseph Tagert, February 17, 1809, Historical Records, Box 1, 1807–1820, Accession 1658. Farmers and Mechanics National Bank Collection, HML; CPA, *An Act to Incorporate the Farmers and Mechanics Bank* (Philadelphia: Jane Aitken, 1809).

33. Wallis, Sylla, and Legler, "Interaction," 121–44; Biddle, *Autobiography*, 345.

34. Sylla, Legler, and Wallis, "Banks," 401; Richard Bache to William Meredith, January 1, 1824, Meredith Papers, HSP.

35. Simon Gratz to William Meredith, January 15, 1824; Meredith Collection, HSP.

36. BPA, "An Act to Incorporate the Subscribers to the Bank of Pennsylvania," in BPA, *Charters . . . Bank of Pennsylvania*, 3–30; Rowland Berthoff, "Conventional Mentality: Free Blacks, Women, and Business Corporations as Unequal Persons, 1820–1870," *JAH* 76 (Nov. 1989): 753–84.

37. CPA, *An Act to Incorporate . . . The Farmers and Mechanics Bank* (1809); Philadelphia Bank, *The Philadelphia Bank; Containing the Articles of Association, the Original Charter, and All the Acts of Assembly Extending and Relating to it, with the General Banking Law of April 16, 1850* (Philadelphia: Wm. F. Murphy & Sons, 1859).

38. BPA, *Charters . . . Bank of Pennsylvania,* 9–10.

39. Ibid., 3–30.

40. Brown, *Knowledge Is Power,* 110–31.

41. February 2, 1798, Minutes of the Stockholders of the BPA, 1793–1842, HSP.

42. Jeffrey A. Cohen and Charles E. Brownell, eds., *The Architectural Drawings of Benjamin Henry Latrobe* (New Haven: Yale University Press, 1994), 2: 188–227; Hamlin, *Latrobe,* 152–58; Fiske Kimball, "The Bank of Pennsylvania, an Unknown Masterpiece of American Classicism," *Architectural Record* 43 (Aug. 1918): 132–39; January 29, 1802, Minutes of the Stockholders of the BPA, 1793–1842, HSP.

43. Owen Biddle, *The Young Carpenter's Assistant, or, A System of Architecture, Adapted to the Style of Building in the United States* (Philadelphia: Benjamin Johnson, 1805), 54; A. B. Duncan, *Travels through Part of the United States and Canada in 1818 and 1819,* vol. 1. (Glasgow: University Press, 1823), 190; Kenneth Hafertepe, "Banking Houses in the United States: The First Generation, 1781–1811," *Winterthur Portfolio* 35, no. 1 (Spring 2000), 1–52; Deborah C. Andrews, "Bank Buildings in Nineteenth-Century Philadelphia," in *The Divided Metropolis: Social and Spatial Dimensions of Philadelphia, 1800–1975,* ed. William W. Cutler III and Howard Gillette, Jr., 57–84 (Westport, CT: Greenwood Press, 1980).

44. Stephen Mihm, "Making Money, Creating Confidence: Counterfeiting and Capitalism in the United States, 1789–1877" (PhD diss., New York University, 2003), 1–24.

45. James Sharswood to Joseph Tagert, March 13, 1807; Historical Records, Box 1, 1807–1820, Farmers and Mechanics National Bank records, Accession 1658, HML.

46. Philemon Dickinson to Jonathan Smith, December 17, 1803, Gratz Collection, HSP.

47. February 1809 (?), Historical Records, Box 1, 1807–1820, Farmers and Mechanics National Bank records, Accession 1658, HML.

48. CPA, *Report and Documents of the Committee Appointed to Enquire into the Conduct of the Cashier and Directors of the Bank of Pennsylvania* (n.p., 1815), 5–6; BPA, *An Address to the Stockholders of the Bank of Pennsylvania. December 22, 1829* (Philadelphia: Clark & Raser, 1829); CPA, *Report of the Committee of State Directors, of the Bank of Pennsylvania, Appointed November 14, 1829, upon the Loans of 1828 and 1829* (Philadelphia: n.p., 1829).

49. Lawrence A. Peskin, *Manufacturing Revolution: The Intellectual Origins of Early American Industry* (Baltimore: Johns Hopkins University Press, 2003), 145–52; "Petition to Pennsylvania Legislature, February 9, 1827," Historical Records, Box 2, 1821–1863, Farmers and Mechanics National Bank records, Accession 1658, HML.

50. BPA, *Charters . . . Bank of Pennsylvania* (1830), 15, 23; George Edward Reed, ed., *Papers of the Governors: Pennsylvania Archives,* 4th ser., vol. 5 (Harrisburg: Commonwealth of Pennsylvania, 1931), 152, 153.

51. CPA, *Report . . . into the Conduct of the BPA* [1815]; Hartz, *Economic Policy,* 254–67.

52. Biddle, *Autobiography,* 273–74; Stockholder Minutes, January 30, 1806, Minutes of the Stockholders of the BPA, 1793–1842, HSP.

53. *Bank of North America* v. *Wycoff,* Supreme Court of Pennsylvania, 4 U.S. 151; 1 L. Ed 778; 1796 U.S. Lexis 415; 4 Dall. 151.

54. *Farmers and Mechanics Bank* v. *Greiner executor of Massey,* Supreme Court of Pennsylvania, Eastern District, Philadelphia 2 Serg. & Rawle 114; 1815 Lexis 87.

55. For the best brief biography of Carey, see James Green, *Mathew Carey, Publisher and Patriot* (Philadelphia: Library Company of Philadelphia, 1985).

56. Mathew Carey, *Private and confidential . . . the case that occurred on Saturday at the Bank of Pennsylvania, February 24, 1817* (Philadelphia: Mathew Carey, 1817).

57. Mathew Carey, *Reflections on the Renewal of the Charter of the Bank of Pennsylvania, Together with a View of the Immoderate Power Possessed by a Small Number of That Body* (Philadelphia: M. Carey, 1829), 7; Mathew Carey to Joseph P. Norris, January 20, 1825, Edward Carey Gardiner Papers, Mathew Carey Section, HSP.

58. Carey, *Reflections on the Renewal*, 4–10.

59. Redlich, *Molding*, 1:17; Lamoreaux, *Insider Lending*, 11–30; Bodenhorn, *State Banking*, 11–94, 123–82.

4—INCORPORATING THE CITY

1. Elaine Forman Crane, ed., *The Diary of Elizabeth Drinker* (Boston: Northeastern University Press, 1991), 2:1381; Hamlin, *Latrobe*, 165.

2. Harrison, ed., *Philadelphia Merchant*, 56; Blake, *Water*, 18; Crane, *Diary of Elizabeth Drinker*, 2:1382.

3. Gary B. Nash, "The Social Evolution of Preindustrial American Cities, 1700–1820," *Journal of Urban History* 13 (Feb. 1987): 113–45; Gideon Sjoberg, *The Preindustrial City, Past and Present* (Glencoe, Il: Free Press, 1960).

4. Hartog, *Public Property;* Joseph S. Lewis to Mathew Carey, July 1, 1824, Edward Carey Gardiner Papers, Mathew Carey Section, Miscellaneous Correspondence on Internal Improvement, HSP.

5. Simeon Crowther, "Urban Growth in the Mid-Atlantic States, 1785–1850," *JEH* 36, no. 3 (Sept. 1976): 624–44; Henry B. Latrobe, *The Journal of Latrobe . . . from 1796 to 1820* (New York: D. Appleton, 1905), 97; Martin V. Melosi, *The Sanitary City: Urban Infrastructure from Colonial Times to the Present* (Baltimore: Johns Hopkins University Press, 2000), 17–42.

6. Leonard P. Curry, *The Corporate City: The American City as a Political Entity, 1800–1850* (Westport, CT: Greenwood Press, 1997), 1–32; Teaford, *Municipal Revolution*, 16–34; Michael McMahon, "'Publick Service,'" 114–47.

7. Teaford, *Municipal Revolution*, 64–78.

8. Delaware and Schuylkill Canal Company, *Address of the Committee;* B. Henry Latrobe, *Remarks on the Address of the Committee of the Delaware and Schuylkill Canal Company . . . Printed by order of the Committee of the Councils* (Philadelphia: Zachariah Poulson, Jr., 1799), 14; David Freeman Hawke, *Nuts and Bolts of the Past: A History of American Technology, 1776–1860* (New York: Harper & Row, 1988), 63–68; January 31, 1799, Series II, Subseries 2, Delaware & Schuylkill Navigation Company, Board of Managers Minutes, Accession 1520, Reading Company Collection, HML.

9. Charles Zable and Jonathan Zeitling, "Historical Alternatives to Mass Production: Politics, Markets, and Technology in Nineteenth-Century Industrialization," *Past and Present*, no. 108 (Aug. 1985): 161; Latrobe, *View*.

10. Carroll W. Pursell, *Early Stationary Steam Engines in America: A Study in the Migration of Technology* (Washington, DC: Smithsonian Institution, 1969), 32; John C. Van Horne and Lee W. Formwalt, eds., *Correspondence and Miscellaneous Papers: The Papers of Benjamin Henry Latrobe*, 4th ser., vol. 1 (New Haven: Published for the Maryland Historical Society by Yale University Press, 1984), 141–42; Darwin Stapleton, "Benjamin Henry Latrobe and the Transfer of Technology," in *Technology in America: A History of Individuals and Ideas*, ed. Carroll Pursell, 34–44 (Cambridge: MIT Press, 1982); Darwin H. Stapleton, ed., *The Engineering Drawings of Benjamin Henry Latrobe* (New Haven: Yale University Press, 1980), 144–98.

11. Joseph Jackson, *Market Street Philadelphia: The Most Historic Highway in America, Its Merchants, and Its Story* (Philadelphia: Patterson & White, 1918), 176–77; Leo Marx, *The Machine in the Garden: Technology and the Pastoral Ideal in America* (New York: Oxford University Press, 1967), 145–226; Blake, *Water*, 18–43.

12. Abigail Adams to Mary Crouch, February 15, 1798, in *Passing Through: Letters and Documents Written in Philadelphia by Famous Visitors*, ed. Clive E. Driver (Philadelphia: Rosenbach Museum & Library, 1982), 49.

13. Harrison, ed. *Philadelphia Merchant*, 383; Blake, *Water*, 161, 223, 265. John Kasson, *Civilizing the Machine: Technology and Republican Values in America, 1776–1900* (New York: Grossman, 1976), 1–52; Fritz Redlich, "Notes and Documents: The Philadelphia Water Works in Relation to the Industrial Revolution in the United States," *PMHB* 69 (July 1945): 247.

14. Pursell, *Early Stationary Steam Engines*, 42–43; Thomas Green Fessenden, *The Register of Arts, or A Compendious View of Some of the Most Useful Modern Discoveries and Inventions* (Philadelphia: Fessenden, 1808), 333.

15. Patrick O'Bannon, "Inconsiderable Progress: Commercial Brewing in Philadelphia before 1840," in McGaw, ed., *Early American Technology*, 161; Smith, "Dawn," 33; Carolyn C. Cooper, "A Patent Transformation: Woodworking Mechanization in Philadelphia, 1830–1856," in McGaw, ed., *Early American Technology*, 285; Eugene S. Ferguson, *Oliver Evans: Inventive Genius of the American Industrial Revolution* (Greenville, RI: Hagley Museum, 1980), 51; Pursell, *Early Stationary Steam Engines*, 87, 94; Department for Supplying the City with Water, *Annual Report of the Chief Engineer of the Water Department of the City of Philadelphia for the Year 1875* (Philadelphia: City of Philadelphia, 1876), 18, as quoted in Pursell, *Early Stationary Steam Engines*, 32–33.

16. Harrison, ed., *Philadelphia Merchant*, 61; "Report of the Watering Committee on the subject of obtaining Water power from the River Schuylkill," City Council 120.42 Committee on Water, Papers 1804–1854, Box A3118, PCA; Blake, *Water*, 78–99.

17. Charles A. Poulson, Extracts from Various Works of Travel &c. &c. Relating to the City of Philadelphia, 1688–1862, Library Company of Philadelphia.

18. CCP, *Report to the Select and Common Councils on the Progress and State of the Water Works on the 24th of November, 1799* (Philadelphia: Zachariah Poulson, Jr., 1799), CCP, *An Ordinance for Raising Supplies . . . for the Year 1799* (Philadelphia: Zachariah Poulson, Jr., 1799); February 17, 1799, Select Council Minutes, October 14, 1796–April 14, 1799, PCA.

19. December 4, 1797, Select Council Minutes, October 14, 1796–April 14, 1799, PCA; Asa Earl Martin, "Lotteries in Pennsylvania prior to 1833," *PMHB* 47, no. 4 (Winter 1923): 307–27.

20. CCP, *Ordinance for Raising Supplies*, 3.

21. August 1, 1799, Common Council Minutes, vol. 2, February 18, 1799–January 13, 1803 (mss.), PCA.

22. CCP, *Ordinance for Raising Supplies*, 3.

23. Statistics compiled from Loan Certificate Transfer Journal, City Treasurer, February 1801–August 1820, PCA; CCP, *Report of the Watering Committee to the Select and Common Councils, November 2, 1809* (Philadelphia: Jane Aitken, 1809), 16.

24. Curry, *Corporate City*, 36–37; Mary M. Schweitzer, "The Spatial Organization of Federalist Philadelphia, 1790," *Journal of Interdisciplinary History*, 24, no. 1 (Summer 1993): 54; Carey, *Cursory Reflections*, 42.

25. CCP, *Ordinance for Raising Supplies*, 5, *Report of the Joint Committee of the Select and Common Councils, on the Subject of Bringing Water to the City* (Philadelphia: Zachariah Poulson, Jr., 1798); Donald F. Swanson and Andrew P. Trout, "Alexander Hamilton's Hidden Sinking Fund," *WMQ*, 3rd ser., 49 (Jan. 1992): 108–16; John C. Lowber, ed., *Ordinances of the Corporation of the City of Philadelphia; to Which Are refixed, the Original Charter, the Act of Incorporation, and Other Acts of Assembly Relating to the City* (Philadelphia: Moses Thomas, 1812), 212–14.

26. Lowber, ed., *Ordinances*, 212–14; CCP, *Ordinances of the Corporation of the City of Philadelphia. Passed since the Third Day of August, One Thousand Eight Hundred and Twenty* (Philadelphia: City Councils, 1822), 168–69, *Ordinances of the Corporation of the City of Philadelphia. Passed Since the Twenty-Seventh Day of December, One Thousand Eight Hundred and Twenty-One* (Philadelphia: City Councils, 1823), 209–10, 221, *Accounts of the Corporation of the City of Philadelphia from the First of April, 1819, to the First of April, 1823* (Philadelphia: The Councils, 1823).

27. Lowber, ed., *Ordinances*, 212–14, 239–40; CCP, *Ordinances of the Corporation of the City of Philadelphia; Passed Since the Fourteenth Day of September, One Thousand Eight Hundred and Fifteen* (Philadelphia: City Councils, 1817), 69–71, *Ordinances of the Corporation of the City of Philadelphia. Passed Since the Sixteenth of July, One Thousand Eight Hundred and Seventeen* (Philadelphia: City Councils, 1819), 117–18, 126–28, *Ordinances*

(1822), 164–65, 171–72, *Ordinances of the Corporation of the City of Philadelphia. Passed Since the Twenty-Second Day of April, One Thousand Eight Hundred and Nineteen* (Philadelphia: City Councils, 1821), 158–59, *Accounts* (1823), 36; March 1, 1830, Philadelphia City Councils, Committee on the Sinking Fund, Minutes 1824–1834, Series 120.32, PCA.

28. Curry, *Corporate City*, 57–58; CCP, *Committee of Ways and Means Report for Appropriations for 1807, Accompanied by An Ordinance for Raising Supplies and Making Appropriations for the Services of the City . . .* (Philadelphia: [Jane Aitken], 1806), 3.

29. Lowber, ed., *Ordinances*, 191, 239–40; CCP, *Ordinances* (1817), 87, *Ordinances* (1822), 168–69, *Ordinances of the Corporation of the City of Philadelphia. Passed since the Fourth Day of February, One Thousand Eight Hundred and Twenty-Three* (Philadelphia: City Councils, 1824), 253–54, *Ordinances of the Corporation of the City of Philadelphia. Passed Since the Eighth Day of January, One Thousand Eight Hundred and Twenty-Four* (Philadelphia: City Councils, 1825), 280–82, *Committee of Ways and Means* (1806), 5; *Ordinances of the Corporation of the City of Philadelphia; Passed since the Eighteenth Day of June, One Thousand Eight Hundred and Twelve* (Philadelphia: Philadelphia Councils, 1815), 11, 12–13, 54; *Ordinances* (1821), 158–59; *Ordinances* (1823), 182; *Ordinances* (1824), 248–50; *Ordinances* (1817), 69–71.

30. CCP, *Ordinances* (1825), 275; November 13, 1824, Philadelphia City Councils, Committee on the Sinking Fund, Minutes 1824–1834, Series 120.32, PCA.

31. In 1817, for example, the city owed the Bank of Pennsylvania $54,000 and the Philadelphia Bank $59,000; *Statements Submitted to the Senate, from the Pennsylvania, Philadelphia, and Farmers' and Mechanics' Banks* ([Harrisburg]: n.p., 1817).

32. CCP, *Report of the Committee for the Introduction of Wholesome Water into the City of Philadelphia* (Philadelphia: Zachariah Poulson, Jr., 1801), *Report of the Watering Committee to the Select and Common Councils, November 1, 1803* (Philadelphia: William Duane, 1803), 5, *Report of the Watering Committee to the Select and Common Councils, November 1, 1804* (Philadelphia: Robert Cochran, 1804), 13, *Report of the Watering Committee* (1809), 15.

33. The figures cited here and displayed on p. 127 were calculated from published city accounts of expenditures from 1799 to 1825 as well as from the General Accounts, Corporation of Philadelphia, vols. 3–5, PCA. For further information regarding the sources and methodology of these calculations, consult the essay, "Methodology and Sources," herein.

34. CCP, *Ordinances* (1823), 227–31; Common Council Minutes, vol. 2, February 18, 1799–January 13, 1803, 204, PCA.

35. Lindstrom, *Economic Development*, 25.

36. Lowber, ed., *Ordinances*, 78–179, 229; CCP, *Report of the Watering Committee* (1803), 20, *Ordinances* (1815), 9–10.

37. Common Council Minutes, vol. 2, February 18, 1799–January 13, 1803, PCA; *Ordinances* (1798), 5; Lowber, ed., *Ordinances* (1812), 178, 196, 198, 227, 229; CCP, *Ordinances* (1819), 110, 120, *Ordinances* (1822), 93.

38. CCP, *Ordinances* (1798), 172, 178.

39. Lowber, ed., *Ordinances;* 198; Robert Wharton to William Eaton, March 3, 1915, City Council 120.42 Committee on Water, Papers 1804–1854, Box A3118, PCA.

40. Select Council Minutes, October 14, 1796–April 14, 1799, 265, PCA; Common Council Minutes, vol. 2, February 18, 1799–January 13, 1803, 284, PCA.

41. March 4, 1828, Samuel Breck Diary, Breck Collection, HSP.

42. *Poulson's Daily Advertiser,* January 29, 1801, quoted in Blake, *Water,* 18; James Hosmer Penniman, *Philadelphia in the Early Eighteen Hundreds* (Philadelphia: St. Stephen's Church, 1923), 43; *Philadelphia Gazette and Daily Advertiser,* September 25, 1833.

43. "Report of the Watering Committee on the Subject of Obtaining Water Power from the River Schuylkill," February 5, 1819, City Council 120.42, Committee on Water, Papers 1804–1854, Box A3118, PCA.

44. "Contract between Corporation of Philadelphia and Spring Garden, February 16, 1827," City Council 120.42, Committee on Water, Papers 1804–1854, Box A3118, PCA; Howard Gillette, Jr., "The Emergence of the Modern Metropolis: Philadelphia in

the Age of Its Consolidation," in William W. Cutler, III and Howard Gillette, Jr., eds., *The Divided Metropolis: Social and Spatial Dimensions of Philadelphia, 1800–1975* (Westport, CT: Greenwood Press, 1980), 3–26.

45. Smith, "Dawn," 243–72; *Report of the Watering Committee, to the Select and Common Councils. Read January 23, 1835* (Philadelphia: Lydia R. Bailey, 1835); September 8, 1825, Select Council Minutes, Series 120.3, PCA.

46. Frederick Graff to Judith Sweyer, October 1, 1806, Graff Family Papers, HSP; Frederick Graff to Judith Graff, March 6, 1807, Graff Family Papers, HSP; Frederick Graff to Joseph S. Lewis, July 14, 1819, Committee on Water, Papers 1804–1854, City Council, PCA; Frederick Graff to Judith Graff, July 3, 1824, Graff Family Papers, HSP.

47. *Poulson's Daily Advertiser,* May 26, 1812; CCP, *Report of the Watering Committee, Read in Select Council, November 12, 1818* (Philadelphia: William Fry, 1818).

48. Frederick Graff to Joseph Watson, September 27, 1827, Stauffer Collection, HSP.

49. Frederick Graff to Judith Graff, July 3, 1824, Graff Collection, HSP; Office of the Watering Committee, Resolution, April 30, 1847, Graff Collection, HSP.

50. Hidy, *House of Baring,* 22.

51. August 20, 1827, Breck Diary, 1827–1831, Breck Collection, HSP.

52. Subscription book for loans of 1823 and 1824, SNC, Accession #1215, SNC Records, HML; October 20, 1823, SNC Minute Books, 1815–1849, SNC Records, PSA.

53. CCP, *Report of the Watering Committee, to the Select and Common Councils. Read January 12, 1832* (Philadelphia: Lydia R. Bailey, 1832), 6; Gillette, "Emergence," 3–26.

5—INCORPORATING THE COUNTRYSIDE

1. James Weston Livingood, *The Philadelphia-Baltimore Trade Rivalry, 1780–1860* (Harrisburg: Pennsylvania Historical and Museum Commission, 1947); Curry, *Corporate City,* 223–40; Richard C. Wade, *The Urban Frontier: The Rise of Eastern Cities, 1790–1830* (Cambridge: Harvard University Press, 1959), 39–71.

2. Taylor, *Transportation Revolution;* Goodrich, ed., *Canals.*

3. Pottsville *Miner's Journal,* October 3, 1829, quoted in Nolan, *Schuylkill,* 29.

4. David Willer, "Power-at-a-Distance," *Social Forces* 81, no. 4 (June 2003): 1295–334.

5. [Samuel Mifflin], *Observations on the Importance of Improving the Navigation of the River Schuylkill . . .* ([Philadelphia]: n.p., 1818), 3; H. Benjamin Powell, *Philadelphia's First Fuel Crisis: Jacob Cist and the Developing Market for Pennsylvania Anthracite* (University Park: Pennsylvania State University Press, 1978); Adams, *Old Dominion,* 48–83.

6. Berks County petition to the Pennsylvania legislature from 1814, quoted in New-York and Schuylkill Coal Company, *History of the Coal Lands, and Other Real Estate, Owned by the New-York and Schuylkill Coal Company* (New York: Geo. F. Hopkins, 1826), 15.

7. Charles V. Hagner, *Early History of the Falls of Schuylkill, Manayunk, Schuylkill and Lehigh Navigation Companies, Fairmount Waterworks, Etc.* (Philadelphia: Claxton, Remsen, and Haffelfinger, 1869), 42–44.

8. Edward S. Gibbons, "The Building of the Schuylkill Navigation System, 1815–1828," *PH* 57 (Jan. 1990): 17.

9. Paleske, *Observations,* 4.

10. Delaware and Schuylkill Navigation broadside, Secretary of the Commonwealth, Internal Improvements File, Canal and Navigation Companies, Delaware and Schuylkill Navigation, File 14, Record Group 26, Pennsylvania Department of State, PSA.

11. Irma A. Watts, "Pennsylvania Lotteries of Other Days," *PH* 2 (Winter 1935): 40–53; Gertrude MacKinney, ed. *Executive Minutes of the Governors,* vol. 4. Pennsylvania Archives, no. 9 (Harrisburg: State of Pennsylvania, 1931), 979–80; "Plan for Lottery," April 27, 1795, Secretary of the Commonwealth, Internal Improvements File, Canal & Navigation Companies, Schuylkill & Susquehanna Canal & Lock Navigation Company, no. 41, Folder 2, Department of State, PSA; "Memorial to the Senate and

House of Representatives of the Commonwealth of Pennsylvania, by the President, Mannagers [sic] and Company of the Schuylkill and Susquehanna Navigation," Society Miscellaneous Collection, HSP; Delaware and Schuylkill Canal Navigation, and Schuylkill and Susquehanna Navigation [ledgers for 1810], Box 4-b (mss., 1810), Society Miscellaneous Collection, HSP.

12. William J. Duane, *Letters, Addressed to the People of Pennsylvania Respecting the Internal Improvement, of the Commonwealth; By Means of Roads and Canals* (Philadelphia: Jane Aitken, 1811), 69; Charles G. Paleske, *Observations*, 6.

13. Christopher Roberts, *The Middlesex Canal, 1793–1860* (Cambridge: Harvard University Press, 1938), 186; Donald C. Jackson, "Roads Most Traveled: Turnpikes in Southeastern Pennsylvania in the Early Republic," in McGaw, ed., *Early American Technology*, 231; Anonymous to Mathew Carey, March 25, 1825, Edward Carey Gardiner Papers, Mathew Carey Section, Miscellaneous Correspondence on Internal Improvement, HSP.

14. Majewski, *House Dividing*, 37–58.

15. William Smith to Governor, May 26, 1792, Secretary of the Commonwealth, Internal Improvements File, Canal & Navigation Companies, Delaware and Schuylkill Canal Navigation, no. 14, Pennsylvania Department of State, Record Group 26, PSA; UCC, *Acts of the Legislature of Pennsylvania, Relating to the Union Canal Company of Pennsylvania* (Philadelphia: Lydia R. Bailey, 1825), 13.

16. Memorial to the Senate and House of Representatives of the Commonwealth of Pennsylvania, by the President, Mannagers [sic] and Company of the Schuylkill and Susquehanna Navigation, HSP Misc. Collection, Box 4-B, HSP; Report of the Commissioners Appointed to receive subscriptions to the Capital Stock for opening a Canal between the waters of the Quittapahila and Tulpehocken in the Counties of Berks and Dauphine, Secretary of the Commonwealth, Internal Improvements File, Canal & Navigation Companies, Schuylkill & Susquehanna Canal & Lock Navigation Company, no. 41, Folder Pennsylvania Department of State, Record Group #26, PSA.

17. François-Alexandre-Frédéric, duc de La Rochefoucauld-Liancourt, *Travels through the United States of North America . . .* (London: R. Phillips, 1799); Delaware and Schuylkill Navigation Company, Board of Managers Minutes, Reading Collection, HML; *Govett* v. *Reed et al.*, Supreme Court of Pennsylvania, Eastern District, 4 Yeates 456 (1807).

18. Nathan Miller, "Private Enterprise in Inland Navigation: The Mohawk Route prior to the Erie Canal," *New York History* 31, 398–413; December 12, 1798, Series II, Subseries 2, Delaware & Schuylkill Navigation Company, Board of Managers Minutes, Reading Company Collection, Accession 1520, HML; Delaware and Schuylkill Canal Navigation, and Schuylkill and Susquehanna Navigation [ledgers for 1810], Society Miscellaneous Collection, HSP.

19. Goodrich, *Government Promotion;* Hartz, *Economic Policy,* 84–85; CPA, *Report on Roads* (1822), tables 4, 5, and 6.

20. CPA, *Report on Roads* (1822), tables 4, 5; SNC, *Report of the President and Managers of the Schuylkill Navigation Company, to the Stockholders. January 2, 1826* (Philadelphia: Lydia R. Bailey, 1826), 10.

21. Statistics compiled from C-Miscellaneous Records; Reel 3327; Stock subscription book, SNC, Manuscript Group 110, PSA; August 22, 1817, Minutes, Board of Managers, Roll 1, October 7, 1815–January 5, 1846, SNC, Manuscript Group 110, PSA.

22. SNC Board of Managers to Stephen Girard, February 5, 1823, Letter Books, Box 1, June 5, 1816–November 25, 1824, MG-110, SNC, PSA.

23. January 2, 1826, Minute Books, October 1815–November 26, 1849, Box 1, MG-110, SNC, PSA; Philip Justice and Seth Craige to William Findlay, Governor of Pennsylvania, January 30, 1819, Pennsylvania Department of State, Record Group 26, Secretary of the Commonwealth, Internal Improvements File, Canal & Navigation Companies, SNC no. 42, Folder 1, PSA.

24. SNC, *Report of the President and Managers of the Schuylkill Navigation Company, to the Stockholders, January 4, 1830* (Philadelphia: James Kay, Jun. & Co., 1830), 6.

25. Lindstrom, *Economic Development,* 121–51; SNC, *Report of the President and*

Managers of the Schuylkill Navigation Company, to the Stockholders, January 7, 1828 (Philadelphia: Lydia R. Bailey, 1828), 9; Nolan, *Schuylkill,* 29.

26. Lindstrom, *Economic Development,* 18; Alfred D. Chandler, Jr., "Anthracite Coal and the Beginnings of the Industrial Revolution in the United States," *BHR* 46 (Summer 1972): 141–81.

27. Sellers, *Market Revolution;* Sean Wilentz, "Society, Politics, and the Market Revolution," in Eric Foner, ed., *The New American History,* rev. and expanded (Philadelphia: Temple University Press, 1997), 61–84; "Petition to Pennsylvania General Assembly, Read January 23, 1804, from Citizens in Bucks County," Folder January 23, 1804, McAllister Collection, HSP; Feller, *Jacksonian Promise;* Appleby, *Inheriting the Revolution;* SNC, *Acts of the Legislature of Pennsylvania, Relating to the Schuylkill Navigation Company* (Philadelphia: Joseph & William Kite, 1838), 3, 24.

28. Taylor, *Transportation Revolution;* Goodrich, ed., *Canals.*

29. Langdon Winner, *The Whale and the Reactor: A Search for Limits in an Age of High Technology* (Chicago: University of Chicago Press, 1986), 19–58.

30. The population of Philadelphia, Montgomery, Berks, and Schuylkill counties and the northern half of Chester County. 1830 United States Census, United States Census browser, <http://fisher.lib.virginia.edu/cgi-local/censusbin/census/cen.pl>, accessed February 25, 2003; SNC, *Report of the President and Managers of the Schuylkill Navigation Company, to the Stockholders, January 1, 1827* (Philadelphia: Lydia R. Bailey, 1827), 9; *Acts . . . Relating to the Schuylkill Navigation Company,* 3; Minute Books, Box 1, October 15–November 26, 1849, MG-100, Schuylkill Navigation Company, PSA.

31. Petitions, March 11, 1825, House File, 49th Session, Folder 5, PSA.

32. Letter from Schuylkill Navigation Company to Joseph S. Lewis, June 6, 1820. Letter Books, Box 1, June 5, 1816–November 25, 1824. Manuscript Group 11, SNC, PSA.

33. SNC, *Acts . . . Relating to the Schuylkill Navigation Company,* 28.

34. Ibid., 3, 5; Morton J. Horwitz, *The Transformation of American Law, 1780–1860* (Cambridge: Harvard University Press, 1977), 67–70.

35. Samuel Breck, Diary, August 18, 1820, Breck Collection, HSP; Petition to General Assembly, House File, 46th Session-1, 1821–1822 (Canal and Navigation Companies, Roads, Turnpikes), Pennsylvania General Assembly, Records of General Assembly, Record Group 7, PSA; Carol Sheriff, *The Artificial River: The Erie Canal and the Paradox of Progress, 1817–1862* (New York: Hill & Wang, 1996), 138–71.

36. SNC, *Acts . . . Relating to the Schuylkill Navigation Company,* 24.

37. Chandler, "Anthracite Coal," 141–81.

38. SNC, *Report of the . . . Schuylkill Navigation Company,* 5; UCC, *Annual Report of the President and Managers of the Union Canal Company of Pennsylvania, to the Stockholders, November 15, 1825* (Philadelphia: Lydia R. Bailey, 1825), 5; SNC, *Report of the . . . Schuylkill Navigation Company,* 11; Rilling, *Making Houses,* 91–128.

39. SNC, *Report of the . . . Schuylkill Navigation Company* (1827), 6; Lindstrom, *Economic Development,* 106.

40. Pottsville *Miner's Journal,* October 3, 1829, quoted in Nolan, *The Schuylkill,* 29; Paul E. Johnson, *A Shopkeepers' Millennium: Society and Revivals in Rochester, New York, 1815–1837* (New York: Hill & Wang, 1978); Mary P. Ryan, *Cradle of the Middle Class: The Family in Oneida County, New York, 1790–1865* (New York: Cambridge University Press, 1981); Sheriff, *Artificial River,* 138–71.

41. "Original Draft Bill for Improving the River Schuylkill Presented in 1812–1813 by Josiah White & others," SNC Folder, Society Miscellaneous Collection, HSP; SNC, *Acts . . . Relating to the Schuylkill Navigation Company,* 3; CCP, *Agreements of June 3, 1819, July 20, 1820, and June 14, 1824, Between the Mayor, Aldermen & Citizens of Philadelphia, and the Schuylkill Navigation Company, Relative to the Water Power, &c., at Fairmount* (Philadelphia: F. C. Markley & Son, 1869), *Report . . . on the Disposal of Surplus Water,* 5.

42. Peter Way, *Common Labour: Workers and the Digging of North American Canals, 1780–1860* (New York: Cambridge University Press, 1993); "Report of the Watering Committee on the Subject of Obtaining Water Power from the River Schuylkill, February 5, 1819," City Council Papers, Box 3118, PCA; Cadwalader Evans, Jr., to Joseph S. Lewis, August 22, 1821, SNC Manuscripts, PSA; Cadwalader Evans, Jr., to Samuel Mifflin, January 11, 1821, SNC Manuscripts, PSA; Paul E. Johnson, *Sam Patch, the Famous Jumper* (New York: Hill & Wang, 2003).

43. Samuel Breck, Diary, August 8, 1820, Breck Papers, HSP; Latrobe, *Remarks*, 6; Samuel Breck, Diary, January 9, 1826, Breck Collection, HSP; P. Maxwell to William Meredith, February 28, 1826, Box 89, Folder 19, Meredith Papers, HSP.

44. Nash, *Forging Freedom*, 246–53; Julie Winch, *Philadelphia's Black Elite: Activism, Accommodation, and the Struggle for Autonomy, 1787–1848* (Philadelphia: Temple University Press, 1988); Smith, "Dawn," 167–74.

45. Horwitz, *Transformation of American Law;* Stanley I. Kutler, *Privilege and Creative Destruction: The Charles River Bridge Case* (New York: Norton, 1978); Steinberg, *Nature Incorporated;* Freyer, *Producers,* 137–66; Peter Karsten, "Supervising the 'Spoiled Children of Legislation': Judicial Judgments Involving Quasi-Public Corporations in the Nineteenth Century," *American Journal of Legal History* 41, no. 3 (July 1997): 315–67; William J. Novak, *The People's Welfare: Law and Regulation in Nineteenth-Century America* (Chapel Hill: University of North Carolina, 1996), 132–36; Nathan Eldred to Lewis Coryell, May 1, 1830, Lewis Coryell Collection, HSP.

46. *The President, Managers and Company of the Schuylkill and Susquehanna Navigation v. Diffebach et al.,* Supreme Court of Pennsylvania, 1 Yeates 367 (1794) Pa. Lexis 19.

47. *The President, Managers, and Company of the Schuylkill Navigation Company* v. *Thoburn,* Supreme Court of Pennsylvania, Eastern District, 7 Serg. & Rawle 411; 1821 Pa. Lexis 118.

48. *The President, Managers, and Company of the Schuylkill Navigation Company* v. *Thoburn,* Supreme Court of Pennsylvania, Eastern District, 7 Serg. & Rawle 411; 1821 Pa. Lexis 118; Petition, House File, 46th Session, 1821–1822 (Canal and Navigation Companies, Roads, Turnpikes), Pennsylvania General Assembly, Records of General Assembly, PSA.

49. John R. Logan and Harvey L. Molotch, *Urban Fortunes: The Political Economy of Place* (Berkeley: University of California Press, 1987); Letter dated August 4, 1825, quoted January 25, 1828, V-1674, Minutes of Board of Managers of Union Canal Company, 7/30/1827–12/31/1831, Reading Company, Accession 1520, HML.

50. SNC, *Report of the President and Managers of the Schuylkill Navigation Company, to the Stockholders. January 3, 1831* (Philadelphia: James Kay, Jun. & Co., 1831), 13; "Report of the Committee Appointed on December 24, 1827," Minutes of the Board of Managers of the UCC, HML.

51. Cynthia J. Shelton, *The Mills of Manayunk: Industrialization and Social Conflict in the Philadelphia Region, 1787–1837* (Baltimore: Johns Hopkins University Press, 1986), 103; Samuel Breck, *Sketch of the Internal Improvements Already Made by Pennsylvania . . . ,* 2nd ed. (Philadelphia: M. Thomas, 1818), 17; Charles V. Hagner, *Early History of the Falls of Schuylkill, Manayunk, Schuylkill and Lehigh Navigation Companies, Fairmount Waterworks, Etc.* (Philadelphia: Claxton, Remsen, and Haffelfinger, 1869), 54.

52. *The Northern Traveler: Containing the Routes to Niagara, Quebec, and the Springs, with the Tour of New-England, and the Route to the Coal Mines of Pennsylvania* (New York: A. T. Goodrich, 1826), 12; Samuel Breck, Diary, August 3, 1826, Breck Collection, HSP; *Democratic Press,* September 24, 1827, quoted in Shelton, *Mills,* 88; Shelton, *Mills,* 93–94; "Statement of the Manayunk Working People's Committee," *Pennsylvanian,* August 28, 1833, quoted in Seth Rockman, ed., *Welfare Reform in the Early Republic: A Brief History with Documents* (Boston: Bedford/St. Martin's Press, 2003), 160.

53. Duane, *Letters;* Lewis Mumford, *Technics and Civilization* (New York: Harcourt, Brace, 1934); Jacques Ellul, *The Technological System,* trans. Joachim Neugroschel (New York: Continuum, 1980).

54. Josiah White, *Josiah White's History Given by Himself* (Philadelphia: Lehigh Coal and Navigation Company, 1909), 18.

55. Ibid., 23–26.

56. Ibid., 27; Evans, *British Corporate Finance;* May 25, 1821, MG-311 Lehigh Coal and Navigation Company Records, Roll 1, Minutes of the Stockholders, 1821–1831, PSA.

57. [Josiah White], *History of the Lehigh Coal and Navigation Company* (Philadelphia: William S. Young, 1840), 18, 54.

58. [Josiah White], *To the Committee on Corporations of the Senate [in Answer to Charges Against the Lehigh Coal and Navigation Company]* (Harrisburg: Hamilton & Son, 1832), 6, 8; Commonwealth of Pennsylvania, *Extract Relative to the Importance of the Lehigh Navigation, to the Commonwealth, from the Report of the Committee of the Senate of Pennsylvania, upon the Subject of the Coal Trade* (Harrisburg: Hugh Hamilton & Son, 1835), 5.

59. Josiah White, *Circular* (Harrisburg: Hamilton & Son, 1832), 1; [Josiah White], *To the Committee on Corporations,* 5; Lehigh Navigation and Coal Mine Company, *Statement of the Lehigh Navigation and Coal Mine Company, with the Terms of Subscription for Stock* (Philadelphia: William Brown, 1818), 6; White, *Circular,* 1.

60. *United States Gazette,* 2 February 1833.

61. Josiah White to Lewis Coryell, January 28, 1824, Lewis Coryell Collection, HSP; Petition, House File, 49th Session-1, 1824–1825, Pennsylvania Canal folder, HSP; Josiah White to George Hollenback et al., December 4, 1824, quoted in Norris Hansell, *Josiah White, Quaker Entrepreneur* (Easton, PA: Canal History and Technology Press, 1992), 69.

62. Commonwealth of Pennsylvania, *Extract Relative to the . . . Lehigh Navigation,* 4, 5–6; *United States Gazette,* February 2, 1833.

63. James Pierce was writing for *Hazard's Register of Pennsylvania,* a periodical published by the brother of White's partner Erskine Hazard. Quoted in Hansell, *Josiah White,* 72; *United States Gazette,* February 2, 1833; Burton W. Folsom, Jr., *Urban Capitalists: Entrepreneurs and City Growth in Pennsylvania's Lackawanna and Lehigh Regions, 1800–1920* (Baltimore: Johns Hopkins University Press, 1981).

64. Majewski, *House Dividing,* 37–58.

65. Harvey Segal, "Canals and Economic Development," in *Canals and American Economic Development,* ed. Carter Goodrich (New York: Columbia University Press, 1961), 224; Sheriff, *Artificial River,* 3; Steinberg, *Nature Incorporated,* 50–98; Majewski, *House Dividing,* 111–41; John Lauritz Larson, *Bonds of Enterprise: John Murray Forbes and Western Development in America's Railway Age* (Cambridge: Harvard University Press, 1984).

66. Sheriff, *Artificial River,* 27–51; Lindstrom, *Economic Development,* 93–120.

6—CREATING A CORPORATE SPHERE

1. Philip Shriver Klein, *Pennsylvania Politics, 1817–1832: A Game without Rules* (Philadelphia: Historical Society of Pennsylvania, 1940), 56–58.

2. Samuel Breck, Diary, August 12, 1820, Breck Collection, HSP.

3. Warner, *Private City,* 79–98.

4. Miller, *Philadelphia—The Federalist City,* 26.

5. Curry, *Corporate City,* 156–58; *Philadelphia Gazette,* October 9, 1833.

6. Edgar P. Richardson, "Athens of America, 1800–1825," in Weigley, ed., *Philadelphia,* 209.

7. John Wurts to Maurice Wurts, March 10, 1823, Vanuxem Collection, Series 2, Maurice Wurts Papers, HML.

8. Analysis of stockholder election results in Stockholder Minutes, Pennsylvania Company for Insurance on Lives and Granting Annuities, HML, and stockholder election results in Stockholder Minutes, Farmers and Mechanics Bank, Historical Records, Farmers and Mechanics National Bank Records, HML.

9. These and the ensuing statistics and analysis of board memberships derive from a database compiled from city directories and company records; for further information, see "Methodology and Sources," herein.

10. Winslow, *Biographies,* 132.

11. Henry Drinker to Samuel W. Fisher, June 8, 1814, Society Miscellaneous Collection, HSP; Abraham Ritter, *Philadelphia and Her Merchants, As Constituted Fifty & Seventy Years Ago, Illustrated by Diagrams of the River Front, and Portraits of Some of its Prominent Occupants* (Philadelphia: Abraham Ritter, 1860), 57; Winslow, *Biographies,* 107–10.

12. Compiled from *The Philadelphia Directory and Register, for 1821* (Philadelphia: M'Carty & Davis, 1821) and Minutes, Board of Managers, SNC, Roll 1, October 7, 1815–January 5, 1846, PSA.

13. CCP, *Ordinance for Raising Supplies,* 3.

14. William Meredith, *Eulogium of the Character and Services of the Late John Sergeant* (Philadelphia: Crissy & Markley, 1858).

15. Mark S. Mizruchi, "What Do Corporate Interlocks Do? An Analysis, Critique, and Assessment of Research on Interlocking Directorates," *Annual Review of Sociology* 22 (1996): 271–98.

16. October 26, 1825, Minute Books, October 5, 1815–November 26, 1849, Box 1, SNC Papers, PSA.

17. Ibid.

18. Winslow, *Biographies,* 55.

19. H. J. Levis to William Meredith, January 25, 1823, Correspondence Box 2, Meredith Papers, HSP.

20. [White], *History,* 11–13.

21. Samuel Breck, Diary, quoted from "Philadelphia Museum of Art: Fairmount Park Houses," <http://www.philamuseum.org/collections/parkhouse/sweetbriar.shtml>, accessed June 6, 2003; Samuel Breck, "Recollections," mss. Breck Collection, HSP.

22. Ibid.

23. Breck Diary, August 3, 1821, Breck Papers, HSP.

24. Breck Diary, April 19, 1822, October 9, 1822, August 29, 1820, Breck Papers, HSP.

25. Smith, "Dawn," 28.

26. Nash, *Urban Crucible,* 396; Smith, "Dawn," 153.

27. For an example of a full British corporate charter exhibiting many of the same features as those described above, see Rochdale Canal Company, *Bill.*

28. October 17, 1823, SNC Minute Books, October 5, 1815–November 26, 1849, Box 1, PSA.

29. Lehigh Coal and Navigation Company, *Act . . . Concerning the Lehigh Coal and Navigation Company* (1837), 25–26; American Fire Insurance Company, *An Act to Incorporate the Subscribers to the American Fire Insurance Company* (Philadelphia: John Binns, 1810), 7.

30. Robert Morris, *Plan alluded to by the Resolution of Congress of the 17th of May, 1781. . . .* [broadside] (Philadelphia: Hall & Sellers, 1781); Samuel Breck Diary, August 20, 1827, Breck Collection, HSP; [Joseph Tagert to Joseph Clay], n.d. Historical Records, Box 1, 1807–1820, Farmers and Mechanics Bank, Accession 1858, HML.

31. Wright, "Bank Ownership," 47–48.

32. *President, &c. of the Delaware and Schuylkill Canal Navigation* v. *Sansom,* Supreme Court of Pennsylvania, 1 Binn 70; 1803 Pa. Lexis 18.

33. Commonwealth of Pennsylvania, *An Act of Incorporation, for that Part of the Northern Liberties, Lying Between the West of Sixth Street and the River Delaware, and between Vine-Street and Cohocksink Creek* (Philadelphia: John Geyer, 1805), 22.

34. CCP, *Ordinances of the City* (1798), 61; February 25, 1802, Common Council Minutes, vol. 2, February 1799–January 1803, PCA.

35. Mathew Carey, *Letter from a Citizen of Philadelphia, to a Member of the Legislature at Harrisburg* ([Philadelphia]: n.p., 1829); *An Act to Incorporate the Farmers and Mechanics Bank,* 9.

36. Philadelphia Bank, *By-Laws of the Philadelphia Bank. . . .* (Philadelphia: William Fry, 1820), 13; Samuel Breck Diary, November 11, 1822, Breck Collection, HSP.

37. Anon., November 6, 1810, Historical Records, Box 1, 1807–1820, Farmers and Mechanics National Bank Collection, HML; Robert Ralston to Samuel Richards, July 24, 1811, Historical Records, Box 1, 1807–1820, Farmers and Mechanics National Bank Collection, HML.

38. June 17, 1814, Excerpt of Minutes of Board of Directors, Historical Records, Box 1, 1807–1820, Farmers and Mechanics Bank Collection, HML; Farmers and Mechanics Bank, *An Act to Re-Charter Certain Banks. To Which Are Added the Several Acts of Assembly Relative to Banks, and the By-Laws of the Farmers and Mechanics Bank* (Philadelphia: R. Desilver, 1824), 36.

39. Rothbard, *Panic.*

40. Farmers and Mechanics Bank to William Jones, May 25, 1813; Commonwealth of Pennsylvania, *Report of the Senate . . . General Distress,* 8–10.

41. Sellers, *Market Revolution,* 163; CPA, *Journal of the Twenty-Seventh House of Representatives* (Harrisburg: James Peacock, 1817), 511.

42. Harvey Molotch, "The City as a Growth Machine: Toward a Political Economy of Place," *American Journal of Sociology* 82, no. 2 (Sept. 1976): 309–22; Alan Harding, "Elite Theory and Growth Machines," in *Theories of Urban Politics,* ed. David Judge, Gerry Stoker, and Harold Wolman (Thousand Oaks, CA: Sage, 1995).

43. August 20, 1817, and April 13, 1821, Minutes, Board of Directors, vol. 1. Pennsylvania Company for Insuring Lives and Granting Annuities, Accession 1476, HML; Subscription book for loans of 1823 and 1824, SNC, Accession 1215, HML; Philadelphia City Councils, Committee on the Sinking Fund, Minutes 1824–1834, Series 120.32, PCA.

44. Philadelphia Bank, *Philadelphia Bank,* 15, 40; Thomas Wilson, *The Philadelphia Directory and Stranger's Guide, for 1825* (Philadelphia: John Bioren, 1825).

45. CCP, *Agreements . . . between . . . Philadelphia, and the Schuylkill Navigation Company,* 16–18.

46. J. L. Sullivan, *Suggestions on the Canal Policy of Pennsylvania, in Reference to the Effects of the Inland Navigation of the Adjoining States, on the Commerce of Philadelphia* (Philadelphia: John Young, 1824), 20; SNC statistics compiled from Minute Books, Box 1, October 5, 1815–November 26, 1849, SNC Records, MG-110, PSA; John Gotwalt to Frederick Graff, November 2, 1825, and Joseph S. Lewis to John Gotwalt, December 8, 1832, in CCP, *Correspondence of the Watering Committee with the Schuylkill Navigation Company . . .* (Philadelphia: Lydia R. Bailey, 1833), 4–5.

47. *United States Gazette,* October 7, 1833.

48. Lindstrom, *Economic Development,* 102; Joseph S. Lewis to John Sergeant, Horace Binney, and Charles Chauncey, December 17, 1832, in John Sergeant et al., *Opinion of Counsel, on the Right of the Schuylkill Navigation Company to Make Another Lock and Canal for the Use of the Navigation at the Fair Mount Dam* (Philadelphia: James Kay, Jun. & Co., 1833), 2.

49. March 2, 1799, Select Council Minutes, October 14, 1796–April 14, 1799, CNL15 (mss.), PCA; CCP, *Report . . . on the Progress* (1799); CCP, *Report of the Watering Committee* (Philadelphia, 1812); CCP, *Report of the Watering Committee* (1818); February 5, 1819, City Council 120.42 Committee on Water, Papers 1804–1854, Box A3118, PCA; Bernhard, Duke of Saxe-Weimar-Eisenach, *Travels through North America, during the Years 1825 and 1826* (Philadelphia: Carey, Lea & Carey, 1828), 137; John P. Wetherill to Joseph S. Lewis, February 13, 1832, in CCP, *Correspondence of the Watering Committee,* 36–40.

50. City Cororation of Philadephia, *Accounts of the Corporation of the City of Philadelphia: From April 1, 1823 to January 1, 1828* (Philadelphia: Philadelphia Councils, 1828); John P. Wetherill to Joseph S. Lewis, November 15, 1832, in CCP, *Correspondence of the Watering Committee* (1833), 10.

51. SNC, *Acts . . . Relating to the Schuylkill Navigation Company* (1838), 28; Blake, *Water,* 92.

52. Joseph S. Lewis to John P. Wetherill, November 27, 1832, in CCP, *Correspondence of the Watering Committee,* 10; Sergeant et al., *Opinion of Counsel, on the Right of the SNC.*

53. Peter Bachrach and Morton S. Baratz, "Two Faces of Power," *American Political Science Review* 56, no. 4 (Dec. 1962): 947–52; Anon., *The Water Works. The Misconduct of the Present City Councils in Relation to the Fair Mount Water Works, Illustrated and Proved from Official Documents* (Philadelphia, 1833), 8; *United States Gazette,* October 4, 1833.

54. Sven Beckert, "Merchants and Manufacturers in the Antebellum North," in *Ruling America*, ed. Fraser and Gerstle, 92–122.

55. Donald R. Adams, *Wage Rates in Philadelphia, 1790–1830* (New York: Arno Press, 1975), 167–90; Lindstrom, *Economic Development*, 93–120.

56. Smith, "Dawn," 134–75; Shelton, *Mills*.

CONCLUSION

1. Quoted in George Wilson Pierson, *Tocqueville in America* (Baltimore: Johns Hopkins University Press, 1996), 457–58; Lindstrom, *Economic Development*, 104–5.

2. Pierson, *Tocqueville*, 485; Alexis de Tocqueville, *Democracy in America*, ed. J. P. Mayer and Max Lerner, trans. George Lawrence (New York: Harper & Row, 1966), 164, 241.

3. Alexis de Tocqueville, *Journey to America*, ed. J. P. Mayer, trans. George Lawrence (Garden City, NY: Anchor Books, 1971), 58; Carey, "Private and confidential" (1817); Tocqueville, *Democracy*, 164.

4. Adam Rothman, "The Slave Power in the United States, 1783–1865," in *Ruling America*, ed. Fraser and Gerstle, 64–91; Wood, *Radicalism*, 271–86.

5. Wood, *Radicalism*, 229–70; Karsten, "Supervising," 315–67; Jennifer L. Goloboy, "The Early American Middle Class," *JER* 25, no. 4 (Winter 2005): 537–46.

6. Rilling, *Making Houses*, viii, 40–69; Harold C. Livesay and Glenn Porter, "The Financial Role of Merchants in the Development of U. S. Manufacturing, 1815–1860," *Explorations in Economic History* 9, no. 1 (Fall 1971): 63–88; Hartz, *Economic Policy*, 40–41; Julius Rubin, "Canal or Railroad? Imitation and Innovation in the Response to the Erie Canal in Philadelphia, Baltimore, and Boston," *Transactions of the American Philosophical Society*, new ser., 51, no. 7 (1961): 1–106; Hartog, *Public Property and Private Power*, 205–39.

7. Frank Otto Gatell, "Spoils of the Bank War: Political Bias in the Selection of Pet Banks," *American Historical Review* 70, no. 1 (Oct. 1964): 35–58; Larry Schweikart, "U.S. Commercial Banking: A Historiographical Survey," *BHR* 65 (Autumn 1991): 612–18; Harry L. Watson, *Liberty and Power: The Politics of Jacksonian America* (New York: Hill & Wang, 1990), 132–71.

8. Davis, "Charters," 432; William Miller, "A Note on the Business Corporations in Pennsylvania, 1800–1860," *Quarterly Journal of Economics* 55 (Nov. 1940): 155; Hartz, *Economic Development*, 39–41; Ershkowitz and Shade, "Consensus," 519–621; Bruce Laurie, *Working People of Philadelphia, 1800–1850* (Philadelphia: Temple University Press, 1980); Grace Palladino, *Another Civil War: Labor, Capital, and the State in the Anthracite Regions of Pennsylvania, 1840–1868* (Urbana: University of Illinois Press, 1990).

9. Bodenhorn, *State Banking*, 95–248; Howard Bodenhorn, *A History of Banking in Antebellum America: Financial Markets and Economic Development in an Era of Nation-Building* (New York: Cambridge University Press, 2000).

10. Wade, *Urban Frontier*, 27, 90, 285, 291, 297; Blake, *Water*, 78–99; Gary A. Donaldson, "Bringing Water to the Crescent City: Benjamin Latrobe and the New Orleans Waterworks System," *Louisiana History* 28, no. 4 (1987): 381–96; Melosi, *Sanitary City*, 73–103; Curry, *Corporate City*, 33–86; Gillette, "Emergence," 3–26; Mike Wallace and Edwin G. Burrows, *Gotham: A History of New York City to 1898* (New York: Oxford University Press, 1998), 1219–35.

11. Larson, *Internal Improvement*, 195–256; Benjamin W. Labaree, "The Making of an Empire: Boston and Essex County, 1790–1850," in Conrad Edick Wright and Katheryn P. Viens, eds., *Entrepreneurs: The Boston Business Community, 1700–1850* (Boston: Massachusetts Historical Society, 1997), 343–64; Curry, *Corporate City*, 229; Alfred D. Chandler, Jr., "Patterns of American Railroad Finance, 1830–1850," *BHR* 28, no. 3. (Sep. 1954): 248–63.

12. Baltzell, *Philadelphia Gentlemen;* Joseph F. Rishel, *Founding Families of Pittsburgh;* Robert F. Dalzell, Jr., *Enterprising Elite: The Boston Associates and the World They Made* (Cambridge: Harvard University Press, 1987); Sven Beckert, *The Monied Metropolis: New*

York City and the Consolidation of the American Bourgeoisie, 1850–1896 (New York: Cambridge University Press, 2001); Harold L. Platt, *The Electric City: Energy and the Growth of the Chicago Area, 1880–1930* (Chicago: University of Chicago Press, 1991).

13. Feller, *Jacksonian Promise*, 1–14; Naomi R. Lamoreaux and Christopher Glaisek, "Vehicles of Privilege or Mobility? Banks in Providence, Rhode Island, during the Age of Jackson," *BHR* 65, no. 3 (Autumn 1991): 502–27; Edward Pessen, "The Egalitarian Myth and American Social Reality: Wealth, Mobility, and Equality in the 'Era of the Common Man,'" *American Historical Review* 76, no. 4 (Oct. 1971): 989–1034; Naomi R. Lamoreaux, "Rethinking the Transition to Capitalism in the Early American Northeast," *JAH* (Sept. 2003), <http://www.historycooperative.org/cgi-bin/justtop.cgi?act=justtop&url=http://www.historycooperative.org/journals/jah/90.2/lamoreaux.html> (accessed May 2, 2005), pars. 18–35; Sellers, *Market Revolution*, 396–428; Robert E. Wright, "The First Phase of the Empire State's 'Triple Transition': Banks' Influence on the Market, Democracy, and Federalism in New York, 1776–1838," *Social Science History* 21, no. 4 (Winter 1997): 521–58.

14. Philip H. Burch, Jr., *Elites in American History: The Federalist Years to the Civil War* (New York: Holmes & Meier, 1981). Beckert, "Merchants," 92–122; Julie Winch, *Philadelphia's Black Elite: Activism, Accommodation, and the Struggle for Autonomy, 1787–1848* (Philadelphia: Temple University Press, 1988); Anthony F. C. Wallace, *Rockdale: The Growth of an American Village in the Early Industrial Revolution* (New York: Norton, 1978).

15. Allan R. Pred, *Urban Growth and the Circulation of Information: The United States System of Cities, 1790–1840* (Cambridge: Harvard University Press, 1973).

16. Larry Lyon, Lawrence G. Felice, M. Ray Perryman, and E. Stephen, "Community Power and Population Increase: An Empirical Test of the Growth Machine Model," *American Journal of Sociology* 86, no. 6 (May 1981): 1387–400.

17. Scranton, *Proprietary Capitalism*, 133–34; Jeremy Atack, Fred Bateman, Thomas Weiss, "The Regional Diffusion and Adoption of the Steam Engine in American Manufacturing," *JEH* 40, no. 2 (June 1980): 281–308.

18. Maier, "Revolutionary Origins," 83–85.

19. Knight, *Institutions*, 188–94; Wood, *Radicalism*, 229–370.

20. Chandler, *Visible Hand*.

21. Francis X. Sutton, ed., *The American Business Creed* (Cambridge: Harvard University Press, 1956); David Vogel, *Kindred Strangers: The Uneasy Relationship between Business and Politics in America* (Princeton: Princeton University Press, 1996), 29–72, 298–323. Mark A. Smith, *American Business and Political Power: Public Opinion, Elections, and Democracy* (Chicago: University of Chicago Press, 2000), 13–36; David A. Moss, *When All Else Fails: Government as the Ultimate Risk Manager* (Cambridge: Harvard University Press, 2002).

22. Peter Temin, "The American Business Elite in Historical Perspective," NBER Working Paper, no. H0104 (Oct. 1997).

WORKS CITED

PERIODICALS

American Sentinel. Philadelphia.
Aurora General Advertiser. Philadelphia.
Pennsylvania Gazette. Philadelphia.
Philadelphia Directory. Philadelphia: [various publishers], 1785–1830.
Philadelphia Gazette & Universal Daily Advertiser.
Miner's Journal. Pottsville.
Poulson's American Daily Advertiser. Philadelphia.
United States Gazette. Philadelphia.

MANUSCRIPT SOURCES

Acts of Incorporation and Supplementary Acts, SNC, HML.
Bank of North America Collection, HSP.
BPA Papers, Society Miscellaneous Collection, HSP.
Breck, Samuel. Diaries. Breck Collection, HSP.
3/M. Recollections. Breck Collection, HSP.
Burnside,Thomas. Papers. Gratz Collection, HSP.
Carey, Mathew. Section. Edward Carey Gardiner Papers, HSP.
Chambers, Gordon. Collection, HSP.
Committee on Water. Papers 1804–1854. CCP. PCA.
Common Council Minutes. CCP. PCA.
Commonwealth of Pennsylvania (CPA). House Committee Files. Records of General Assembly. PSA.
———. House of Representatives. Committee Books. Records of General Assembly. PSA.
———. House of Representatives. Records of General Assembly. Journals. PSA.
———. Records of the Senate. Committee Books. Records of General Assembly. PSA.
———. Records of the Senate. Journals. Records of General Assembly. PSA
———. Senate Committee Files. Records of General Assembly. PSA.
Coryell, Lewis. Collection, HSP.
Delaware & Schuylkill Navigation Company, List of Stockholders who have compleated Shares, 1807, HSP Society Miscellaneous Collection, HSP.
Delaware & Schuylkill Navigation Company Records. Board of Managers Minutes. Reading Company Collection, HML.
Dickinson, Philemon. Correspondence. Society Miscellaneous Collection, HSP.
Farmers and Mechanics Bank. Minutes. Farmers' & Mechanics' National Bank. HML.
3/M. Corporate series. Farmers' & Mechanics' National Bank. HML.
3/M. Historical Records. Farmers' & Mechanics' National Bank. HML.

First Congress Under the Constitution, Gratz Collection, HSP.

Graff Family Papers. Letters, HSP.

Leach Collection, HSP.

Lewis, Joseph S. Correspondence. Society Miscellaneous Collection, HSP.

McAllister Collection. HSP.

Memorial to the Senate and House of Representatives of the Commonwealth of Pennsylvania, by the President, Mannagers [sic] and Company of the Schuylkill and Susquehanna Navigation, 12 December 1805. HSP Miscellaneous Collection. HSP

Meredith Papers. Correspondence. HSP.

Minutes of the Stockholders of the Bank of Pennsylvania, 1793–1842, HSP.

Morris, Robert. Collection. Huntington Library.

Newbold, Thomas. Papers. Society Miscellaneous Collection, HSP.

Patterson, Robert. Papers, ALS Collection, HSP.

Pemberton Papers, HSP.

Peters, Richard. Correspondence. Society Miscellaneous Collection. HSP.

Petitions, Society Miscellaneous Collection, HSP.

Poulson, Charles A. Extracts from Various Works of Travel &c. &c. Relating to the City of Philadelphia, 1688–1862. Library Company of Philadelphia.

SNC Loan Subscription Book for Loans of 1823 and 1824, HML.

SNC Manuscript Group, PSA.

SNC Papers. Society Miscellaneous Collection, HSP.

Select Council Minutes. CCP. PCA.

Sergeant, John. Papers. Society Miscellaneous Collection. HSP.

Stauffer Collection, HSP.

The First Subscribers for the City Water from Center Square Works. HSP.

Thomson, Charles. Papers. Gratz Collection, HSP.

Vanuxem, James. Papers. Wurts Family Papers Collection, HML.

Vaux Family Papers, HSP.

Wurts, Maurice. Papers. Wurts Family Papers Collection, HML.

PUBLISHED SOURCES

Adams, Donald R., Jr. *Finance and Enterprise in Early America: A Study of Stephen Girard's Bank, 1812–1831.* Philadelphia: University of Pennsylvania Press, 1978.

———. "Portfolio Management and Profitability in Early-Nineteenth-Century Banking." *BHR* 52, no. 1 (Spring 1978): 61–79.

———. *Wage Rates in Philadelphia, 1790–1830.* New York: Arno Press, 1975.

Adams, Sean Patrick. *Old Dominion, Industrial Commonwealth: Coal, Politics, and Economy in Antebellum America.* Baltimore: Johns Hopkins University Press, 2004.

Adrian, Charles R. *A History of American City Government: The Foundation of Traditions, 1775–1870.* New York: Praeger, 1976.

Alberts, Robert C. *The Golden Voyage: The Life and Times of William Bingham, 1752–1804.* Boston: Houghton-Mifflin, 1969.

Alexander, John K. "The Fort Wilson Incident of 1779: A Case Study of the Revolutionary Crowd." *WMQ*, 3rd ser., 31, no. 4 (Oct. 1974): 589–612.

Allen, James. "Diary of James Allen, Esq., of Philadelphia, Counsellor-at-Law, 1770–1778." *PMHB* 9 (1885): 176–96, 278–96, 424–40.

American Fire Insurance Company. *An Act to Incorporate the Subscribers to the American Fire Insurance Company.* Philadelphia: John Binns, 1810.

Andrews, Deborah C. "Bank Buildings in Nineteenth-Century Philadelphia." In *The Divided Metropolis: Social and Spatial Dimensions of Philadelphia, 1800–1975*, ed. William W. Cutler III and Howard Gillette, Jr., 57–84. Westport, CT: Greenwood Press, 1980.

Anon. *An Address to the Assembly of Pennsylvania, on the Abolition of the Bank of North-America.* Philadelphia: Robert Aitken, 1785.

———. *Order of Procession, in Honor of the Establishment of the Constitution of the United States* . . . Philadelphia: Hall & Sellers, 1788.

———. *Proposals for Establishing Another Bank in the City of Philadelphia, by the Name of the Bank of Pennsylvania.* [Philadelphia: n.p., 1784.]

———. *Remarks on a Pamphlet, Entitled, "Considerations on the Bank of North-America."* Philadelphia: John Steele, 1785.

———. *A Shot from a Backwoods-Marksman, Most Respectfully Addressed to the People of the Commonwealth of Pennsylvania, by their Humble Servant, a Shinglemaker.* [Philadelphia?]: n.p., 1832.

———. *To the Senate and House of Representatives of the Commonwealth of Pennsylvania, in General Assembly Met. The Memorial of the Subscribers, Inhabitants of the Borough of Pittsburgh, and Its Vicinity.* Pittsburgh: n.p., 1810.

———. *The Water Works. The Misconduct of the Present City Councils in Relation to the Fair Mount Water Works, Illustrated and Proved from Official Documents.* Philadelphia: n.p., 1833.

Appleby, Joyce. *Capitalism and a New Social Order: The Republican Vision of the 1790s.* New York: New York University Press, 1984.

———. *Inheriting the Revolution: The First Generation of Americans.* Cambridge: Harvard University Press, 2000.

Arbuckle, Robert D. *Pennsylvania Speculator and Patriot: The Entrepreneurial John Nicholson, 1757–1800.* University Park: Pennsylvania State University Press, 1975.

Armor, William Crawford. *The Lives of the Governors of Pennsylvania: With the Incidental History of the State, from 1609 to 1872.* Philadelphia: J. K. Simon, 1872.

Arnold, Douglas M. *A Republican Revolution: Ideology and Politics in Pennsylvania, 1776–1790.* New York: Garland, 1989.

Atack, Jeremy, Fred Bateman, and Thomas Weiss. "The Regional Diffusion and Adoption of the Steam Engine in American Manufacturing." *JEH* 40, no. 2 (June 1980): 281–308.

Bachrach, Peter, and Morton S. Baratz. "Two Faces of Power." *American Political Science Review* 56, no. 4 (Dec. 1962): 947–52.

Bailyn, Bernard. *Ideological Origins of the American Revolution.* Cambridge: Belknap Press, 1967.

Balch, Thomas Willing. *The Philadelphia Assemblies.* Philadelphia: Allen, Lane, & Scott, 1916.

Ball, Terence. "New Faces of Power." In *Rethinking Power,* edited by Thomas Wartenburg, 14–31. Albany: State University of New York, 1992.

Balleisen, Edward J. *Navigating Failure: Bankruptcy and Commercial Society in Antebellum America.* Chapel Hill: University of North Carolina Press, 2001.

Baltzell, E. Digby. *Philadelphia Gentlemen: The Making of a National Upper Class.* New York: Free Press, 1958.

[Barton, William]. *Observations on the Nature and Use of Paper-Credit . . . Including Proposals for Founding a National Bank.* Philadelphia: R. Aitken, 1781.

Beckert, Sven. "Merchants and Manufacturers in the Antebellum North." In Fraser and Gerstle, *Ruling America,* 92–122.

———. *The Monied Metropolis: New York City and the Consolidation of the American Bourgeoisie, 1850–1896.* New York: Cambridge University Press, 2001.

Beeman, Richard R. *The Varieties of Political Experience in Eighteenth-Century America.* Philadelphia: University of Pennsylvania Press, 2004.

Benson, Barbara E., ed. *Benjamin Henry Latrobe & Moncure Robinson: The Engineer as Agent of Technological Transfer.* Regional Conference on Economic History, May 14, 1974. Philadelphia: Eleutherian Mills Historical Library, 1975.

Bernhard, Duke of Saxe-Weimar-Eisenach. *Travels through North America, during the Years 1825 and 1826.* Philadelphia: Carey, Lea & Carey, 1828.

Berthoff, Rowland. "Conventional Mentality: Free Blacks, Women, and Business Corporations as Unequal Persons, 1820–1870." *JAH* 76, no. 3 (Dec. 1989): 753–84.

Bezanson, Anne. *Prices and Inflation during the American Revolution.* Philadelphia: University of Pennsylvania Press, 1951.

Bezanson, Anne, Robert D. Gray, and Miriam Hussey. *Wholesale Prices in Philadelphia, 1784–1861*. Philadelphia: University of Pennsylvania Press, 1936.

Biddle, Charles. *Autobiography of Charles Biddle, Vice-President of the Supreme Executive Council of Pennsylvania, 1745–1821*. Philadelphia: E. Claxton, 1883.

Biddle, Owen. *The Young Carpenter's Assistant, or, A System of Architecture, Adapted to the Style of Building in the United States*. Philadelphia: Benjamin Johnson, 1805.

Blackson, Robert M. "Pennsylvania Banks and the Panic of 1819: A Reinterpretation." *JER* 9, no. 3 (Autumn 1989): 335–58.

Blake, Nelson Manfred. *Water for the Cities: A History of the Urban Water Supply Problem in the United States*. Syracuse, NY: Syracuse University, 1956.

Bodenhorn, Howard. *A History of Banking in Antebellum America: Financial Markets and Economic Development in an Era of Nation-Building*. New York: Cambridge University Press, 2000.

———. *State Banking in Early America: A New Economic History*. New York: Oxford University Press, 2003.

Bouton, Terry. "A Road Closed: Rural Insurgency in Post-Independence Pennsylvania." *JAH* 87, no. 3 (Dec. 2000): 855–87.

Bank of Pennsylvania (BPA). *An Address to the Stockholders of the Bank of Pennsylvania. December 22, 1829*. Philadelphia: Clark & Raser, 1829.

———. *Charters, Laws, and By-Laws, of the Bank of Pennsylvania*. Philadelphia: Clark & Raser, 1830.

———. *Laws of the Bank of Pennsylvania*. Philadelphia: John Binns, 1811.

———. *List of Stockholders in the Bank of Pennsylvania*. [Philadelphia]: E. Oswald, 1790.

———. *To the Senate and House of Representatives of the Commonwealth of Pennsylvania, the Memorial of the President and Directors of the Bank of Pennsylvania*. [Philadelphia?]: n.p., 1805.

———. *To the Senate . . . the Memorial of the President and Directors of the Bank of North America . . . Founded on the Representation Given by the Stock Books of the Bank of North America . . .* [Philadelphia]: n.p., 1807.

———. *Statements Submitted to the Senate, from the Pennsylvania, Philadephia, and Farmers' and Mechanics' Banks. Read January 20, 1817*. [Harrisburg]: n.p., 1817.

Breck, Samuel. *Sketch of the Internal Improvements Already Made by Pennsylvania*. 2nd ed. Philadelphia: M. Thomas, 1818.

[Brindley, James]. *The History of Inland Navigations*. 2nd ed. London: T. Lowndes, 1769.

Brissot de Warville, J.-P. *New Travels in the United States of America. Performed in the Year 1788*. Dublin: W. Corbet, 1792.

Brock, Leslie. *The Currency of the American Colonies, 1700–1764: A Study in Colonial Finance and Imperial Relations*. New York: Arno Press, 1975.

Brown, Richard D. *Modernization: The Transformation of American Life*. New York: Hill & Wang, 1967.

———. *Knowledge Is Power: The Diffusion of Information in Early America, 1700–1865*. New York: Oxford University Press, 1989.

Brunhouse, Robert L. *The Counter-revolution in Pennsylvania, 1776–1790* (originally published in 1942). New York: Octagon Books, 1971.

Burch, Philip H., Jr. *Elites in American History: The Federalist Years to the Civil War*. New York: Holmes & Meier, 1981.

Burn, Robert Scott. *The Steam Engine: Its History and Mechanism. . . .* London: J. Ogden, n.d.

Burrows, Edwin G., and Mike Wallace. *Gotham: A History of New York City to 1898*. New York: Oxford University Press, 1998.

Caldwell, John. *William Findley from West of the Mountains: A Politician in Pennsylvania, 1783–1791*. Gig Harbor, WA: Red Apple, 2000.

Callender, Guy S. "The Early Transportation and Banking Enterprises of the States in Relation to the Growth of Corporations." *Quarterly Journal of Economics* 17, no. 1 (Nov. 1902): 111–62.

Calomoris, Charles. "Institutional Failure, Monetary Scarcity, and the Depreciation of the Continental." *JEH* 48, no. 1 (Mar. 1988): 47–68.

Carey, Mathew. *Cursory Reflections on the System of Taxation.* . . . Philadelphia: Mathew Cary, 1806.

———, ed. *Debates and Proceedings of the General Assembly of Pennsylvania, on the Memorials Praying a Repeal or Suspension of the Law Annulling the Charter of the Bank.* Philadelphia: Carey, 1786.

[———]. *Letter from a Citizen of Philadelphia, to a Member of the Legislature at Harrisburg.* [Philadelphia]: n.p., 1829.

———. *Private and confidential . . . the case that occurred on Saturday at the Bank of Pennsylvania . . . February 24, 1817.* Philadelphia: Mathew Carey, 1817.

———. *Reflections on the Renewal of the Charter of the Bank of Pennsylvania . . . Together with a View of the Immoderate Power Possessed by a Small Number of That Body.* Philadelphia: M. Carey, 1829.

Carter, Edward C., II. *Benjamin Henry Latrobe and Public Works: Professionalism, Private Interest, and Public Policy in the Age of Jefferson.* Washington, DC: Public Works Historical Society, 1976.

———, ed. *The Virginia Journals of Benjamin Henry Latrobe, 1795–1798.* New Haven: Yale University Press, 1977.

Catalano, Kathleen M. "Cabinetmaking in Philadelphia, 1820–1840: Transition from Craft to Industry." In *American Furniture and Its Makers,* edited by Ian M. G. Quimby, 81–138. Winterthur Portfolio, vol. 13. Chicago: Published for the Henry Francis du Pont Winterthur Museum by the University of Chicago Press, 1979.

Chandler, Alfred D. "Patterns of American Railroad Finance, 1830–1850." *BHR* 28, no. 3 (Sep. 1954): 248–63.

———. *The Visible Hand: The Managerial Revolution in American Business.* Cambridge: Belknap Press, 1977.

Chastellux, François Jean, marquis de. *Travels in North-America, in the Years 1780–81–82.* . . . New York: [s.n.], 1828.

City Corporation of Philadelphia (CCP). *Accounts of the Corporation of the City of Philadelphia: From April 1, 1823, to January 1, 1828.* Philadelphia: City Councils, 1828.

———. *Accounts of the Corporation of the City of Philadelphia from the First of April, 1819, to the First of April, 1823.* Philadelphia: The Councils, 1823.

———. *Agreements of June 3, 1819, July 20, 1820, and June 14, 1824, between the Mayor, Aldermen & Citizens of Philadelphia, and the Schuylkill Navigation Company, Relative to the Water Power, &c., at Fairmount.* Philadelphia: F. C. Markley & Son, 1869.

———. *Committee of Ways and Means Report for Appropriations for 1807, Accompanied by an Ordinance for Raising Supplies and Making Appropriations for the Services of the City, for the Year One Thousand Eight Hundred and Seven.* Philadelphia: [Jane Aitken?], 1806.

———. *Correspondence of the Watering Committee with the Schuylkill Navigation Company, in Relation to the Fair Mount Water Works: Together with the Reports of the Watering Committee to Councils, Made Dec'r. 11, 1832, and Feb'y. 11, 1833.* Philadelphia: Lydia R. Bailey, 1833.

———. *An Ordinance for Raising Supplies, and Making Appropriations, for the Services and Exigencies of the City of Philadelphia, for the Year 1799.* Philadelphia: Zachariah Poulson, Jr., 1799.

———. *The Ordinances of the City of Philadelphia: To Which Are Prefixed, the Act of Incorporation and the Several Supplements Thereto, Together with the Address of George Washington, Late President of the United States, to His Fellow Citizens.* Philadelphia: Zachariah Poulson, Jr., 1798.

———. *Ordinances of the Corporation of the City of Philadelphia; Passed since the Eighteenth Day of June, One Thousand Eight Hundred and Twelve.* Philadelphia: Philadelphia Councils, 1815.

———. *Ordinances of the Corporation of the City of Philadelphia. Passed since the Eighth Day of January, One Thousand Eight Hundred and Twenty-Four.* Philadelphia: City Councils, 1825.

———. *Ordinances of the Corporation of the City of Philadelphia. Passed since the Fourth Day of February, One Thousand Eight Hundred and Twenty-Three*. Philadelphia: City Councils, 1824.

———. *Ordinances of the Corporation of the City of Philadelphia; Passed Since the Fourteenth Day of September, One Thousand Eight Hundred and Fifteen*. Philadelphia: City Councils, 1817.

———. *Ordinances of the Corporation of the City of Philadelphia. Passed since the Sixteenth of July, One Thousand Eight Hundred and Seventeen*. Philadelphia: City Councils, 1819.

———. *Ordinances of the Corporation of the City of Philadelphia. Passed since the Third Day of August, One Thousand Eight Hundred and Twenty*. Philadelphia: City Councils, 1822.

———. *Ordinances of the Corporation of the City of Philadelphia. Passed Since the Twenty-Second Day of April, One Thousand Eight Hundred and Nineteen*. Philadelphia: City Councils, 1821.

———. *Ordinances of the Corporation of the City of Philadelphia. Passed since the Twenty-Seventh Day of December, One Thousand Eight Hundred and Twenty-One*. Philadelphia: City Councils, 1823.

———. *Report of the Committee for the Introduction of Wholesome Water into the City of Philadelphia*. Philadelphia: Zachariah Poulson, Jr., 1801.

———. *Report of the Joint Committee of the Select and Common Councils, on the Subject of Bringing Water to the City*. Philadelphia: Zachariah Poulson, Jr., 1798.

———. *Report of the Watering Committee, on the Disposal of the Surplus Water Power of the River Schuylkill, and the Construction of a Canal between the Schuylkill and the Delaware*. Philadelphia: City Councils, 1825.

———. *Report of the Watering Committee, Read in Select Council, November 12, 1818*. Philadelphia: William Fry, 1818.

———. *Report of the Watering Committee to the Select and Common Councils, November 1, 1803*. Philadelphia: William Duane, 1803.

———. *Report of the Watering Committee to the Select and Common Councils, November 1, 1804*. Philadelphia: Robert Cochran, 1804.

———. *Report of the Watering Committee to the Select and Common Councils, November 2, 1809*. Philadelphia: Jane Aitken, 1809.

———. *Report of the Watering Committee, to the Select and Common Councils. Read January 12, 1832*. Philadelphia: Lydia R. Bailey, 1832.

———. *Report of the Watering Committee, to the Select and Common Councils. Read January 23, 1835*. Philadelphia: Lydia R. Bailey, 1835.

———. *Report to the Select and Common Councils on the Progress and State of the Water Works on the 24th of November, 1799*. Philadelphia: Zachariah Poulson, Jr., 1799.

Cochran, Thomas C., and William Miller. *The Age of Enterprise: A Social History of Industrial America*. New York: Macmillan, 1942.

Cohen, Jeffrey A., and Charles E. Brownell, eds. *The Architectural Drawings of Benjamin Henry Latrobe*. New Haven: Yale University Press, 1994.

Cooper, Carolyn C. "A Patent Transformation: Woodworking Mechanization in Philadelphia, 1830–1856." In McGaw, *Early American Technology*, 278–327.

Cornell, Saul. "Aristocracy Assailed: The Ideology of Backcountry Anti-Federalism." *JAH* 76, no. 4 (Mar. 1990): 1148–72.

Countryman, Edward. *The American Revolution*, 2nd ed. New York: Hill & Wang, 2003.

Commonwealth of Pennsylvania (CPA). *An Act of Incorporation, for That Part of the Northern Liberties Lying between the West of Sixth Street and the River Delaware, and between Vine Street and Cohocksink Creek*. Philadelphia: John Geyer, 1805.

———. *Extract Relative to the Importance of the Lehigh Navigation, to the Commonwealth, from the Report of the Committee of the Senate of Pennsylvania, upon the Subject of the Coal Trade*. Harrisburg: Hugh Hamilton & Son, 1835.

———. *Journal of the Twenty-Seventh House of Representatives of the Commonwealth of Pennsylvania* [1816–1817]. Harrisburg: James Peacock, 1817.

———. *Proceedings and Debates of the Convention of the Commonwealth of Pennsylvania to Propose Amendments to the Constitution. Commenced and Held at Harrisburg on the Second Day of May, 1837.* Harrisburg: Packer, Barrett, and Parke, 1837.

———. *Report and Documents of the Committee Appointed to Enquire into the Conduct of the Cashier and Directors of the Bank of Pennsylvania.* [Harrisburg]: n.p., 1815.

———. *Report of the Committee of State Directors, of the Bank of Pennsylvania, Appointed November 14, 1829, upon the Loans of 1828 and 1829.* Philadelphia: n.p., 1829.

———. *Report of the Senate, Appointed to Enquire into the Extent and Causes of the Present General Distress.* Lancaster: Pennsylvania Senate, 1820.

———. *Report on Roads, Bridges and Canals, Read in the Senate, March 23, 1822.* Harrisburg: C. Mowry, 1822.

Crane, Elaine Forman, ed. *The Diary of Elizabeth Drinker.* Boston: Northeastern University Press, 1991.

Crowther, Simeon. "Urban Growth in the Mid-Atlantic States, 1785–1850." *JEH* 36, no. 3 (Sept. 1976): 624–44.

Cummings, Hubertis. "Robert Morris and the Episode of the Polacre 'Victorious.'" *PMHB* 70, no. 3 (July 1946): 239–57.

Currie, William. *Memoirs of the Yellow Fever. . . .* Philadelphia: John Bioren, 1798.

Curry, Leonard P. *The Corporate City: The American City as a Political Entity, 1800–1850.* Westport, CT: Greenwood Press, 1997.

Dalzell, Robert F., Jr. *Enterprising Elite: The Boston Associates and the World They Made.* Cambridge: Harvard University Press, 1987.

Davis, Gerald F. "Agents without Principles? The Spread of the Poison Pill through the Intercorporate Network." *Administrative Science Quarterly* 36, no. 4 (Dec. 1991): 586–613.

Davis, Joseph P. "Charters for American Business Corporations in the Eighteenth Century." *Publications of the American Statistical Association* 15, no. 116 (Dec. 1916): 426–35.

Davis, Joseph S. *Essays in the Earlier History of American Corporations.* 2 vols. Cambridge: Harvard University Press, 1917.

Delaware and Schuylkill Canal Company. *Address of the Committee of the Delaware and Schuylkill Canal Company, to the Committees of the Senate and House of Representatives on the Memorial of Said Company.* Philadelphia: John Ormrod, 1799.

Diamondstone, Judith Marion. "The Philadelphia Corporation, 1701–1776." PhD diss., University of Pennsylvania, 1969.

Doerflinger, Thomas M. *A Vigorous Spirit of Enterprise: Merchants and Economic Development in Revolutionary Philadelphia.* Chapel Hill: University of North Carolina Press, 1986.

Donaldson, Gary A. "Bringing Water to the Crescent City: Benjamin Latrobe and the New Orleans Waterworks System." *Louisiana History* 28, no. 4 (1987): 381–96.

Driver, Clive E., ed. *Passing Through: Letters and Documents Written in Philadelphia by Famous Visitors.* Philadelphia: Rosenbach Museum & Library, 1982.

Duane, William J. *Letters, Addressed to the People of Pennsylvania Respecting the Internal Improvement, of the Commonwealth; By Means of Roads and Canals.* Philadelphia: Jane Aitken, 1811.

Duncan, A. B. *Travels through Part of the United States and Canada in 1818 and 1819,* vol. 1. Glasgow: University Press, 1823.

Ellul, Jacques. *The Technological System.* Translated by Joachim Neugroschel. New York: Continuum, 1980.

Ershkowitz, Herbert, and William G. Shade. "Consensus or Conflict? Political Behavior in the State Legislatures during the Jacksonian Era." *JAH* 58, no. 3 (Dec. 1971): 591–621.

Evans, George Heberton, Jr. *British Corporation Finance, 1775–1850: A Study of Preference Shares.* Baltimore: Johns Hopkins University Press, 1936.

Farmers and Mechanics Bank. *An Act to Incorporate the Farmers and Mechanics Bank.* Philadelphia: Jane Aitken, 1809.

————. *An Act to Re-Charter Certain Banks. To Which Are Added the Several Acts of Assembly Relative to Banks, and the By-laws of the Farmers and Mechanics Bank*. Philadelphia: R. Desilver, 1824.

Feller, Daniel. *The Jacksonian Promise: America, 1815–1840*. Baltimore: Johns Hopkins University Press, 1995.

Fenstermaker, J. Van. *The Development of American Commercial Banking: 1782–1837*. Kent, OH: Kent State University, 1965.

Ferguson, E. James. *The Papers of Robert Morris, 1781–1784*. Pittsburgh: University of Pittsburgh Press, 1973–1980.

————. *The Power of the Purse: A History of American Public Finance, 1776–1790*. Chapel Hill: University of North Carolina Press, 1961.

Ferguson, Eugene S. *Oliver Evans: Inventive Genius of the American Industrial Revolution*. Greenville, RI: Hagley Museum, 1980.

Fessenden, Thomas Green. *The Register of Arts, or A Compendious View of Some of the Most Useful Modern Discoveries and Inventions*. Philadelphia: Fessenden, 1808.

Findley, William. "William Findley of Westmore, PA., Author of 'History of the Insurrection in the Western Counties of Pennsylvania'—An Autobiographical Letter." *PMHB* 5, no. 4 (1881): 440–51.

Folsom, Burton W., Jr. *Urban Capitalists: Entrepreneurs and City Growth in Pennsylvania's Lackawanna and Lehigh Regions, 1800–1920*. Baltimore: Johns Hopkins University Press, 1981.

Foner, Eric. *Tom Paine and Revolutionary America*. New York: Oxford University Press, 1976.

Francis, Joseph Hume. *History of the Bank of England*. Chicago: Euclid, 1888.

Franklin, Benjamin. *The Interest of Great Britain Considered. . . .* London: T. Becket, 1761.

Fraser, Steve, and Gary Gerstle, eds. *Ruling America: A History of Wealth and Power in a Democracy*. Cambridge: Harvard University Press, 2005.

Freyer, Tony A. *Producers versus Capitalists: Constitutional Conflict in Antebellum America*. Charlottesville: University Press of Virginia, 1994.

Friedman, Walter A., and Richard S. Tedlow. "Statistical Portraits of American Business Elites: A Review Essay." *Business History* 45, no. 4 (Oct. 2003): 89–113.

Gallatin, Albert. *Report of the Secretary of the Treasury, on the Subject of Public Roads and Canals; Made in Pursuance of a Resolution of Senate, of March 2, 1807. April 12, 1808*. Washington, DC: R. C. Weightman, 1808.

Garraty, John A., and Mark C. Carnes. *American National Biography*. New York: Oxford University Press, 1999.

Geib, George Winthrop. "A History of Philadelphia, 1776–1789." PhD diss., University of Wisconsin, 1969.

Gibbons, Edward S. "The Building of the Schuylkill Navigation System, 1815–1828." *PH* 57, no. 1 (Jan. 1990): 13–43.

Gilje, Paul. *Wages of Independence: Capitalism in the Early American Republic*. Madison, WI: Madison House, 1997.

Gillette, Howard, Jr. "The Emergence of the Modern Metropolis: Philadelphia in the Age of Its Consolidation." In *The Divided Metropolis: Social and Spatial Dimensions of Philadelphia, 1800–1975*, edited by William W. Cutler III and Howard Gillette, Jr., 3–26. Westport, CT: Greenwood Press, 1980.

Glasberg, Davita Silfen. "Corporate Power and Control: The Case of Leasco Corporation versus Chemical Bank." *Social Problems* 29, no. 2 (Dec. 1991): 104–16.

Godbeer, Richard. *Sexual Revolution in Early America*. Baltimore: Johns Hopkins University Press, 2002.

Goloboy, Jennifer L. "The Early American Middle Class." *JER* 25, no. 4 (Winter 2005): 536–46.

Goodrich, Carter, ed. *Canals and American Economic Development*. New York: Columbia University Press, 1961.

————, ed. *The Government and the Economy, 1783–1861*. Indianapolis: Bobbs-Merrill, 1967.

────. *Government Promotion of American Canals and Railroads, 1800–1890.* New York: Columbia University Press, 1960.

────. "Internal Improvements Reconsidered." *JEH* 30 (June 1970): 289–311.

Gorton, Gary, and Warren E. Weber. "Quoted Discounts on State Bank Notes in Philadelphia, 1832–1858." Research Dept., Federal Reserve Bank of Minneapolis <http://minneapolisfed.org/research/economists/wewproj.html/>.

Gough, Robert. "Can a Rich Man Favor Revolution? The Case of Philadelphia in 1776." *PH* 48, no. 3 (July 1981): 235–50.

────. "Towards a Theory of Class and Social Conflict: A Social History of Wealthy Philadelphia, 1775–1800." PhD diss, University of Pennsylvania, 1978.

Gunn, L. Ray. *The Decline of Authority: Public Economic Policy and Political Development in New York, 1800–1860.* Ithaca, NY: Cornell University Press, 1988.

Hafertepe, Kenneth. "Banking Houses in the United States: The First Generation, 1781–1811." *Winterthur Portfolio* 35, no. 1 (Spring 2000): 1–52.

Hagner, Charles V. *Early History of the Falls of Schuylkill, Manayunk, Schuylkill and Lehigh Navigation Companies, Fairmount Waterworks, Etc.* Philadelphia: Claxton, Remsen, and Haffelfinger, 1869.

Hall, Mark David. *The Political and Legal Philosophy of James Wilson, 1742–1798.* Columbia: University of Missouri Press, 1997.

Hamilton, Henry. *An Economic History of Scotland in the Eighteenth Century.* Oxford: Clarendon Press, 1963.

Hamlin, Talbot. *Benjamin Henry Latrobe.* New York: Oxford University Press, 1955.

Hammond, Bray. *Banks and Politics in America, from the Revolution to the Civil War.* Princeton: Princeton University Press, 1957.

Hancock, David. *Citizens of the World: London Merchants and the Integration of the British Atlantic Community, 1735–1785.* New York: Cambridge University Press, 1995.

Handlin, Oscar, and Mary Flug Handlin. *Commonwealth: A Study of the Role of Government in the American Economy.* Cambridge: Harvard University Press, 1947.

────. "Origins of the American Business Corporation." *JEH* 5 (May 1945): 1–23.

Hansell, Norris. *Josiah White, Quaker Entrepreneur.* Easton, PA: Canal History and Technology Press, 1992.

Harding, Alan. "Elite Theory and Growth Machines." In *Theories of Urban Politics,* edited by David Judge, Gerry Stoker, and Harold Wolman, 35–53. Thousand Oaks, CA: Sage, 1995.

Harris, Ron. *Industrializing English Law: Entrepreneurship and Business Organization, 1720–1844.* New York: Cambridge University Press, 2000.

Harrison, Eliza Cope, ed. *Philadelphia Merchant: The Diary of Thomas P. Cope.* South Bend, IN: Gateway Editions, 1978.

Hartog, Hendrik. *Public Property and Private Power: The Corporation of the City of New York in American Law, 1730–1870.* Chapel Hill: University of North Carolina Press, 1983.

Hartz, Louis. *Economic Policy and Democratic Thought: Pennsylvania, 1776–1860.* Cambridge: Harvard University Press, 1948.

Hawke, David Freeman. *Nuts and Bolts of the Past: A History of American Technology, 1776–1860.* New York: Harper & Row, 1988.

Heideking, Jurgen. "Simon Snyder." In *American National Biography,* vol. 20, edited by John A. Garraty and Mark C. Carnes, 350–51. New York: Oxford University Press, 1999.

Hidy, Ralph. *The House of Baring in American Trade and Finance: English Merchant Bankers at Work, 1763–1861.* Cambridge: Harvard University Press, 1949.

Higginbotham, Sanford Wilson. *The Keystone in the Democratic Arch: Pennsylvania Politics, 1800–1816.* Philadelphia: University of Pennsylvania, 1952.

Hirschman, Albert O. *The Passions and the Interests: Political Arguments for Capitalism before Its Triumph.* Princeton: Princeton University Press, 1977.

Hoffman, Susan. *Politics and Banking: Ideas, Public Policy, and the Creation of Financial Institutions*. Baltimore: Johns Hopkins University Press, 2001.

Horwitz, Morton J. *The Transformation of American Law, 1780–1860*. Cambridge: Harvard University Press, 1977.

Hurst, James W. *The Legitimacy of the Business Corporation in the Law of the United States, 1780–1970*. Charlottesville: University Press of Virginia, 1970.

Hutson, James H. *Pennsylvania Politics, 1746–1770: The Movement for Royal Government and Its Consequences*. Princeton: Princeton University Press, 1972.

Illick, Joseph E. *Colonial Pennsylvania: A History*. New York: Scribner, 1976.

Jackson, Donald C. "Roads Most Traveled: Turnpikes in Southeastern Pennsylvania in the Early Republic." In McGaw, *Early American Technology*, 197–239.

Jackson, Joseph. *Market Street Philadelphia: The Most Historic Highway in America, Its Merchants, and Its Story*. Philadelphia: Patterson & White, 1918.

Johnson, Paul E. *Sam Patch, the Famous Jumper*. New York: Hill & Wang, 2003.

———. *A Shopkeeper's Millennium: Society and Revivals in Rochester, New York, 1815–1837*. New York: Hill & Wang, 1978.

Karmel, James. "Banking on the People: Banks, Politics, and Market Evolution in Early National Pennsylvania, 1781–1824." PhD diss., University of Buffalo, 1999.

———. "The Market Moment: Banking and Politics in Jeffersonian Pennsylvania, 1810–1815." *PH* 70, no. 1 (Winter 2003): 55–80.

Karsten, Peter. "Supervising the 'Spoiled Children of Legislation': Judicial Judgments Involving Quasi-Public Corporations in the Nineteenth Century." *American Journal of Legal History* 41, no. 3 (July 1997): 315–67.

Kasson, Michael. *Civilizing the Machine: Technology and Republican Values in America*. New York: Grossman, 1976.

Kehl, James A. *Ill Feeling in the Era of Good Feelings: Western Pennsylvania Political Battles, 1815–1825*. Pittsburgh: University of Pittsburgh Press, 1956.

Keller, Kenneth. *Rural Politics and the Collapse of Pennsylvania Federalism*. Philadelphia: American Philosophical Society, 1982.

Kimball, Fiske. "The Bank of Pennsylvania, an Unknown Masterpiece of American Classicism." *Architectural Record* 43 (Aug. 1918): 132–39.

Kippis, Andrew. *Biographia Britannica; or, The Lives of the Most Eminent Persons Who Have Flourished in Great Britain and Ireland*, vol. 2. 2nd ed. London: W. and A. Strahan, 1780.

Klein, Daniel B. "The Voluntary Provision of Public Goods? The Turnpike Companies of Early America." *Economic Inquiry* 28 (Oct. 1990): 788–812.

Klein, Philip Shriver. *Pennsylvania Politics, 1817–1832: A Game without Rules*. Philadelphia: Historical Society of Pennsylvania, 1940.

Knight, Jack. *Institutions and Social Conflict*. New York: Cambridge University Press, 1992.

Kornblith, Gary J., and John M. Murrin. "The Dilemmas of Ruling Elites in Revolutionary America." In Fraser and Gerstle, *Ruling America*, 27–64.

Kutler, Stanley I. *Privilege and Creative Destruction: The Charles River Bridge Case*. New York: Norton, 1978.

La Rochefoucauld-Liancourt, François-Alexandre-Frédéric, Duc de. *Travels through the United States of North America*. . . . London: R. Phillips, 1799.

Labaree, Benjamin W. "The Making of an Empire: Boston and Essex County, 1790–1850." In *Entrepreneurs: The Boston Business Community*, edited by Conrad Edick Wright and Katheryn P. Viens, 343–64. Boston: Massachusetts Historical Society, 1997.

Lamoreaux, Naomi R. "Constructing Firms: Partnerships and Alternative Contractual Arrangements in Early Nineteenth-Century American Business." *Business and Economic History* 24 (Winter 1995): 43–71.

———. *Insider Lending: Banks, Personal Connections, and Economic Development in Industrial New England*. New York: Cambridge University Press, 1994.

Lamoreaux, Naomi R., and Christopher Glaisek. "Vehicles of Privilege or Mobility? Banks in Providence, Rhode Island, during the Age of Jackson." *BHR* 65, no. 3 (Autumn 1991): 502–27.

Larson, John Lauritz. *Bonds of Enterprise: John Murray Forbes and Western Development in America's Railway Age.* Cambridge: Harvard University Press, 1984.

———. *Internal Improvement: National Public Works and the Promise of Popular Government in the Early United States.* Chapel Hill: University of North Carolina Press, 2001.

Latrobe, B. Henry. *The Journal of Latrobe . . . from 1796 to 1820.* New York: D. Appleton, 1905.

———. *Remarks on the Address of the Committee of the Delaware and Schuylkill Canal Company . . . Printed by order of the Committee of the Councils.* Philadelphia: Zachariah Poulson, Jr., 1799.

———. *View of the Practicability and Means of Supplying the City of Philadelphia with Wholesome Water: In a Letter to John Miller, Esquire, from B. Henry Latrobe, Engineer, December 29, 1798.* Philadelphia: Zachariah Poulson, Jr., 1799.

Laurie, Bruce. *Working People of Philadelphia, 1800–1850.* Philadelphia: Temple University Press, 1980.

Lehigh Coal and Navigation Company. *Act of the General Assembly of Pennsylvania concerning the Lehigh Coal and Navigation Company; Together with the Bye-Laws, Etc.* Philadelphia: James Kay, Jun. and Brother, 1837.

Lehigh Navigation and Coal Mine Company. *Statement of the Lehigh Navigation and Coal Mine Company, with the Terms of Subscription for Stock.* Philadelphia: William Brown, 1818.

Levering, Joseph Mortimer. *A History of Bethlehem, Pennsylvania, 1741–1892.* Bethlehem: Times, 1903.

Library Company of Philadelphia. *Catalogue of the Books, Belonging to the Library Company of Philadelphia; To Which Is Prefixed, a Short Account of the Institution, with the Charter, Laws, and Regulations.* Philadelphia: Bartram & Reynolds, 1787.

Library of Congress. *The First Booklist of the Library of Congress.* Washington, DC: Library of Congress, 1981.

Lindstrom, Diane. *Economic Development in the Philadelphia Region, 1810–1850.* New York: Columbia University Press, 1978.

Linebaugh, Peter, and Marcus Rediker. *The Many-Headed Hydra: Sailors, Slaves, Commoners and the Hidden History of the Revolutionary Atlantic.* Boston: Beacon Press, 2000.

Livermore, Shaw. *Early American Land Companies: Their Influence on Corporate Development.* New York: Commonwealth Fund, 1939.

Livesay, Harold C., and Glenn Porter. "The Financial Role of Merchants in the Development of U.S. Manufacturing, 1815–1860." *Explorations in Economic History* 9, no. 1 (Fall 1971): 63–88.

Livingood, James Weston. *The Philadelphia–Baltimore Trade Rivalry, 1780–1860.* Harrisburg: Pennsylvania Historical and Museum Commission, 1947.

Logan, John R., and Harvey L. Molotch. *Urban Fortunes: The Political Economy of Place.* Berkeley: University of California Press, 1987.

Lowber, John C. *Ordinances of the Corporation of the City of Philadelphia; to Which Are Prefixed, the Original Charter, the Act of Incorporation, and Other Acts of Assembly Relating to the City.* Philadelphia: Moses Thomas, 1812.

Lyon, Larry, Lawrence G. Felice, M. Ray Perryman, and E. Stephen Parker. "Community Power and Population Increase: An Empirical Test of the Growth Machine Model." *American Journal of Sociology* 86, no. 6 (May 1981): 1387–400.

Maass, Eleanor. "A Public Watchdog: Thomas Pym Cope and the Philadelphia Waterworks." *Proceedings of the American Philosophical Society* 125 (Apr. 1981): 135–54.

MacKinney, Gertrude, ed. *Pennsylvania Archives.* 9th ser. Harrisburg: Commonwealth of Pennsylvania, 1931.

Maier, Pauline. "The Revolutionary Origins of the American Corporation." *WMQ,* 3rd ser., 50 (1993): 51–84.

Majewski, John D. *A House Dividing: Economic Development in Pennsylvania and Virginia before the Civil War.* New York: Cambridge University Press, 2000.

Mann, Bruce H. *Republic of Debtors: Bankruptcy in the Age of American Independence.* Cambridge: Harvard University Press, 2002.

Martin, Asa Earl. "Lotteries in Pennsylvania prior to 1833." *PMHB* 47, no. 4 (Winter 1923): 307–27.

Martin, Scott C., ed. *Cultural Change and the Market Revolution in America.* Lanham: Rowman & Littlefield, 2005.

Marx, Leo. *The Machine in the Garden: Technology and the Pastoral Ideal in America.* New York: Oxford University Press, 1967.

Matson, Cathy, and Peter Onuf. *A Union of Interests: Political and Economic Thought in Revolutionary America.* Lawrence: University Press of Kansas, 1990.

McCoy, Drew. *The Elusive Republic: Political Economy in Jeffersonian America.* Chapel Hill: University of North Carolina Press, 1980.

McCulloch, Robert. *The Pennsylvania Main Line Canal.* York, PA: American Canal and Transportation Center, 1976.

McCusker, John J. *Money and Exchange in Europe and America, 1600–1775: A Handbook.* Chapel Hill: University of North Carolina Press, for the Institute of Early American History and Culture, 1978.

McCusker, John, and Russell Menard. *The Economy of British America, 1607–1789.* Chapel Hill: University of North Carolina Press, for the Institute of Early American History and Culture, 1987.

McGaw, Judith, ed. *Early American Technology: Making and Doing Things from the Colonial Era to 1850.* Chapel Hill: University of North Carolina Press, 1994.

McMahon, Michael. "'Publick Service' versus 'Mans Properties': Dock Creek and the Origins of Urban Technology in Eighteenth-Century Philadelphia." In McGaw, *Early American Technology,* 114–47.

Melosi, Martin V. *The Sanitary City: Urban Infrastructure from Colonial Times to the Present.* Baltimore: Johns Hopkins University Press, 2000.

Meredith, William. *Eulogium of the Character and Services of the Late John Sergeant.* Philadelphia: Crissy & Markley, 1858.

[Mifflin, Samuel]. *Observations on the Importance of Improving the Navigation of the River Schuylkill, for the Purpose of Connecting It with the Susquehanna, and through That River Extending Our Communication to the Genesee Lakes and the Ohio.* [Philadelphia]: n.p., 1818.

Mihm, Stephen. "Making Money, Creating Confidence: Counterfeiting and Capitalism in the United States, 1789–1877." PhD diss., New York University, 2003.

Miller, Richard G. *Philadelphia—The Federalist City: A Study of Urban Politics, 1789–1801.* Port Washington, NY: Kennikat Press, 1976.

Miller, William. "A Note on the Business Corporations in Pennsylvania, 1800–1860." *Quarterly Journal of Economics* 55, no. 1 (Nov. 1940): 150–60.

Mizruchi, Mark S. *The Structure of Corporate Political Action: Interfirm Relations and Their Consequences.* Cambridge: Harvard University Press, 1992.

———. "What Do Corporate Interlocks Do? An Analysis, Critique, and Assessment of Research on Interlocking Directorates." *Annual Review of Sociology* 22 (1996): 271–98.

Molotch, Harvey. "The City as a Growth Machine: Toward a Political Economy of Place." *American Journal of Sociology* 82, no. 2 (Sep. 1976): 309–22.

Monkkonen, Erik H. *America Becomes Urban: The Development of U.S. Cities and Towns, 1780–1980.* Berkeley: University of California Press, 1988.

Morris, Robert. *State of Pennsylvania. In General Assembly, Tuesday, February 26, 1782. P.M. on Motion, Resolved, That the Plan alluded to by the Resolution of Congress of the 17th of May, 1781, said to have been submitted to their Consideration by Robert Morris, Esq; be published in the News-papers, and that one Hundred Copies be Struck off in Handbills for the Use of the House.* Philadelphia: Hall & Sellers, 1781.

Moss, David A. *When All Else Fails: Government as the Ultimate Risk Manager.* Cambridge: Harvard University Press, 2002.

Moyer, Paul. "Wild Yankees: Settlement, Conflict, & Localism along Pennsylvania's Northeast Frontier, 1760–1820." PhD diss., College of William and Mary, 1999.

Mumford, Lewis. *Technics and Civilization.* New York: Harcourt, Brace, 1934.

Nash, Gary B. *Forging Freedom: The Formation of Philadelphia's Black Community, 1720–1840.* Cambridge: Harvard University Press, 1988.

———. "The Social Evolution of Preindustrial American Cities, 1700–1820." *Journal of Urban History* 13, no. 2 (Feb. 1987): 113–45.

———. *Urban Crucible: Social Change, Political Consciousness, and the Origins of the American Revolution.* Cambridge: Harvard University Press, 1979.

New-York and Schuylkill Coal Company. *History of the Coal Lands, and Other Real Estate, Owned by the New-York and Schuylkill Coal Company.* New York: Geo. F. Hopkins, 1826.

Nolan, J. Bennett. *The Schuylkill.* New Brunswick, NJ: Rutgers University Press, 1951.

Novak, William J. *The People's Welfare: Law and Regulation in Nineteenth-Century America.* Chapel Hill: University of North Carolina, 1996.

Nye, David E. *American Technological Sublime.* Cambridge: MIT Press, 1994.

O'Bannon, Patrick. "Inconsiderable Progress: Commercial Brewing in Philadelphia before 1840." In McGaw, *Early American Technology,* 148–63.

Olton, Charles S. *Artisans for Independence: Philadelphia Mechanics and the American Revolution.* Syracuse, NY: Syracuse University Press, 1975.

Paine, Thomas. *Dissertations on Government, on the Affairs of the Bank, and Paper-Money.* Philadelphia: Charles Cist, 1786.

Paleske, Charles G. *Observations on the Application for a Law to Incorporate "The Union Canal Company" Respectfully Submitted to the Members of Both Houses of the Legislature of Pennsylvania.* Philadelphia: William Duane, 1808.

Palladino, Grace. *Another Civil War: Labor, Capital, and the State in the Anthracite Regions of Pennsylvania, 1840–1868.* Urbana: University of Illinois Press, 1990.

Penniman, James Hosmer. *Philadelphia in the Early Eighteen Hundreds.* Philadelphia: St. Stephen's Church, 1923.

Perkins, Edwin J. *American Public Finance and Financial Services, 1700–1815.* Columbus: Ohio State University Press, 1994.

Pernick, Martin S. "Politics, Parties, and Pestilence: Epidemic Yellow Fever in Philadelphia and the Rise of the First Party System." *WMQ,* 3rd ser., 29 (October 1972): 559–86.

Peskin, Lawrence A. *Manufacturing Revolution: The Intellectual Origins of Early American Industry.* Baltimore: Johns Hopkins University Press, 2003.

Philadelphia Bank. *By-laws of the Philadelphia Bank. . . .* Philadelphia: William Fry, 1820.

———. *The Philadelphia Bank; Containing the Articles of Association, the Original Charter, and All the Acts of Assembly Extending and Relating to It, with the General Banking Law of April 16, 1850.* Philadelphia: Wm. F. Murphy & Sons, 1859.

Phillips, John. *A General History of Inland Navigation . . . with Considerations on Those Projected.* London: I. and J. Taylor, 1792.

Pierson, George Wilson. *Tocqueville in America.* Baltimore: Johns Hopkins University Press, 1996.

Platt, Harold L. *The Electric City: Energy and the Growth of the Chicago Area, 1880–1930.* Chicago: University of Chicago Press, 1991.

Postlethwayt, Malachy. *The Universal Dictionary of Trade and Commerce.* London: n.p., 1751.

Powell, H. Benjamin. *Philadelphia's First Fuel Crisis: Jacob Cist and the Developing Market for Pennsylvania Anthracite.* University Park: Pennsylvania State University Press, 1978.

Powell, J. H. *Bring Out Your Dead: The Great Yellow Fever Plague in Philadelphia in 1793.* Philadelphia: University of Pennsylvania Press, 1993.

Pred, Allan R. *Urban Growth and the Circulation of Information: The United States System of Cities, 1790–1840.* Cambridge: Harvard University Press, 1973.

Priestley, Joseph. *Historical Account of the Navigable Rivers, Canals and Railways throughout Great Britain.* London: n.p., 1831.

Pursell, Carroll W. *Early Stationary Steam Engines in America: A Study in the Migration of Technology.* Washington, DC: Smithsonian Institution Press, 1969.

Rappaport, George David. *Stability and Change in Revolutionary Pennsylvania: Banking, Politics, and Social Structure.* University Park: Pennsylvania State University Press, 1996.

Redlich, Fritz. *The Molding of American Banking: Men and Ideas.* New York: Johnson Reprint, 1968.

———. "The Philadelphia Waterworks in Relation to the Industrial Revolution in the United States." *PMHB* 69 (1945): 243–56.

Reed, George Edward, ed. *Pennsylvania Archives.* 4th ser., vol. 5. Harrisburg: State of Pennsylvania, 1900.

Remer, Rosalind. *Printers and Men of Capital: Philadelphia Book Publishers in the New Republic.* Philadelphia: University of Pennsylvania Press, 1996.

Richardson, Edgar P. "Athens of America, 1800–1825." In Weigley, *Philadelphia,* 208–57.

Rilling, Donna J. *Making Houses, Crafting Capitalism: Builders in Philadelphia, 1790–1850.* Philadelphia: University of Pennsylvania Press, 2001.

———. "Sylvan Enterprise and the Philadelphia Hinterland, 1790–1840." *PH* 67, no. 2 (Apr. 2000): 194–217.

Rishel, Joseph F. *Founding Families of Pittsburgh: The Evolution of a Regional Elite, 1760–1910.* Pittsburgh: University of Pittsburgh Press, 1990.

Ritter, Abraham. *Philadelphia and Her Merchants, As Constituted Fifty & Seventy Years Ago, Illustrated by Diagrams of the River Front, and Portraits of Some of its Prominent Occupants.* Philadelphia: Abraham Ritter, 1860.

Roberts, Kenneth, and Anna M. Roberts, eds. *Moreau de St. Méry's American Journey, 1793–1798.* Garden City, NY: Doubleday, 1947.

Rochdale Canal Company. *Bill for Making and Maintaining a Navigable Canal from the Calder Navigation, at or near Sowery Bridge Wharf, in the Parish of Halifax, in the West Riding of the County of York, to Manchester, in the County Palatine of Lancaster; and also several Collateral Cuts from the said Canal.* [London]: n.p., 1792.

Rockman, Seth, ed. *Welfare Reform in the Early Republic: A Brief History with Documents.* Boston: Bedford/St. Martin's Press, 2003.

Rodgers, Daniel T. "Republicanism: The Career of a Concept." *JAH* 79, no. 1 (June 1992): 11–38.

Rothbard, Murray N. *The Panic of 1819: Reactions and Policy.* New York: Columbia University Press, 1962.

Rothman, Adam. "The Slave Power in the United States, 1783–1865." In Fraser and Gerstle, *Ruling America,* 64–91.

Roy, William G. *Socializing Capital: The Rise of the Large Industrial Corporation in America.* Princeton: Princeton University Press, 1997.

Rubin, Julius. "Canal or Railroad? Imitation and Innovation in the Response to the Erie Canal in Philadelphia, Baltimore, and Boston." *Transactions of the American Philosophical Society,* n.s., 51, no. 7 (1961): 1–106.

Ryan, Mary. *Cradle of the Middle Class: The Family in Oneida County, New York, 1790–1865.* New York: Cambridge University Press, 1981.

Ryerson, Richard Alan. *The Revolution Is Now Begun: The Radical Committees of Philadelphia, 1765–1776.* Philadelphia: University of Pennsylvania Press, 1978.

Sabel, Jonathan, and Charles Zeitlin. "Historical Alternatives to Mass Production: Politics, Markets, and Technology in Nineteenth-Century Industrialization." *Past and Present,* no. 108 (Aug. 1985): 133–76.

Schiesl, Martin J. *The Politics of Efficiency: Municipal Administration and Reform in America, 1800–1920.* Berkeley: University of California Press, 1977.

Schultz, Ronald. "The Small-Producer Tradition and the Moral Origins of Artisan Radicalism in Philadelphia 1720–1810." *Past and Present,* no. 127 (May 1990): 84–116.

Schuylkill Navigation Company (SNC). *Acts of the Legislature of Pennsylvania, Relating to the Schuylkill Navigation Company.* Philadelphia: Josephy & William Kite, 1838.

———. *Report of the President and Managers of the Schuylkill Navigation Company, to the Stockholders. January 2, 1826.* Philadelphia: Lydia R. Bailey, 1826.

———. *Report of the President and Managers of the Schuylkill Navigation Company, to the Stockholders, January 1, 1827.* Philadelphia: Lydia R. Bailey, 1827.

———. *Report of the President and Managers of the Schuylkill Navigation Company, to the Stockholders. January 7, 1828.* Philadelphia: Lydia R. Bailey, 1828.

———. *Report of the President and Managers of the Schuylkill Navigation Company, to the Stockholders. January 3, 1831.* Philadelphia: James Kay, Jun. & Co., 1831.

Schwartz, Anna Jacobson. "The Beginning of Competitive Banking in Philadelphia, 1782–1809." *Journal of Political Economy* 55, no. 5 (Oct. 1947): 417–31.

Schweikart, Larry. "U.S. Commercial Banking: A Historiographical Survey." *BHR* 65, no. 3 (Autumn 1991): 606–61.

Schweitzer, Mary M. *Custom and Contract: Household, Government, and the Economy in Colonial Pennsylvania.* New York: Columbia University Press, 1987.

———. "The Spatial Organization of Federalist Philadelphia, 1790." *Journal of Interdisciplinary History* 24, no. 1 (Summer 1993): 31–57.

———. "State-Issued Currency and the Ratification of the U.S. Constitution." *JEH* 49, no. 2 (June 1989): 311–22.

Scott, William Robert. *The Constitution and Finance of English, Scottish and Irish Joint-Stock Companies to 1720, Vol. 3: Water Supply, Postal, Street-Lighting, Manufacturing, Banking, Finance and Insurance Companies; Also Statements Relating to the Crown Finances.* New York: Peter Smith, 1951.

Scranton, Philip. *Proprietary Capitalism: The Textile Manufacture at Philadelphia, 1800–1885.* New York: Cambridge University Press, 1983.

Seavoy, Ronald E. *The Origins of the American Business Corporation, 1784–1855: Broadening the Concept of Public Service during Industrialization.* Westport, CT: Greenwood Press, 1982.

Segal, Harvey. "Canals and Economic Development." In Goodrich, *Canals and American Economic Development,* 216–48.

Sellers, Charles. *The Market Revolution: Jacksonian America, 1815–1846.* New York: Oxford University Press, 1991.

Sergeant, John, et al. *Opinion of Counsel, on the Right of the Schuylkill Navigation Company to Make Another Lock and Canal for the Use of the Navigation at the Fair Mount Dam.* Philadelphia: James Kay, Jun. & Co., 1833.

Shankman, Andrew. *Crucible of American Democracy: The Struggle to Fuse Egalitarianism & Capitalism in Jeffersonian Pennsylvania.* Lawrence: University Press of Kansas, 2004.

Shaw, Ronald E. *Canals for a Nation: The Canal Era in the United States, 1790–1860.* Lexington: University Press of Kentucky, 1990.

Shelton, Cynthia J. *The Mills of Manayunk: Industrialization and Social Conflict in the Philadelphia Region, 1787–1837.* Baltimore: Johns Hopkins University Press, 1986.

Sheriff, Carol. *The Artificial River: The Erie Canal and the Paradox of Progress, 1817–1862.* New York: Hill & Wang, 1996.

Shlakman, Vera. *The Economic History of a Factory Town: A Study of Chicopee, Massachusetts.* Northampton, MA: Smith College Press, 1935.

Sicilia, David B. "Industrialization and the Rise of Corporations, 1860–1900." In *A Companion to 19th-Century America,* edited by William L. Barney, 139–51. Malden, MA: Blackwell, 2001.

Sjoberg, Gideon. *The Preindustrial City, Past and Present.* Glencoe, IL: Free Press, 1960.

Sklar, Martin J. *The Corporate Reconstruction of American Capitalism, 1890–1916: The Market, the Law, and Politics.* New York: Cambridge University Press, 1987.

Slaughter, Thomas. *The Whiskey Rebellion: Frontier Epilogue to the American Revolution.* New York: Oxford University Press, 1987.

Smith, Billy G. *The "Lower Sort": Philadelphia's Laboring People, 1750–1800.* Ithaca, NY: Cornell University Press, 1990.

Smith, Mark A. *American Business and Political Power: Public Opinion, Elections, and Democracy*. Chicago: University of Chicago Press, 2000.

Smith, Tom W. "The Dawn of the Urban-Industrial Age: The Social Structure of Philadelphia, 1790–1830." PhD diss., University of Chicago, 1980.

Smith, William. *An Historical Account of the Rise, Progress and Present State of the Canal Navigation in Pennsylvania. . . .* Philadelphia: Zachariah Poulson, Jr., 1795.

Stapleton, Darwin H. "Benjamin Henry Latrobe and the Transfer of Technology." In *Technology in America: A History of Individuals and Ideas*, edited by Carroll Pursell, 34–44. Cambridge: MIT Press, 1982.

———, ed. *The Engineering Drawings of Benjamin Henry Latrobe*. New Haven: Yale University Press, 1980.

Steinberg, Theodore. *Nature Incorporated: Industrialization and the Waters of New England*. New York: Cambridge University Press, 1991.

Stoker, Gerry. "Regime Theory and Urban Politics." In *Theories of Urban Politics*, edited by David Judge, Gerry Stoker, and Harold Wolman, 54–71. Thousand Oaks, CA: Sage, 1995.

Sullivan, J. L. *Suggestions on the Canal Policy of Pennsylvania, in Reference to the Effects of the Inland Navigation of the Adjoining States, on the Commerce of Philadelphia*. Philadelphia: John Young, 1824.

Sutton, Francis X., ed. *The American Business Creed*. Cambridge: Harvard University Press, 1956.

Sylla, Richard. "American Banking and Growth in the Nineteenth Century: A Partial View of the Terrain." *Explorations in Economic History* 9, no. 2 (Winter 1972): 197–229.

———. "Forgotten Men of Money: Private Bankers in Early U.S. History." *JEH* 36, no. 1 (March 1976): 173–88.

———. "Monetary Innovation in America." *JEH* 42, no. 1 (March 1982): 21–30.

Sylla, Richard, John Legler, and John Wallis. "Banks and State Public Finance in the New Republic: The United States, 1790–1860." *JEH* 47, no. 2 (June 1987): 391–403.

Syrett, Harold C., and Jacob E. Cooke, eds. *The Papers of Alexander Hamilton*, vol. 2: 1779–1781. New York: Columbia University Press, 1961.

Taylor, Alan. *William Cooper's Town: Power and Persuasion on the Frontier of the Early American Republic*. New York: Vintage Books, 1995.

Taylor, George Rogers. *The Transportation Revolution*. New York: Harper & Row, 1951.

Teaford, Jon. *The Municipal Revolution in America: The Origins of Modern Urban Government, 1650–1825*. Chicago: University of Chicago Press, 1975.

Temin, Peter. "The American Business Elite in Historical Perspective." NBER Working Paper, no. H0104 (Oct. 1997).

Thayer, Theodore. "The Land Bank System in the American Colonies." *JEH* 13, no. 2 (Spring 1953): 145–59.

Thompson, E. P. "The Moral Economy of the English Crowd in the Eighteenth Century." *Past and Present*, no. 50 (Feb. 1971): 76–136.

Tinkcom, Harry M. "The Revolutionary City, 1765–1783." In Weigley, *Philadelphia*, 109–54.

Tocqueville, Alexis de. *Democracy in America*. Edited by J. P. Mayer and Max Lerner. Translated by George Lawrence. New York: Harper & Row, 1966.

———. *Journey to America*. Edited by J. P. Mayer and Max Lerner. Translated by George Lawrence. Garden City, NY: Anchor Books, 1971.

Tolles, Frederick B. *Meeting House and Counting House: The Quaker Merchants of Colonial Philadelphia, 1682–1763*. Chapel Hill: University of North Carolina Press, 1948.

Tooker, Elva C. "A Merchant Turns to Money-Lending in Philadelphia." *Bulletin of the Business Historical Society* 2, no. 3 (June 1946): 71–85.

Union Canal Company (UCC). *Acts of the Legislature of Pennsylvania, Relating to the Union Canal Company of Pennsylvania*. Philadelphia: Lydia R. Bailey, 1828.

———. *Annual Report of the President and Managers of the Union Canal Company of Pennsylvania, to the Stockholders*. November 15, 1825. Philadelphia: Lydia R. Bailey, 1825.

———. *Report and Memorial of the President and Managers, of the Union Canal Company, of Pennsylvania. Made and Presented to the Legislature of the State of Pennsylvania, at Their Session, 1812–13.* Philadelphia: John Binns, 1812.

———. *Report of the President and Managers of the Union Canal Company of Pennsylvania; to the Stockholders. Made in Compliance with the Provisions Contained in Their Act of Incorporation.* Philadelphia: John Bioren, 1818.

Vallancey, Charles. *A Treatise on Inland Navigation, or, The Art of Making Rivers Navigable, of Making Canals in All Sorts of Soils, and of Constructing Locks and Sluices.* Dublin: George and Alexander Ewing, 1763.

Van Horne, John C., and Lee W. Formwalt, eds. *Correspondence and Miscellaneous Papers: The Papers of Benjamin Henry Latrobe,* 4th ser., vol. 1. New Haven: Published for the Maryland Historical Society by Yale University Press, 1984.

Vogel, David. *Kindred Strangers: The Uneasy Relationship between Business and Politics in America.* Princeton: Princeton University Press, 1996.

———. "Why Businessmen Distrust Their State: The Political Consciousness of American Corporate Executives." *British Journal of Political Science* 8, no. 1 (Jan. 1978): 45–78.

Wade, Richard C. *The Urban Frontier: The Rise of Eastern Cities, 1790–1830.* Cambridge: Harvard University Press, 1959.

Wallace, Anthony F. C. *Rockdale: The Growth of an American Village in the Early Industrial Revolution.* New York: Norton, 1978.

Wallis, John, Richard Sylla, and John Legler. "The Interaction of Taxation and Regulation in Nineteenth-Century Banking." In *The Regulated Economy: A Historical Approach to Political Economy,* edited by Claudia Goldin and Gary D. Libecap, 121–44. Chicago: University of Chicago Press, 1994.

Wansey, Henry. *The Journals of an Excursion to the United States of North America, in the Summer of 1794.* Salisbury: J. Easton, 1796.

Warner, Sam Bass, Jr. *The Private City: Philadelphia in Three Periods of Its Growth.* Philadelphia: University of Pennsylvania Press, 1968.

Watson, Harry L. *Liberty and Power: The Politics of Jacksonian America.* New York: Hill & Wang, 1990.

Watts, Irma A. "Pennsylvania Lotteries of Other Days." *PH* 2, no. 1 (Jan. 1935): 40–53.

Way, Peter. *Common Labour: Workers and the Digging of North American Canals, 1780–1860.* New York: Cambridge University Press, 1993.

Webster, Pelatiah. *An Essay on Credit: In Which the Doctrine of Banks Is Considered, and Some Remarks Are Made on the Present State of the Bank of North America.* Philadelphia: Eleazer Oswald, 1786.

Weigley, Russell F., ed. *Philadelphia: A 300-Year History.* New York: Norton, 1982.

Weil, François. "Capitalism and Industrialization in New England, 1815–1845." *JAH* 84, no. 4 (March 1998): 1334–54.

White, Josiah. *Circular.* Harrisburg: Hamilton & Son, 1832.

[———]. *History of the Lehigh Coal and Navigation Company.* Philadelphia: William S. Young, 1840.

———. *Josiah White's History Given by Himself.* Philadelphia: Lehigh Coal and Navigation Company, 1909.

———. *To the Committee on Corporations of the Senate (in Answer to Charges against the Lehigh Coal and Navigation Company).* Harrisburg, PA: Hamilton & Son, 1832.

Whitworth, Richard. *The Advantages of Inland Navigation; or, Some Observations Offered to the Public, to Shew That an Inland Navigation May Be Easily Effected between the Three Great Ports of Bristol, Liverpool, and Hull; Together with a Plan for Executing the Same.* London: R. Baldwin, 1766.

Wicker, Elmus. "Colonial Monetary Standards Contrasted: Evidence from the Seven Years' War." *JEH* 45, no. 4 (Dec. 1985): 869–84.

Wilentz, Sean. "Society, Politics, and the Market Revolution." In *The New American History,* edited by Eric Foner, 61–84. Philadelphia: Temple University Press, 1997.

Willer, David. "Power-at-a-Distance." *Social Forces* 81, no. 4 (June 2003): 1295–334.

Wilson, James. *Considerations on the Bank of North-America.* Philadelphia: Hall & Sellers, 1785.

Winch, Julie. *Philadelphia's Black Elite: Activism, Accommodation, and the Struggle for Autonomy, 1787–1848.* Philadelphia: Temple University Press, 1988.

Winner, Langdon. *The Whale and the Reactor: A Search for Limits in an Age of High Technology.* Chicago: University of Chicago Press, 1986.

Winslow, Stephen N. *Biographies of Successful Philadelphia Merchants.* Philadelphia: James K. Simon, 1864.

Wood, Gordon S. *The Creation of the American Republic, 1776–1787.* Chapel Hill: University of North Carolina Press, 1969.

———. "The Enemy Is Us: Democratic Capitalism in the Early Republic." *JER* 16, no. 2 (Summer 1996): 293–308.

———. *The Radicalism of the American Revolution.* New York: Vintage Books, 1992.

Wright, Robert E. "Artisans, Banks, Credit, and the Election of 1800." *PMHB* 132, no. 3 (Autumn 1998): 211–40.

———. "Bank Ownership and Lending Patterns in New York and Pennsylvania, 1781–1831." *BHR* 73, no. 1 (Spring 1999): 40–60.

———. "The First Phase of the Empire State's 'Triple Transition': Banks' Influence on the Market, Democracy, and Federalism in New York, 1776–1838." *Social Science History* 21, no. 4 (Winter 1997): 521–58.

———. *Origins of Commercial Banking in America, 1750–1800.* New York: Rowman & Littlefield, 2001.

———. "Thomas Willing (1731–1832): Philadelphia Financier and Forgotten Family Founder." *PH* 63, no. 4 (Autumn 1996): 525–60.

Yearley, Clifton K. *Enterprise and Anthracite: Economics and Democracy in Schuylkill County, 1820–1875.* Baltimore: Johns Hopkins University Press, 1961.

Zable, Charles, and Jonathan Zeitling. "Historical Alternatives to Mass Production: Politics, Markets, and Technology in Nineteenth-Century Industrialization." *Past and Present,* no. 108 (Aug. 1985): 161.

Zunz, Olivier. *Making America Corporate, 1870–1920.* Chicago: University of Chicago Press, 1990.

INDEX